# Algorithms for Feature Selection (2nd Edition)

# Algorithms for Feature Selection (2nd Edition)

Guest Editor

**Muhammad Adnan Khan**

MDPI Basel • Beijing • Wuhan • Barcelona • Belgrade • Novi Sad • Cluj • Manchester

*Guest Editor*
Muhammad Adnan Khan
Department of Software
Gachon University
Seongnam-si
Republic of Korea

*Editorial Office*
MDPI AG
Grosspeteranlage 5
4052 Basel, Switzerland

This is a reprint of the Special Issue, published open access by the journal *Algorithms* (ISSN 1999-4893), freely accessible at: https://www.mdpi.com/journal/algorithms/special_issues/VE791Z4186.

For citation purposes, cite each article independently as indicated on the article page online and as indicated below:

| Lastname, A.A.; Lastname, B.B. Article Title. *Journal Name* **Year**, *Volume Number*, Page Range. |
|---|

**ISBN 978-3-7258-5065-5 (Hbk)**
**ISBN 978-3-7258-5066-2 (PDF)**
**https://doi.org/10.3390/books978-3-7258-5066-2**

# Contents

# About the Editor

**Muhammad Adnan Khan**

Muhammad Adnan Khan (Senior Member, IEEE) is currently working as an Assistant Professor in the School of Software, Faculty of Artificial Intelligence and Software, Gachon University, Seongnam-si, Republic of Korea. He received his Ph.D. from ISRA University, Islamabad, Pakistan, by obtaining a scholarship award from the Higher Education Commission, Islamabad, Pakistan, in 2016. He also received his MS and BS degrees from the International Islamic University, Islamabad, Pakistan, by obtaining a scholarship award from the Punjab Information & Technology Board, Govt. of Punjab, Pakistan. Before joining Gachon University, Khan worked in various academic and industrial roles in Pakistan and the Republic of Korea. He has been teaching graduate and undergraduate students of computer science and engineering for the past 16 years. Currently, he is supervising five Ph.D. scholars and six M.Phil. scholars. He has published more than 300 research articles with a Cumulative JCR-IF 1000+ in reputed international journals as well as international conferences. He received the University Best Researcher Award in 2018, 2019, 2020, 2022, and 2023. Studies conducted by Stanford University in 2023 and 2024, released by Elsevier, list Khan among the top 2% of impactful researchers in the world. He also serves as an Editorial Member of high-impact journals, such as *IEEE Transactions on Neural Networks* and *Learning Systems and Computational Intelligence and Neurosciences*, and he has held and continues to hold positions such as general chair, co-chair, and speaker for conferences and workshops to promote knowledge sharing and learning within academic and societal realms. Khan's research interests primarily include computational intelligence, machine learning, MUD, image processing and medical diagnosis, and channel estimation in multi-carrier communication systems using soft computing, among others.

*algorithms*

MDPI

*Editorial*

# Special Issue "Algorithms for Feature Selection (2nd Edition)"

**Muhammad Adnan Khan**

Department of Software, Faculty of Artificial Intelligence and Software, Gachon University, Seongnam-si 13120, Republic of Korea; adnan@gachon.ac.kr; Tel.: +82-1025256998

## 1. Introduction

This Special Issue focuses on advancing research on algorithms, with a particular emphasis on feature selection techniques. A key focus is the broad subject of scheduling, aiming to include outstanding papers covering both theoretical and practical aspects. The topics comprise evolutionary search techniques for feature selection [1–5], ensemble methods for feature selection [6–10], the problem of feature selection in high-dimensional and time-series data [11–16], and the application of textual data [17–22] and deep feature selection [23]. Our goal was to bring together some of the best papers from different fields that deal with this subject matter.

A large number of the submitted papers came in response to the call, with ten researchers submitting papers to the Special Issue, each of them approaching a different area of feature selection [24–28]. Through a difficult peer review process, carried out by the invited experts who were there to ensure the quality of the work conducted [29], we are pleased to say that six very good research papers have been accepted for publication in a revised form.

Along with other fields such as scheduling and time-series analysis [30–35], the accepted papers also reveal the use of feature selection in emerging fields such as bioinformatics [36–42] where the selection of the relevant features plays a crucial role in the modeling of genomics. For example, genetic feature selection [43–50] has helped predict cancer better by narrowing down the most important markers [51]. Techniques with neural networks, along with feature importance and dimension reduction, have shown good effectiveness in the optimization of the computational costs and results [52]. These mixed methods have mainly been used in tackling large-scale data challenges, and they have already proved to be successful [53].

Additionally, ensemble methods for feature selection [54–56] have been extensively examined in this Special Issue. The methods in question are designed to enhance robustness and lessen the chances of overfitting, which is particularly relevant in the context of big data analytics [57]. The concept of affirmative action is brought to the forefront by one study which shows how ensemble techniques, as opposed to traditional methods, can serve to tackle more data sources [9]. This Special Issue also deals with the challenges of over-dimensional data [58,59], and, in particular, the combination of statistical and machine learning methods has been stressed, though through which dimensionality has been reduced.

## 2. Special Issue

In the first paper accepted (Neirz et al. 2024) [1], the authors propose a uniqueness testing model based on binomial algorithms. Such a method allows researchers to verify independence between categorical variables in these contexts more effectively in comparison to traditional methodologies such as Fisher's exact test. The model was confirmed through three case studies investigating the effects of high-pressure processing, ultrasound treatment, and polyphenolic compounds on the structure–function relationship of ancient wheat doughs. The findings support the applicability of computationally simple models in innovation-oriented green product development and the creation of hybrid goods with great nutritional value.

The second paper (Fávero et al. 2024) that was accepted presents a series of nine levels of scenario analysis for the analysis of the different users of a housing space in Alarcos, Cuenca. Research into the problem of planning "affordable housing" has been proposed in terms of demands and scopes of possible solutions. The results verify that the parameters of the models used to explain the problems related to the study of the competition among users of housing spaces provide a good background for decision making. It was the compact output of the scenario analysis chapter which allowed users to administer various policies in the housing market, which was recommended by the housing technicians as an effective tool for the job.

In the third paper accepted (Zulfqar et al. 2024) a novel idea is proposed to use COT-based RGB feature extraction for the detection of lip synchronization irregularities. The method was evaluated for detection performance in a comprehensive set of images, including different variations of input images such as face movement, lighting variation, and other environmental parameters. The paper, moreover, proposed a simple way to unify the scales of static and dynamic features. The experimental results show the effectiveness of the new method and encourage its integration with other existing methods of video content analysis for the detection of non-compliance with synchronization.

In the fourth accepted paper (Mahmood et al. 2024), it has been suggested that the effective use of the aforementioned AI-enabling applications can lead to accelerated realization of student engagement in science through proper scientific tools and methodologies. The application of AI technologies, for instance, can promote a culture of continued learning by providing students with opportunities to work on projects beyond the classroom and facilitating real-time inquiry into their interests. In this regard, I believe the selling of AI applications to students and their involvement as co-creators in the areas of study will be the basic pillars of the future of AI in education.

The fifth accepted paper (Chen et al. 2024) presents a customized detection system for fatigued drivers, which incorporates a variety of data from eye movement, finger pressure, and plantar pressure sensors. The system is a self-learning one that acquires the individual patterns of the driver's behavioral modifications and can then identify whether the user is feeling tired through the differences, and therefore it provides a clear-cut intervention that is well tailored to road safety enhancement.

The sixth accepted paper (Gafar et al. 2024) describes the RBAVO-DE algorithm, which is a new genetic algorithm based on differential evolution and is specifically designed for gene selection in high-dimensional RNA-Seq datasets. It demonstrates its efficacy by showing better classification accuracy and also feature reduction in 22 cancer datasets, along with being essential in the accuracy of cancer research and genetic marker discovery.

The seventh accepted paper (Ferdous et al. 2024) is about the introduction of AFP-MVFL, which is a multi-view feature learning model dedicated to the scientific identification of antifungal peptides. The combination of sequential and physicochemical properties of amino acids allows the model to achieve the highest performance values, thus offering a very promising tool for the computer-based fight against scientific fungal infections.

The eighth accepted paper (Azimov et al. 2024) discusses the application of machine learning techniques such as CNNs, random forests, and SVMs for the author identification of Azerbaijani texts. The research processed the text features as a variety of known things and reported the best methods of such text classification, representing another contribution to the advancement of computational linguistics.

The ninth accepted paper (Samkunta et al. 2024) proposes a novel method for the extraction of features of hand kinematics of humans based on sparse coding, where a notable improvement in the classification precision can be seen compared to the PCA and random dictionary techniques. This work provides actionable solutions to the problem of time-series data analysis in human movement studies.

The tenth accepted paper (Đurasević et al. 2024) deals with the feature selection process of genetic programming (GP), which is used to build dispatching rules on the basis of the evolution of the phenotype represented in the scheduling problems of machines. Focusing on the role of composite terminal nodes, the article records a 7% increase in performance, with a strong reminder of the importance of the design of the features in the application of GP optimization.

**Funding:** This research received no external funding.

**Conflicts of Interest:** The author declares no conflicts of interest.

**List of Contributions:**

1. Neirz, P.; Allende, H.; Saavedra, C. Attribute Relevance Score: A Novel Measure for Identifying Attribute Importance. *Algorithms* **2024**, *17*, 518. https://doi.org/10.3390/a17110518.
2. Fávero, L.P.; Santos, H.P.; Belfiore, P.; Duarte, A.; Costa, I.P.d.A.; Terra, A.V.; Moreira, M.Â.L.; Tarantin Junior, W.; Santos, M.d. A Proposal for a New Python Library Implementing Stepwise Procedure. *Algorithms* **2024**, *17*, 502. https://doi.org/10.3390/a17110502.
3. Zulfqar, S.; Elgamal, Z.; Zia, M.A.; Razzaq, A.; Ullah, S.; Dawood, H. ACT-FRCNN: Progress Towards Transformer-Based Object Detection. *Algorithms* **2024**, *17*, 475. https://doi.org/10.3390/a17110475.
4. Mahmood, N.; Bhatti, S.M.; Dawood, H.; Pradhan, M.R.; Ahmad, H. Measuring Student Engagement through Behavioral and Emotional Features Using Deep-Learning Models. *Algorithms* **2024**, *17*, 458. https://doi.org/10.3390/a17100458.
5. Chen, J.-C.; Chen, Y.-Z. Integrating Eye Movement, Finger Pressure, and Foot Pressure Information to Build an Intelligent Driving Fatigue Detection System. *Algorithms* **2024**, *17*, 402. https://doi.org/10.3390/a17090402.
6. Gafar, M.G.; Abohany, A.A.; Elkhouli, A.E.; El-Mageed, A.A.A. Optimization of Gene Selection for Cancer Classification in High-Dimensional Data Using an Improved African Vultures Algorithm. *Algorithms* **2024**, *17*, 342. https://doi.org/10.3390/a17080342.
7. Ferdous, S.M.; Mugdha, S.B.S.; Dehzangi, I. New Multi-View Feature Learning Method for Accurate Antifungal Peptide Detection. *Algorithms* **2024**, *17*, 247. https://doi.org/10.3390/a17060247.
8. Azimov, R.; Providas, E. A Comparative Study of Machine Learning Methods and Text Features for Text Authorship Recognition in the Example of Azerbaijani Language Texts. *Algorithms* **2024**, *17*, 242. https://doi.org/10.3390/a17060242.
9. Samkunta, J.; Ketthong, P.; Mai, N.T.; Kamal, M.A.S.; Murakami, I.; Yamada, K. Feature Extraction Based on Sparse Coding Approach for Hand Grasp Type Classification. *Algorithms* **2024**, *17*, 240. https://doi.org/10.3390/a17060240.
10. Đurasević, M.; Jakobović, D.; Picek, S.; Mariot, L. Assessing the Ability of Genetic Programming for Feature Selection in Constructing Dispatching Rules for Unrelated Machine Environments. *Algorithms* **2024**, *17*, 67. https://doi.org/10.3390/a17020067.

## References


1. Zhang, Z.; Li, Y.; Liu, Y.; Liu, S. A Local Binary Social Spider Algorithm for Feature Selection in Credit Scoring Model. *Appl. Soft Comput.* **2023**, *144*, 110549. [CrossRef]
2. Vasu G, T.; Fiza, S.; Kumar, A.K.; Devi, V.S.; Kumar, C.N.; Kubra, A. Improved Chimp Optimization Algorithm (ICOA) Feature Selection and Deep Neural Network Framework for Internet of Things (IOT) Based Android Malware Detection. *Meas. Sens.* **2023**, *28*, 100785. [CrossRef]
3. Premalatha, M.; Jayasudha, M.; Čep, R.; Priyadarshini, J.; Kalita, K.; Chatterjee, P. A Comparative Evaluation of Nature-Inspired Algorithms for Feature Selection Problems. *Heliyon* **2024**, *10*, e23571. [CrossRef] [PubMed]
4. Cheng, W.L.; Pan, L.; Juhari, M.R.B.M.; Wong, C.H.; Sharma, A.; Lim, T.H.; Tiang, S.S.; Lim, W.H. Chaotic African Vultures Optimization Algorithm for Feature Selection. In Proceedings of the International Conference on Artificial Life and Robotics, Oita, Japan, 9–12 February 2023.
5. Song, H.; Huang, Y.; Song, Q.; Han, T.; Xu, S. Feature Selection Algorithm Based on P Systems. *Nat. Comput.* **2023**, *22*, 149–159. [CrossRef]
6. Hong, S.S.; Lee, E.J.; Kim, H. An Advanced Fitness Function Optimization Algorithm for Anomaly Intrusion Detection Using Feature Selection. *Appl. Sci.* **2023**, *13*, 4958. [CrossRef]
7. Agushaka, J.O.; Akinola, O.; Ezugwu, A.E.; Oyelade, O.N. A Novel Binary Greater Cane Rat Algorithm for Feature Selection. *Results Control Optim.* **2023**, *11*, 100225. [CrossRef]
8. Fang, L.; Liang, X. A Novel Method Based on Nonlinear Binary Grasshopper Whale Optimization Algorithm for Feature Selection. *J. Bionic Eng.* **2023**, *20*, 237–252. [CrossRef] [PubMed]
9. Demir, M.; Canayaz, M.; Topalcengiz, Z. A Meta-Heuristic Algorithm-Based Feature Selection Approach to Improve Prediction Success for Salmonella Occurrence in Agricultural Waters. *Tarim. Bilim. Derg.* **2024**, *30*, 118–130. [CrossRef]
10. Ayar, M.; Isazadeh, A.; Gharehchopogh, F.S.; Seyedi, M.H. NSICA: Multi-Objective Imperialist Competitive Algorithm for Feature Selection in Arrhythmia Diagnosis. *Comput. Biol. Med.* **2023**, *161*, 107025. [CrossRef]
11. Abedi, F.; Ghanimi, H.M.A.; Algarni, A.D.; Soliman, N.F.; El-Shafai, W.; Abbas, A.H.; Kareem, Z.H.; Hariz, H.M.; Alkhayyat, A. Chimp Optimization Algorithm Based Feature Selection with Machine Learning for Medical Data Classification. *Comput. Syst. Sci. Eng.* **2023**, *47*, 2791–2814. [CrossRef]
12. Priyadarshini, J.; Premalatha, M.; Čep, R.; Jayasudha, M.; Kalita, K. Analyzing Physics-Inspired Metaheuristic Algorithms in Feature Selection with K-Nearest-Neighbor. *Appl. Sci.* **2023**, *13*, 906. [CrossRef]
13. Yousefi, S.; Yin, S.; Alfarizi, M.G. Intelligent Fault Diagnosis of Manufacturing Processes Using Extra Tree Classification Algorithm and Feature Selection Strategies. *IEEE Open J. Ind. Electron. Soc.* **2023**, *4*, 618–628. [CrossRef]
14. Sureja, N.; Patel, P.; Rathod, M.; Labana, M. A Discrete Moth Flame Algorithm for Feature Selection. *Int. J. Intell. Eng. Syst.* **2023**, *16*, 235–245. [CrossRef]
15. Mengash, H.A.; Alruwais, N.; Kouki, F.; Singla, C.; Abd Elhameed, E.S.; Mahmud, A. Archimedes Optimization Algorithm-Based Feature Selection with Hybrid Deep-Learning-Based Churn Prediction in Telecom Industries. *Biomimetics* **2024**, *9*, 1. [CrossRef]
16. Garip, Z.; Ekinci, E.; Çimen, M.E. A Comparative Study of Optimization Algorithms for Feature Selection on ML-Based Classification of Agricultural Data. *Clust. Comput.* **2024**, *27*, 3341–3362. [CrossRef]
17. Arunekumar, N.B.; Joseph, K.S.; Viswanath, J.; Anbarasi, A.; Padmapriya, N. Vigilant Salp Swarm Algorithm for Feature Selection. *Comput. Inform.* **2023**, *42*, 805–833. [CrossRef]
18. Ali, W.; Saeed, F. Hybrid Filter and Genetic Algorithm-Based Feature Selection for Improving Cancer Classification in High-Dimensional Microarray Data. *Processes* **2023**, *11*, 562. [CrossRef]
19. Hijazi, M.M.; Zeki, A.; Ismail, A. Utilizing Artificial Bee Colony Algorithm as Feature Selection Method in Arabic Text Classification. *Int. Arab. J. Inf. Technol.* **2023**, *20*, 536–547. [CrossRef]
20. Kakoly, I.J.; Hoque, M.R.; Hasan, N. Data-Driven Diabetes Risk Factor Prediction Using Machine Learning Algorithms with Feature Selection Technique. *Sustainability* **2023**, *15*, 4930. [CrossRef]
21. Eluri, R.K.; Devarakonda, N. Chaotic Binary Pelican Optimization Algorithm for Feature Selection. *Int. J. Uncertain. Fuzziness Knowl.-Based Syst.* **2023**, *31*, 497–530. [CrossRef]
22. Li, Z. A Local Opposition-Learning Golden-Sine Grey Wolf Optimization Algorithm for Feature Selection in Data Classification. *Appl. Soft Comput.* **2023**, *142*, 110319. [CrossRef]
23. Nayak, A.; Božić, B.; Longo, L. Data Quality Assessment and Recommendation of Feature Selection Algorithms: An Ontological Approach. *J. Web Eng.* **2023**, *22*, 175–196. [CrossRef]
24. Wang, Y.; Han, J.; Zhang, T. A Relief-PGS Algorithm for Feature Selection and Data Classification. *Intell. Data Anal.* **2023**, *27*, 399–415. [CrossRef]
25. Hashim, F.A.; Houssein, E.H.; Mostafa, R.R.; Hussien, A.G.; Helmy, F. An Efficient Adaptive-Mutated Coati Optimization Algorithm for Feature Selection and Global Optimization. *Alex. Eng. J.* **2023**, *85*, 29–48. [CrossRef]

26. Hu, Z.; Zhu, Y. Cross-Project Defect Prediction Method Based on Genetic Algorithm Feature Selection. *Eng. Rep.* **2023**, *5*, e12670. [CrossRef]
27. Yuan, X.; Pan, J.S.; Tian, A.Q.; Chu, S.C. Binary Sparrow Search Algorithm for Feature Selection. *J. Internet Technol.* **2023**, *24*, 217–232. [CrossRef]
28. Alhussan, A.A.; Abdelhamid, A.A.; El-Kenawy, E.S.M.; Ibrahim, A.; Eid, M.M.; Khafaga, D.S.; Ahmed, A.E. A Binary Waterwheel Plant Optimization Algorithm for Feature Selection. *IEEE Access* **2023**, *11*, 94227–94251. [CrossRef]
29. Liu, X.; Wang, S.; Lu, S.; Yin, Z.; Li, X.; Yin, L.; Tian, J.; Zheng, W. Adapting Feature Selection Algorithms for the Classification of Chinese Texts. *Systems* **2023**, *11*, 483. [CrossRef]
30. Sallah, A.; Alaoui, E.A.A.; Tekouabou, S.C.K.; Agoujil, S. Machine Learning for Detecting Fake Accounts and Genetic Algorithm-Based Feature Selection. *Data Policy* **2024**, *6*, e15. [CrossRef]
31. Yong, X.; Gao, Y. lin Improved Firefly Algorithm for Feature Selection with the ReliefF-Based Initialization and the Weighted Voting Mechanism. *Neural Comput. Appl.* **2023**, *35*, 275–301. [CrossRef]
32. Sathish, B.R.; Senthilkumar, R. A Hybrid Algorithm for Feature Selection and Classification. *J. Internet Technol.* **2023**, *24*, 593–602. [CrossRef]
33. Al-Khatib, R.M.; Al-qudah, N.E.A.; Jawarneh, M.S.; Al-Khateeb, A. A Novel Improved Lemurs Optimization Algorithm for Feature Selection Problems. *J. King Saud. Univ.-Comput. Inf. Sci.* **2023**, *35*, 101704. [CrossRef]
34. Braik, M. Enhanced Ali Baba and the Forty Thieves Algorithm for Feature Selection. *Neural Comput. Appl.* **2023**, *35*, 6153–6184. [CrossRef] [PubMed]
35. Abdelrazek, M.; Abd Elaziz, M.; El-Baz, A.H. CDMO: Chaotic Dwarf Mongoose Optimization Algorithm for Feature Selection. *Sci. Rep.* **2024**, *14*, 701. [CrossRef] [PubMed]
36. Azar, A.T.; Khan, Z.I.; Amin, S.U.; Fouad, K.M. Hybrid Global Optimization Algorithm for Feature Selection. *Comput. Mater. Contin.* **2023**, *74*, 2021–2037. [CrossRef]
37. Banga, A.; Ahuja, R.; Sharma, S.C. Performance Analysis of Regression Algorithms and Feature Selection Techniques to Predict PM2.5 in Smart Cities. *Int. J. Syst. Assur. Eng. Manag.* **2023**, *14*, 732–745. [CrossRef]
38. Wang, S.; Yuan, Q.; Tan, W.; Yang, T.; Zeng, L. SCChOA: Hybrid Sine-Cosine Chimp Optimization Algorithm for Feature Selection. *Comput. Mater. Contin.* **2023**, *77*, 3057–3075. [CrossRef]
39. Shahsavari, M.; Mohammadi, V.; Alizadeh, B.; Alizadeh, H. Application of Machine Learning Algorithms and Feature Selection in Rapeseed (*Brassica napus* L.) Breeding for Seed Yield. *Plant Methods* **2023**, *19*, 57. [CrossRef] [PubMed]
40. Chen, Y.; Ye, Z.; Gao, B.; Wu, Y.; Yan, X.; Liao, X. A Robust Adaptive Hierarchical Learning Crow Search Algorithm for Feature Selection. *Electronics* **2023**, *12*, 3123. [CrossRef]
41. Jain, S.; Dharavath, R. Memetic Salp Swarm Optimization Algorithm Based Feature Selection Approach for Crop Disease Detection System. *J. Ambient. Intell. Humaniz. Comput.* **2023**, *14*, 1817–1835. [CrossRef]
42. Shaheen, M.; Naheed, N.; Ahsan, A. Relevance-Diversity Algorithm for Feature Selection and Modified Bayes for Prediction. *Alex. Eng. J.* **2023**, *66*, 329–342. [CrossRef]
43. Ramdhani, Y.; Putra, C.M.; Alamsyah, D.P. Heart Failure Prediction Based on Random Forest Algorithm Using Genetic Algorithm for Feature Selection. *Int. J. Reconfig. Embed. Syst.* **2023**, *12*, 205–214. [CrossRef]
44. Abd Elaziz, M.; Dahou, A.; Al-Betar, M.A.; El-Sappagh, S.; Oliva, D.; Aseeri, A.O. Quantum Artificial Hummingbird Algorithm for Feature Selection of Social IoT. *IEEE Access* **2023**, *11*, 66257–66278. [CrossRef]
45. Saibene, A.; Gasparini, F. Genetic Algorithm for Feature Selection of EEG Heterogeneous Data. *Expert. Syst. Appl.* **2023**, *217*, 119488. [CrossRef]
46. Altarabichi, M.G.; Nowaczyk, S.; Pashami, S.; Mashhadi, P.S. Fast Genetic Algorithm for Feature Selection—A Qualitative Approximation Approach. *Expert. Syst. Appl.* **2023**, *211*, 118528. [CrossRef]
47. Espinosa, R.; Jiménez, F.; Palma, J. Multi-Surrogate Assisted Multi-Objective Evolutionary Algorithms for Feature Selection in Regression and Classification Problems with Time Series Data. *Inf. Sci.* **2023**, *622*, 1064–1091. [CrossRef]
48. Ay, Ş.; Ekinci, E.; Garip, Z. A Comparative Analysis of Meta-Heuristic Optimization Algorithms for Feature Selection on ML-Based Classification of Heart-Related Diseases. *J. Supercomput.* **2023**, *79*, 11797–11826. [CrossRef] [PubMed]
49. Zaimoğlu, E.A.; Yurtay, N.; Demirci, H.; Yurtay, Y. A Binary Chaotic Horse Herd Optimization Algorithm for Feature Selection. *Eng. Sci. Technol. Int. J.* **2023**, *44*, 101453. [CrossRef]
50. Xu, M.; Song, Q.; Xi, M.; Zhou, Z. Binary Arithmetic Optimization Algorithm for Feature Selection. *Soft Comput.* **2023**, *27*, 11395–11429. [CrossRef]
51. Oh, S.; Ahn, C.W. Evolutionary Approach for Interpretable Feature Selection Algorithm in Manufacturing Industry. *IEEE Access* **2023**, *11*, 46604–46614. [CrossRef]
52. Kovács, L. Feature Selection Algorithms in Generalized Additive Models under Concurvity. *Comput. Stat.* **2024**, *39*, 461–493. [CrossRef]

53. Zhao, L.; Li, Y.; Li, S.; Ke, H. A Frequency Item Mining Based Embedded Feature Selection Algorithm and Its Application in Energy Consumption Prediction of Electric Bus. *Energy* **2023**, *271*, 126999. [CrossRef]
54. Zhang, Z.; Song, F.; Zhang, P.; Chao, H.C.; Zhao, Y. A New Online Field Feature Selection Algorithm Based on Streaming Data. *J. Ambient. Intell. Humaniz. Comput.* **2024**, *15*, 1365–1377. [CrossRef]
55. Yang, F.; Xu, Z.; Wang, H.; Sun, L.; Zhai, M.; Zhang, J. A Hybrid Feature Selection Algorithm Combining Information Gain and Grouping Particle Swarm Optimization for Cancer Diagnosis. *PLoS ONE* **2024**, *19*, e0290332. [CrossRef]
56. Zhu, Z. Analysis of the Innovation Path of University Education Management Informatization in the Era of Big Data. *Appl. Math. Nonlinear Sci.* **2024**, *9*, 1–14. [CrossRef]
57. Yilmaz, M.; Yalcin, E.; Kifah, S.; Demir, F.; Sengur, A.; Demir, R.; Mehmood, R.M. Improving the Classification Performance of Asphalt Cracks After Earthquake With a New Feature Selection Algorithm. *IEEE Access* **2024**, *12*, 6604–6614. [CrossRef]
58. SabbaghGol, H.; Saadatfar, H.; Khazaiepoor, M. Evolution of the Random Subset Feature Selection Algorithm for Classification Problem. *Knowl. Based Syst.* **2024**, *285*, 111352. [CrossRef]
59. Almutairi, M.S. Evolutionary Multi-Objective Feature Selection Algorithms on Multiple Smart Sustainable Community Indicator Datasets. *Sustainability* **2024**, *16*, 1511. [CrossRef]

*algorithms*

MDPI

*Article*

# Attribute Relevance Score: A Novel Measure for Identifying Attribute Importance

**Pablo Neirz †, Hector Allende † and Carolina Saavedra *,†**

Departamento de Informática, Universidad Técnica Federico Santa María, Valparaíso 1680, Chile; pneira@usm.cl (P.N.); hector.allende@usm.cl (H.A.)
* Correspondence: carolina.saavedra@usm.cl
† These authors contributed equally to this work.

**Abstract:** This study introduces a novel measure for evaluating attribute relevance, specifically designed to accurately identify attributes that are intrinsically related to a phenomenon, while being sensitive to the asymmetry of those relationships and noise conditions. Traditional variable selection techniques, such as filter and wrapper methods, often fall short in capturing these complexities. Our methodology, grounded in decision trees but extendable to other machine learning models, was rigorously evaluated across various data scenarios. The results demonstrate that our measure effectively distinguishes relevant from irrelevant attributes and highlights how relevance is influenced by noise, providing a more nuanced understanding compared to established methods such as Pearson, Spearman, Kendall, MIC, MAS, MEV, GMIC, and $Phi_k$. This research underscores the importance of phenomenon-centric explainability, reproducibility, and robust attribute relevance evaluation in the development of predictive models. By enhancing both the interpretability and contextual accuracy of models, our approach not only supports more informed decision making but also contributes to a deeper understanding of the underlying mechanisms in diverse application domains, such as biomedical research, financial modeling, astronomy, and others.

**Keywords:** feature importance; feature selection; feature ranking; dependency measures; machine learning explainability; all-relevant problem

## 1. Introduction

In recent years, there has been significant advancement in methods for feature relevance and dependency assessment across a range of fields, from biomedical research to artificial intelligence and data engineering. Traditional approaches, such as those based on linear correlations, are well suited for capturing monotonic relationships but often fail in the presence of complex, nonlinear dependencies. Recent studies emphasize the limitations of these classical metrics and advocate for robust methods that adapt to diverse data characteristics. For instance, Khan et al. (2023) [1] highlight the challenges posed by high-dimensional data and underscore the need for feature selection methods that ensure computational efficiency without sacrificing relevance accuracy. Similarly, in biomedical contexts, methods that go beyond linear dependencies are essential for identifying complex, nonlinear relationships that could otherwise be overlooked by conventional techniques [2].

The rise of Big Data has intensified the need for scalable metrics capable of managing noisy and complex datasets [3]. Advanced methods, including metaheuristic algorithms, have demonstrated strong potential in unsupervised feature selection and clustering, offering robustness and adaptability for diverse data analysis needs. These methods are increasingly relevant for applications requiring reliable feature relevance assessment in complex, high-dimensional settings [4,5].

In the context of high-dimensional data analysis, identifying relevant attributes is critical for the effective implementation of machine learning methods and statistical analysis. This challenge can be approached from two primary perspectives: the "minimal optimal problem" and the "all-relevant problem". The former focuses on determining the smallest set of attributes that optimizes model performance, while the latter aims to identify all attributes that exhibit a relationship with the target variable, regardless of noise, redundancy, or indirect interactions [6]. The "all-relevant problem" is particularly valuable when seeking to understand the underlying mechanisms of the phenomenon under study, rather than merely building a predictive model. For example, in the medical field, when working with large datasets containing multiple attributes potentially related to cancer, the goal is to identify which of these attributes are truly relevant for prediction, even if they have been previously overlooked due to noise, complex interactions, or redundancy.

To address the "all-relevant problem", there is a growing preference for wrapper methods over classical statistical approaches. Wrapper methods combine a machine learning algorithm, a relevance criterion, and a search procedure that explores potential subsets of relevant features. These procedures are often heuristic and guided by the performance of an underlying model, frequently based on decision trees due to their interpretability and ability to handle complex variable interactions. However, wrapper algorithms have limitations, such as the absence of a measure that distinguishes the magnitude of relevance and the inability to clearly identify interactions among attributes or assess the likelihood of results being due to chance.

According to Kohavi and John (1997) [7], the relevance of a feature in a classification context should be defined in terms of its impact on the performance of an optimal Bayes classifier. A feature $\mathbf{x}$ is considered strongly relevant if its removal alone causes a deterioration in the performance of the optimal Bayes classifier. In other words, a strongly relevant feature is indispensable for maintaining the classifier's prediction accuracy. Conversely, a feature is considered weakly relevant if it is not strongly relevant, but there exists a subset of attributes $S$ such that the performance of the Bayes classifier on $S$ is worse than its performance on $S \cup \{\mathbf{x}\}$. This implies that while a weakly relevant feature may not always be critical, it can still contribute to improving the classifier's accuracy in specific contexts. A feature is deemed irrelevant if it is neither strongly nor weakly relevant; that is, its inclusion or exclusion does not affect the performance of the classifier. Understanding these distinctions is essential for determining the contribution and interaction of each feature within the dataset, which is a fundamental aspect of effective feature selection.

A notable issue with Kohavi and John's definition is that if we have two identical attributes $\mathbf{x}_1$ and $\mathbf{x}_2$, both strongly correlated with the target $\mathbf{y}$, removing one will not degrade the classifier's performance. Thus, according to their definition, $\mathbf{x}_1$ and $\mathbf{x}_2$ would not be considered strongly relevant, despite their strong relationship with the target. This limitation raises questions about whether Kohavi and John's definition intuitively captures relevance, particularly when an attribute that fully conveys information about the target could be categorized as weakly relevant [8].

Permutation feature importance, introduced by Breiman [9], is a fundamental technique for evaluating feature importance in supervised learning models. It involves randomly shuffling (i.e., randomly permuting) each feature's values and measuring the resulting performance drop, directly estimating each feature's relevance. A feature is relevant if its permutation significantly decreases the model's predictive accuracy, indicating its critical role. However, Strobl et al. [10] found that permutation-based measures can be biased, favoring high-cardinality features due to their higher chance of reducing impurity by chance. They proposed conditional permutation and tree-growing algorithm modifications to mitigate these biases, enhancing interpretability and validity in random forest models.

Stoppiglia et al. [11] introduced an innovative approach to the "all-relevant problem" in wrapper methods by incorporating a "test attribute" into the feature selection process. This randomly generated attribute, expected to be unrelated to the target variable, is added to the candidate attributes. The importance of other attributes is then evaluated based on their performance relative to the test attribute, determining relevance based on whether an attribute is ranked higher or lower than the test attribute. Unlike Kohavi and John's relevance definition, which may underestimate important attributes, Stoppiglia's approach considers an attribute relevant if its contribution exceeds that of a random attribute acting as a risk threshold, offering a more intuitive and practical perspective on relevance.

However, Stoppiglia's approach presents challenges, such as determining an acceptable risk threshold. In large datasets, more permissive risk thresholds may lead to the inclusion of irrelevant attributes. Additionally, heuristic-based selection may reduce the score of collinear attributes, and random attributes might, by chance, improve model performance, falsely indicating relevance. These issues can lead to the undervaluation or exclusion of potentially relevant attributes, complicating comprehensive identification of all relevant features. Such challenges highlight the limitations of Stoppiglia's method in effectively addressing the "all-relevant problem".

Stoppiglia's concept of outperforming test attributes has been adopted by algorithms designed to solve the "all-relevant problem", such as the Boruta algorithm [12]. These algorithms use admissible risk thresholds, addressing issues identified by Stoppiglia and reducing the arbitrariness introduced by random attributes.

Boruta, named after a Slavic forest god, was developed to address the "all-relevant problem" in multivariate classification. It combines concepts from Stoppiglia and Breiman. Stoppiglia's idea involved comparing predictor variables against a randomly generated benchmark attribute, while Breiman introduced permuting attribute values to assess feature importance. In Boruta, "shadow" attributes, created by permuting original attribute values, are used as benchmarks. These shadow attributes, unrelated to the target but retaining key statistical properties, ensure that both original and shadow attributes come from the same distribution. Boruta rigorously evaluates feature relevance by comparing original attributes against the highest-performing shadow attribute through statistical tests and multiple iterations of random forest. An attribute is deemed relevant if it consistently outperforms the best-performing shadow attribute, setting a high threshold and mitigating biases in feature selection processes [13]. While Boruta excels in multivariate contexts, in this work we focus on applying its principles in a univariate framework. In practical applications, relationships between variables are rarely symmetrical, and attributes with low cardinality often provide limited predictive power for those with high cardinality. For instance, an attribute with only three unique values is unlikely to effectively predict another with 100 unique values, whereas the attribute with higher cardinality could serve as a near-perfect predictor of the one with fewer values. This challenge, particularly evident in real-world scenarios, was highlighted by Wetschoreck (2020) [14].

### 1.1. Reproducibility

The challenges of reproducibility in machine learning, particularly in the context of high-dimensional data analysis, have been extensively examined. Goodman, Fanelli, and Ioannidis [15] categorize reproducibility into three essential types: methods reproducibility, which ensures that technical procedures can be precisely replicated; results reproducibility, which guarantees that reimplementations of a method produce statistically consistent outcomes; and inferential reproducibility, the most crucial of the three, which ensures that conclusions drawn from data are robust and generalizable across different experimental conditions. Bouthillier et al. [16] built upon this framework, emphasizing its importance in the context of machine learning, where these forms of reproducibility are essential for validating research findings and ensuring that they are not mere artifacts of specific experimental designs.

Moreover, factors such as data sampling, model initialization, and hyperparameter optimization introduce variability that can obscure true model performance. Addressing and modeling these sources of variability is essential for enhancing the reliability of machine learning benchmarks [17]. These principles are particularly related in the context of feature selection, where rigorous and reproducible methods are vital to ensure that the identified features genuinely contribute to the model's predictive power. Collectively, these approaches highlight the necessity of careful experimental design and robust evaluation criteria, which are indispensable for accurately determining the relevance of features in high-dimensional datasets.

A/B testing, a widely used technique in experimental design and digital marketing, shares several key principles with reproducibility-focused methodologies. A/B testing involves comparing two versions of a product or feature (commonly referred to as A and B versions) to determine which performs better according to a predefined metric [18]. This process relies on statistical hypothesis testing to assess whether observed differences in performance are statistically significant, thereby informing decisions about which version should be adopted [19].

### *1.2. Phenomenon-Centric Explainability*

In the rapidly evolving field of machine learning, the concept of explainability has become increasingly critical, particularly as models grow in complexity and are applied in high-stakes domains. Techniques such as SHAP (SHapley Additive exPlanations) [20], LIME (Local Interpretable Model-agnostic Explanations) [21], and the frameworks proposed by Sokol [22] exemplify this approach by providing insights into how individual predictions are made. These methods aim to enhance user trust and enable validation of complex models by attributing importance scores to individual features, thereby making the model's decisions more transparent and comprehensible.

However, recent work by Lapuschkin et al. [23], in "Unmasking Clever Hans predictors and assessing what machines really learn", highlights the significant limitations of relying solely on traditional explainability techniques. Their study demonstrates that models can generate seemingly accurate predictions based on spurious correlations within the training data, reminiscent of the "Clever Hans" effect observed in psychology [24].

Similarly, machine learning models may appear to perform well by leveraging incidental patterns in the data patterns that do not genuinely reflect the underlying phenomena. These issues become particularly evident in studies where models achieve high predictive accuracy by leveraging spurious correlations in the training data [25,26]. Similarly, in computer vision, research has shown that models can misclassify images due to subtle perturbations that are imperceptible to the human eye [27]. Additionally, recent work by Wang et al. [28] has demonstrated how dataset biases can influence the conclusions drawn from SHAP values. These examples underscore the necessity of ensuring that model predictions are grounded in genuine, relevant patterns that accurately capture the true underlying processes, rather than being influenced by misleading artifacts.

In light of these findings, we propose a paradigm shift towards *phenomenon-centric explainability*, which emphasizes understanding the underlying phenomena that models are designed to capture. This approach is particularly critical in scientific research and in addressing complex challenges such as the "all-relevant problem". In these contexts, the primary objective is to gain deep insights into domain-specific processes, recognizing the importance of uncovering relationships—whether causal, dependent, or instrumental—rather than merely optimizing predictive accuracy. This perspective suggests that phenomenon-centric explainability represents a logical and necessary evolution, aligning with the traditional goals of scientific inquiry, such as exploring complex relationships and underlying mechanisms, without relying on interpretations that may be influenced by spurious correlations in the training data.

## 2. Proposal: Attribute Relevance Score

In this work, within the framework of the all-relevant problem, we introduce a novel univariate approach for evaluating attribute relevance, designed to tackle the inherent challenges of feature selection in high-dimensional datasets. Our approach builds upon the concept of shadow attributes, introduced by L. Breiman and later used by M.B. Kursa in the Boruta algorithm, to create a more robust measure of individual attribute importance. Unlike traditional methods, which may produce biased results due to specific data splits or data assumptions, our technique systematically evaluates each attribute's contribution by comparing it against its permuted versions. This process ensures that the relevance identified for each feature truly reflects underlying patterns in the data rather than artifacts from specific data splits or model configurations, enhancing both the reliability and interpretability of the results.

Consider an attribute matrix $\mathbf{X} \in \mathbb{R}^{n \times m}$, where $n$ represents the number of samples and $m$ denotes the number of attributes, along with its corresponding labels $\mathbf{y} \in \mathbb{R}^n$. To evaluate a specific attribute $\mathbf{x} = [x_1, x_2, \ldots, x_n]^T$, where each $x_i$ represents an observation, we begin by partitioning $\mathbf{x}$ into training and testing subsets, denoted as $\mathbf{x}_{\text{train}}$ and $\mathbf{x}_{\text{test}}$, respectively, such that $\mathbf{x} = \mathbf{x}_{\text{train}} \cup \mathbf{x}_{\text{test}}$ and $\mathbf{x}_{\text{train}} \cap \mathbf{x}_{\text{test}} = \varnothing$.

A model $\mathcal{M}$ (e.g., a decision tree) is then trained using the training subset $\mathbf{x}_{\text{train}}$ and its corresponding labels $\mathbf{y}_{\text{train}}$. Subsequently, a shadow model, $\mathcal{M}_s$, is trained using a permutation of $\mathbf{x}_{\text{train}}$, denoted as $\mathbf{x}_s$, with the same labels $\mathbf{y}_{\text{train}}$.

We then consider a performance measure $F$ that results from evaluating the output of a model on the test subset $\mathbf{x}_{\text{test}}$, compared to the correct labels $\mathbf{y}_{\text{test}}$. The choice of $F$ should be made according to the specific problem at hand.

The core premise of our approach is that the performance measure $F$ of the model $\mathcal{M}$, trained on the original attribute $\mathbf{x}_{\text{train}}$, should consistently be superior to that of the shadow model $\mathcal{M}_s$, trained on the permuted attribute $\mathbf{x}_s$, when both are evaluated on the same test subset $\mathbf{x}_{\text{test}}$ with labels $\mathbf{y}_{\text{test}}$.

$$\text{Opt}(F(\mathcal{M})) > \text{Opt}(F(\mathcal{M}_s)), \tag{1}$$

where $\text{Opt}(\cdot)$ represents an optimization criterion for $F$. Depending on the nature of $F$, this criterion could aim to maximize or minimize its value.

To minimize biases from specific test subsets, which could distort evaluations, we employ random sampling across multiple test subsets. This ensures a comprehensive and robust assessment of attribute relevance, capturing the magnitude of the observed effects and articulating them with a level of detail that supports precise and actionable conclusions.

We propose Equation (2) to calculate the attribute relevance score (ARS) for performance metrics $F$, where "the closer to 1, the better", such as those commonly used in classification tasks (e.g., accuracy, F1 score, recall, and precision).

$$\text{ARS} = \max\left(0, \frac{\overline{F}(\mathcal{M}) - (\overline{F}(\mathcal{M}_s) + \epsilon)}{1 - (\overline{F}(\mathcal{M}_s) + \epsilon)}\right), \tag{2}$$

where $\overline{F}(\mathcal{M})$ represents the median performance of model $\mathcal{M}$ across multiple test subsets, $\overline{F}(\mathcal{M}_s)$ is the median performance of the shadow model over the same subsets, and $\epsilon$ is a small positive constant indicating the minimum acceptable effect size threshold. The ARS algorithm for classification is detailed in Algorithm 1.

The primary objective of our measure is to answer two fundamental questions:

1. Is there a significant dependency between an attribute $\mathbf{x}$ and another attribute or target variable $\mathbf{y}$, independent of factors such as cardinality, specific distributions, or artifacts from the data or model configuration? A score of $\text{ARS}(\mathbf{x}) > 0$ would indicate such a genuine dependency.
2. How effectively can $\mathbf{y}$ be approximated based on $\mathbf{x}$ using a specific error measure and a chosen algorithm? The attribute relevance score (ARS) quantifies the practical capability of $\mathbf{x}$ to predict or approximate $\mathbf{y}$, capturing not only the existence of a statistical dependency but also the magnitude of its predictive power in the context of the selected model and performance metric. This ensures that any detected relevance corresponds to a genuine and meaningful predictive capacity, rather than an artifact of the statistical properties of $\mathbf{x}$ or models based on chance.

To illustrate the behavior of the ARS and build intuition, consider the simple equation $\mathbf{y} = \mathbf{x}_1 + \mathbf{x}_2 + \mathbf{x}_3$, where $\mathbf{x}_i$ are three independent, nonredundant predictor attributes within the same range. Suppose that, for the first attribute, we obtain $\overline{F}(\mathcal{M}_s) + \epsilon = 0.5$ and $\overline{F}(\mathcal{M}) = 0.75$; for the second attribute, $\overline{F}(\mathcal{M}_s) + \epsilon = 0.5$ and $\overline{F}(\mathcal{M}) = 0.65$; and for the third attribute, $\overline{F}(\mathcal{M}_s) + \epsilon = 0.5$ and $\overline{F}(\mathcal{M}) = 0.6$. Calculating the attribute relevance score (ARS) for each attribute yields scores of 0.5, 0.3, and 0.2, respectively. Notably, in the ideal case, the sum of these scores is 1.0, which suggests that these three independent variables, collectively, have the capacity to fully represent the target variable. This example illustrates how the ARS quantifies the cumulative relevance of independent attributes, capturing the extent to which a set of predictors can collectively account for the target variable.

**Algorithm 1** Attribute relevance score for classification.

1: **Set up model:** (e.g., `DecisionTreeClassifier`)
2: **Set up performance metric** $F$**:** (e.g., $f_1$-score)
3: **Set up acceptable error margin:** $\epsilon$
4: **Set significance level:** $\alpha$ (e.g., $\alpha = 0.05$)
5: **Initialize** lists to store performance metrics of the original and shadow models
6: **for** iteration from 1 to $N$ **do**
7: Split the data into training and testing sets: $\mathbf{X}_{\text{train}}, \mathbf{X}_{\text{test}}, \mathbf{y}_{\text{train}}, \mathbf{y}_{\text{test}}$
8: Train the original model $\mathcal{M}$ on $\mathbf{X}_{\text{train}}$ and $\mathbf{y}_{\text{train}}$
9: Generate shadow attributes by permuting the original attributes to obtain $\mathbf{X}_{\text{shadow}}$
10: Train the shadow model $\mathcal{M}_s$ on $\mathbf{X}_{\text{shadow}}$ and $\mathbf{y}_{\text{train}}$
11: Evaluate and store the performance metric $F$ of both models $\mathcal{M}$ and $\mathcal{M}_s$ on $\mathbf{X}_{\text{test}}, \mathbf{y}_{\text{test}}$
12: **end for**
13: Compute the median performances $\overline{F}(\mathcal{M})$ and $\overline{F}(\mathcal{M}_s)$
14: **Conduct statistical test:** Perform a test of means (e.g., a $t$-test) on the performance metrics collected from $\mathcal{M}$ and $\mathcal{M}_s$ to obtain a $p$-value
15: **if** $p$-value $< \alpha$ **then**
16: Compute the Attribute Relevance Score (ARS) using the following formula:

$$\text{ARS} = \max\left(0, \frac{\overline{F}(\mathcal{M}) - (\overline{F}(\mathcal{M}_s) + \epsilon)}{1 - (\overline{F}(\mathcal{M}_s) + \epsilon)}\right)$$

17: **else**
18: **Set** ARS $= 0$
19: **end if**
20: **return** ARS and the $p$-value from the statistical test

In Step 13 of Algorithm 1, we conduct a statistical test (e.g., a $t$-test) to compare the performance metrics of the original model $\mathcal{M}$ and the shadow model $\mathcal{M}_s$. This test provides a $p$-value that quantifies the likelihood that the observed difference in performance occurred by chance. If the $p$-value is less than the significance level $\alpha$, we consider the difference in performance to be statistically significant. In this case, we proceed to compute the attribute relevance score (ARS) using the formula provided. If the $p$-value is greater than or equal to $\alpha$, we conclude that there is no statistically significant difference between the models. Therefore, we set ARS $= 0$, indicating that the attribute is not considered relevant.

By incorporating this statistical test, we embed statistical significance into our attribute relevance score. However, it is important to recognize that a low $p$-value is a necessary but not sufficient condition for establishing attribute relevance. Additional factors such as effect size, consistency across iterations, and practical significance should also be considered to ensure that the identified relevance corresponds to meaningful patterns rather than random fluctuations. This holistic approach emphasizes the importance of not relying solely on statistical significance but also assessing the practical implications of the findings to confirm that they align with genuine data relationships.

This scoring system not only facilitates the identification of relevant attributes but also significantly enhances the reliability and validity of the constructed predictive models. By incorporating multiple test subsets and focusing on statistical robustness, our approach ensures that the results are both generalizable and reproducible across diverse experimental conditions, thereby contributing to the advancement of more robust and credible data analysis in high-dimensional settings.

Moreover, with slight modifications, Algorithm 1 can also be adapted for performance metrics $F$ where "closer to zero is better" such as mean absolute error (MAE), mean absolute percentage error (MAPE), and root mean square error (RMSE), which are more common in regression problems, illustrated in Algorithm 2.

**Algorithm 2** Attribute relevance score for regression.

**Set up model:** (e.g., `DecisionTreeRegressor`)
**Set up performance metric** $F$**:** (e.g., Mean Absolute Error)
**Set up acceptable error margin:** $\epsilon$
**Set significance level:** $\alpha$ (e.g., $\alpha = 0.05$)
**Initialize** lists to store performance metrics of the original and shadow models
**for** iteration from 1 to $N$ **do**
    Split the data into training and testing sets: $\mathbf{X}_{\text{train}}, \mathbf{X}_{\text{test}}, \mathbf{y}_{\text{train}}, \mathbf{y}_{\text{test}}$
    Train the original model $\mathcal{M}$ on $\mathbf{X}_{\text{train}}$ and $\mathbf{y}_{\text{train}}$
    Generate shadow attributes by permuting the original attributes to obtain $\mathbf{X}_{\text{shadow}}$
    Train the shadow model $\mathcal{M}_s$ on $\mathbf{X}_{\text{shadow}}$ and $\mathbf{y}_{\text{train}}$
    Evaluate and store the performance metric $F$ (e.g., MAE) of both models $\mathcal{M}$ and $\mathcal{M}_s$ on $\mathbf{X}_{\text{test}}, \mathbf{y}_{\text{test}}$
**end for**
Compute the median performances $\overline{F}(\mathcal{M})$ and $\overline{F}(\mathcal{M}_s)$
**Conduct statistical test:** Perform a test of means (e.g., a $t$-test) on the performance metrics collected from $\mathcal{M}$ and $\mathcal{M}_s$ to obtain a $p$-value
**if** $p$-value $< \alpha$ **then**
    Compute the Attribute Relevance Score (ARS) using the following formula:

$$\text{ARS} = \max\left(0, \frac{(\overline{F}(\mathcal{M}_s) - \epsilon) - \overline{F}(\mathcal{M})}{(\overline{F}(\mathcal{M}_s) - \epsilon) - 0}\right)$$

**else**
    **Set** ARS $= 0$
**end if**
**return** ARS and the $p$-value from the statistical test

By using models that directly accept categorical variables, such as CatBoost [29], and selecting appropriate performance metrics for multilabel and multioutput problems, the ARS method can be seamlessly extended to handle a wide variety of data types and problem settings. This flexibility ensures that the method remains robust and effective across different domains, making it a valuable tool for feature selection and attribute relevance evaluation in diverse applications.

## 3. Materials and Methods

### 3.1. Pearson's Correlation

Among the most widely used filtering methods for determining attribute relevance, we first encounter Pearson's correlation, denoted by $r_{xy}$ (see Equation (3)).

$$r_{xy} = \frac{\sum_{i=1}^{n}(x_i - \bar{x})(y_i - \bar{y})}{\sqrt{\sum_{i=1}^{n}(x_i - \bar{x})^2 \sum_{i=1}^{n}(y_i - \bar{y})^2}} \tag{3}$$

where $x_i$ and $y_i$ are the individual observations of the variables, $\bar{x}$ and $\bar{y}$ denote the means, and $n$ denotes the total number of observations.

This technique identifies attributes that exhibit a high linear correlation with the target variable, potentially suggesting attribute relevance. Pearson's correlation values range between $-1$ and 1. The closer the coefficient is to 1 or $-1$, the stronger the linear correlation.

A coefficient of 1 indicates a perfect positive correlation, meaning that as one variable increases, the other variable increases in constant proportion. Conversely, a coefficient of $-1$ indicates a perfect negative correlation, meaning that as one variable increases, the other decreases in constant proportion. A coefficient of 0 indicates the absence of a linear relationship between the two variables, implying no linear correlation.

It is important to note the limitations of Pearson's correlation in detecting nonlinear relationships between variables, as well as its sensitivity to outliers, which can lead to biased or inaccurate interpretations in the attribute selection process.

### 3.2. Spearman's Correlation

Another classical option is Spearman's correlation (Equation (4)), denoted by $\rho$. Spearman's correlation, or Spearman's rank correlation coefficient, is a statistical measure that evaluates the relationship between two variables. Unlike Pearson's correlation, which assesses a linear relationship, Spearman's coefficient examines monotonic relationships, meaning that as one variable increases or decreases, the other also tends to increase or decrease, without requiring a strictly linear relationship.

For its calculation, Spearman's correlation relies on the ranks of the data rather than the actual values. That is, each value in a variable is replaced by its position or rank in magnitude within its respective dataset.

$$\rho = 1 - \frac{6\sum d_i^2}{n(n^2-1)} \tag{4}$$

where $d_i$ denotes the rank differences between the observations. If the variables $x_i$ and $y_i$ have ranks $r_{xi}$ and $r_{yi}$, respectively, then $d_i = r_{xi} - r_{yi}$, and $n$ denotes the total number of observations.

Similar to Pearson's correlation, Spearman's correlation values also range between $-1$ and 1, but their interpretation is slightly different. A coefficient of 1 indicates a perfect positive correlation, meaning that as one variable increases, the other variable also tends to increase in a monotonic relationship. Similarly, a coefficient of $-1$ indicates a perfect negative correlation, meaning that as one variable increases, the other variable tends to decrease in a monotonic relationship. A coefficient of 0 indicates the absence of a monotonic correlation between the two variables.

### 3.3. Kendall's Correlation

Kendall's correlation, or Kendall's rank correlation coefficient, denoted by $\tau$ (Equation (5)), is a statistical measure that evaluates the association between two ordinal variables. It is based on the concept of concordance and discordance between pairs of observations. A pair of observations is concordant if the relative order between the two variables is the same (i.e., if one observation is higher in both variables or lower in both). A pair is discordant if the relative order is different. Similar to Spearman's correlation, $\tau$ is useful for measuring monotonic relationships, and its range of values and interpretation are equivalent, ranging between $-1$ and 1. A value of 1 indicates a perfectly positive monotonic relationship, and a value of $-1$ indicates a perfectly negative monotonic relationship. The main advantage of $\tau$ over Spearman's correlation is its reduced sensitivity to outliers.

$$\tau = \frac{2}{n(n-1)} \sum_{i<j} sgn(x_i - x_j) sgn(y_i - y_j) \tag{5}$$

where $sgn(x_i - x_j)$ and $sgn(y_i - y_j)$ are the sign functions that return 1 if $x_i > x_j$ or $y_i > y_j$, $-1$ if $x_i < x_j$ or $y_i < y_j$, and 0 if $x_i = x_j$ or $y_i = y_j$. The sum counts the concordant and discordant pairs of observations. A pair of observations $(i, j)$ is concordant if both ($x_i > x_j$ and $y_i > y_j$) or ($x_i < x_j$ and $y_i < y_j$); otherwise, the pair is discordant.

### 3.4. Phi$_k$ Correlation

$\phi_k$ is a correlation coefficient developed by Baak et al. (2020) [30] to measure the association between two variables, including categorical and mixed variables (categorical and continuous), without the need for prior transformations. The aim of this coefficient is to provide a robust and more informative measure than traditional coefficients previously mentioned. Another difference is that its values range between 0 and 1, where 0 indicates no correlation and 1 indicates a perfect correlation. Since its calculation involves several rules, it does not have a closed-form formula:

1. Variable transformation: Categorical variables are handled using encoding, while numerical variables must be discretized if necessary. It is suggested to use 10 uniformly spaced bins per variable.
2. Contingency table: A contingency table is created with the transformed variables, where each pair contains $N$ observations, $r$ rows, and $k$ columns.
3. Pearson's chi-square test ($\chi^2$): The chi-square statistic is calculated for the contingency table, as described in Equation (6), to evaluate the independence between variables.
4. Calculation of $\phi_k$: The value of $\chi^2$ is interpreted as if it were derived from a bivariate normal distribution without statistical fluctuations, using Equations (7) and (8).
    - If $\chi^2 < \chi^2_{ped}$, then set $\rho$ to zero.
    - Else, with fixed $N, r, k$, invert the $\chi^2_{b.n.}$ function and numerically solve for $\rho$ in the range $[0, 1]$.
    - The solution for $\rho$ defines the correlation coefficient $\phi_k$

$$\chi^2 = \sum_{i=1}^{r}\sum_{j=1}^{k} \frac{(O_{ij} - E_{ij})^2}{E_{ij}} \tag{6}$$

where $O_{ij}$ represents the observed frequency in cell $ij$ of the contingency table, $E_{ij}$ represents the expected frequency in cell $ij$ under the null hypothesis of independence of the variables, $r$ is the number of rows in the contingency table, and $k$ is the number of columns in the contingency table.

$$\chi^2_{b.n.}(\rho, N, r, k) = \sum_{i=1}^{r}\sum_{j=1}^{k} \frac{(F_{ij}(\rho = \rho) - F_{ij}(\rho = 0))^2}{F_{ij}(\rho = 0)} \tag{7}$$

$$\chi^2_{b.n.}(\rho, N, r, k) = \chi^2_{ped} + \left(\frac{\chi^2_{max}(N, r, k) - \chi^2_{ped}}{\chi^2_{b.n.}(1, N, r, k)}\right) \cdot \chi^2_{b.n.}(\rho, N, r, k) \tag{8}$$

### 3.5. Mutual Information

From a perspective grounded in information theory, mutual information (MI) offers a distinct approach to understanding correlations by measuring how much information the knowledge of one variable provides about another. In other words, mutual information quantifies the reduction of uncertainty about one variable given information about the other variable (Equation (9)). The minimum value of MI is 0, indicating that two variables are completely independent, or that the knowledge of one variable provides no information about the other. It does not have a fixed upper limit; the maximum value can be as large as allowed by the entropy of each of the variables.

$$I(\mathbf{x}; \mathbf{y}) = \sum_{i=1}^{n}\sum_{j=1}^{m} P(x_i, y_j) \log\left(\frac{P(x_i, y_j)}{P(x_i)P(y_j)}\right) \tag{9}$$

where $P(x_i, y_j)$ is the joint probability that $\mathbf{x}$ takes the value $x_i$ and $\mathbf{y}$ takes the value $y_j$, while $P(x_i)$ and $P(y_j)$ are the marginal probabilities of $\mathbf{x}$ and $\mathbf{y}$, respectively. Mutual information is generally calculated over discrete probability distributions. Therefore, if the numerical variables are continuous, they may need to be discretized into intervals or categories. Since discretization can affect the accuracy of the calculation and lead to the loss of important information, in this work, we will use the scikit-learn implementation based on the work of Ross BC (2014) [31], which avoids discretization by using an entropy estimation based on K-nearest neighbor distances.

### 3.6. Maximal Information-Based Nonparametric Exploration Suite

The Maximal Information-Based Nonparametric Exploration (MINE) suite is a collection of statistical tools designed to detect a wide range of relationships between variables in large datasets. Unlike traditional correlation measures that often focus on linear associations, MINE is tailored to capture both linear and nonlinear dependencies without making strong assumptions about the underlying data distribution. Developed by Reshef et al. (2011) [32], the MINE suite includes several measures, such as the maximal information coefficient (MIC), maximal asymmetry score (MAS), maximal edge value (MEV), and generalized mean information coefficient (GMIC), each designed to identify different types of associations in a data-driven manner.

One of the primary measures in the MINE suite, the maximal information coefficient (MIC), represents a significant advancement in detecting complex associations within data. MIC is specifically designed to identify both linear and nonlinear dependencies between two variables, making it particularly valuable in scenarios where relationships are complex or nonlinear and difficult to capture with conventional methods.

The methodology behind MIC involves optimizing the partitioning of the data space to maximize the normalized mutual information between variables (Equation (10)). It systematically explores all possible ways of dividing the data into grids and evaluates the strength of the relationship within each partition, selecting the configuration that maximizes normalized mutual information:

$$MIC(\mathbf{x};\mathbf{y}) = \max_{G\in\text{Grids}(\mathbf{x},\mathbf{y})} \left\{ \frac{I(\mathbf{x};\mathbf{y} \mid G)}{\log(\min\{|\mathbf{x}|,|\mathbf{y}|\})} \right\} \tag{10}$$

where $I(\mathbf{x};\mathbf{y} \mid G)$ is the mutual information conditioned on a specific grid partition $G$, and $|\mathbf{x}|$ and $|\mathbf{x}|$ denote the cardinalities of variables $\mathbf{x}$ and $\mathbf{y}$. The normalization ensures that MIC values range between 0 and 1, where 1 indicates a perfect association.

MIC has been recognized for its ability to uncover complex patterns in data, and software tools like "minepy" version 1.2.6, created by Davide Albanese under a GNU General Public License (GPL). Refs. [33,34] have made it accessible for large-scale analyses. However, the exhaustive evaluation of multiple data partitions can be computationally intensive. To address this, Reshef et al. introduced optimizations to improve computational efficiency, especially in high-dimensional datasets.

The MINE suite also includes the maximal asymmetry score (MAS), which extends the capability of detecting asymmetrical relationships that symmetric measures often overlook. MAS quantifies the degree of asymmetry in the relationship between two variables, offering a more nuanced perspective:

$$MAS(\mathbf{x};\mathbf{y}) = \max_{G\in\text{Grids}(\mathbf{x},\mathbf{y})} \left\{ \frac{|(\mathbf{x};\mathbf{y} \mid G) - I(Y;X \mid G)|}{\log(\min\{|\mathbf{x}|,|\mathbf{y}|\})} \right\} \tag{11}$$

where $(\mathbf{x};\mathbf{y} \mid G)$ and $I(Y;X \mid G)$ are mutual information measures calculated in opposite directions. MAS values between 0 and 1 reflect the extent of asymmetry in the association.

Additionally, the maximal edge value (MEV) focuses on identifying the strongest dependencies within subsets of data, which may not be uniformly strong across all points but exhibit significant relationships in specific regions:

$$MEV(\mathbf{x};\mathbf{y}) = \max_{G\in\text{Grids}(\mathbf{x},\mathbf{y})} \{\text{EdgeValue}((\mathbf{x};\mathbf{y} \mid G))\} \tag{12}$$

where $\text{EdgeValue}((\mathbf{x}; \mathbf{y} \mid G))$ is the mutual information at the boundaries of a grid partition $G$, highlighting local dependencies that might be averaged out in global measures like MIC.

### *3.7. Generalized Mean Information Coefficient*

The generalized mean information coefficient (GMIC), proposed by Luedtke and Tran [35], extends the maximal information coefficient (MIC) by introducing a more flexible framework for detecting associations, particularly in finite sample settings. The GMIC enhances the sensitivity of MIC by incorporating a generalized mean approach, which allows for a more nuanced detection of statistical dependencies between variables.

The core innovation of GMIC lies in its use of a maximal characteristic matrix, defined as follows:

$$C^*(\mathbf{x}, \mathbf{y})_{i,j} = \max_{kl \le ij} \{C(\mathbf{x}, \mathbf{y})_{kl}\}, \tag{13}$$

where $i, j \ge 2$. This matrix captures the highest normalized mutual information that can be obtained with grid sizes up to $ij$, providing a robust measure of the strongest possible association achievable for each grid resolution.

GMIC itself is calculated using a generalized mean, which is defined as follows:

$$GMIC_p(\mathbf{x}, \mathbf{y}) = \left( \frac{1}{Z} \sum_{ij \le B(n)} (C^*(\mathbf{x}, \mathbf{y})_{i,j})^p \right)^{1/p}, \tag{14}$$

where $p$ is a tuning parameter that adjusts the measure's sensitivity to different aspects of the data, and $Z = \#\{(i,j) : ij \le B(n)\}$ denotes the number of grid sizes considered. By varying $p$, GMIC can emphasize different features of the data's structure; for example, when $p \to \infty$, it approaches the original MIC, while for $p \to -\infty$, GMIC converges to the minimal value from the maximal characteristic matrix

The introduction of the tuning parameter $p$ provides flexibility, allowing GMIC to detect a broader range of complex associations across various data types. In simulations, GMIC has demonstrated improved power over MIC for detecting associations, particularly in finite samples. It retains desirable properties, such as convergence to zero for independent variables as the sample size increases, and convergence to one for noiseless, monotonic relationships.

Overall, GMIC enhances the capabilities of the MINE suite by offering a more adaptive and sensitive approach to uncovering diverse relationships in complex datasets, making it a valuable tool for exploratory data analysis in high-dimensional contexts.

## 4. Simulation Results

### *4.1. Experiment #1: Computer-Generated Data*

This study utilizes a synthetically generated dataset to evaluate the performance of the proposed methods under various types of bivariate relationships, including both linear and nonlinear dependencies. The data were created using multiple transformations and multivariate normal distributions to simulate distinct scenarios that reflect complexities commonly observed in real-world datasets. The goal is to assess the robustness and effectiveness of the proposed attribute relevance score (ARS) (using decision trees as the base model), and other established dependency measures across diverse data configurations.

- **Multivariate normal distributions**: Seven datasets, each containing 1000 samples, were generated using multivariate normal distributions with correlation coefficients ranging from $-1.0$ to 1.0. These datasets represent different degrees of linear relationships between variables, labeled from (A) to (G) in Figure 1.
- **Rotated normal distributions**: To examine the effect of rotational transformations on normally distributed data, seven datasets of 1000 samples each were created by applying specific rotation angles (ranging from 0 to $\pi/2$) to a bivariate normal

distribution with equal variance and high covariance. These are labeled from (H) to (N) in Figure 1. A special case, labeled (K) with unique horizontal distribution, was included to demonstrate a scenario with zero correlation. These transformations model linear relationships oriented in diverse directions.

- **Other nonlinear and complex distributions**: This category includes seven distinct datasets representing various nonlinear, asymmetric, and complex dependencies. They are labeled from (O) to (U) in Figure 1. Key examples are the following:
  - (O): Displays a quadratic dependency with added noise.
  - (P) and (Q): Represent sequential rotations applied to uniformly distributed data.
  - (R) and (S): Exhibit parabolic and partially symmetric patterns.
  - (T): Simulates a trigonometric relationship combining sinusoidal and cosinusoidal transformations.
  - (U): Comprises a clustered structure formed by four multivariate normal distributions centered at distinct locations, resembling spatially separated clusters.

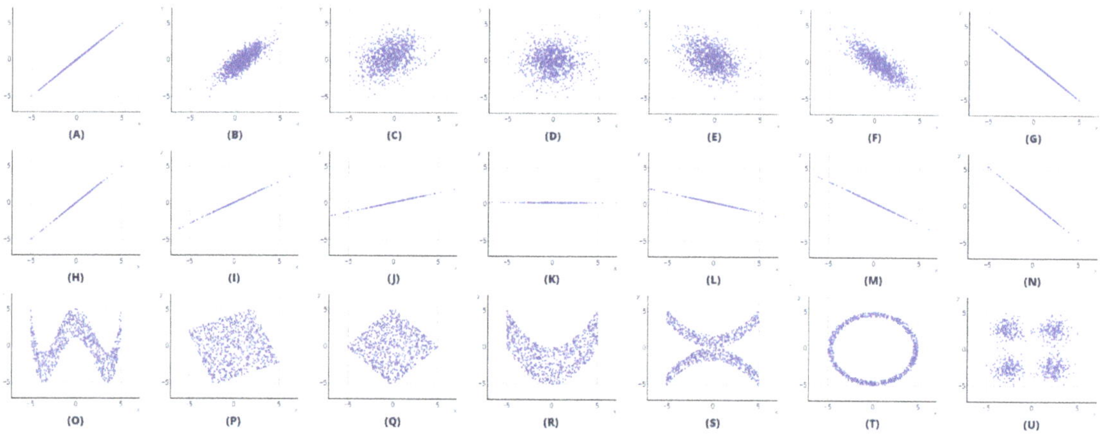


**Figure 1.** Scatter plots illustrating various bivariate relationships generated. Each subplot represents a different synthetic dataset: (**A–G**) are datasets generated from multivariate normal distributions with varying correlations; (**H–N**) are datasets generated from rotated normal distributions, illustrating different linear relationships; (**O–U**) represent other complex, nonlinear patterns.

To ensure comparability across subsets, all data were scaled using MinMax scaling within the range of −5 to 5, preserving the inherent structural relationships while normalizing their ranges, as illustrated in Figure 1.

Results #1

Table 1 presents the performance of various dependency measures applied to the synthetically generated datasets described in the previous section. Each dataset was designed to capture different types of bivariate relationships, including both linear and nonlinear dependencies, to assess the robustness and effectiveness of the proposed attribute relevance score (ARS) and other correlation measures.

The results demonstrate that for datasets based on **multivariate normal distributions (A–G)**, the ARS and other linear measures such as Pearson and Spearman coefficients perform as expected when the relationship between variables is linear. In particular, datasets (A) and (G), which exhibit perfect linear correlation, yield maximum values (1.000) for most measures, including Pearson, Spearman, Kendall, and $Phi_k$, with corresponding high ARS scores of 0.996. Similarly, datasets with moderate to low correlation levels (e.g., (B) and (F)) show a consistent decline in these measures, with ARS scores reflecting these variations (0.429 and 0.394, respectively).

**Table 1.** Comparison of various dependency measures across different datasets. The columns represent different metrics: $r_{xy}$ is the Pearson correlation coefficient, $\rho$ is the Spearman rank correlation coefficient, and $\tau$ is Kendall's tau coefficient. These metrics assess the linear and monotonic relationships between variables, while other columns represent measures of mutual information (MI), maximal information coefficient (MIC), maximal asymmetry score (MAS), maximum edge-value (MEV), generalized mean information coefficient (GMIC), and the proposed attribute relevance score (ARS).

| Set | $r_{xy}$ | $\rho$ | $\tau$ | $\phi_k$ | MI | MIC | MAS | MEV | GMIC | ARS Proposed |
|---|---|---|---|---|---|---|---|---|---|---|
| (A) | 1.000 | 1.000 | 1.000 | 1.000 | 5.984 | 1.000 | 0.000 | 1.000 | 1.000 | 0.996 |
| (B) | 0.805 | 0.783 | 0.587 | 0.859 | 0.575 | 0.519 | 0.030 | 0.519 | 0.461 | 0.429 |
| (C) | 0.378 | 0.378 | 0.258 | 0.373 | 0.081 | 0.200 | 0.017 | 0.200 | 0.148 | 0.049 |
| (D) | 0.009 | 0.016 | 0.010 | 0.157 | 0.007 | 0.126 | 0.007 | 0.126 | 0.054 | 0.000 |
| (E) | 0.394 | 0.383 | 0.261 | 0.407 | 0.054 | 0.215 | 0.015 | 0.215 | 0.158 | 0.089 |
| (F) | 0.809 | 0.800 | 0.606 | 0.817 | 0.508 | 0.512 | 0.015 | 0.512 | 0.465 | 0.394 |
| (G) | 1.000 | 1.000 | 1.000 | 1.000 | 5.984 | 1.000 | 0.000 | 1.000 | 1.000 | 0.996 |
| (H) | 1.000 | 1.000 | 1.000 | 1.000 | 4.373 | 1.000 | 0.000 | 1.000 | 1.000 | 0.980 |
| (I) | 1.000 | 1.000 | 1.000 | 1.000 | 4.373 | 1.000 | 0.000 | 1.000 | 1.000 | 0.980 |
| (J) | 1.000 | 1.000 | 1.000 | 1.000 | 4.373 | 1.000 | 0.000 | 1.000 | 1.000 | 0.980 |
| (K) | 0.606 | 0.624 | 0.483 | 0.784 | 0.697 | 0.498 | 0.038 | 0.498 | 0.412 | 0.000 |
| (L) | 1.000 | 1.000 | 1.000 | 1.000 | 4.373 | 1.000 | 0.000 | 1.000 | 1.000 | 0.980 |
| (M) | 1.000 | 1.000 | 1.000 | 1.000 | 4.373 | 1.000 | 0.000 | 1.000 | 1.000 | 0.980 |
| (N) | 1.000 | 1.000 | 1.000 | 1.000 | 4.373 | 1.000 | 0.000 | 1.000 | 1.000 | 0.980 |
| (O) | 0.052 | 0.046 | 0.033 | 0.732 | 0.733 | 0.773 | 0.626 | 0.773 | 0.670 | 0.477 |
| (P) | 0.014 | 0.014 | 0.006 | 0.525 | 0.240 | 0.195 | 0.026 | 0.195 | 0.136 | 0.046 |
| (Q) | 0.036 | 0.044 | 0.023 | 0.526 | 0.315 | 0.163 | 0.025 | 0.138 | 0.121 | 0.024 |
| (R) | 0.028 | 0.028 | 0.018 | 0.688 | 0.534 | 0.416 | 0.245 | 0.416 | 0.382 | 0.297 |
| (S) | 0.020 | 0.021 | 0.018 | 0.783 | 0.902 | 0.450 | 0.037 | 0.262 | 0.208 | 0.135 |
| (T) | 0.025 | 0.020 | 0.003 | 0.836 | 1.421 | 0.566 | 0.079 | 0.376 | 0.443 | 0.215 |
| (U) | 0.013 | 0.025 | 0.017 | 0.000 | 0.012 | 0.134 | 0.009 | 0.134 | 0.065 | 0.000 |

For the **rotated normal distributions (H–N)**, the ARS effectively captures the directional dependencies across different orientations. Datasets (H) to (J) and (L) to (N) maintain high scores across all measures (1.000), including ARS values around 0.980, indicating the robustness of the ARS in identifying dependencies even when the data are rotated. Notably, dataset (K), which presents no linear or clear directional correlation, shows an ARS value of 0.000, while other measures still return nonzero values. This highlights the ARS's unique sensitivity to the absence of any meaningful relationship, effectively distinguishing it from traditional dependency measures.

The results for the **other nonlinear and complex distributions (O–U)** highlight the limitations of traditional linear measures in capturing intricate dependencies. For instance, in dataset (O), which exhibits a quadratic dependency, the ARS score (0.477) is notably higher than those of other measures, such as Pearson (0.052) and Spearman (0.046), demonstrating ARS's ability to detect nonlinear patterns. Similarly, datasets (R) and (T), featuring parabolic and trigonometric relationships, yield ARS values (0.297 and 0.215, respectively) that surpass those of the linear measures, suggesting that ARS offers a more refined assessment of these complex dependencies. Notably, datasets (D) and (K), which do not exhibit any significant linear or nonlinear relationships, have ARS scores of 0.000, whereas other measures still return nonzero values. This distinction underscores the ARS's unique sensitivity to the absence of meaningful relationships, effectively setting it apart from traditional dependency measures. However, for dataset (U), which represents a clustered structure formed by four multivariate normal distributions centered at distinct locations, it may be arguable whether any of the measures presented, including ARS, effectively capture the inherent clustering pattern. In this case, all measures, including ARS, tend to produce the lowest values observed, indicating the potential limitations of these metrics in identifying complex clustering structures.

Overall, the results indicate that ARS is a robust metric for capturing both linear and nonlinear dependencies across diverse types of relationships. In comparison to traditional measures such as Pearson, Spearman, and Kendall—which are effective at identifying monotonic dependencies but limited with more complex nonlinear relationships—the ARS consistently outperformed these classical methods, particularly on datasets (O) to (U). By using ARS alongside conventional metrics, a more comprehensive framework is established for evaluating bivariate dependencies, fulfilling the objectives of this study and providing valuable insights across a broad range of real-world scenarios.

### 4.2. Experiment #2: Benchmark Dataset

This section aims to compare our proposed method against established predictive approaches using a synthetic dataset that has been used in prior research [12,36]. The selected benchmark dataset is particularly suitable for this evaluation as it incorporates both informative and noninformative variables, with varying degrees of noise, thus providing a comprehensive framework for assessing model performance under realistic conditions.

The dataset is generated using a set of equations designed to create correlated predictor variables that combine both signal and noise components, allowing for a critical evaluation of each method's ability to discern relevant features in the presence of spurious or irrelevant variables. The data generation process is defined as follows:

$$\mathbf{y} = 0.25\exp(4\mathbf{x}_1) + \frac{4}{1+\exp(-20(\mathbf{x}_2 - 0.5))} + 3\mathbf{x}_3 + \eta, \tag{15}$$

where $\mathbf{y}$ is the output variable, $\eta$ is normally distributed with mean 0 and standard deviation 0.2, and the predictor variables $\mathbf{x}_1$, $\mathbf{x}_2$, and $\mathbf{x}_3$ are uniformly distributed between 0 and 1 ($U(0,1)$).

Each relationship in Equation (15) contributes uniquely to $\mathbf{y}$, reflecting the distinct characteristics of their functional forms. The exponential dependency on $\mathbf{x}_1$ acts as the primary driver of variability in $\mathbf{y}$. Due to its exponential nature, even small increases in $\mathbf{x}_1$ can produce substantial shifts in $\mathbf{y}$, especially when $\mathbf{x}_1$ reaches higher values within its range. This makes $\mathbf{x}_1$ a dominant factor influencing the output variable. In contrast, the logistic dependency on $\mathbf{x}_2$ provides a significant but bounded effect on $\mathbf{y}$. The logistic function has its strongest impact around the midpoint ($\mathbf{x}_2 = 0.5$), where it introduces notable changes in $\mathbf{y}$. However, this effect stabilizes outside of that range, introducing a controlled nonlinear influence that is considerable near the midpoint but limited in other regions. The linear dependency on $\mathbf{x}_3$ has a more modest contribution to $\mathbf{y}$. Although this linear relationship ensures proportional adjustments in $\mathbf{y}$ with changes in $\mathbf{x}_3$, its effect can be easily overshadowed by the more pronounced variations introduced by $\mathbf{x}_1$ and $\mathbf{x}_2$, as well as by the error term $\eta$. This suggests that, in the presence of more dominant influences and noise, the contribution of $\mathbf{x}_3$ may be less perceptible and could, therefore, receive a lower score in certain attribute importance measures.

#### 4.2.1. Results #2.1

Examining the results without the noise term $\eta$ offers additional insight into the ARS measure's effectiveness in isolating informative dependencies. To highlight this, we present the ARS behavior derived from Equation (15) after excluding $\eta$. This "noise-free" version of ARS is evaluated using three distinct base models: decision trees, linear regression, and k-nearest neighbors (k = 5). By removing the noise component, we aim to reveal how well each model captures the inherent relationships between $\mathbf{x}_1$, $\mathbf{x}_2$, and $\mathbf{x}_3$ and the target variable $\mathbf{y}$, thereby underscoring the relative strengths of each approach in detecting true signal (see Figure 2).

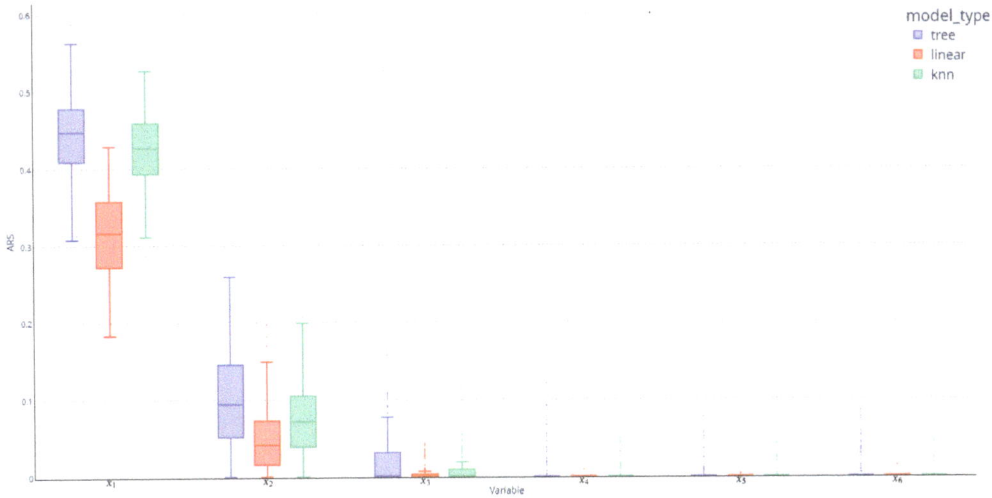


**Figure 2.** Performance of ARS with different base models on Equation (15) without the noise term $\eta$ on the benchmark dataset. The informative variables ($\mathbf{x}_1$, $\mathbf{x}_2$, and $\mathbf{x}_3$) and noninformative variables ($\mathbf{x}_4$, $\mathbf{x}_5$, and $\mathbf{x}_6$) are evaluated across three base models: decision trees, linear regression, and k-nearest neighbors.

**Performance on benchmark dataset without noise for different base models**: Figure 2 illustrates the ARS measure's sensitivity to both informative variables ($\mathbf{x}_1$, $\mathbf{x}_2$, and $\mathbf{x}_3$) and noninformative variables ($\mathbf{x}_4$, $\mathbf{x}_5$, and $\mathbf{x}_6$) under different base models (decision trees, linear regression, and k-nearest neighbors) with the noise term $\eta$ excluded. The decision tree and k-nearest neighbors models demonstrate a stronger capacity to capture the inherent dependencies, particularly for the nonlinear relationships in $\mathbf{x}_1$ and $\mathbf{x}_2$. In contrast, the linear regression model struggles to detect these dependencies, reflecting its limitations with nonlinear data. For the noninformative variables $\mathbf{x}_4$, $\mathbf{x}_5$, and $\mathbf{x}_6$, ARS consistently returns zero across all quartiles, with only occasional nonzero outliers, highlighting ARS's robustness in distinguishing relevant features from noise. This behavior underscores ARS's reliability in filtering out noninformative attributes, even in the absence of noise.

#### 4.2.2. Results #2.2

To increase the dataset's complexity, additional noninformative predictor variables $\mathbf{x}_4$, $\mathbf{x}_5$, and $\mathbf{x}_6$ are generated uniformly within the range 0 to 1 ($U(0,1)$). These variables do not contribute directly to $\mathbf{y}$, simulating the presence of noise and further challenging the model's ability to differentiate between relevant and irrelevant features. To further enrich the dataset, we simulates the presence of progressively weaker signal-to-noise ratios, allowing the method to be tested on its ability to identify relevant variables in the presence of noise. To achieve this, we generate noise versions of the predictor variables using the following equation:

$$\mathbf{v}_i^{(j)} = \mathbf{x}_i + \left(0.01 + \frac{0.5(j-1)}{10-1}\right) N(0;0.3), \tag{16}$$

for $j = 1, \ldots, 10$ the level of noise, where the correlation between $\mathbf{x}_i$ and $\mathbf{v}_i^{(j)}$ systematically decreases as $j$ increases. $i = 1, \ldots, 6$ corresponds to the index values of the original $\mathbf{x}_i$. This formula generates multiple noisy versions of the base variables $\mathbf{x}_i$. This experimental setup enables a robust comparison of our method against alternative techniques by specifically evaluating their capacity to distinguish between relevant and nonrelevant features, even in the presence of noise. By conducting 100 repetitions with 100 observations each, we aim to thoroughly assess the robustness, accuracy, and adaptability of the methods when faced with scenarios that include a mixture of informative and noninformative variables.

The evaluation of our proposed attribute relevance score (ARS) method, using decision trees as the base model, conducted alongside established dependency measures, was performed using the benchmark dataset described above. This dataset provides a challenging environment, containing both informative and noninformative variables with varying levels of noise, designed to test the robustness and discriminative ability of each method.

**Performance on informative variables**: For the variable $\mathbf{v}_1^{(j)}$, both versions $\mathbf{v}_1^{(1)}$ and $\mathbf{v}_1^{(10)}$ exhibit high mean ARS scores (0.435 and 0.264, respectively) compared to the other predictors, indicating strong relevance (see Figure 3). This aligns with the role of $\mathbf{x}_1$ as the primary driver of variability in $\mathbf{y}$ due to its exponential dependency. Furthermore, the low standard deviation of the ARS across both versions highlights the stability and robustness of this measure in consistently capturing the predictive power of $\mathbf{v}_1^{(j)}$.

In the case of $\mathbf{v}_2^{(j)}$, represented by $\mathbf{v}_2^{(1)}$ and $\mathbf{v}_2^{(10)}$, the mean ARS scores indicate relevance (0.087, std: 0.063 and 0.069, std: 0.064, respectively); however, these scores are notably lower than those obtained for $\mathbf{v}_1^{(j)}$ and other methods. This discrepancy is expected, considering the second objective of our study, which assesses the effectiveness of approximating $\mathbf{y}$ from $\mathbf{x}$ using a specific error measure and algorithm. ARS quantifies this practical capability, capturing not only the statistical dependence but also the magnitude of predictive power within the context of the selected model and performance metric. In this context, despite the added structured noise in $\mathbf{v}_2^{(j)}$, the mean ARS remains relatively stable, suggesting that the relevance of $\mathbf{v}_2^{(j)}$ is not significantly diminished by noise alone. This stability may imply that the ARS effectively captures a fundamental relationship between $\mathbf{v}_2^{(j)}$ and $\mathbf{y}$ that remains informative despite the noise corruption. The resilience of $\mathbf{v}_2^{(j)}$'s ARS score under noise indicates that the relationship retains predictive utility, though at a much lower magnitude compared to $\mathbf{v}_1^{(j)}$.

For $\mathbf{v}_3^{(j)}$, both versions $\mathbf{v}_3^{(1)}$ and $\mathbf{v}_3^{(10)}$ register low mean ARS scores (0.019, std: 0.033 and 0.018, std: 0.039, respectively), which is consistent with the weaker dependency of $\mathbf{x}_3$ on $\mathbf{y}$, particularly in the presence of external variability and more dominant dependencies.

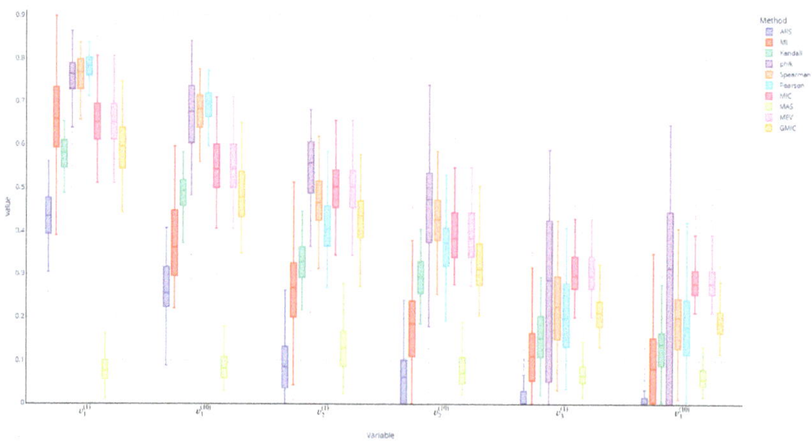


**Figure 3.** Performance of various dependency measures on informative variables $\mathbf{v}_1^{(j)}$, $\mathbf{v}_2^{(j)}$, and $\mathbf{v}_3^{(j)}$ across different noise levels ($j$). This figure illustrates the mean and standard deviation of each measure, highlighting the stability of ARS compared to other metrics.

In comparison, traditional methods such as Pearson and Spearman correlations displayed higher mean values for informative variables. For instance, the Pearson correlation for $\mathbf{v}_1^{(1)}$ was 0.781 (std: 0.028), indicating strong linear relationships. This pattern persisted across other informative variables, with measures like GMIC and MIC showing similarly elevated means (e.g., GMIC for $\mathbf{v}_1^{(1)}$ was 0.595, std: 0.065), apparently reflecting substantial associations. However, it is important to note that this situation also arises for noninformative variables, as we will show in the next results.

**Performance on noninformative variables**: In the case of noninformative variables $\mathbf{v}_4^{(j)}$, $\mathbf{v}_5^{(j)}$, and $\mathbf{v}_6^{(j)}$, ARS effectively identified the lack of relevance by consistently returning scores of zero across all instances, with only occasional nonzero values attributable to random chance (see Figure 4). The ARS scores for these variables were zero in the vast majority of cases, resulting in extremely low mean values and minimal standard deviations. For example, for $\mathbf{v}_4^{(1)}$, ARS returned a mean score of 0.009 with a standard deviation of 0.024, indicating that most scores were zero except for rare outliers. This demonstrates ARS's robustness in correctly identifying noise and nonrelevant attributes, as the minimal nonzero scores observed can be attributed to expected statistical fluctuations in practical datasets.

However, other dependency measures exhibited higher variability and occasionally elevated scores, even for noninformative attributes, suggesting spurious associations. Metrics such as GMIC and MIC presented mean values of 0.139 (std: 0.027) and 0.240 (std: 0.035), respectively, for $\mathbf{v}_4^{(1)}$, suggesting a tendency to overestimate the relevance of noisy attributes. Similarly, traditional correlation measures, such as Spearman and Pearson also showed notable variability (e.g., mean Spearman for $\mathbf{v}_4^{(1)}$ was 0.088, std: 0.068), indicating their limitations in distinguishing between informative patterns and noise.

Overall, the attribute relevance score (ARS) outperformed traditional and information-based metrics by providing a more stable and reliable assessment of attribute relevance across both informative and noninformative variables. While measures like Pearson, Spearman, and MIC can capture strong relationships when present, their high values—especially in noninformative scenarios—reduce their effectiveness in complex, noisy datasets. The fact that ARS returned zero scores for all noninformative variables, except for occasional outliers, underscores its robustness and practical utility in feature selection processes. By effectively filtering out noise and avoiding false positives, ARS stands out as a particularly powerful tool for distinguishing between meaningful and spurious relationships, thereby enhancing the reliability of feature selection in predictive modeling.

## 5. Discussion

This study introduces the attribute relevance score (ARS), a novel metric designed to robustly identify relevant attributes in complex datasets exhibiting both linear and nonlinear relationships with varying levels of noise. For instance, ARS consistently returned scores close to zero for noninformative variables, with mean scores below 0.01 and minimal standard deviations, whereas traditional metrics often yielded higher scores with greater variability. This distinguishes ARS from traditional dependency measures, which often exhibit significant fluctuations, especially when assessing noninformative variables.

A key finding from our experiments is ARS's robustness to noise. Traditional metrics such as Pearson, Spearman, and Kendall correlations struggle to maintain consistency in the presence of noise, frequently showing inflated scores for noninformative variables. This issue is particularly problematic in high-dimensional settings, where distinguishing between signal and noise is crucial. In contrast, ARS consistently produces low scores for noninformative attributes $\mathbf{v}_4^{(j)}$, $\mathbf{v}_5^{(j)}$, and $\mathbf{v}_6^{(j)}$ with minimal variability, as shown in Figure 4. This stability suggests that ARS more reliably filters out irrelevant features, enhancing the quality and interpretability of predictive models. Further supporting ARS's robustness, the analysis of ARS in the noise-free scenario (Figure 2) yields results closely aligned with those observed in noisier conditions. ARS maintains consistent sensitivity to informative variables ($\mathbf{x}_1$, $\mathbf{x}_2$, and $\mathbf{x}_3$) across both scenarios, with decision trees and k-nearest neighbors models effectively capturing the dependencies. The consistency of these results, even in the absence of noise, underscores ARS's ability to reliably identify relevant features regardless of noise levels. Likewise, noninformative variables ($\mathbf{x}_4$, $\mathbf{x}_5$, and $\mathbf{x}_6$) continue to exhibit near-zero ARS scores, reinforcing ARS's capacity to filter out irrelevant features accurately. These findings demonstrate that ARS provides a stable assessment of attribute relevance, with minimal influence from random noise—essential for feature selection applications that demand reliability despite fluctuations in data quality.

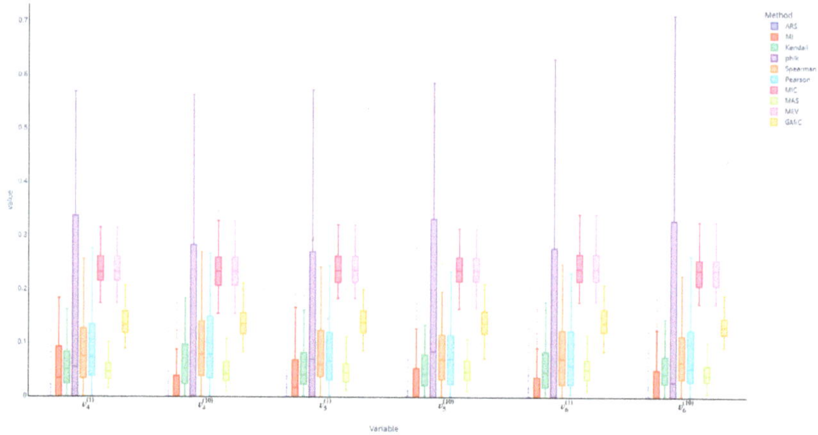


**Figure 4.** Performance of various dependency measures on noninformative variables $\mathbf{v}_4^{(j)}$, $\mathbf{v}_5^{(j)}$, and $\mathbf{v}_6^{(j)}$ across different noise levels (j). This figure shows the mean and standard deviation for each measure, demonstrating the high variability of traditional metrics compared to the consistently low scores of ARS. Absolute values are considered for readability.

Our comparative analysis against established metrics such as GMIC, MAS, and MIC further underscores the strengths of ARS. While these metrics aim to capture complex nonlinear relationships, they exhibit higher variability and occasionally assign moderate relevance scores to noninformative attributes, reflecting their susceptibility to noise. The high standard deviations observed indicate a lack of robustness, potentially leading to inconsistent feature selection. In contrast, ARS accurately identifies relevant attributes such as $\mathbf{v}_1^{(j)}$, $\mathbf{v}_2^{(j)}$, and $\mathbf{v}_3^{(j)}$ while maintaining low scores for noise variables, effectively balancing sensitivity to true relationships with resilience to random fluctuations.

The ability of ARS to consistently differentiate between relevant and irrelevant attributes has significant implications for high-dimensional data analysis, particularly in fields where data complexity and noise pose challenges, such as genomics, finance, and environmental modeling. By integrating statistical rigor with practical applicability, ARS contributes to more reliable feature selection, enhancing reproducibility and reducing the risk of overfitting. This is crucial in scientific research, where the goal is not only to build predictive models but also to uncover meaningful relationships that drive further understanding.

The significance of reproducibility in machine learning cannot be overstated, particularly in high-dimensional data analysis. Reproducibility concerns often arise when results depend heavily on specific data splits or model configurations, leading to conclusions that may not generalize. In feature selection, these issues are critical, as identifying relevant attributes is pivotal for subsequent analysis.

Our methodology incorporates concepts from reproducibility and A/B testing. Similar to A/B testing, we compare models trained on original attributes with those trained on *shadow attributes*, which are permuted versions of the original attributes. By evaluating whether the model using the original attributes consistently outperforms the one using shadow attributes across various data samples, we assess the relevance of each attribute. This comparison grounds attribute selection in robust statistical principles, ensuring that the selected attributes are genuinely informative and that the results are reproducible under diverse conditions.

By employing a probabilistic approach to assessing feature relevance, ARS reduces the risk of findings being artifacts of particular experimental setups. The use of shadow attributes and random sampling provides a rigorous framework for quantifying feature importance while controlling for variability introduced by data sampling and model configurations. Moreover, the ARS framework strengthens inferential reproducibility by ensuring that identified relevant attributes consistently contribute to model performance across various scenarios. This aligns with principles of methods reproducibility, results reproducibility, and inferential reproducibility.

We acknowledge that ARS computational complexity increases linearly with the number of input features. Specifically, for datasets with a large number of attributes, the need to train separate models for each attribute can become computationally intensive, posing practical challenges in high-dimensional machine learning applications. However, because each attribute is evaluated independently, ARS can leverage parallel computing resources by distributing computations across multiple processors or computational nodes. This parallelization significantly reduces total processing time, enabling ARS to remain scalable and maintain practical performance even with a large number of attributes.

While ARS offers clear strengths, it is not without limitations. The current implementation relies on decision trees, which may not capture all forms of attribute interactions, especially in highly nonlinear or interaction-heavy scenarios. Moreover, ARS is inherently a univariate approach, evaluating each attribute's relevance independently. This means it lacks the capability to detect redundancies and interactions between attributes. Synergistic effects, where combinations of attributes contribute significantly to the target variable, may be overlooked. This limitation can be critical in domains where attribute interactions play a crucial role. Future research should explore extending ARS to incorporate multivariate analysis techniques or models that can account for attribute interactions.

In summary, our work advances feature selection methodologies in high-dimensional data analysis and enhances the reproducibility and generalizability of results. By embedding statistical significance into a measure of attribute relevance and ensuring robustness across different conditions, we contribute to developing more reliable and reproducible machine learning models. Future work will focus on expanding the applicability of ARS to a broader range of models and exploring its integration into automated machine learning frameworks.

## 6. Conclusions and Future Work

The ARS method represents a versatile approach that can be adapted to various types of data and problem settings. Its application extends beyond standard regression and classification tasks to exploratory data analysis and feature engineering, where the identification of significant predictors is crucial. ARS's ability to provide consistent and reliable relevance scores, particularly in noisy and complex environments, aligns with the increasing need for robust, interpretable, and reproducible methods in data science. Its stability under noisy conditions and superior performance in distinguishing informative attributes position it as a valuable tool for researchers and practitioners. By addressing key challenges in feature selection for complex datasets, ARS improves predictive model accuracy and interpretability, paving the way for more robust data-driven decision making.

However, the relevance of an attribute should not depend solely on its individual contribution to model performance but also on its interactions with other attributes. This perspective highlights the need for a more holistic evaluation of attribute relevance within complex predictive models. In many scenarios, attributes do not function in isolation; their true value emerges through interactions with other features. Ignoring these interactions can lead to underestimating the importance of certain attributes that may appear irrelevant when considered univariately but have a significant impact in combination with others. Moreover, attribute redundancy should not unduly diminish an attribute's univariate relevance or intrinsic predictive capability. Two redundant attributes might share valuable information, and removing one could result in a loss of crucial insights. Therefore, it is essential to consider redundancy in a way that does not unduly penalize the relevance of attributes that, despite being redundant, are predictively valuable.

To address these considerations, future research should explore integrating ARS with other feature selection frameworks capable of effectively evaluating both attribute interactions and redundancies. Additionally, adapting ARS to more advanced learning models, such as deep neural networks, could enhance its applicability across different contexts. Expanding the evaluation of ARS on real-world datasets from various domains would further validate its effectiveness and uncover additional insights into its utility.

In conclusion, a robust evaluation of attribute relevance that carefully considers both interactions among attributes and the potential for redundancy is essential for developing predictive models that are not only accurate but also interpretable and reliable. Furthermore, this strategy emphasizes the critical distinction between a model that consistently improves performance due to meaningful insights and one that does so merely by chance. By focusing on selecting nonredundant variables, even at the expense of optimal performance in some metrics, we align the model's outcomes more closely with the realities of the underlying phenomena. This approach moves us towards a more robust definition of understanding within the field of machine learning. Through the development of a multivariate relevance measure, we can assess when a model is not just learning correlations but is genuinely comprehending the underlying phenomena. This deeper level of understanding enables models to generalize more effectively, providing reliable interpretations and fostering the model's capacity to make informed decisions across diverse scenarios. Consequently, this advancement enhances the fidelity and reliability of model interpretations, contributing to a more nuanced and scientifically sound understanding of the model's ability to generalize and adapt.

**Author Contributions:** Conceptualization, P.N. and C.S.; methodology, C.S.; software, P.N.; validation, P.N. and C.S.; resources, C.S.; writing—original draft preparation, P.N.; writing—review and editing, C.S. and H.A.; visualization, P.N.; supervision, C.S.; project administration, C.S. and H.A.; funding acquisition, C.S. All authors have read and agreed to the published version of the manuscript.

**Funding:** This research was funded by Project USM PI_LIR_24_14.

**Data Availability Statement:** The data can be found at the following link: https://github.com/Pneirz/Attribute-Relevance-Score/ (accessed on 5 November 2024).

**Conflicts of Interest:** The authors declare no conflicts of interest.

## References

1. Ullah, S.; Mahmood, Z.; Ali, N.; Ahmad, T.; Buriro, A. Machine Learning-Based Dynamic Attribute Selection Technique for DDoS Attack Classification in IoT Networks. *Computers* **2023**, *12*, 115. [CrossRef]
2. Kang, I.A.; Njimbouom, S.N.; Kim, J.D. Optimal Feature Selection-Based Dental Caries Prediction Model Using Machine Learning for Decision Support System. *Bioengineering* **2023**, *10*, 245. [CrossRef] [PubMed]
3. Kiratsoudis, S.; Tsiantos, V. Enhancing Personnel Selection through the Integration of the Entropy Synergy Analysis of Multi-Attribute Decision Making Model: A Novel Approach. *Information* **2024**, *15*, 1. [CrossRef]
4. AL-Gburi, A.F.J.; Nazri, M.Z.A.; Yaakub, M.R.B.; Alyasseri, Z.A.A. Multi-Objective Unsupervised Feature Selection and Cluster Based on Symbiotic Organism Search. *Algorithms* **2024**, *17*, 355. [CrossRef]
5. Đurasević, M.; Jakobović, D.; Picek, S.; Mariot, L. Assessing the Ability of Genetic Programming for Feature Selection in Constructing Dispatching Rules for Unrelated Machine Environments. *Algorithms* **2024**, *17*, 67. [CrossRef]
6. Nilsson, R.; Peña, J.M.; Björkegren, J.; Tegnér, J. Consistent Feature Selection for Pattern Recognition in Polynomial Time. *J. Mach. Learn. Res.* **2007**, *8*, 589–612.
7. Kohavi, R.; John, G.H. Wrappers for feature subset selection. *Artif. Intell.* **1997**, *97*, 273–324. [CrossRef]
8. Mnich, K.; Rudnicki, W.R. All-relevant feature selection using multidimensional filters with exhaustive search. *Inf. Sci.* **2020**, *524*, 277–297. [CrossRef]
9. Breiman, L. Random forests. *Mach. Learn.* **2001**, *45*, 5–32. [CrossRef]
10. Strobl, C.; Boulesteix, A.L.; Zeileis, A.; Hothorn, T. Bias in random forest variable importance measures: Illustrations, sources and a solution. *BMC Bioinform.* **2007**, *8*, 25. [CrossRef]

11. Stoppiglia, H.; Dreyfus, G.; Dubois, R.; Oussar, Y. Ranking a Random Feature For Variable And Feature Selection. *J. Mach. Learn. Res.* **2003**, *3*, 1399–1414. [CrossRef]
12. Degenhardt, F.; Seifert, S.S. Evaluation of variable selection methods for random forests and omics data sets. *Briefings Bioinform.* **2019**, *20*, 492–503. [CrossRef] [PubMed]
13. Kursa, M.B.; Rudnicki, W.R. Feature selection with the Boruta package. *J. Stat. Softw.* **2010**, *36*, 1–13. [CrossRef]
14. Wetschoreck, F. RIP Correlation. Introducing the Predictive Power Score. Towards Data Science, Medium. 2020. Available online: https://towardsdatascience.com/rip-correlation-introducing-the-predictive-power-score-3d90808b9598 (accessed on 7 November 2024).
15. Goodman, S.; Fanelli, D.; Ioannidis, J. What does research reproducibility mean? *Sci. Transl. Med.* **2016**, *8*, 341ps12. [CrossRef] [PubMed]
16. Bouthillier, X.; Laurent, C.; Vincent, P. Unreproducible Research is Reproducible. In Proceedings of the 36th International Conference on Machine Learning, Long Beach, CA, USA, 9–15 June 2019.
17. Bouthillier, X.; Delaunay, P.; Bronzi, M.; Trofimov, A.; Nichyporuk, B.; Szeto, J.; Mohammadi Sepahvand, N.; Raff, E.; Madan, K.; Voleti, V.; et al. Accounting for Variance in Machine Learning Benchmarks. *Proc. Mach. Learn. Syst.* **2021**, *3*, 747–769.
18. Kohavi, R.; Longbotham, R. Online Controlled Experiments and A/B Testing. In *Encyclopedia of Machine Learning and Data Mining*; Sammut, C., Webb, G.I., Eds.; Springer: Boston, MA, USA, 2017; pp. 922–929. [CrossRef]
19. Deng, A.; Xu, Y.; Kohavi, R.; Walker, T. Improving the sensitivity of online controlled experiments by utilizing pre-experiment data. In Proceedings of the Sixth ACM International Conference on Web Search and Data Mining, New York, NY, USA, 4–8 February 2013; WSDM'13; pp. 123–132. [CrossRef]
20. Lundberg, S.M.; Lee, S.I. A unified approach to interpreting model predictions. In Proceedings of the 31st International Conference on Neural Information Processing Systems, Red Hook, NY, USA, 4–9 December 2017; NIPS'17; pp. 4768–4777.
21. Ribeiro, M.T.; Singh, S.; Guestrin, C. "Why Should I Trust You?". In Proceedings of the 22nd ACM SIGKDD International Conference on Knowledge Discovery and Data Mining, ACM, San Francisco, CA, USA, 13–17 August 2016. Available online: https://arxiv.org/pdf/1602.04938.pdf (accessed on 7 November 2024). [CrossRef]
22. Sokol, K.; Flach, P. Explainability fact sheets: A framework for systematic assessment of explainable approaches. In Proceedings of the 2020 Conference on Fairness, Accountability, and Transparency, New York, NY, USA, 27–30 January 2020; FAT*'20; pp. 56–67. [CrossRef]
23. Lapuschkin, S.; Wäldchen, S.; Binder, A.; Montavon, G.; Samek, W.; Müller, K.R. Unmasking Clever Hans predictors and assessing what machines really learn. *Nat. Commun.* **2019**, *10*, 1096. [CrossRef]
24. Pfungst, O. *Clever Hans (The Horse of Mr. von Osten): A Contribution to Experimental, Animal, and Human Psychology*; Holt, Rinehart, and Winston: New York, NY, USA, 1911.
25. Roberts, M.; Driggs, D.; Thorpe, M.; Gilbey, J.; Yeung, M.; Ursprung, S.; Aviles-Rivero, A.; Etmann, C.; McCague, C.; Beer, L.; et al. Common pitfalls and recommendations for using machine learning to detect and prognosticate for COVID-19 using chest radiographs and CT scans. *Nat. Mach. Intell.* **2021**, *3*, 199–217. [CrossRef]
26. DeGrave, A.J.; Janizek, J.D.; Lee, S.I. AI for radiographic COVID-19 detection selects shortcuts over signal. *Nat. Mach. Intell.* **2021**, *3*, 610–619. [CrossRef]
27. Szegedy, C.; Zaremba, W.; Sutskever, I.; Bruna, J.; Erhan, D.; Goodfellow, I.; Fergus, R. Intriguing properties of neural networks. In Proceedings of the International Conference on Learning Representations (ICLR), Banff, AB, Canada, 14–16 April 2014.
28. Thomas, T.; Straub, D.; Tatai, F.; Shene, M.; Tosik, T.; Kersting, K.; Rothkopf, C.A. Modelling dataset bias in machine-learned theories of economic decision-making. *Nat. Hum. Behav.* **2024**, *8*, 679–691. [CrossRef]
29. Prokhorenkova, L.; Gusev, G.; Vorobev, A.; Dorogush, A.V.; Gulin, A. CatBoost: Unbiased boosting with categorical features. *Adv. Neural Inf. Process. Syst.* **2018**, *31*, 6638–6648. [CrossRef]
30. Baak, M.; Koopman, R.; Snoek, H.; Klous, S. A new correlation coefficient between categorical, ordinal and interval variables with Pearson characteristics. *Comput. Stat. Data Anal.* **2020**, *152*, 107043. [CrossRef]
31. Ross, B.C. Mutual information between discrete and continuous data sets. *PLoS ONE* **2014**, *9*, e87357. [CrossRef] [PubMed]
32. Reshef, D.N.; Reshef, Y.A.; Finucane, H.K.; Grossman, S.R.; McVean, G.; Turnbaugh, P.J.; Lander, E.S.; Mitzenmacher, M.; Sabeti, P.C. Detecting novel associations in large data sets. *Science* **2011**, *334*, 1518–1524. [CrossRef] [PubMed]
33. Albanese, D.; Riccadonna, S.; Donati, C.; Franceschi, P. A practical tool for maximal information coefficient analysis. *GigaScience* **2018**, *7*, giy032. [CrossRef] [PubMed]
34. Albanese, D.; Filosi, M.; Visintainer, R.; Riccadonna, S.; Jurman, G.; Furlanello, C. minerva and minepy: A C engine for the MINE suite and its R, Python and MATLAB wrappers. *Bioinformatics* **2012**, *29*, 407–408. [CrossRef]
35. Luedtke, A.; Tran, L.H. The Generalized Mean Information Coefficient. *arXiv* **2013**, arXiv:1308.5712. [CrossRef]
36. Chen, Z.; Zhang, W. Integrative analysis using module-guided random forests reveals correlated genetic factors related to mouse weight. *PLoS Comput. Biol.* **2013**, *9*, e1002956. [CrossRef]

*algorithms*

MDPI

*Article*

# A Proposal for a New Python Library Implementing Stepwise Procedure

**Luiz Paulo Fávero [1], Helder Prado Santos [1], Patrícia Belfiore [2], Alexandre Duarte [3], Igor Pinheiro de Araújo Costa [4,*], Adilson Vilarinho Terra [4], Miguel Ângelo Lellis Moreira [4], Wilson Tarantin Junior [1] and Marcos dos Santos [5]**

1 Faculty of Economics, Administration, and Accounting, University of Sao Paulo, Sao Paulo 05508-900, Brazil; lpfavero@usp.br (L.P.F.); helderprado@gmail.com (H.P.S.); wilsontarantin@yahoo.com.br (W.T.J.)

2 Department of Management Engineering, Federal University of ABC, Sao Bernardo do Campo 09606-045, Brazil; patricia.favero@ufabc.edu.br

3 Polytechnic School, University of Sao Paulo, Sao Paulo 05508-010, Brazil; alexandre.duarte@usp.br

4 Production Engineering Department, Fluminense Federal University, Niteroi 24210-240, Brazil; adilsonvilarinho@id.uff.br (A.V.T.); miguellellis@hotmail.com (M.Â.L.M.)

5 Systems and Computing Department, Military Institute of Engineering, Rio de Janeiro 22290-270, Brazil

* Correspondence: costa_igor@id.uff.br

**Abstract:** Carefully selecting variables in problems with large volumes of data are extremely important, as it reduces the complexity of the model, improves the interpretation of the results, and increases computational efficiency, ensuring more accurate and relevant analyses. This paper presents a comprehensive approach to selecting variables in multiple regression models using the stepwise procedure. As the main contribution of this study, we present the stepwise function implemented in Python to improve the effectiveness of statistical analyses, allowing the intuitive and efficient selection of statistically significant variables. The application of the function is exemplified in a real case study of real estate pricing, validating its effectiveness in improving the fit of regression models. In addition, we presented a methodological framework for treating joint problems in data analysis, such as heteroskedasticity, multicollinearity, and nonadherence of residues to normality. This framework offers a robust computational implementation to mitigate such issues. This study aims to advance the understanding and application of statistical methods in Python, providing valuable tools for researchers, students, and professionals from various areas.

**Keywords:** supervised machine learning; stepwise function; Python function

## 1. Introduction

Data-driven culture, based on data-informed decision-making, has become increasingly relevant across diverse industries, driven by the increasing availability of data and technological advancements [1]. At the same time, big data have presented new challenges regarding analyzing and interpreting these massive volumes of information [2].

In this context, Chowdhury and Turin [3] state that it is possible to apply several variable selection techniques to construct a statistical model. Among them, the stepwise procedure is applied to identify a limited number of variables in statistical models, especially in prediction problems or situations with many original variables [4]. However, there are other techniques, such as lasso-like regularization procedures, which may be more suitable and perform better in certain cases [5]. Ultimately, it is up to the researcher to determine which method best fits their needs.

The stepwise procedure has the property of automatically deleting or maintaining the $\beta$ parameters of the linear regression model according to the criteria presented and offering the final model only with parameters $\beta$ statistically different from zero for a given level of significance [6].

Also, stepwise provides a systematic approach to building models, which is especially useful when dealing with many variables. It allows analysts to focus on the most relevant variables, simplifying the interpretation of results [7]. Stepwise ensures the validity and importance of the chosen variables and reduces the additional error introduced by redundant variables [8].

Considering that the practical selection of variables plays a crucial role in constructing regression models, the computational implementation of the stepwise procedure offers an automated and efficient approach to selecting variables, allowing the construction of more robust models. In this sense, it is possible to perform the computational implementation of the stepwise regression procedure in several programming languages, each offering specific packages or libraries to assist in this process.

The stepwise procedure is widely found in the literature, with multidisciplinary applications, such as storm prediction [9]; modeling of real estate sales prices [10]; agricultural production forecast [11,12]; environment-related analyses [13–17]; regression models in healthcare [18–20]; and analyses related to human behavior [21]. These are just a few of the many applications of the stepwise procedure in machine-learning models of multiple regressions.

As for the computational implementation of stepwise, we observe packages and libraries in several programming languages and software, such as R (v. 4.3.1), SAS (v. 9.4M8), MATLAB (v. R2024b), Julia (v. 1.9.3), SPSS (v. 29.0.1.1), Stata (v. 18), Java (v. 21), and C++ (v. 20), among others. However, Python (v. 3.13.0) requires a specific library that implements stepwise selection based on the statistical significance of the variables. As the most popular programming language for data science [22], Python has gained widespread adoption for statistical analysis and machine learning [23]. This highlights the importance of having tools that cater to rigorous statistical methodologies within such a versatile programming environment.

It is possible to perform the stepwise selection procedure based on the statistical significance of the variables manually; however, for models with a large number of variables, it is convenient to have a package that automates this process, making it easier to select relevant and statistically significant independent variables for the model.

In Python, there is the mlxtend library, which has the SequentialFeatureSelector (SFS) function that performs stepwise selection. However, two caveats are necessary. First, the package only selects the variables, and it is necessary to adjust the model again after selecting them. Second, and more importantly, the package selects the variables based on some metric, such as $R^2$, MSE, MAE, RMSE, AIC, and BIC, among others, and it does not consider the statistical significance of the variables.

The stepwise procedure is applied to models with multiple independent variables ($X$), where the issue of multicollinearity arises. [24]. A variable may be removed during the stepwise process for several reasons: if its parameter is not statistically different from zero at a given significance level (i.e., the variable $X_i$ is not significant on its own); or if multicollinearity is present, meaning there is a correlation between variables, making it unnecessary to include two variables when one may already explain the behavior of the other. From a predictive standpoint, in cases of multicollinearity, one of the independent variables $X_i$ will be removed to avoid prediction issues caused by multicollinearity. In other words, if an independent variable whose beta is not statistically different from zero is not excluded, the model loses its predictive power [6]. This is because that $\beta$ parameter, in the presence of other variables, ceteris paribus, does not contribute to the predictive composition, making the variable statistically insignificant in explaining the behavior of the dependent variable $Y$ alongside other $X_i$ variables. Including such a $\beta$ parameter could alter the magnitude and potentially even the sign of the other beta parameters, without contributing meaningfully to the construction of a predictive model [6,24,25].

In this sense, it is important to provide an implementation alternative that uses the statistical significance of the variables as a criterion. According to [6], metrics such as the $R^2$ adjustment coefficient do not inform researchers whether a given explanatory variable is statistically significant and whether it is the true cause of changes in the behavior of the dependent variable. Moreover, this metric does not allow for an assessment of potential omitted variable bias or whether the choice of the explanatory variables included in the proposed model was appropriate. Thus, regarding the application of stepwise selection, it is insufficient to consider only adjustment or accuracy metrics; it is essential to take into account the statistical significance of the explanatory variables when selecting which ones remain in the final model after stepwise selection, since a model built from sample data that includes statistically insignificant beta parameters is not considered a final model when the goal is prediction [6,24,26].

It is important to note that this approach is more commonly used in applied sciences, such as statistics, engineering, and economics, where there is a need to develop models that identify sample phenomena and align the estimated model with the real-world sample data. However, in some contexts, the focus on the statistical significance of beta parameters is less emphasized, such as in the study of deterministic phenomena [6].

Despite the wealth of features offered by libraries such as "stats models" and "scikit-learn", there was no specific function for the stepwise procedure based on the statistical significance of the variables in Python. This gap limits the efficiency and practicality of implementing this procedure in research projects and practical applications. The absence of a specific library not only complicates the adoption of the stepwise procedure but also makes it difficult to standardize and reproduce experiments, resulting in additional efforts for users who wish to adopt and explore the various methods of variable selection, which can be based on metrics or statistical significance. Filling this gap represents an opportunity to advance the development of specialized tools for automated variable selection.

This article proposes the development of a library in Python that implements the stepwise procedure based on the statistical significance of the variables as a simple and intuitive function. This function fills the gap in the literature by providing specialized functionalities for the automated selection of variables in multiple regression models. The library was developed based on the best practices of programming, modularity, and precise documentation to facilitate users' use and understanding. In addition, the library will promote the standardization and reproduction of experiments, simplifying the research process and the development of statistical projects.

In summary, the present study presents the following objectives:

1. Propose and detail the stepwise function based on the statistical significance of the variables in Python;
2. Exemplify how the application of the proposed stepwise function can help in retaining only the statistically significant variables, potentially improving the overall model performance and enhancing the statistical reliability of the results;
3. Present a methodological framework for the treatment and mitigation of problems of heteroskedasticity, multicollinearity, and nonadherence of residues to normality, providing its computational implementation;
4. Consolidate the concepts discussed in a real case study of real estate pricing, considering linear and nonlinear multiple regression models stepwise.

Given the above, this paper aims to advance the understanding and application of statistical methods in Python, allowing researchers, students, and professionals from various areas to use these techniques in a way that is more effective, intuitive, and grounded. The results presented here may raise new debates and contributions to data analysis and statistical modeling.

## 2. Background

### 2.1. Multiple Linear Regression

Multiple linear regression (MLR) models are a class of statistical models used to analyze the relationship between a continuous dependent variable and several independent variables (or predictors) [27–29].

Favero et al. [25] state that MLR primarily enables analyses of the relationship between several explanatory variables, presented in linear form, and a quantitative dependent variable. Thus, it is possible to define a general MLR model as Equation (1):

$$Y_i = \alpha + \beta_1 X_{i1} + \beta_2 X_{2i} + \cdots + \beta_k X_{ki} + u_i \tag{1}$$

where $Y$ represents the dependent variable; $\alpha$ matches the intercept; $\beta_j$ (j = 1, 2, ..., k) are the coefficients of each variable (angular coefficients); $X_j$ is the explanatory variables (metrics or dummies); $u$ is the error term (difference between the actual and predicted values of $Y$ through the model for each observation). The subscript $i$ represents each sample's observations under analysis ($i$ = 1, 2, ..., n, where $n$ is the sample size).

It is possible to write the error term $u_i$, for each observation $i$, as presented in Equation (2):

$$u_i = Y_i - \hat{Y}_i \tag{2}$$

$\hat{Y}_i$ represents the predicted value of the dependent variable that the estimated model will generate for the observation $i$ [6]. The error terms $u$ occur due to some reasons that need to be known and considered by researchers [25,30,31], such as the existence of aggregated and non-random variables, failures during model specification, and errors in data collection.

One of the most used techniques for estimating a multiple linear regression model is the ordinary least squares (OLS) method [6]. A model estimated by OLS must determine $\alpha$ and $\beta$, making the sum of the residues' squares as small as possible [32].

In this context, an important concept related to the explanatory power of the regression model is the coefficient of adjustment or explanation ($R^2$) [6]. Considering a multiple regression model, $R^2$ represents how much of the behavior of variable $Y$ is explained by the joint variation of variable $X$ considered in the model. However, Fávero and Belfiore [32] point out that there is not necessarily a cause-and-effect relationship between variables $X$ and $Y$.

Stock and Watson [33] define the $R^2$ coefficient as the fraction of the variance of the $Y_I$ sample explained by the explanatory variables. It is possible to use the $R^2$ coefficient to measure the degree of fit of the proposed model [31].

Empirical studies highlight the importance of including a comprehensive set of independent variables in MLR models [34,35]. However, it is essential to consider the challenges associated with including many independent variables, such as multicollinearity, which can distort the results and hinder the interpretation of the estimated coefficients [36].

Furthermore, as discussed in the introduction, it is well-known in the context of applied sciences that, for predictive purposes, including irrelevant independent variables can reduce not only the model's efficiency but also its interpretability [6,24,26]. In this regard, selecting the appropriate variables is crucial to avoid introducing unnecessary elements that do not contribute to the model's predictive power [37,38].

Therefore, including an adequate number of independent variables in MLR models requires a careful analysis of the theoretical and empirical relationships between variables. It is essential to seek a balance between the inclusion of relevant variables and the consideration of the problems associated with multicollinearity [3], since it is unnecessary to include variables when one may already explain the behavior of the other [6].

Another relevant point to discuss when applying regression models refers to qualitative explanatory variables, such as gender, age range, or classification of a given client, when these are on the right side of the regression models to estimate [32].

In these cases, according to [6], assigning values to each of the categories of the qualitative variable (a procedure known as arbitrary weighting) is an incorrect approach. The correct way to treat such types of variables is to resort to the artifice of dummy, or binary, variables, which assume 0 or 1, stratifying the sample to, from there, be included in the model under analysis [32].

### 2.2. Normality of Residuals

The normality of the residuals is an essential assumption for the hypothesis tests of the regression models to be validated, such as the *p*-value of the *t* and F tests [6]. According to [32], this assumption is constantly violated when estimating OLS regression models. However, normality is vital for defining the best functional form and determining confidence intervals for model prediction, with exceptions for sufficiently large samples.

In this context, the Shapiro–Francia statistical test, applied to the model's error terms, allows for verifying the assumption of the normality of the residuals [32]. This test, proposed by Shapiro and Francia [39], can be applied to samples of size $5 \leq n \leq 5000$. The Shapiro–Francia test assumes the following hypotheses [6].

**H0.** *The sample comes from a population with normal distribution.*

**H1.** *The sample does not come from a population with a normal distribution.*

It is possible to see the Shapiro–Francia statistic ($W'_{cal}$) calculation in Equation (3):

$$W\prime_{cal} = \frac{\left[\sum_{i=1}^{n} m_i.X_{(i)}\right]}{\sum_{i=1}^{n} m_i^2.\sum_{i=1}^{n}\left(X_i - \overline{X}\right)^2}, \quad for\, i = 1, \ldots, n \tag{3}$$

where $X_{(i)}$ are the statistics of the i-th ordered observation so that $X_{(1)} \leq X_{(2)} \leq X_{(3)} \leq \ldots \leq X_{(n-1)} \leq X_{(n)}$; $m_i$ is the approximate expected value of the i-th observation ($Z_{score}$) [6].

For the diagnosis of multicollinearity, the critical values $W'_c$ should be considered, such that $P\left(W'_{cal} < W'_c\right) = \alpha$ (considering a unilateral test on the left), with the *p*-values being established by a correspondence table, found in [6]; The parameter $\alpha$ corresponds to the level of statistical significance established. For the null hypothesis $H0$ to be rejected, $W'_{cal} < W'_c$; otherwise, $H0$ is not rejected [32].

Another form of analysis is the comparison of the *p*-value (probability associated with $W'_{cal}$), obtained in the same table of correspondences [6]. In this case, $H0$ is rejected if pvalue $\leq \alpha$. In short, if $H0$ is rejected, the residues do not adhere to normality.

### 2.3. The Problem of Multicollinearity

Multicollinearity occurs when there are very high correlations between the model's explanatory variables, which can be caused by the presence of variables with the same trend or the use of databases with few observations [32].

As forms of multicollinearity diagnosis, we highlight the statistics *Tolerance* and Variance Inflation Factor ($VIF$) based on estimating auxiliary regressions [40], according to Equations (4) and (5):

$$Tolerance = 1 - R_K^2 \tag{4}$$

$$VIF = \frac{1}{Tolerance} \tag{5}$$

$R_k^2$ is the adjustment coefficient of each of the estimated $k$ auxiliary regressions. According to [32], if *Tolerance* is too low (which implies a high $VIF$ statistic), there is evidence of multicollinearity problems. In this case, the explanatory variable depends on this auxiliary regression, sharing a high percentage of variance with the other explanatory variables [6].

As reference values for diagnosing multicollinearity problems, many authors establish a $VIF$ threshold above 10. However, Favero and Belfiore [32] warn that a $VIF$ value equal to 4 will result in an $R_k^2$ of 0.75 for a given auxiliary regression, a relatively high percentage of shared variance. If the VIF exceeds the established limits, it indicates the presence of multicollinearity in the proposed model. Therefore, the use of stepwise is recommended so that only statistically significant variables remain in the model, thus avoiding the problem of multicollinearity.

### 2.4. Diagnosis of Heteroskedasticity

In addition to the assumptions and statistical tests presented above, each random error term's probability distribution is represented by $u_i$ in Equations (2) and (3) must present the same variance; that is, they must be homoscedastic [6].

As Favero and Belfiore [32] explain, heteroskedasticity can indicate a correlation between the terms of the error and the explanatory variables, causing problems with the hypothesis tests of the t statistics [41,42]. However, it does not necessarily affect the consistency of the parameter estimates, and it can be addressed by robust standard errors, such as Huber-White, in order to provide valid inference by adjusting the standard errors of the estimated coefficients, ensuring that statistical tests remain reliable even in the presence of heteroscedasticity.

For the diagnosis of heteroscedasticity, the Breusch–Pagan/Cook–Weisberg test stands out, based on the Lagrange multiplier, with $H0$ corresponding to the variance of the constant error terms (homoskedasticity) [6]; hypothesis $H1$ corresponds to the variance of error terms non-constantly, indicating that the terms $u_i$ are a function of one or more explanatory variables (heteroskedastic errors) [32]. Favero and Belfiore [6] indicate this test when the assumption of normality of the residues is verified.

It is necessary to obtain each standardized residual using Equation (6) to apply the Breusch–Pagan test:

$$u_{BP,i} = \frac{u_i^2}{\sum_{i=1}^{n} u_i^2 / n} \tag{6}$$

where $u_i$ represents the residual vector, and $n$ is the sample size. Next, the regression model, Equation (7), through which the sum of squares of the regression is calculated, divided by two, obtaining the $\chi^2_{BP}$ statistic [6].

$$u_{BP,i} = \alpha + \beta \hat{Y}_i + \varepsilon_i \tag{7}$$

$\hat{Y}_i$ represents the dependent variable's predicted value vector, and $\varepsilon_i$ corresponds to the regression's error term.

The Breusch–Pagan test presents $H0$ as the calculated statistic $\chi^2_{BP}$ with a chi-square distribution with 1 degree of freedom for a given significance level. In practice, if the error terms are homoskedastics, the squared residues do not increase or decrease with the increase of $\hat{Y}_i$ [6].

### 2.5. Nonlinear Regression Models

The definition of the best functional form of a regression model is an empirical question to be decided in favor of the best fit of the analyzed data [43]. According to [6], such a definition is based on the highest $R^2$, considering equal samples and with the same amount of parameters. Otherwise, one should choose the functional form whose model presents the highest adjusted $R^2$.

Box and Cox [44] proposed a general regression model as the basis for all functional forms in this context. From the linear regression model with a single variable, $X$, it is possible to obtain a transformed model, replacing $Y$ by $(Y^{\lambda} - 1)/\lambda$ and from $X$ by $(X^{\theta} - 1)/\theta$, where $\lambda$ and $\theta$ are the parameters of the transformation [25,44,45]. Thus, it is possible to represent the model by Equation (8):

$$\frac{(Y_i^{\lambda} - 1)}{\lambda} = \alpha + \beta \frac{(X_i^{\theta} - 1)}{\theta} + u_i \tag{8}$$

From Equation (8), values are assigned to $\lambda$ and $\theta$ that provide adherence to the primary functional forms, such as Semilogarithmic to the right, to the left, Logarithmic Inverse, Quadratic, and Cubic [6]. When applied to an original variable, the Box–Cox transformation generates a new variable, which presents a new distribution [32]. When applying the Box–Cox transformation to a regression model with multiple independent variables $X$, each variable can be transformed individually using its own parameter $\theta_i$. The parameters $\lambda$ and $\theta_i$ are estimated through maximum likelihood before fitting the linear regression model to the transformed variables.

According to [46], problems related to residuals in regression models may arise from specification failures in the model's functional form. In this sense, the Box–Cox transformation can help define the functional form most adherent to the data, maximizing adherence to normality [6].

### 2.6. The Stepwise Procedure

The main approaches to stepwise regression are forward selection, backward elimination, and bidirectional elimination [47]. The forward selection procedure begins with an equation without variables. At each step, the technique involves adding the variable with the highest F-statistic or the lowest $p$-value until there is none left to be added to the model [8].

The backward elimination procedure starts from a "complete" model, with all the predictive input variables and the intercept. Then, at each step, the variable that least improves the model is deleted, one at a time, until no other excluded variable can significantly improve the model's performance [48].

Bidirectional elimination corresponds to a forward selection procedure but with the possibility of excluding a selected variable at each stage, as in backward elimination. This approach is commonly applied to stepwise regression, mainly when there are correlations between variables [48].

#### 2.6.1. Forward Selection

The inclusion criteria forward selection is a procedure that determines whether to include an independent variable in the model based on its statistically significant contribution to the model's fit.

This inclusion is assessed through the significance test, which compares the statistical improvement from adding the variable to the model with a predetermined significance level [27].

It is possible to see the general equation for the inclusion criteria below (Equation (9)):

$$Y = \beta_0 + \beta_1 X_1 + \varepsilon \tag{9}$$

where $Y$ represents the dependent variable, $X_1$ represents the independent variable for inclusion in the model, and $\varepsilon$ is the error term, which captures the variation not explained by the model [27].

The inclusion criteria seek to determine whether adding the variable $X_1$ to the model results in a statistically significant improvement in the ability to explain the variability of the dependent variable. The procedure takes place by calculating test statistics such as the $p$-value. If the $p$-value is less than the predetermined significance level, the variable $X_1$ is considered statistically significant and is included in the model [49].

Thus, the inclusion criteria in the stepwise procedure allow the selection of independent variables that present a statistically significant relationship with the dependent variable, contributing to a better adjustment and explanation of the MLR model [50].

It is important to mention that, when new variables $X_i$ are added to the model, it is possible that other variables already included, which were previously statistically significant, may lose their significance. This occurs because the inclusion of additional variables can alter the relationships between covariates, affecting their $p$-values. Therefore, it is crucial to thoroughly explore all independent variables and select a set in which all remain statistically significant in the presence of others. This ensures that each variable meaningfully contributes to the predictive power of the model based on the sample data, avoiding redundancy [3,6,24,26].

#### 2.6.2. Backward Elimination

The exclusion criteria (Backward Elimination) guide the decision-making process: whether or not to remove an independent variable from the model based on statistical criteria. In this criterion, the independent variables are initially included in the model and then removed one by one if their exclusion results in a statistically significant improvement in model fit. The measure of improvement is usually assessed using the significance test, using a predetermined significance level [27].

It is possible to see the general equation for the exclusion criteria below (Equation (10)):

$$Y = \beta_0 + \beta_1 X_1 + \beta_2 X_2 + \cdots + \beta_P X_P + \varepsilon \tag{10}$$

In this equation, $Y$ represents the dependent variable; $X_1, X_2, \ldots, X_P$ represent the independent variables, and $\varepsilon$ is the error term. The exclusion criteria remove independent variables one by one based on their statistically insignificant contribution to explaining the variability of the dependent variable [50].

Statistical tests guide the decision to remove a variable, such as a $p$-value, which compares the relationship between each independent and dependent variable. Suppose the $p$-value is more significant than the predetermined significance level, indicating that the variable does not contribute statistically significantly to the model. In that case, the exclusion criteria remove it from the model [50].

Thus, the exclusion criterion in the stepwise procedure allows for refining the multiple linear regression model, eliminating the independent variables that are not statistically significant [27]. If an independent variable with a beta that is not statistically different from zero is not excluded, the model loses predictive power. This beta does not contribute to the predictive composition in the presence of other variables, ceteris paribus, rendering it statistically insignificant in explaining the dependent variable $Y$. Including such a variable can also distort the magnitude and sign of other beta parameters, without adding meaningful value to the predictive model [3,6,24,26].

#### 2.6.3. Bidirectional Elimination

The Bidirectional Elimination is a flexible approach to selecting variables in a MLR model. This criterion can add or removes independent variables based on their statistical contribution to the model fit. The significance test usually evaluates the contribution measure and determines the statistical significance from a pre-established confidence level [51].

### 2.7. *Applications of the Stepwise Procedure in Multiple Regressions*

The academic literature presents several relevant applications of the stepwise procedure in multiple regression machine learning models, as shown in Table 1.

Based on the examples of the application of the stepwise procedure in machine learning models of multiple regressions, a wide range of studies are observed, covering several areas of research.

Its use aims to identify and select the most relevant and statistically significant variables, in the most diverse applications, for example, in the prediction of meteorological events, understanding of factors that affect prices and production in different sectors, such as real estate and agriculture, as well as providing valuable information in environmental fields, such as studies on soil, deforestation and air quality.

The approach also has applications in medicine, helping to estimate ages, predict disease and analyze the impact of health conditions on drug responses. Its versatility allows employment in socioeconomic and urban issues, such as impact and balance analyses in various contexts.

Notably, this literature review is not exhaustive since the stepwise procedure has an extensive and multifaceted scope. However, the various studies analyzed in this section allowed us to demonstrate its multidisciplinary applicability.

From predicting meteorological phenomena to analyzing socioeconomic impacts and evaluating health issues, the stepwise procedure has proven to be a versatile and valuable tool for the judicious selection of statistically significant variables in various research fields. In the study of sample data within applied sciences, it is essential to select only those variables that demonstrate statistical significance. A model constructed from sample data that includes betas that are not statistically significant, particularly for predictive purposes, cannot be considered the final model [3,6,24,26].

**Table 1.** Examples of stepwise applications in regression models.

| Reference | Journal | Objective |
|---|---|---|
| [9] | Mausam | Select statistically significant variables for forecasting storms |
| [10] | Landscape and Urban Planning | Select hedonic variables in modeling real estate sales prices |
| [12] | Poultry Science | Predict total egg production in European quail based on phenotypes |
| [13] | Ecosphere | To analyze the depth distribution of organic carbon in the soils of eastern Australia |
| [19] | Forensic Science International: Genetics | Estimation of chronological age using specific DNA methylation patterns |
| [17] | Environmental and Ecological Statistics | Relate deforestation and forest fragmentation metrics to socioeconomic and bio geophysical factors |
| [14] | Air Quality, Atmosphere and Health | Evaluate and provide hourly air quality forecasting |
| [18] | Clinical Pharmacokinetics | Predicting the Effect of Renal Failure on Pharmacokinetics of Drugs |
| [11] | Small Ruminant Research | Predict marketable carcass characteristics and cuts of meat |
| [52] | Plant Methods | Evaluate the detection capacity of terrestrial light and range data in the estimation of corn biomass in precision agriculture practices |
| [15] | Ecological Indicators | Estimate the above-ground biomass indicator of degraded grasslands using machine learning methods |
| [53] | Land Use Policy | Apply and compare stepwise regression with the Random Forest algorithm for mass evaluation in an urban residential area |
| [54] | Applied Soft Computing | Predict mortality from COVID-19 |
| [55] | Hydrology and Earth System Sciences | Estimate the regionalization of hydrological model parameters |
| [56] | Building and Environment | To analyze the impacts of urbanization characteristics on carbon emissions from road passenger transport |
| [57] | Sustainability (Switzerland) | To analyze the performance of stepwise multiple regression methods to estimate the biomass distribution of eucalyptus |
| [21] | IEEE Engineering Management Review | Analyze the work–life balance of women in information technology organizations |
| [58] | Applied Water Science | Predict irrigation water quality indices based on machine learning and regression models |
| [20] | Journal of Craniofacial Surgery | Predict changes in head index after cranioplasty |
| [59] | Information Systems and e-Business Management | Predict the influence of climate variations on the spread of COVID-19 |

### 2.8. Computational Implementation of Stepwise

This section briefly describes implementations in some of the main languages used in the statistical analysis and data modeling.

The R language is widely known for its efficiency in statistical analyses and has a variety of packages that support the stepwise procedure [60]. The "MASS" package (v. 7.3-61) provides the "stepAIC()" function, which allows for the implementation of the stepwise forward, backward, and bidirectional methods. In addition, the "leaps", "stepwise", and "caret" packages also provide additional functionality for variable selection and statistical modeling.

The stepwise procedure is available through the PROC REG command for users of SAS (v. 9.4M8), a statistical tool widely used in industry and research. This command allows the automatic selection of variables using different input methods, such as the forward, backward, or stepwise method.

In MATLAB (v. R2023b), a programming platform commonly used in engineering and science, the "Statistics and Machine Learning Toolbox" package assists in implementing the stepwise procedure. This package provides functionality for adjusting regression models, including the stepwise method.

In addition to the languages mentioned above, other programming languages implement the stepwise procedure. Julia, for example, offers the "GLM" (v. 1.9.0) and "StatsModels.jl" (v. 0.6.35) packages that provide functionality for stepwise regression. For SPSS software users (v. 29.0.1.1), the "REGRESSION" command, and the appropriate options to specify the variable selection method, help to perform the stepwise procedure. In the Stata environment (v. 18), the "stepwise" command allows for the implementation of the stepwise procedure.

Other languages like Java, C++, and C# support the stepwise procedure through different packages and libraries. Java, for example, relies on the Weka package (v. 3.8), which provides methods for selecting variables, including stepwise, based on *p*-values as well as accuracy metrics. Weka allows for forward, backward, or mixed selection approaches. In the case of C++, the Mlpack library (v. 4.5.0) offers functionality for stepwise regression, primarily based on performance metrics rather than *p*-values, and does not implement a traditional stepwise method but allows for forward or backward approaches based on model performance. C# has the Accord.NET package (v. 3.8.0), which also focuses on accuracy metrics rather than *p*-values, providing features for variable selection using forward and backward methods.

## 3. Methodology

The proposed library aims to apply the stepwise procedure to perform a regression analysis. This procedure makes it possible to select a subset of the independent variables that best explain the variability of a dependent variable, in such a way that all the independent variables selected are statistically significant at a pre-established confidence level.

The technological approach used is the Python language, which we used to propose and implement the regression model, facilitating its integration into studies that involve the application of a specific regression model. Figure 1 illustrates the methodological workflow of the stepwise library to validate and select the statistically significant variables.

After collecting the data, processing and structuring it using Extraction, Transform, and Load (ETL) techniques is essential. Defining the variables that we want to predict and the variables that explain that prediction is critical to building a supervised machine learning model. In addition, it is essential to perform an exploratory analysis of the variables using unsupervised modeling to complement the evaluation process.

When we have one or more explanatory variables of a qualitative nature, it is necessary to transform them into dummy variables, creating $n - 1$ dummies, where $n$ is the number of categories present in each explanatory variable. Next, we built a general regression model to evaluate the statistical importance of all the variables involved. Next, if there are variables that are not statistically significant, a diagnosis of multicollinearity should be performed using the VIF and Tolerance statistics.

Then, the main contribution of this paper is implemented: the stepwise procedure based on the statistical significance of variables as a function of the Python programming language. Stepwise automatically excludes variables that are not statistically significant from the model.

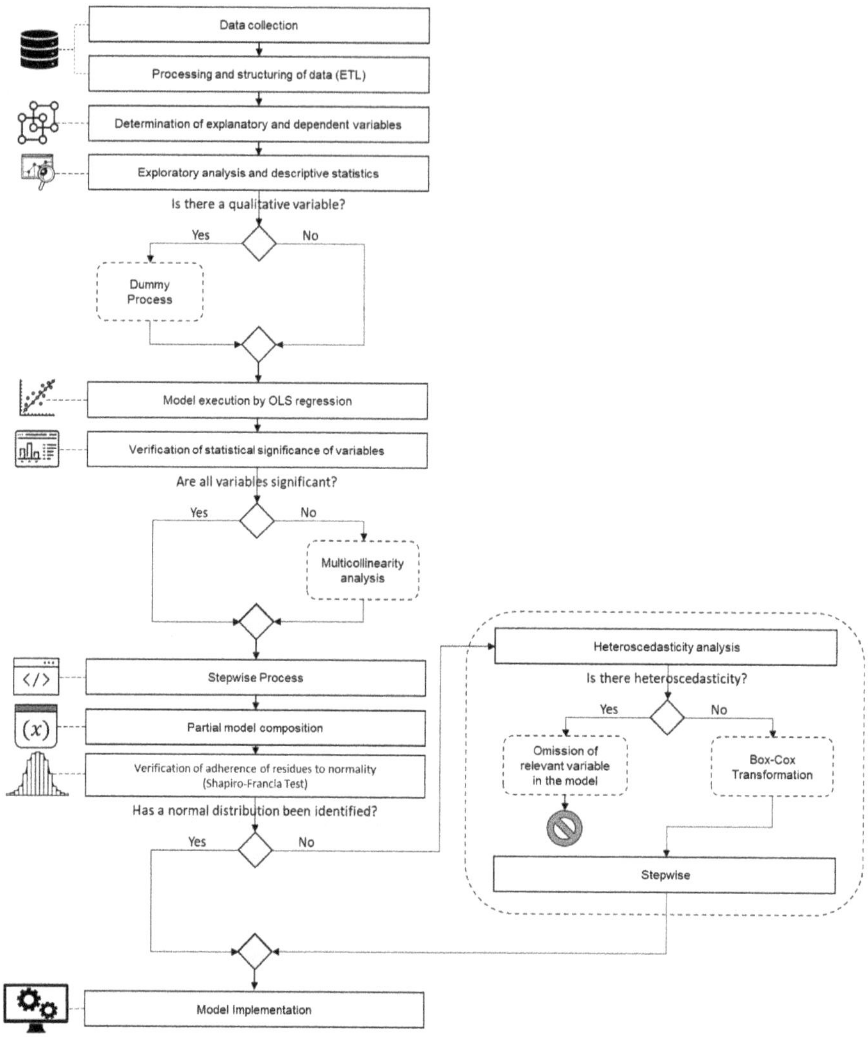


**Figure 1.** Methodological workflow.

The variable selection process is automated, allowing the model to select independent variables without manual intervention. In situations with many independent variables available, the stepwise method can reduce the dimensionality of the model, avoiding overfitting problems and improving the model's generalization to new data. During this process, variables may be added and then removed, as their statistical significance can change in the presence of other variables, even if they were significant initially. The algorithm retains those variables that, together, are all statistically significant, providing the best fit with all relevant predictors [3]. This is crucial for maintaining the model's predictive capability [6]. It is essential that all considered variables are statistically representative to explain the behavior of the dependent variable $y$ alongside the other $X_i$ variables, thereby preventing the $\beta$ parameters from being altered by the inclusion of a variable whose $\beta$ is not statistically different from zero [3,30]. It is important to note that the implemented package allows you to define the desired error term. If the "error_type" argument is omitted, by default the stepwise function considers conventional error terms. However, if we set "error_type" to "robust", the algorithm considers Huber-White standard errors.

After stepwise, a partial model is composed. The next step is to verify the adherence of the residuals to normality, using the Shapiro–Francia test, also implemented in the 'statstests.tests' package (v. 1.0.7) in Python and presented in this article.

If there is no adherence of the residues to normality, the next analysis is the diagnosis of heteroscedasticity. If there is heteroscedasticity in the model, applying the Breusch–Pagan test, which may indicate the omission of a relevant variable in the model.

Following the flow of Figure 1, considering that the residuals are not adherent to normality and the data present heteroscedasticity, an efficient procedure is the Box–Cox transformation in the dependent variable, to maximize its adherence to normality.

To confirm whether the nonlinear model performs better, the stepwise procedure and multicollinearity, normality, and heteroscedasticity tests should be performed again.

All this process established in the methodological flow shown in Figure 1 and described in this section is part of a general model of construction and analysis of a multiple regression model. In this process, stepwise is of great value in building a model with the guarantee of using variables with statistical significance for predictive purposes.

You can find all the information regarding the process of installing and using the stepwise library at: https://pypi.org/project/statstests/ (accessed on 24 June 2024). The script for the implementation of the stepwise Function in Python can be found in the Supplementary Material.

To exemplify the flowchart, in the next section a real case study of real estate pricing will be carried out, which runs through all the steps described in this section.

## 4. Case Study

To exemplify the use of the proposed library for implementing the stepwise procedure in Python, an estimation of a multiple linear regression model for evaluating apartments in the city of São Paulo, Brazil, will be performed. We used real estate data from 200 apartments in three neighborhoods (Vila Nova, Brooklin, and Moema).

We evaluated four explanatory variables: Apartment area ($X_1$), measured in $m^2$, represented in the database by 'area'; Number of rooms ($X_2$), represented by the number of compartments of the property, represented by 'rooms'; Land area ($X_3$), in $m^2$, represented by 'land_area'; and the neighborhood where the property is located ($X_4$), a qualitative variable represented by 'neighborhood'. As a dependent variable, the price of the property ($Y$), $R\$/\text{m}^2$, represented by 'price', was considered. Notably, among the explanatory variables, the apartment area, number of rooms, and land area are quantitative, while the neighborhood is a qualitative variable with three categories (neighborhoods).

Equation (11) below represents the proposed MLR model, where $i$ varies from 1 to 200 since the database consists of 200 apartments.

$$price_i = \alpha + \beta_1 area_i + \beta_2 rooms_i + \beta_3 land\_area_i + \beta_4 neighborhood_i + \varepsilon_i \tag{11}$$

We applied the Python script available in the Supplementary Material to perform all the analyses presented and discussed in this section.

Figure 2 presents the descriptive statistics of the quantitative variables of the model.

| | price | area | rooms | land_area |
|---|---|---|---|---|
| count | 200.000000 | 200.000000 | 200.000000 | 200.000000 |
| mean | 3223.668000 | 100.020000 | 4.705000 | 1500.660000 |
| std | 848.941684 | 25.095588 | 1.670908 | 378.796142 |
| min | 1774.600000 | 64.000000 | 2.000000 | 948.000000 |
| 25% | 2522.800000 | 76.000000 | 3.000000 | 1140.000000 |
| 50% | 3100.000000 | 98.000000 | 4.000000 | 1464.000000 |
| 75% | 3952.450000 | 126.000000 | 6.000000 | 1896.000000 |
| max | 5384.000000 | 136.000000 | 7.000000 | 2040.000000 |

**Figure 2.** Descriptive statistics of the quantitative variables.

The descriptive statistics show that there are 200 observations for each variable; that is, there are no missing values in the sample. We also verified that the neighborhood variable is a polychotomous categorical variable with three categories.

Figure 3 shows the heatmap of the Pearson correlations matrix between the metric variables. The values of the main diagonal are all equal to 1 because they represent the correlation of a given variable with itself. A high correlation (practically equal to 1) between the variables 'area' and 'land_area' stands out.

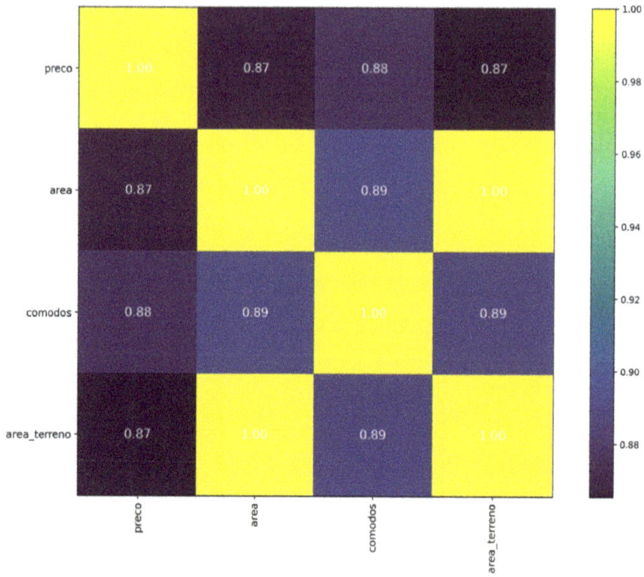


**Figure 3.** Heatmap of the Pearson correlation correlations matrix between the metric variables.

Figure 4 consolidates the distributions of the metric variables on the main diagonal, scatters, values of correlations (r), and respective statistical significance ($p$), all lower than 0.01, with a confidence level greater than 99%.

Next, the analysis of the frequency table of the qualitative variable is performed, with the number of apartments for each of the three neighborhoods: 72 apartments in Vilanova, 66 in Moema, and 62 in Brooklyn. As the variable 'neighborhood' is qualitative, to avoid the arbitrary weighting procedure, the $n-1$ dummies procedure is applied.

In the proposed case study, the Brooklyn neighborhood was used as a reference category, as it is the first in alphabetical order, which will have its behavior captured by the $\alpha$ intercept. Notably, the choice of the reference category does not affect the final result of the analysis since there will be a rearrangement of the $\beta$ values.

Estimating the multiple linear regression model with $n-1$ dummies, we arrive at the results of Figure 5.

The model equation, after the $n-1$ dummies procedure, is represented in Equation (12). The 'neighborhood' variable will be summarized by 'neighb'.

$$price_i = 1532.96 + 89.2area_i + 134.46rooms_i - 5.63land\_area_i + 474.93neighb\_moema_i + 1175.3neighb\_vilanova_i + \varepsilon_i \quad (12)$$

The value of $R^2$ is equal to 0.87; that is, the variable $X$ explains 87% of the behavior of the variable $Y$. However, we verified that the $p$-values of the variables 'area' and 'land_area' are, respectively, 0.109 and 0.124. Such values are not statistically significant, at a confidence level of 95%, in the presence of the other variables. In this case, the multicollinearity diagnosis was performed using the statistics Variance Inflation Factor (VIF) and Tolerance, according to Figure 6.

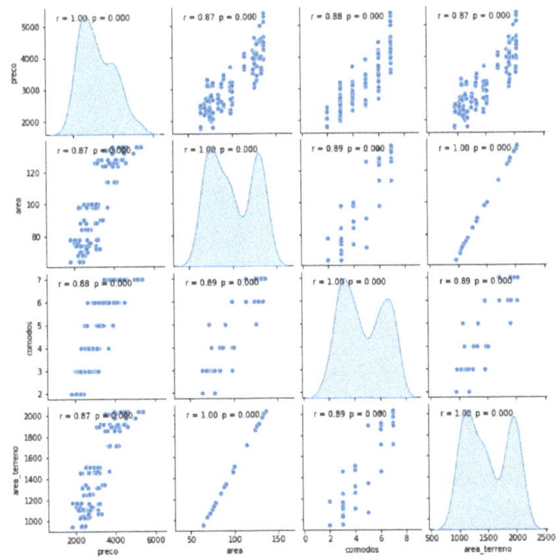


**Figure 4.** Distribution of the metric variables.

```
                            OLS Regression Results
==============================================================================
Dep. Variable:                  preco   R-squared:                       0.871
Model:                            OLS   Adj. R-squared:                  0.868
Method:                 Least Squares   F-statistic:                     262.3
Date:                Thu, 31 Oct 2024   Prob (F-statistic):           2.89e-84
Time:                        15:22:44   Log-Likelihood:                -1427.2
No. Observations:                 200   AIC:                             2866.
Df Residuals:                     194   BIC:                             2886.
Df Model:                           5
Covariance Type:            nonrobust
=============================================================================================
                                coef    std err          t      P>|t|      [0.025      0.975]
---------------------------------------------------------------------------------------------
const                      1532.6217    156.527      9.791      0.000    1223.908    1841.335
area                         89.2355     55.491      1.608      0.109     -20.207     198.678
rooms                       134.4406     32.006      4.200      0.000      71.316     197.565
land_area                    -5.6290      3.643     -1.545      0.124     -12.814       1.556
neighborhood_moema          475.0474     63.235      7.512      0.000     350.331     599.764
neighborhood_vilanova      1175.4929    121.510      9.674      0.000     935.842    1415.143
==============================================================================
Omnibus:                       25.075   Durbin-Watson:                   1.774
Prob(Omnibus):                  0.000   Jarque-Bera (JB):               48.368
Skew:                           0.622   Prob(JB):                     3.14e-11
Kurtosis:                       5.063   Cond. No.                     1.33e+04
==============================================================================
```

**Figure 5.** MLR model.

| | VIF | Tolerance |
|---|---|---|
| const | 51.431258 | 0.019443 |
| area | 4050.486419 | 0.000247 |
| rooms | 5.973655 | 0.167402 |
| land_area | 3977.022693 | 0.000251 |
| neighborhood_moema | 1.855901 | 0.538822 |
| neighborhood_vilanova | 7.140927 | 0.140038 |

**Figure 6.** Variance Inflation Factor and Tolerance.

Although no cutoff point is established in the literature to define whether or not there is multicollinearity between explanatory variables, it is necessary to observe VIF values greater than ten. In this sense, the variables 'area' and 'land_area' present VIF values close to 4000, with Tolerance practically equal to 0, representing a practically maximum $R^2$, representing a preliminary indication of multicollinearity in the proposed model.

To confirm the multicollinearity and establish the set of statistically significant variables, we arrive at the main contribution of this work: the implementation of the stepwise procedure based on the statistical significance of the variables as a function of the Python programming language. To apply stepwise through the function proposed in this paper, run the following command:

from stats tests.process import stepwise

model_step_apartments = stepwise(model_apartments, pvalue_limit = 0.05)

where 'model_apartments' is the MLR model in Figure 5; 'model_step_apartments' is the MLR model obtained after the stepwise procedure; 'pvalue_limit' refers to the level of statistical significance (in this case, equal to 0.05). Figure 7 shows the new model obtained after applying the stepwise.

```
 Atributes discarded on the process...:

{'atribute': "Q('land_area')", 'p-value': 0.12392157729883521}
{'atribute': "Q('area')", 'p-value': 0.11512639854800828}

 Model after stepwise process...:
 preco ~ Q('rooms') + Q('neighborhood_moema') + Q('neighborhood_vilanova')

                            OLS Regression Results
==============================================================================
Dep. Variable:                  preco   R-squared:                       0.868
Model:                            OLS   Adj. R-squared:                  0.866
Method:                 Least Squares   F-statistic:                     429.1
Date:                Thu, 31 Oct 2024   Prob (F-statistic):           7.56e-86
Time:                        15:25:06   Log-Likelihood:                -1429.7
No. Observations:                 200   AIC:                             2867.
Df Residuals:                     196   BIC:                             2881.
Df Model:                           3
Covariance Type:            nonrobust
=============================================================================================
                                coef    std err          t      P>|t|      [0.025      0.975]
---------------------------------------------------------------------------------------------
Intercept                  1788.3928     92.330     19.369      0.000    1606.304    1970.482
Q('rooms')                  171.6374     26.672      6.435      0.000     119.036     224.239
Q('neighborhood_moema')     506.7849     61.567      8.231      0.000     385.366     628.204
Q('neighborhood_vilanova') 1277.9567    106.091     12.046      0.000    1068.731    1487.183
==============================================================================
Omnibus:                       29.828   Durbin-Watson:                   1.756
Prob(Omnibus):                  0.000   Jarque-Bera (JB):               62.000
Skew:                           0.707   Prob(JB):                     3.44e-14
Kurtosis:                       5.332   Cond. No.                         31.0
==============================================================================
```

**Figure 7.** New model ('model_step_apartments') obtained after applying the stepwise.

According to the preliminary analysis by $VIF$ and *Tolerance* statistics, the variables 'area' and 'land_area' present multicollinearity, being excluded from the multiple regression model after the stepwise procedure, leaving only the variables 'rooms' and 'neighborhood' (with two categories, since 'Brooklyn' was the reference category).

The following analysis consists of the verification of adherence of the residues to normality using the Shapiro–Francia test, implemented by the 'Shapiro–Francia' function of the 'statstests.tests' package, also presented in this article, according to the commands below:

from stats tests.tests import shapro-francia

shapiro_francia = (model_step_apartments.resid)

where 'model_step_apartments' is the MLR model after performing the stepwise procedure. The Shapiro-Francia test is shown in Figure 8. As a result, a $p$-value of 0.00002 was obtained, lower than the established significance level of 0.05. Therefore, we rejected the hypothesis, which means there is no adherence to the normality of the residues of the analyzed model.

```
method  :  Shapiro-Francia normality test
statistics W  :  0.9428879585951422
statistics z  :  4.610630444107969
p-value  :  2.0072482113803717e-06
Statistics W=0.94289, p-value=0.000002
```

**Figure 8.** Shapiro–Francia test.

As a result of nonadherence to normality, another essential analysis is the diagnosis of heteroskedasticity using the Breusch–Pagan test. It is possible to see the result of which in Figure 9. The $p$-value was approximately $6.41 \times 10^{-15}$, lower than the significance level of 0.05. Thus, there is heteroskedasticity in the data, which means that there is correlation between the residues and one or more explanatory variables. In short, relevant variables are omitted from the model.

```
Breusch-Pagan Test (model_step_apartament)
chisq: 60.790590590891995
p-value: 6.449304131067478e-15
```

**Figure 9.** Breusch–Pagan test.

Considering that the residues of the model in question are not adherent to normality and the data present heteroskedasticity, a solution is the Box–Cox transformation in the dependent variable 'price', aiming to maximize the adherence of variable $Y$ to normality. Figure 10 shows the $p$-values of the model variables after applying the Box–Cox transformation.

```
                            OLS Regression Results
==============================================================================
Dep. Variable:               bc_preco   R-squared:                       0.893
Model:                            OLS   Adj. R-squared:                  0.891
Method:                 Least Squares   F-statistic:                     325.4
Date:                Thu, 31 Oct 2024   Prob (F-statistic):           2.85e-92
Time:                        15:34:58   Log-Likelihood:                 440.99
No. Observations:                 200   AIC:                            -870.0
Df Residuals:                     194   BIC:                            -850.2
Df Model:                           5
Covariance Type:            nonrobust
===========================================================================================
                              coef    std err          t      P>|t|      [0.025      0.975]
-------------------------------------------------------------------------------------------
Intercept                   4.5966      0.014    334.628      0.000       4.570       4.624
area                        0.0048      0.005      0.980      0.328      -0.005       0.014
rooms                       0.0151      0.003      5.359      0.000       0.010       0.021
land_area                  -0.0003      0.000     -0.924      0.357      -0.001       0.000
neighborhood_moema          0.0633      0.006     11.407      0.000       0.052       0.074
neighborhood_vilanova       0.1167      0.011     10.945      0.000       0.096       0.138
==============================================================================
Omnibus:                        3.303   Durbin-Watson:                   1.828
Prob(Omnibus):                  0.192   Jarque-Bera (JB):                2.890
Skew:                          -0.247   Prob(JB):                        0.236
Kurtosis:                       3.320   Cond. No.                     1.33e+04
==============================================================================
```

**Figure 10.** $p$-values of the model variables after the Box–Cox transformation.

Considering the level of statistical significance of 5%, as in the previous model, we verified that the variables 'area' and 'land_area' were not statistically significant in the presence of the other variables. In addition, there is an increase in $R^2$ to 0.893.

Applying the stepwise procedure to the 'model_bc_apartments', obtained after the Box–Cox transformation, we arrive at the result of Figure 11.

```
Atributes discarded on the process...:

{'atribute': "Q('land_area')", 'p-value': 0.3565392251671068}
{'atribute': "Q('area')", 'p-value': 0.16497153382004484}

Model after stepwise process...:
bc_preco ~ Q('rooms') + Q('neighborhood_moema') + Q('neighborhood_vilanova')

                            OLS Regression Results
==============================================================================
Dep. Variable:               bc_preco   R-squared:                       0.892
Model:                            OLS   Adj. R-squared:                  0.890
Method:                 Least Squares   F-statistic:                     539.3
Date:                Thu, 31 Oct 2024   Prob (F-statistic):           2.11e-94
Time:                        15:36:53   Log-Likelihood:                 439.56
No. Observations:                 200   AIC:                            -871.1
Df Residuals:                     196   BIC:                            -857.9
Df Model:                           3
Covariance Type:            nonrobust
==================================================================================================
                                   coef    std err          t      P>|t|      [0.025      0.975]
--------------------------------------------------------------------------------------------------
Intercept                        4.6147      0.008    572.576      0.000       4.599       4.631
Q('rooms')                       0.0176      0.002      7.579      0.000       0.013       0.022
Q('neighborhood_moema')          0.0656      0.005     12.202      0.000       0.055       0.076
Q('neighborhood_vilanova')       0.1244      0.009     13.438      0.000       0.106       0.143
==============================================================================
Omnibus:                        2.472   Durbin-Watson:                   1.806
Prob(Omnibus):                  0.291   Jarque-Bera (JB):                2.087
Skew:                          -0.186   Prob(JB):                        0.352
Kurtosis:                       3.334   Cond. No.                         31.0
==============================================================================

Notes:
[1] Standard Errors assume that the covariance matrix of the errors is correctly specified.
```

**Figure 11.** Stepwise procedure applied to the 'model_bc_apartments'.

At the significance level established, the variables 'area' and 'land_area' were once again removed from the final model by the stepwise procedure.

Comparing the initial models and after the Box–Cox transformation, both having undergone the stepwise procedure through the function proposed in this article, we arrive at Figure 12.

```
=======================================================================
                             STEPWISE MODEL | STEPWISE MODEL WITH BOX-COX
-----------------------------------------------------------------------
Intercept                    1788.3928***     4.6147***
                             (92.3305)        (0.0081)
Q('rooms')                   171.6374***      0.0176***
                             (26.6724)        (0.0023)
Q('neighborhood_moema')      506.7849***      0.0656***
                             (61.5671)        (0.0054)
Q('neighborhood_vilanova') 1277.9567***       0.1244***
                             (106.0908)       (0.0093)
R-squared                    0.8679           0.8919
R-squared Adj.               0.8658           0.8903
N                            200              200
=======================================================================
Standard errors in parentheses.
* p<.1, ** p<.05, ***p<.01
```

**Figure 12.** Comparison between the two models.

We observed that the $R^2$ of the Box–Cox model was higher than the initial one (0.8920 to 0.8679), which reflects a gain in adherence to the nonlinear model. Once again, applying the Shapiro–Francia test, we arrive at the result of Figure 13.

```
method  :  Shapiro-Francia normality test
statistics W  :  0.9868704088633033
statistics z  :  1.570841156128166
p-value  :  0.058109774822529804
Statistics W=0.98687, p-value=0.058110
```

**Figure 13.** Application of the Shapiro–Francia test.

The $p$-value was approximately 0.0584 higher than the established significance level. Therefore, we did not reject the null hypothesis; that is, there is adherence to the normality of the residues. Then, by evaluating the heteroskedasticity, the result of the Breusch–Pagan test is obtained (Figure 14).

```
Breusch-Pagan Test (modelo_step_bc_apartamentos)
chisq: 1.0130847799601872
p-value: 0.47767069834924153
```

**Figure 14.** Breusch–Pagan test.

A $p$-value of approximately 0.48 is observed, higher than the established significance level. Thus, there is no more heteroskedasticity in the data, only by the adequacy of the dependent variable to a nonlinear form. Given the above, we arrive at the Equation (13) which is the equation of the final model proposed after the Box–Cox transformation and application of stepwise, proposed and implemented in this paper. The 'neighborhood' variable will be summarized by 'neighb'.

$$\left(\frac{price_i^{-0.144}-1}{-0.144}\right) = 4.6147 + 0.0176 * rooms_i + 0.0656 * neighb\_moema_i + 0.1244 * neighb\_vilanova_i \quad (13)$$

## 5. Conclusions

The present research has achieved the proposed objectives, contributing significantly to data analyses and statistical modeling in Python. First, we presented the stepwise function based on the statistical significance of the variables in Python, detailed and exemplified, offering researchers, students, and professionals a practical and intuitive tool for carefully selecting variables in multiple regression models. This new tool differs from existing ones, which rely on accuracy metrics, as it is fundamentally based on the statistical significance of the variables. This approach is extremely important in the context of regression models within applied sciences, as failing to exclude variables whose $\beta$ parameters lack statistical significance can lead to a loss of predictive capability. Such inclusion can alter the magnitude and even the effect of other $\beta$ parameters in the predictive model.

Then, practical examples demonstrated how applying the proposed stepwise function can enhance the reliability of multiple regression models by removing non-significant variables, leading to more accurate and trustworthy model adjustments and predictions. In addition, we presented a comprehensive methodological framework to address common problems in data analyses, such as heteroskedasticity, multicollinearity, and nonadherence of residues to normality, providing a robust and user-friendly computational implementation.

The current case study of real estate pricing, considering linear and nonlinear multiple regression models through stepwise, allowed us to consolidate the concepts discussed and validate the effectiveness of the proposed approach. The results showed that the correct application of the stepwise procedure could lead to more accurate models and a better interpretation of the factors that influence real estate pricing.

In conclusion, this research fully achieved the proposed objectives, contributing significantly to advancing the understanding and application of statistical methods in Python. The results presented in this paper can be widely used and inspire new debates and contributions in data analysis and statistical modeling. The availability of the stepwise function based on the statistical significance of the variables in Python and the methodological framework will provide practitioners with a more informed and practical approach to handling complex data, driving significant advances in their respective research and application areas.

Despite the promising results achieved in this study, it is essential to recognize some limitations that may open space for future research. First, while the stepwise procedure based on the statistical significance of the variables is a valuable approach to variable selection, there may be better options in some scenarios. Additionally, this stepwise process can also be conducted using metrics of fit and accuracy, leaving it to the researcher to decide which method best suits their study. In addition, we focused the case study on real estate pricing, which may limit the generalization of the results to other application areas. Future research could explore the applicability of the proposed stepwise function in different contexts, addressing specific problems and testing the approach's effectiveness in other modeling tasks.

Another aspect to consider is that we addressed heteroskedasticity problems, multicollinearity, and nonadherence of residues to normality in this study. Still, the complexity of these problems can vary widely in different data sets. Future research could explore more sophisticated and specific strategies to address these issues, considering their particularities in different scenarios.

Finally, although the methodological framework developed has demonstrated effectiveness in mitigating common problems in data analysis, it is possible to improve its performance and generality through more advanced approaches and adapt to different contexts. Future research could seek methodological improvements and the validation of the approach in other types of problems, contributing to a better understanding and application of statistical methods in Python in an even broader spectrum of research areas and challenges.

**Supplementary Materials:** The following supporting information can be downloaded at: https://www.mdpi.com/article/10.3390/a17110502/s1. Supplementary File: A Proposal for a new Python Library Implementing Stepwise Procedure.

**Author Contributions:** Conceptualization, L.P.F., H.P.S. and P.B.; methodology, L.P.F., P.B., I.P.d.A.C., A.D. and M.Â.L.M.; software, L.P.F., H.P.S., M.Â.L.M. and W.T.J.; validation, L.P.F., P.B. and W.T.J.; formal analysis, I.P.d.A.C. and M.Â.L.M.; investigation, L.P.F., P.B., I.P.d.A.C. and M.Â.L.M.; resources, A.D., I.P.d.A.C., A.V.T. and M.Â.L.M.; data curation, I.P.d.A.C., A.V.T. and M.Â.L.M.; writing—original draft preparation, L.P.F., I.P.d.A.C., A.V.T. and M.Â.L.M.; writing—review and editing, L.P.F., A.D., I.P.d.A.C., A.V.T. and M.Â.L.M.; visualization, I.P.d.A.C., M.Â.L.M., W.T.J. and M.d.S.; supervision, I.P.d.A.C., M.Â.L.M., W.T.J. and M.d.S.; project administration, M.d.S.; funding acquisition, I.P.d.A.C.; Supplementary Material, A.D. and I.P.d.A.C.; All authors have read and agreed to the published version of the manuscript.

**Funding:** This research received no external funding.

**Data Availability Statement:** Data are contained within the article.

**Conflicts of Interest:** The authors declare no conflicts of interest.

## References

1. Provost, F.; Fawcett, T. Data Science and Its Relationship to Big Data and Data-Driven Decision Making. *Big Data* **2013**, *1*, 51–59. [CrossRef]
2. Philip Chen, C.L.; Zhang, C.-Y. Data-Intensive Applications, Challenges, Techniques and Technologies: A Survey on Big Data. *Inf. Sci.* **2014**, *275*, 314–347. [CrossRef]
3. Vidaki, A.; Ballard, D.; Aliferi, A.; Miller, T.H.; Barron, L.P.; Syndercombe Court, D.; Cui, S.; Wang, Y.; Wang, D.; Sai, Q.; et al. Variable Selection Strategies and Its Importance in Clinical Prediction Modelling. *Math. Probl. Eng.* **2022**, *8*, 759–771. [CrossRef]
4. Steyerberg, E.W.; Eijkemans, M.J.C.; Habbema, J.D.F. Stepwise Selection in Small Data Sets: A Simulation Study of Bias in Logistic Regression Analysis. *J. Clin. Epidemiol.* **1999**, *52*, 935–942. [CrossRef] [PubMed]
5. Emmert-Streib, F.; Dehmer, M. High-Dimensional LASSO-Based Computational Regression Models: Regularization, Shrinkage, and Selection. *Mach. Learn. Knowl. Extr.* **2019**, *1*, 359–383. [CrossRef]
6. Fávero, L.P.; Belfiore, P. *Manual de Análise de Dados: Estatística e Machine Learning Com Excel®, SPSS®, Stata®, R® e Python®*, 2nd ed.; Grupo Gen: Barueri, Brazil, 2024; ISBN 9788595159921.

7. Wold, S.; Kettaneh, N.; Tjessem, K. Hierarchical Multiblock PLS and PC Models for Easier Model Interpretation and as an Alternative to Variable Selection. *J. Chemom.* **1996**, *10*, 463–482. [CrossRef]
8. Yu, T.; Yu, G.; Li, P.-Y.; Wang, L. Citation Impact Prediction for Scientific Papers Using Stepwise Regression Analysis. *Scientometrics* **2014**, *101*, 1233–1252. [CrossRef]
9. Dhawan, V.B.; Tyagi, A.; Bansal, M.C. Forecasting of Thunderstorms in Pre-Monsoon Season over Northwest India. *Mausam* **2008**, *59*, 433–444. [CrossRef]
10. Yoo, S.; Im, J.; Wagner, J.E. Variable Selection for Hedonic Model Using Machine Learning Approaches: A Case Study in Onondaga County, NY. *Landsc. Urban Plan.* **2012**, *107*, 293–306. [CrossRef]
11. Alves, A.A.C.; Chaparro Pinzon, A.; Costa, R.M.D.; Silva, M.S.D.; Vieira, E.H.M.; Mendonça, I.B.D.; Viana, V.D.S.S.; Lôbo, R.N.B. Multiple Regression and Machine Learning Based Methods for Carcass Traits and Saleable Meat Cuts Prediction Using Non-Invasive in Vivo Measurements in Commercial Lambs. *Small Rumin. Res.* **2019**, *171*, 49–56. [CrossRef]
12. Felipe, V.P.S.; Silva, M.A.; Valente, B.D.; Rosa, G.J.M. Using Multiple Regression, Bayesian Networks and Artificial Neural Networks for Prediction of Total Egg Production in European Quails Based on Earlier Expressed Phenotypes. *Poult. Sci.* **2014**, *94*, 772–780. [CrossRef] [PubMed]
13. Hobley, E.U.; Wilson, B. The Depth Distribution of Organic Carbon in the Soils of Eastern Australia. *Ecosphere* **2016**, *7*, e01214. [CrossRef]
14. Peng, H.; Lima, A.R.; Teakles, A.; Jin, J.; Cannon, A.J.; Hsieh, W.W. Evaluating Hourly Air Quality Forecasting in Canada with Nonlinear Updatable Machine Learning Methods. *Air Qual. Atmos. Health* **2017**, *10*, 195–211. [CrossRef]
15. Xu, K.; Su, Y.; Liu, J.; Hu, T.; Jin, S.; Ma, Q.; Zhai, Q.; Wang, R.; Zhang, J.; Li, Y.; et al. Estimation of Degraded Grassland Aboveground Biomass Using Machine Learning Methods from Terrestrial Laser Scanning Data. *Ecol. Indic.* **2020**, *108*, 105747. [CrossRef]
16. Yang, Q.; Su, Y.; Hu, T.; Jin, S.; Liu, X.; Niu, C.; Liu, Z.; Kelly, M.; Wei, J.; Guo, Q. Allometry-Based Estimation of Forest Aboveground Biomass Combining LiDAR Canopy Height Attributes and Optical Spectral Indexes. *For. Ecosyst.* **2022**, *9*, 100059. [CrossRef]
17. Zanella, L.; Folkard, A.M.; Blackburn, G.A.; Carvalho, L.M.T. How Well Does Random Forest Analysis Model Deforestation and Forest Fragmentation in the Brazilian Atlantic Forest? *Environ. Ecol. Stat.* **2017**, *24*, 529–549. [CrossRef]
18. Borella, E.; Poggesi, I.; Magni, P. Prediction of the Effect of Renal Impairment on the Pharmacokinetics of New Drugs. *Clin. Pharmacokinet.* **2018**, *57*, 505–514. [CrossRef]
19. Vidaki, A.; Ballard, D.; Aliferi, A.; Miller, T.H.; Barron, L.P.; Syndercombe Court, D. DNA Methylation-Based Forensic Age Prediction Using Artificial Neural Networks and next Generation Sequencing. *Forensic Sci. Int. Genet.* **2017**, *28*, 225–236. [CrossRef]
20. Villavisanis, D.F.; Shakir, S.; Zhao, C.; Cho, D.Y.; Barrero, C.; Blum, J.D.; Swanson, J.W.; Bartlett, S.P.; Tucker, A.M.; Taylor, J.A. Predicting Changes in Cephalic Index Following Spring-Mediated Cranioplasty for Nonsyndromic Sagittal Craniosynostosis: A Stepwise and Machine Learning Algorithm Approach. *J. Craniofac. Surg.* **2022**, *33*, 2333–2338. [CrossRef]
21. Gupta, C.; Rajeswara Rao, K.V.S.; Datta, P. Support Vector Machine Based Prediction of Work-Life Balance Among Women in Information Technology Organizations. *IEEE Eng. Manag. Rev.* **2022**, *50*, 147–155. [CrossRef]
22. Gurcan, F. What Issues Are Data Scientists Talking about? Identification of Current Data Science Issues Using Semantic Content Analysis of Q&A Communities. *PeerJ Comput. Sci.* **2023**, *9*, e1361. [PubMed]
23. Asha, V.; Sreeja, S.P.; Saju, B.; Nisarga, C.S.; Prasad, A. Performance Analysis of Olympic Games Using Data Analytics. In Proceedings of the 2023 Second International Conference on Electronics and Renewable Systems (ICEARS), Tuticorin, India, 2–4 March 2023; pp. 1436–1443.
24. Gujarati, D.N. *Essentials of Econometrics*; Sage Publications: New York, NY, USA, 2021; ISBN 1071850407.
25. Fávero, L.P.; Belfiore, P.; da Silva, F.L.; Chan, B.L. *Análise de Dados: Modelagem Multivariada Para Tomada de Decisões*; Campus Elsevier: Rio de Janeiro, Brazil, 2009.
26. Kutner, M.H.; Nachtsheim, C.J.; Neter, J.; Li, W. *Applied Linear Statistical Models*; McGraw-Hill: New York, NY, USA, 2005; ISBN 0072386886.
27. Kuhn, M.; Johnson, K. *Applied Predictive Modeling*; Springer: New York, NY, USA, 2013; ISBN 9781461468493.
28. Li, M.; Wang, J. An Empirical Comparison of Multiple Linear Regression and Artificial Neural Network for Concrete Dam Deformation Modelling. *Math. Probl. Eng.* **2019**, *2019*, 7620948. [CrossRef]
29. Montgomery, D.C.; Peck, E.A.; Vining, G.G. *Introduction to Linear Regression Analysis*; John Wiley & Sons: Hoboken, NJ, USA, 2021; ISBN 1119578752.
30. Kennedy, P. *A Guide to Econometrics*; John Wiley & Sons: Hoboken, NJ, USA, 2008; ISBN 1405182571.
31. Wooldridge, J.M.; Wadud, M.; Lye, J. *Introductory Econometrics: Asia Pacific Edition with Online Study Tools 12 Months*; Cengage AU: Stamford, CT, USA, 2016; ISBN 0170350835.
32. Fávero, L.P.; Belfiore, P. *Data Science for Business and Decision Making*; Academic Press Elsevier: Cambridge, MA, USA, 2019; ISBN 0128112174.
33. Stock, J.H.; Watson, M.W. Econometria. *Agric. Sao Paulo* **2004**, *51*, 85.
34. Barro, R.J. Economic Growth in a Cross Section of Countries. *Q. J. Econ.* **1991**, *106*, 407–443. [CrossRef]

35. Engle, R.F.; Granger, C.W.J. Co-Integration and Error Correction: Representation, Estimation, and Testing. *Econom. J. Econom. Soc.* **1987**, *55*, 251–276. [CrossRef]
36. Belsley, D.A.; Kuh, E.; Welsch, R.E. *Regression Diagnostics: Identifying Influential Data and Sources of Collinearity*; John Wiley & Sons: Hoboken, NJ, USA, 2005; ISBN 0471725145.
37. Chen, J.; Chen, Z. Extended Bayesian Information Criteria for Model Selection with Large Model Spaces. *Biometrika* **2008**, *95*, 759–771. [CrossRef]
38. Hastie, T.; Tibshirani, R.; Friedman, J.H.; Friedman, J.H. *The Elements of Statistical Learning: Data Mining, Inference, and Prediction*; Springer: Berlin/Heidelberg, Germany, 2009; Volume 2.
39. Shapiro, S.S.; Francia, R.S. An Approximate Analysis of Variance Test for Normality. *J. Am. Stat. Assoc.* **1972**, *67*, 215–216. [CrossRef]
40. Fava, V.L. Manual de Econometria. In *Vasconcelos MAS*; Alves, D., Ed.; Editora Atlas: São Paulo, Brazil, 2000.
41. Greene, W. *Econometric Analysis*; Pearson: Harlow, UK, 2012.
42. Vasconcellos, M.A.S.; Alves, D. *Manual de Econometria*; Atlas: São Paulo, Brazil, 2000.
43. Linneman, P. Some Empirical Results on the Nature of the Hedonic Price Function for the Urban Housing Market. *J. Urban Econ.* **1980**, *8*, 47–68. [CrossRef]
44. Box, G.E.P.; Cox, D.R. An Analysis of Transformations. *J. R. Stat. Soc. Ser. B Stat. Methodol.* **1964**, *26*, 211–243. [CrossRef]
45. Favero, L.P.L. O Mercado Imobiliário Residencial Da Região Metropolitana de São Paulo: Uma Aplicação de Modelos de Comercialização Hedônica de Regressão e Correlação Canônica. Ph.D. Thesis, Universidade de São Paulo, São Paulo, Brazil, 2005.
46. Nwakuya, M.T.; Nwabueze, J.C. Application of Box-Cox Transformation as a Corrective Measure to Heteroscedasticity Using an Economic Data. *Am. J. Math. Stat.* **2018**, *8*, 8–12.
47. Chatterjee, S.; Hadi, A.S. *Regression Analysis by Example*; John Wiley & Sons: Hoboken, NJ, USA, 2015; ISBN 1119122732.
48. Wang, M.; Wright, J.; Brownlee, A.; Buswell, R. A Comparison of Approaches to Stepwise Regression on Variables Sensitivities in Building Simulation and Analysis. *Energy Build.* **2016**, *127*, 313–326. [CrossRef]
49. Hair, J.F.; Black, W.C.; Babin, B.J.; Anderson, R.E. *Multivariate Data Analysis: Pearson New International Edition PDF EBook*; Pearson Higher Education: New York, NY, USA, 2013; ISBN 1292035110.
50. Tabachnick, B.G.; Fidell, L.S.; Ullman, J.B. *Using Multivariate Statistics*; Pearson: Boston, MA, USA, 2013; Volume 6.
51. Draper, N. *Applied Regression Analysis*; McGraw-Hill. Inc.: New York, NY, USA, 1998.
52. Jin, S.; Su, Y.; Song, S.; Xu, K.; Hu, T.; Yang, Q.; Wu, F.; Xu, G.; Ma, Q.; Guan, H.; et al. Non-Destructive Estimation of Field Maize Biomass Using Terrestrial Lidar: An Evaluation from Plot Level to Individual Leaf Level. *Plant Methods* **2020**, *16*, 1–19. [CrossRef] [PubMed]
53. Yilmazer, S.; Kocaman, S. A Mass Appraisal Assessment Study Using Machine Learning Based on Multiple Regression and Random Forest. *Land Use Policy* **2020**, *99*, 104889. [CrossRef]
54. Cui, S.; Wang, Y.; Wang, D.; Sai, Q.; Huang, Z.; Cheng, T.C.E. A Two-Layer Nested Heterogeneous Ensemble Learning Predictive Method for COVID-19 Mortality. *Appl. Soft Comput.* **2021**, *113*, 107946. [CrossRef]
55. Song, Z.; Xia, J.; Wang, G.; She, D.; Hu, C.; Hong, S. Regionalization of Hydrological Model Parameters Using Gradient Boosting Machine. *Hydrol. Earth Syst. Sci.* **2022**, *26*, 505–524. [CrossRef]
56. Su, Y.; Wu, J.; Ciais, P.; Zheng, B.; Wang, Y.; Chen, X.; Li, X.; Li, Y.; Wang, Y.; Wang, C.; et al. Differential Impacts of Urbanization Characteristics on City-Level Carbon Emissions from Passenger Transport on Road: Evidence from 360 Cities in China. *Build. Environ.* **2022**, *219*, 109165. [CrossRef]
57. Li, Y.; Wang, R.; Shi, W.; Yu, Q.; Li, X.; Chen, X. Research on Accurate Estimation Method of Eucalyptus Biomass Based on Airborne LiDAR Data and Aerial Images. *Sustainability* **2022**, *14*, 10576. [CrossRef]
58. Mokhtar, A.; Elbeltagi, A.; Gyasi-Agyei, Y.; Al-Ansari, N.; Abdel-Fattah, M.K. Prediction of Irrigation Water Quality Indices Based on Machine Learning and Regression Models. *Appl. Water Sci.* **2022**, *12*, 76. [CrossRef]
59. Butt, N.A.; Gull, H.; Ali, Z.; Muhammad, G.; AlQahtani, S.A. A Multi-Prefecture Study Applying Multivariate Approaches for Predicting and Demystifying Weather Data Variations Affect COVID-19 Spread. *Inf. Syst. E-bus. Manag.* **2023**. [CrossRef]
60. Crawley, M.J. *The R Book*; John Wiley & Sons: Hoboken, NJ, USA, 2012; ISBN 0470973927.

algorithms

MDPI

Article

# ACT-FRCNN: Progress Towards Transformer-Based Object Detection

**Sukana Zulfqar [1], Zenab Elgamal [2,*], Muhammad Azam Zia [1], Abdul Razzaq [3], Sami Ullah [4] and Hussain Dawood [2]**

1 Department of Computer Science, University of Agriculture Faisalabad, Faisalabad 38000, Pakistan; sukanazulfqar5517@gmail.com (S.Z.); mazamzia@uaf.edu.pk (M.A.Z.)
2 School of Computing, Skyline University College, Sharjah P.O. Box 1797, United Arab Emirates; dawood.hussain@skylineuniversity.ac.ae
3 Department of Computer Science & IT, Muhammad Nawaz Sharif University of Agriculture Multan, Multan 59300, Pakistan; abdul.razzaq@mnsuam.edu.pk
4 Department of Computer Science, Government College University Faisalabad, Faisalabad 38000, Pakistan; samiullah@gcuf.edu.pk
* Correspondence: zenab.elgamal@skylineuniversity.ac.ae

**Abstract:** Maintaining a high input resolution is crucial for more complex tasks like detection or segmentation to ensure that models can adequately identify and reflect fine details in the output. This study aims to reduce the computation costs associated with high-resolution input by using a variant of transformer, known as the Adaptive Clustering Transformer (ACT). The proposed model is named ACT-FRCNN. Which integrates ACT with a Faster Region-Based Convolution Neural Network (FRCNN) for a detection task head. In this paper, we proposed a method to improve the detection framework, resulting in better performance for out-of-domain images, improved object identification, and reduced dependence on non-maximum suppression. The ACT-FRCNN represents a significant step in the application of transformer models to challenging visual tasks like object detection, laying the foundation for future work using transformer models. The performance of ACT-FRCNN was evaluated on a variety of well-known datasets including BSDS500, NYUDv2, and COCO. The results indicate that ACT-FRCNN reduces over-detection errors and improves the detection of large objects. The findings from this research have practical implications for object detection and other computer vision tasks.

**Keywords:** adaptive clustering transformer (ACT); object detection; segmentation; computer vision; classification; feature map

## 1. Introduction

The Bidirectional Transformer [1] paradigm has demonstrated outstanding improvements in machine translation [2], question–answering [3], text categorization [4], and document summarization [5], among other NLP issues. This accomplishment is partly due to the transformer's ability to recognize complex relationships among input sequences through self-attention. It uses pre-train models on large datasets without encountering performance saturation due to its scalability [1,4].

Transformers can be directly applied to images by converting an image into a collection of patches. Although attention-based transformer models may not perform as well as convolution-based models on medium-sized datasets, these can be pre-trained on a large amount of data due to their capacity, as seen in NLP transformers [4]. This shows attention-based components have the potential to improve or even replace the traditional convolution approach that has been standard in vision modeling for a long time [5].

The higher-level feature maps of a convolutional network often align with the input's spatial layout. This means that features from objects on the left of an input image tend to appear on the left of higher-level feature maps [5]. This property makes it easy to convert convolutional classifiers into object detectors by adding detection heads that output object classes and positions on high-level convolutional maps. Unlike convolutional networks, transformers can work at each layer of the network, potentially affecting the spatial relationship between input features and those at the middle layers. This raises the question of whether ACT can be adjusted to perform tasks that require more sensitivity to local context, such as object detection or segmentation.

This research proposes an ACT technique to replace the transformer in the encoder of the original FRCNN system as an easy-to-add component. The ACT works well with the classic transformer and does not require new skills. Adding Multi-Task Knowledge Distillation (MTKD) to ACT can improve its accuracy to match the original transformer. MTKD can also allow for a seamless transition between models with different computing resources and accuracy during inference. However, some transformer adjustments can be made to reduce computational complexity [6–9]. If we have enough processing power, one obvious question is if we can improve the performance of FRCNN and strike a balance with computational resources.

In this paper a new model ACT-FRCNN is developed. The model is based on ACT and includes specific task heads for detecting and locating objects in images. The aim is to demonstrate that ACT-FRCNN, with its transformer-based backbone, can effectively preserve crucial spatial information for object detection. The experiment illustrate that ACT-FRCNN shares many of the desired features of transformer-based models while achieving strong performance on various benchmarked datasets including: BSDS500 [10], NC2016 [11], and COCO 2017 [12]. This research examines the benefits of using the extensive pre-training method with transformers for object detection tasks. The experimental results demonstrate a decrease in false positive detections and improved detection performance for large objects, possibly due to the architecture's ability to attend globally.

In this paper a large-scale computer vision models are typically trained on massive datasets and then fine-tuned for specific tasksåå.

The main contributions are threefold:

- Designed an ACT-FRCNN model that can be used for object detection and segmentation.
- Proposed an Adaptive Clustering Transformer (ACT) with Convolutional Neural Network (CNN) as the backbone of ACT-FRCNN.
- ACT-FRCNN is evaluated on three different datasets: BSDS500, NYUDv2, and COCO 2017, and demonstrate significant outcomes.

The remaining manuscript sections are organized: Section 2 discusses related work. Section 3 demonstrates the method and materials used in this research. Section 4 describes the experimental procedure. Finally, Sections 5 and 6 presents the discussion and conclusion respectively.

## 2. Related Work

### 2.1. NLP and CV for Attention Model

The attention model [13] has been widely utilized in computer vision (CV) and NLP due to its inherent capability to gather evolving information that evolves over time. The transformer facilitates the exchange of data between two entities, such as regions in CV or words in NLP. Transformer has achieved cutting-edge results in Machine translation [14], object detection [15], multimodality reasoning [16], picture classifications [17], video classifications [18], and language understanding [1]. The transformer has performed very well in different situations.

However, scaling is complex because the length of the input sequence leads to quadratic complexity. There are many ideas for solving the Transformer's computational issues. Kitaev et al. [19] suggested sharing the key and query, clustering features that are close together into one cluster using Locality Sensitive Hashing (LSH) to perform information exchange into each cluster. Zhu et al. [20] approximates the SoftMax between the key and query interaction with linear complexity, verifiable approximation error, and positive orthogonal random features (PORFs). Using the association property, the authors of linear attention [9] reduce the complexity of key-query value multiplication from quadratic to linear. By eliminating the input of one layer at a time, the method of progressive elimination [8] can reduce the computational cost of the transformer while still achieving the same or better performance as the original. To reduce the computational complexity, asymmetric attention [21] summarizes essential features into a small number of key vectors by pooling over these features at many scales. Global graph reasoning [5] uses weighted pooling to compress input data into globally unique vectors that may then be transmitted. As mentioned earlier, these techniques altered the original transformer's structure and required substantial training and inference resources. Additionally, the performance gap between ACT and the original transformer can be further reduced with a few iterations of fine-tuning knowledge distillation [22].

### 2.2. Deep Learning for Object Detection

The framework for object detection sorts data within a changing time window [22]. The Viola-Jones Sliding window technique was used for face detection with a face detector [23] and AdaBoost [24]. In addition, the CNN method has been used for object classification with great success [25], as will the deep features classification used for object identification. The object detection utilizing in-depth features can be classified into two types: one-stage and two-stage approaches. The two-stage solutions include RCNN [26], Fast RCNN, and Faster RCNN [26], Whereas the one-stage options are YOLO [26] and SSD [27]. Training and deploying earlier techniques for object detection is more difficult due to the extensive post-processing pipeline NMS [28], imbalanced loss, and hand-crafted anchor [29]. Instead of using a sliding window, objects can now be detected by solving a robust set prediction problem against permutations. Liu et al. [30] developed an end-to-end people detection using the CNN encoding of visual features and the LSTM [31] decoding of the bounding box sequentially. Hungarian loss [31] will be applied to the end-to-end training process to ensure the predicted bounding box is consistent with the ground truth. Recurrent instance segmentation [32] superimposes an extra-segmentation head over the end-to-end object identification architecture, testing the concept of instance segmentation with great success. Using the more powerful transformer instead of LSTM [31] has simplified the object detection pipeline by solving the end-to-end set prediction problem, removing the need for custom priors. However, because self-attention has quadratic complexity, end-to-end set prediction converges slowly and requires high inference costs. SMCA [33] increased convergence speed by introducing Gaussian before the transformer decoder.

### 2.3. Self-Attention for Object Detection

DETR [5] is an essential method because it effectively utilizes transformers for object detection. It includes a set-matching loss, a transformer encoder, and a decoder, all integrated with a standard convolutional neural network (CNN) model such as ResNet-50/101. This method stands out because it eliminates the need for non-maximum suppression (NMS), and its decoder design can independently learn to remove redundant bounding box predictions. Deformable DETR [27] addresses a few drawbacks of DETR: (1) achieving relatively poor detection performance on small objects and (2) requiring substantially longer training epochs for convergence than standard detectors. Our proposed ACT aims to reduce the computational cost of DETR's inference without retraining, unlike Deformable DETR and SMCA.

DETR variations have also been suggested as solutions to the issues. By combining a multi-scale deformable encoder with learnable sparse sampling, Deformable DETR [34] speeds up convergence. To address problems mostly created by the insurmountable challenge of processing high-resolution feature maps, deformable DETR implements a deformable attention module that learns to focus on a small fraction of sample points in the feature map. Differently, RelationNet++ [35] benefits from multi-head attention. A "Bridging Visual Representations" (BVR) module built on a transformer decoder is suggested to integrate information from various object representations. These results build on the work conducted by RelationNet [36] and Non-Local Networks (NL) [19] in object recognition by splitting the focus between bounding box features and pixel features.

DETR and Deformable DETR use convolutional networks to encode visual characteristics, while the transformer decodes these features into detection outputs. This article explores a new variation of a transformer-based detector in which the transformer encodes visual information instead of a standard region proposal network (RPN) and also generates the output detections.

### 2.4. Pertaining Model and Self-Training

Numerous studies have used large-scale datasets, like JFT-300M [37] and IG-940M [38], to investigate how useful pre-training is for learning visual representations. Big Transfer (BiT) [39] found that detection transfer performance was aided by extensive classification-based pre-training. He et al. [40] have found that when the detection dataset is large enough, small-scale classification-based pre-training, such as pre-training on ILSVRC-2012 [41], does not always improve detection performance compared to training from scratch. In this paper, the pre-training paradigms for object detection are the primary focus of our attention. However, semi-supervised learning [42] and self-training [43] paradigms are also effective when working with enormous amounts of unlabeled data.

### 2.5. Research Gap

The research discussed in this paper aims to improve our understanding of how transformer models, specifically the ACT model, can be used in object identification and other computer vision tasks. It also aims to enhance object detection systems by addressing the limitations of current methods. The paper proposes an FRCNN model that integrates ACT, leveraging the well-known transformer features of extensive pretraining capability and fast fine-tuning performance. Experimental results demonstrate the superior performance of the ACT-FRCNN model on the BSDS500, NYUDv2, and COCO 2017 benchmark datasets. The findings indicate that the ACT-FRCNN model outperforms many state-of-the-art techniques, achieving higher accuracy using fewer parameters.

## 3. Method and Materials

In ACT-FRCNN, a detection network is used with Adaptive Clustering backbone. This addition allows us to determine bounding box classifications and coordinates. The original transformer's design is identical to the adaptive clustering transformer (ACT) we proposed. ACT reduces the calculation cost of the transformer without requiring retraining. Through a few rounds of knowledge distillation fine-tuning, we can narrow the performance gap between ACT and the base transformer [1]. Figure 1 shows a visual representation of the ACT-FRCNN architecture. The RPN generates multiple predictions for each location on the map to identify exciting areas likely to contain objects. Each prediction corresponds to a specific anchor on the map and has different sizes and aspect ratios. The first step is to determine if an object exists in that area, and then the system determines the coordinates of a box around the object. Parameterization allows us to calculate the bounding boxes as distances from the anchor boxes.

$$\begin{aligned} t_x &= (x - x_a)/w_a & t_x^* &= (x^* - x_a)/w_a \\ t_y &= (y - y_a)/h_a & t_y^* &= (y^* - y_a)/h_a \\ t_w &= \log(w/w_a) & t_w^* &= \log(w^*/w_a) \\ t_h &= \log(h/h_a) & t_h^* &= \log(h^*/h_a) \end{aligned} \tag{1}$$

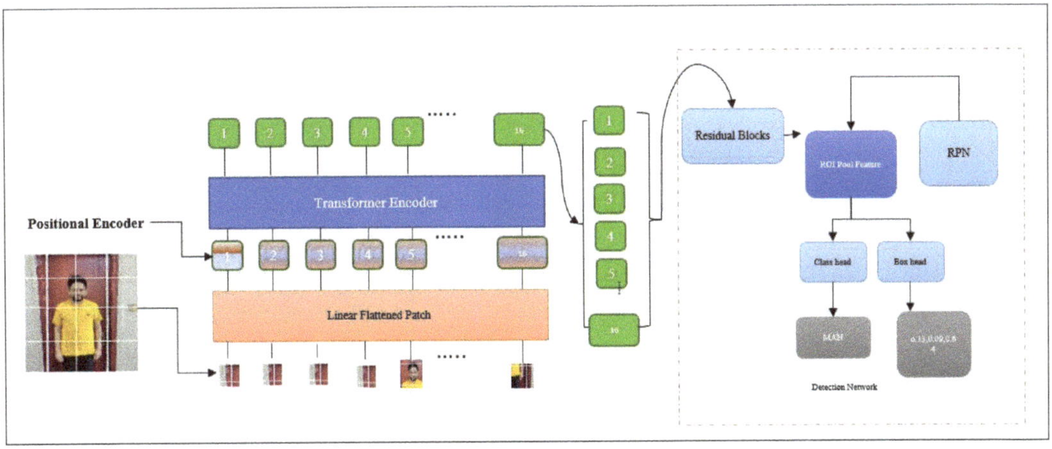


**Figure 1.** The ACT-FRCNN model relies on an ACT framework for its object detection capabilities. It generates a feature map using the last transformer layer's per-patch outputs to feed into a detection model. For precise object detection, this model generates both class predictions and box coordinates. ACT-FRCNN exhibits remarkable performance and shares the benefits of transformer-based models.

The coordinates ($x$, $y$, $w$, $h$) of the box's center, width, and height are denoted by $x$, $x_a$, and $x^*$, whereas $x$, $x_a$, and $x^*$ represent the prediction, anchor, and ground truth, respectively. When comparing the true offsets $t^*$ to the projected offsets $t$, the box training loss is equivalent to a Huber loss. The best candidates are used to RoI-pool regions from the feature map based on the RPN's thorough forecast of object-containing regions, yielding one feature proposal for each region. The same parameterization as before provides these pooled features to a pair of lightweight heads, which then generate bounding box regressions and predictions for object categories (or background).

The DETR encoder includes features that allow it to use the attention mechanism to gather information from nearby positions. Our research shows that similar features in close physical proximity tend to produce identical attention maps. ACT must select prototypes representing the whole and communicate updated characteristics to its neighbor since its self-attention overlaps with its nearest neighbor. The more complex the encoder becomes, the more similar its characteristics grow as they start to share data. Also, each encoder layer shows a significant variation in the distributions of input features. These findings suggest using an adaptive method to determine the required number of prototypes for each data layer instead of relying on a predetermined set of cluster centers.

To tackle the issue of encoder attention redundancy, ACT utilizes key-query attention for representative prototypes. These prototypes are created by clustering similar query features and then averaging them. The modified features of the prototypes are then shared with their neighbors by using the Euclidean distance on the query feature space. Due to the wide variety of encoder characteristics, we need an adaptive clustering method to categorize features based on their location in the input and encoder layers. Our technique called multi-round exact Euclidean locality sensitivity hashing (E2LSH) [19] achieves query feature distribution-aware clustering.

*3.1. Implementation Details*

In this implementation, the used settings are similar to those for ACT-FRCNN and the original Faster R-CNN. The RPN predicts 15 anchors at each spot: the used of five sizes ($32 \times 32$, $64 \times 64$, $128 \times 128$, $256 \times 256$, and $512 \times 512$ pixels) and three different shapes (1:1, 1:2, and 2:1). NMS is applied to the region suggestions generated by the RPN with an overlap threshold of 0.6. During training, the top 22,000 suggestions are sent to the detector heads, and during inference, the top 800 are used. To create our final detections, the perform a final round of NMS at the time of inference using a threshold of 0.4. to explored two ways to use the encoder outputs: combining all intermediate outputs into a single one and using only the last one. The use a learned transformation in both approaches to reduce the spatial feature map's dimensionality to 512 channels. Finally, added intermediate residual blocks between the detection module and the encoder spatial feature map was practical (for a visual representation of the residual block structure, similar to ResNet with some slight modifications, refer to Figure 2).

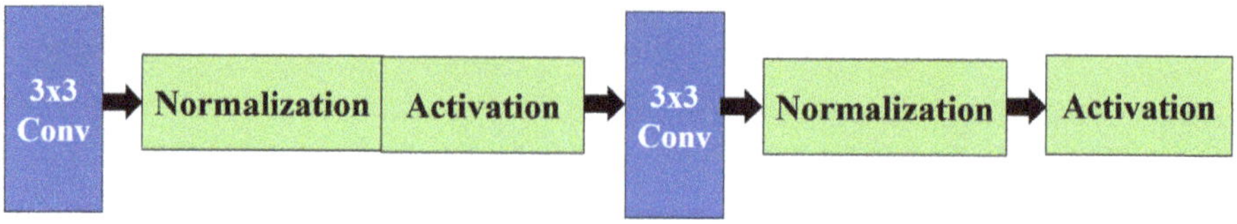


**Figure 2.** The encoder outputs are connected to the detection module using the intermediary residual convolution blocks. Batch normalization and GeLU activation functions are used in all studies.

## 3.2. *Adaptive Clustering Transformer*

### 3.2.1. Determine Prototypes

The locality sensitive hashing (LSH) prototype is used to join queries that are close together based on Euclidean distance. This method effectively solves the nearest neighbor search problem. When vectors are close, they are likely to have the same hash, while those far apart do not. By adjusting the hash function's parameters and the number of hashing iterations, to ensured that all vectors with a distance less than $p$ end up in the same hash bucket. Specifically, the used the exact Euclidean locality sensitive hashing (E2LSH) as our hash function [19].

$$h(\vec{v}) = [\frac{\vec{a}.\vec{v} + b}{r}] \tag{2}$$

where $h : R^d \to Z$ is the hash function, $r$ is a hyper-parameter, and $\vec{a}, b$ are random variables satisfying $\vec{a} = (a_1, a_2, \ldots\ldots, a_d)$, with $a_i \sim N(0,1)$ and $b \sim u(0,r)$. The results carry more weight when LSH is applied iteratively. The final hash value obtained by

$$h(\vec{v}) = \sum_{i=0}^{L-1} B^i h_i(\vec{v}) \tag{3}$$

where each $h_i$ is calculated using Equation (3) with parameters $\vec{a}$ and $b$ drawn at random, and where $B$ is a constant equal to 4 in our trials. The random normal vectors $\vec{a}_1$ $\vec{a}_1$ and offset $b_i$ in each hash function $h_i$ can be visualized as a series of parallel hyperplanes. The hyper-parameter $r$ controls the spacing of the hyperplanes. More significant separation indicates greater importance. In addition, $L$ hash functions partition the search area into a number of cells, each of which contains vectors that are hashed to the same value. The likelihood that the vectors enter the same cell increases as the Euclidean distance decreases.

To obtain the prototypes, the hash value for each query was first computed. The questions that have the same hash value will be clustered together, with the prototype query serving as the group's hub. The $Q \in R^{N \times D_k}$ and the queries $P \in R^{C \times D_k}$ sets as prototypes, where $N$ and $C$ are the number of groups for queries and prototypes, respectively. The $G_i$ represent the index of the cluster to which $Q_i$ belongs. The Prototype of the $j$th group can be obtained by Equation (4).

$$P_j = \frac{\sum_i, G_i = j\, Q_i}{\sum_i, G_i = j\, 1} \tag{4}$$

3.2.2. Estimate Attention Output

After the initial stage, a prototype created to represent each set of questions. Then compute the attention map between the prototypes and keys. After that, the gathered of the specific target vector for each prototype and applied it to the original questions. This allows to estimate the impact on attention roughly. By reducing the number of prototypes and hash rounds, which are much fewer than $N$ and $M$, this significantly reduce the computation's difficulty by a factor of C compared to the exact attention calculation.

Formally, the values $K \in R^{M \times D_k}$ are the keys $V \in R^{C \times D_k}$. The following equations provide us with an approximation of the output of attention:

$$L = L_{pred}(Y, Y_2) + L_{KD}(B_1, B_2) \quad (5)$$

$$\widetilde{W} = \widetilde{A}V \quad (6)$$

$$\widetilde{V}^o = \widetilde{W}_j,\ G_i = j \quad (7)$$

where $G_i$ stands for the index of the cluster $Q_i$. SoftMax function is applied row-wise.

### *3.3. Multi-Task Knowledge Distillation*

ACT has been found to reduce the computational cost of FRCNN without need of retraining. Additionally, it has been discovered that fine-tuning MTKD multiple times, leads to better performance-to-computability ratio. The process for MTKD is shown in Figure 3. Image features will first be extracted using the pre-trained CNN backbone, which is specifically designed to capture intricate spatial hierarchies and patterns within the data. Once extracted, these features will be passed into both the adaptive convolutional transformer (ACT) and the original transformer in parallel, allowing for a comparative analysis of their respective outputs. To ensure a seamless transition and integration between ACT and the original transformer, the training process will be guided by Multi-Task Knowledge Distillation (MTKD). This approach facilitates optimal performance by leveraging the strengths of both models. Below is a notation for the training loss:

$$L = L_{pred}(Y, Y_2) + L_{KD}(B_1, B_2.\text{det}ach()) \quad (8)$$

where $Y$ stands for the real world, $B_1$ for the ACT prediction's bounding box, and $B_2$, $Y_2$ for the whole prediction. The difference between the truth and FRCNN's prediction is denoted by $L_{pred}$ $(Y, Y_2)$. The $L_2$ distance between the ACT and FRCNN predictions is minimized by $L_{KD}$ $(B_1, B_2)$, which is the knowledge distillation loss.

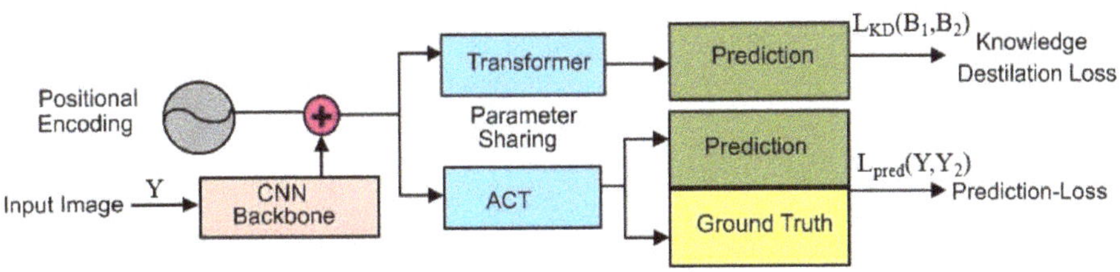


**Figure 3.** Multi-task knowledge Distillation. Initially, the CNN core extract features from images. The transformer kept in parallel with the excised section being fed into it. Training process guided by MTKD to ensure a smooth transition from the original transformer to ACT.

The training loss helps with the smooth transition from ACT to transformer by training the original transformer at the same time. The knowledge transformer includes region categorization and regression distillation features. The impact of ACT's approximation error is more noticeable in the regression sub-branch than in the classification sub-branch. The transferred of knowledge of the bounding box regression technique. Just by moving the box regression branch, the convergence rate is significantly improved.

### 3.4. Datasets

The ACT-FRCNN model is evaluated on the BSDS500 [10], NYUDv2 [11], and COCO 2017 [12] benchmarks to determine how well the suggested strategy performed in different settings. The studies conducted on the BSDS500, NYUDv2, and COCO 2017 benchmarks provide strong evidence for the effectiveness and adaptability of the proposed strategy and demonstrate how it can advance the field of computer vision. The aimed is to illustrate the efficiency and robustness of the proposed method in various image analysis tasks by evaluating it across these three benchmarks. According to the experimental results, this strategy outperforms the state of the art regarding accuracy and efficiency across all three benchmarks. These results showcase the versatility of the technique, indicating its suitability for tasks such as object identification and segmentation, depth estimation, and image segmentation.

#### 3.4.1. BSDS500 Dataset

The Berkeley Segmentation Dataset and Benchmark dataset (BSDS500) comprises 500 natural RGB photos, with 200 allocated for training, 100 for validation, and 200 for testing. Each photograph is meticulously annotated by an average of five different individuals. The ACT-FRCNN model is tested on the evaluation set after being trained on the training and validation sets. To augment the dataset, each image can be flipped and rotated, increasing the dataset size 16-fold. On the other hand, the PASCAL VOC Context Dataset [44], which contains full-scene segmentation annotations with more than 400 classes and comprises 10,103 training images, used as supplementary training data as done in earlier research [45]. In Stage One of model training, the outer borders from the segmentation annotations are used to infer context and semantic signals. Therefore, Stage One is pre-trained using the PASCAL VOC Context Dataset [44] before refining it using the BSDS500 [10]. Stage One training is the only phase that utilizes the PASCAL VOC Context Dataset [44], which offers finer, more specific edge and boundary annotations.

#### 3.4.2. NYUDv2 Dataset

The NYUDv2 dataset is widely used in computer vision research, especially for tasks such as depth estimation, scene understanding, and object detection. It comprises 1449 paired RGB and depth images, divided into 654 training images, 414 validation images, and 381 testing images. A key feature of NYUDv2 is its provision of dense depth maps, where each pixel in the image has a depth value, making it valuable for tasks like depth measurement and 3D reconstruction. The dataset also includes detailed ground truth annotations for object recognition and scene understanding, including scene category labels, object labels, and object borders. To augment the dataset, researchers often combine the training and validation sets and apply techniques such as four-fold rotation, random flipping, and scaling of both images and annotations [46].

#### 3.4.3. COCO 2017 Dataset

The COCO 2017 Dataset experiments are performed using 118,000 training and 5000 validation images from the COCO 2017 detection and panoptic segmentation datasets [47]. The dataset includes bounding boxes and panoptic segmentation annotations for each image. On average, the training set contains seven instances per image, with object sizes varying from very small to large. Unless specified otherwise, the performance is evaluated using Average Precision (AP), measured with a range of Intersection over Union (IoU) thresholds. For the first 1000 photos in the COCO 2017 [12] validation set, the average Floating-point Operations per second (FLOPs) is also measured. The FLOPs computation includes operations involving convolutional layers, fully connected layers, attention matrix operations, and other components like clustering and heuristics.

## 4. Experimental Procedure

The experiments on ACT-FRCNN demonstrate its effectiveness on detection datasets BSDS500 [10], NYUDv2 [11], and COCO 2017 [12]. The experiments conducted on a system with two GPUs, each with 12 GB of memory, 64 GB of RAM and the Intel Core i9 12th generation processor. A thorough set of analyses on ACT-FRCNN is provided, showing how a transformer-based detector might be advantageous due to its simplified training process and ability to generalize well to unknown data. Object detection studies are conducted by torch vision [12] implementations of ResNet and Faster R-CNN (FRCNN. Object detection studies were conducted using the TorchVision [12] ResNet and Faster R-CNN (FRCNN).

### *4.1. Result Discussion*

The Performance and Accuracy

The model's Average Precision (AP) is compared to DETR-DC5, with a specific focus on speed-accuracy trade-offs. Additionally, the adaptive clustering approach is compared to the K-means clustering method used in [46] were the number of clusters is denoted by $C$. When $L$ and $C$ are adjusted and the AP is calculated using various computational budgets, the ACT technique achieves significantly higher AP than K-means under an equalized computational budget. FLOPs are reduced from 168.9 GFLOPs to 164.3 GFLOPs compared to DETR-ACT, with only 0.5% loss in AP. MTKD substantially enhances AP, especially for devices with smaller FLOP capacities. ACT with L = 32 performs similarly to DETR-ACT, while ACT with L = 16 achieves a 4.6% increase in AP due to MTKD.

The advantages of proposed model over K-means clustering. K-means clustering requires the same number of clusters across all encoder levels. However, selecting an appropriate hyper-parameter can be difficult due to the varying distribution of queries based on the input image and encoder layer's index. Misusing the hyper-parameter $C$ can result in inaccurate estimates or unnecessary computational costs. Furthermore, K-means may not converge properly in certain situations, and many clusters can empty if $C$ is relatively large, as it is a hierarchical method. To address these issues, the proposed method employs an adaptive mechanism to dynamically calculate the number of prototypes.

**Detailed AP Comparision:** The Bounding Box Average Precisions (BBox APs) for the large ($AP_L$), medium ($AP_M$), and small ($AP_S$) instances are reported. Faster RCNN [48] and Discrete Event Time Series [15] is compared with these metrics. Both DETR and Faster R-CNN use Dilated ResNet-50 as the backbone. The results are presented in Table 1.

**Table 1.** A comparison of the AP of ACT-FRCNN model with DETR-ACT and Faster RCNN. Dilated ResNet-50 serves as the foundation of DETR-ACT and Faster RCNN. The '+' in the GFLOPs column denotes more flops in comparison to the backbone. The BBox APs for large, medium, and small instances are designated $AP_L$, $AP_M$, and $AP_S$, respectively.

| Model | GFLOPs | AP | $AP_L$ | $AP_M$ | $AP_S$ |
|---|---|---|---|---|---|
| Backbone (ResNet50-DC5) | 110.7 | --- | --- | --- | --- |
| DETR-DC5 [15] | +73.4 | 43.3 | 61.1 | 47.3 | 22.5 |
| FasterRCNN-DC5 [49] | +209.3 | 41.1 | 55.0 | 45.9 | 22.9 |
| DETR-ACT [50] | 168.9 | 43.1 | 61.4 | 47.1 | 22.2 |
| ACT (L = 16) | +47.2 | 41.4 | 60.8 | 43.1 | 17.1 |
| ACT (L = 20) | +51.7 | 40.6 | 61.1 | 46.5 | 18.7 |
| ACT (L = 24) | +55.2 | 39.2 | 61.3 | 47.3 | 20.2 |
| ACT (L = 32) | +59.7 | 44.3 | 62.5 | 48.2 | 23.7 |
| ACT + MTKD (L = 16) | +49.6 | 41.3 | 61.1 | 44.3 | 18.5 |
| ACT + MTKD (L = 20) | +52.5 | 41.9 | 61.9 | 47.1 | 20.2 |
| ACT + MTKD (L = 24) | +56.7 | 40.1 | 61.7 | 48.2 | 21.9 |
| ACT + MTKD (L = 32) | +60.2 | 44.9 | 62.7 | 49.1 | 24.2 |

DETR-ACT performs better than our ACT model, with $L$ equal to 16 while using fewer FLOPs. However, when it comes to detecting items of a certain size, ACT is much better than DETR-ACT. For large objects, our ACT model can provide a better approximation than FasterRCNN-DC5. The most significant AP losses occur with small- and medium-sized objects. Small- and medium-sized items experience the most AP losses. The most significant AP losses occur with small- and medium-sized objects. We suggest that our clustering attention can be considered as a dropout operation that can help prevent overfitting during the distillation of information.

Importantly, we found that the keys grouped using our strategy performed well. We tested query grouping, key grouping, and combining queries and keys. We adjusted the hyper-parameter $L$ and compared the average precision on the validation set to ensure that the computational cost across all three experiments was consistent. Table 2 shows the results. Our model's ability to generalize is demonstrated by the fact that all three methods achieved similar average precision while using the same computational cost. This suggests that, when there are significantly more keys than queries, models can benefit from adaptively grouping the keys to improve performance.

**Table 2.** FLOPs and AP under various clustering targets.

| Cluster Queries | Cluster Keys | FLOPs | AP |
|---|---|---|---|
| L = 24 | × | 165.75 | 0.418 |
| × | L = 18 | 164.90 | 0.419 |
| L = 32 | L = 12 | 164.3 | 0.416 |

**Inference time and memory:** The above analyses were based on FLOPs or theoretical computation costs. We also performed field tests to assess the time and memory requirements. Table 3 shows the inference time and memory cost of the Nvidia GeForce GTX TITAN X for a batch size of 1. It is evident that ACT accelerates in real-world scenarios as predicted by the theoretical study, and it does so with significantly lower memory costs.

**Table 3.** The Nvidia GeForce GTX TITAN X's inference time and memory usage with a batch size of 1.

| Model | Inference Time/Image | Memory |
|---|---|---|
| ACT (L = 16) | 0.175 s | 1010 MiB |
| ACT (L = 20) | 0.190 s | 1385 MiB |
| ACT (L = 24) | 0.196 s | 1500 MiB |
| ACT (L = 32) | 0.201 s | 1700 MiB |
| ACT-FRCNN | 0.216 s | 1850 MiB |

### *4.2. Comparison with the State of Art*

#### 4.2.1. Results on COCO 2017 Dataset

The COCO 2017 dataset enables a comprehensive evaluation of detection models for domain shift. The models are assessed on the corresponding categories without any fine-tuning. The ViT-FRCNN models show significant improvement over the ResNet-FRCNN baselines on this dataset, as illustrated in Table 4. ViT-B/16*-FRCNN achieves a 22.9 AP (a + 7 AP boost) compared to the ResNet101-FRCNN-FPN baseline. Larger pre-training datasets result in better out-of-distribution generalization (+1.8 AP boost). These findings suggest that pre-training detection models with large-scale transformers are promising for enhancing their effectiveness in realistic, high-stakes scenarios.

**Table 4.** ACT-FRCNN outperforms ResNet-FRCNN techniques in terms of out-of-domain performance as measured by average precision (AP) in the COCO dataset.

| Model | AP | $AP_{50}$ | $AP_{75}$ | $AP_{L}$ |
|---|---|---|---|---|
| ResNet101-FRCNN-FPN | 15.9 | 34.1 | 12.9 | 16.1 |
| ResNet50-FRCNN-FPN | 13.9 | 30.8 | 10.2 | 14.1 |
| ViT-B/32*-FRCNN | 17.9 | 36.4 | 15.8 | 18.0 |
| ViT-B/32-FRCNN | 16.4 | 34.5 | 14.0 | 16.5 |
| ViT-B/16*-FRCNN | 22.9 | 46.6 | 20.9 | 23.0 |
| ViT-B/16-FRCNN | 20.2 | 40.5 | 17.8 | 20.4 |
| **ACT-FRCNN** | **24.7** | **48.5** | **22.6** | **25.1** |

4.2.2. BSDS500 Dataset

The model's efficacy is measured against both conventional detectors, such as SCG [51], Sketch Tokens [52], SE [53], and MES [54], and deep learning-based detectors, such as Deep Boundary [55], COB [56], AMHNet [57], CED [58], LPCB [59], BDCN [50], DexiNed [60], PiDiNet [61], and EDTER-MS-VOC [62]. Table 5 displays the numerical outcomes. Our method is superior to all current state-of-the-art edge detectors, with accuracy levels of 86.5% (ODS), 88.3% (OIS), and 92.4% (AP).

**Table 5.** Outcomes on the BSDS500 dataset.

| Method | Year | ODS | OIS | AP |
|---|---|---|---|---|
| SCG [46] | 2012 | 0.739 | 0.758 | 0.773 |
| Sketch Tokens [63] | 2013 | 0.272 | 0.746 | 0.780 |
| SE [64] | 2014 | 0.746 | 0.767 | 0.803 |
| MES [48] | 2015 | 0.756 | 0.776 | 0.756 |
| DeepBoundary [65] | 2015 | 0.813 | 0.831 | 0.866 |
| CED [51] | 2017 | 0.815 | 0.833 | 0.889 |
| LPCB [52] | 2018 | 0.815 | 0.834 | ------ |
| BDCN [45] | 2019 | 0.828 | 0.844 | 0.890 |
| DexiNed [53] | 2020 | 0.729 | 0.745 | 0.583 |
| PiDiNet [54] | 2021 | 0.807 | 0.823 | ----- |
| EDTER-MS-VOC [55] | 2022 | 0.848 | 0.865 | 0.903 |
| **ACT-FRCNN (our)** | ----- | **0.865** | **0.883** | **0.924** |

4.2.3. Results on NYUDv2 Dataset

In NYUDv2, we conducted tests on RGB images and evaluated them in comparison to cutting-edge techniques, such as gPb-ucm [10], Silberman [11], gPb+NG, SE [53], SE+NG+OEF, Semi Contour, HED, RCF [46], AMH-Net [57], LPCB [59], BDCN [50], PiDiNet [61], and EDTER [61]. On a single-scale input, all outcomes are based. The numeric outcomes of our approach and those of our rivals are displayed in Table 6. Our approach results in the top ODS, OIS, and AP scores of 81.3%, 82.0%, and 85.1%, respectively. We improved the results in three categories by 3.9%, 3.1%, and 3.2% when compared to the second-best method.

**Table 6.** Quantitative comparisons on NYUDv2.

| Method | Year | ODS | OIS | AP |
|---|---|---|---|---|
| gPb-ucm [10] | 2011 | 0.632 | 0.661 | 0.562 |
| Silberman [11] | 2012 | 0.658 | 0.661 | - |
| gPb+NG [56] | 2013 | 0.687 | 0.716 | 0.629 |

**Table 6.** *Cont.*

| Method | Year | ODS | OIS | AP |
|---|---|---|---|---|
| SE [64] | 2014 | 0.695 | 0.708 | 0.679 |
| SE+NG+ [57] | 2014 | 0.706 | 0.734 | 0.738 |
| OEF [58] | 2015 | 0.651 | 0.667 | - |
| Semi Contour [59] | 2016 | 0.680 | 0.700 | 0.690 |
| HED [60] | 2015 | 0.720 | 0.734 | 0.734 |
| RCF [61] | 2017 | 0.729 | 0.742 | - |
| AMH-Net [62] | 2017 | 0.744 | 0.758 | 0.765 |
| LPCB [52] | 2018 | 0.739 | 0.754 | - |
| BDCN [45] | 2019 | 0.748 | 0.763 | 0.790 |
| PiDiNet [54] | 2021 | 0.733 | 0.747 | - |
| EDTER [55] | 2022 | 0.774 | 0.789 | 0.797 |
| **ACT-FRCNN (Our)** | ----- | **0.813** | **0.820** | **0.831** |

## 5. Discussion

The developments in object detection have received numerous inputs from different models and algorithms, especially the ACT-FRCNN, which is based on transformers. The results of the experiments on datasets, such as BSDS500, NYUDv2, and COCO, clearly show that our proposed ACT-FRCNN achieved a better performance than the traditional models. Thus, incorporating ACT with the detection task head has helped improve the effectiveness and proficiency in detecting objects within images.

It draws attention to the necessity of an advanced architecture to be incorporated with the increasing efficacy of the object detection task. Using the conditional generative adversarial network utilized in developing the current model further enhances the detection features by creating realistic samples to improve the training procedure. Notably, this architecture of transformers and generative models not only enhances the accuracy of detections but also makes the results invariant to the context and other conditions.

The research has benefited from collaboration between institutions: the University of Agriculture Faisalabad, Skyline University College, Sharjah-UAE, Muhammad Nawaz Sharif University of Agriculture Multan, and Government College University Faisalabad. The collaboration with other institutions, especially in organizations, has helped accrue a wide variety of insights and expertise, thus contributing to the complete development and testing of the ACT-FRCNN mode.

Consequently, our work demonstrates that transformer models have a promising future for object detection tasks. The findings of multiple experiments demonstrate that, even when trained with law-breaking samples, the ACT-FRCNN model does even better than the current state of the art. More research should be carried out on applying such new architectures to further advance the possibilities of object detection.

## 6. Conclusions

An object detection solution based on ACT-FRCNN, which demonstrates robust performance through a transformer backbone, is presented in the proposed research. As described in these findings, alternative architectures, like transformers, are more promising than adaptive clustering transformers (ACTs) for advancing complex vision tasks. Transformer-based models have demonstrated impressive capabilities in pre-training on large datasets without reaching saturation. ACT-FRCNN demonstrates the advantages of using transformers in vision tasks. For instance, in the NYUDv2 dataset, ACT-FRCNN achieved ODS, OIS, and AP scores of 81.3%, 82.0%, and 85.1%, respectively, outperforming the previous best methods by 3.9%, 3.1%, and 3.2%, respectively. These results highlight the advantages of transformer-based models, specifically ACT, in vision tasks. This marks an important milestone, as it is the first exploration of transformer-based architectures for solving various vision problems in the research community. As a result of the success of ACT-FRCNN, further research and development in computer vision using transformer-based models is encouraged. Future research ideas might be built around novel transformer kinds and transformer topologies modified for object-detecting applications. Lastly, more advanced techniques seem promising to improve the results and performance rates of the particular method, such as Conditional Generative Adversarial Networks (CGANs), or conduct additional research into the suitability of transformers in combination with other machine learning frameworks, like federated learning.

**Author Contributions:** The study idea and its execution were contributed to by all authors. Methodology, formal analysis, project administration, data curation, and English language editing performed by S.Z., Z.E., M.A.Z., A.R., S.U. and H.D. All authors have read and agreed to the published version of the manuscript.

**Funding:** This research received no external funding.

**Institutional Review Board Statement:** All procedures performed in studies were in accordance with the ethical standards of the institutional and/or national research committee.

**Data Availability Statement:** Data are contained within the article.

**Conflicts of Interest:** The authors declare that they have no known competing financial interests or personal relationships that could have appeared to influence the work reported in this paper.

## References

1. Portes, J.; Trott, A.; Havens, S.; King, D.; Venigalla, A.; Nadeem, M.; Sardana, N.; Khudia, D.; Frankle, J. MosaicBERT: A bidirectional encoder optimized for fast pretraining. In Proceedings of the Advances in Neural Information Processing Systems, Vancouver, BC, Canada, 9–15 December 2024; Volume 36.
2. Team, I. Internlm: A Multilingual Language Model with Progressively Enhanced Capabilities. 2023. Available online: https://github.com/InternLM/InternLM (accessed on 27 September 2023).
3. Radford, A.; Wu, J.; Child, R.; Luan, D.; Amodei, D.; Sutskever, I. Language models are unsupervised multitask learners. *OpenAI Blog* **2019**, *1*, 1–24.
4. Brown, T.; Mann, B.; Ryder, N.; Subbiah, M.; Kaplan, J.D.; Dhariwal, P.; Neelakantan, A.; Shyam, P.; Sastry, G.; Askell, A. Language models are few-shot learners. *Adv. Neural Inf. Process. Syst.* **2020**, *33*, 1877–1901.
5. Chen, D.; Cao, P.; Yan, L.; Chen, H.; Lin, J.; Li, X.; Yuan, L.; Wu, K. Multi-Scale Mixed Attention Tea Shoot Instance Segmentation Model. *Phyton* **2024**, *93*, 261.
6. Chen, Y.; Rohrbach, M.; Yan, Z.; Shuicheng, Y.; Feng, J.; Kalantidis, Y. Graph-based global reasoning networks. In Proceedings of the IEEE/CVF Conference on Computer Vision and Pattern Recognition, Long Beach, CA, USA, 15–20 June 2019; pp. 433–442.
7. Gao, P.; You, H.; Zhang, Z.; Wang, X.; Li, H. Multi-modality latent interaction network for visual question answering. In Proceedings of the IEEE/CVF International Conference on Computer Vision, Seoul, Republic of Korea, 27 October–2 November 2019; pp. 5825–5835.
8. Goyal, S.; Choudhury, A.R.; Raje, S.; Chakaravarthy, V.; Sabharwal, Y.; Verma, A. PoWER-BERT: Accelerating BERT inference via progressive word-vector elimination. In Proceedings of the International Conference on Machine Learning, Virtual, 13–18 July 2020; pp. 3690–3699.
9. Katharopoulos, A.; Vyas, A.; Pappas, N.; Fleuret, F. Transformers are rnns: Fast autoregressive transformers with linear attention. In Proceedings of the International Conference on Machine Learning, Virtual, 13–18 July 2020; pp. 5156–5165.
10. Arbelaez, P.; Maire, M.; Fowlkes, C.; Malik, J. Contour detection and hierarchical image segmentation. *IEEE Trans. Pattern Anal. Mach. Intell.* **2010**, *33*, 898–916.
11. Silberman, N.; Hoiem, D.; Kohli, P.; Fergus, R. Indoor segmentation and support inference from rgbd images. *ECCV* **2012**, *7576*, 746–760.
12. Lin, T.-Y.; Maire, M.; Belongie, S.; Hays, J.; Perona, P.; Ramanan, D.; Dollár, P.; Zitnick, C.L. Microsoft coco: Common objects in context. In Proceedings of the Computer Vision—ECCV 2014: 13th European Conference, Zurich, Switzerland, 6–12 September 2014; Proceedings, Part V 13. Springer: Berlin/Heidelberg, Germany; pp. 740–755.
13. Jiang, Z.; Gao, P.; Guo, C.; Zhang, Q.; Xiang, S.; Pan, C. Video object detection with locally-weighted deformable neighbors. *Proc. AAAI Conf. Artif. Intell.* **2019**, *33*, 8529–8536. [CrossRef]
14. Zhang, Y.; Liu, C.; Liu, M.; Liu, T.; Lin, H.; Huang, C.B.; Ning, L. Attention is all you need: Utilizing Attention in AI-enabled drug discovery. *Brief. Bioinform.* **2024**, *25*, bbad467.
15. Carion, N.; Massa, F.; Synnaeve, G.; Usunier, N.; Kirillov, A.; Zagoruyko, S. End-to-end object detection with transformers. In Proceedings of the Computer Vision—ECCV 2020: 16th European Conference, Glasgow, UK, 23–28 August 2020; Proceedings, Part I 16. Springer: Berlin/Heidelberg, Germany; pp. 213–229.

16. Gao, P.; Jiang, Z.; You, H.; Lu, P.; Hoi, S.C.; Wang, X.; Li, H. Dynamic fusion with intra-and inter-modality attention flow for visual question answering. In Proceedings of the IEEE/CVF Conference on Computer Vision and Pattern Recognition, Long Beach, CA, 15–20 June 2019; pp. 6639–6648.
17. Liu, Z.; Lin, Y.; Cao, Y.; Hu, H.; Wei, Y.; Zhang, Z.; Lin, S.; Guo, B. Swin transformer: Hierarchical vision transformer using shifted windows. In Proceedings of the IEEE/CVF International Conference on Computer Vision, Montreal, QC, Canada, 11–17 October 2021; pp. 10012–10022.
18. Wu, X.; Zhang, K.; Hu, Y.; He, X.; Gao, X. Multi-scale non-local attention network for image super-resolution. *Signal Process.* **2024**, *218*, 109362.
19. Kitaev, N.; Kaiser, Ł.; Levskaya, A. Reformer: The efficient transformer. *arXiv* **2020**, arXiv:2001.04451.
20. Choromanski, K.; Likhosherstov, V.; Dohan, D.; Song, X.; Gane, A.; Sarlos, T.; Hawkins, P.; Davis, J.; Mohiuddin, A.; Kaiser, L.; et al. Rethinking attention with performers. *arXiv* **2020**, arXiv:2009.14794.
21. Zhu, Z.; Xu, M.; Bai, S.; Huang, T.; Bai, X. Asymmetric non-local neural networks for semantic segmentation. In Proceedings of the IEEE/CVF International Conference on Computer Vision, Seoul, Republic of Korea, 27 October–2 November 2019; pp. 593–602.
22. Zhang, L.; Song, J.; Gao, A.; Chen, J.; Bao, C.; Ma, K. Be your own teacher: Improve the performance of convolutional neural networks via self distillation. In Proceedings of the IEEE/CVF International Conference on Computer Vision, Seoul, Republic of Korea, 27 October–2 November 2019; pp. 3713–3722.
23. Husain, S.; Abolkasim, E. Estimating the Number of People in Digital Still Images Based on Viola-Jones Face Detection Algorithms. *Afr. J. Adv. Pure Appl. Sci. (AJAPAS)* **2024**, *3*, 146–154.
24. Emami, S.; Martínez-Muñoz, G. Sequential training of neural networks with gradient boosting. *IEEE Access* **2023**, *11*, 42738–42750. [CrossRef]
25. Pu, T.; Sun, M.; Wu, H.; Chen, T.; Tian, L.; Lin, L. Semantic representation and dependency learning for multi-label image recognition. *Neurocomputing* **2023**, *526*, 121–130. [CrossRef]
26. Li, J.; Zhu, Z.; Liu, H.; Su, Y.; Deng, L. Strawberry R-CNN: Recognition and counting model of strawberry based on improved faster R-CNN. *Ecol. Inform.* **2023**, *77*, 102210. [CrossRef]
27. Yang, F.; Huang, L.; Tan, X.; Yuan, Y. FasterNet-SSD: A small object detection method based on SSD model. *Signal Image Video Process.* **2024**, *18*, 173–180. [CrossRef]
28. Wang, L.; Zhang, X.; Zhao, F.; Wu, C.; Wang, Y.; Song, Z.; Yang, L.; Xu, B.; Li, J.; Ge, S.S. Fuzzy-nms: Improving 3D object detection with fuzzy classification in nms. *IEEE Trans. Intell. Veh.* 2024; *early access*.
29. Wang, S.; Chen, R.; Wu, H.; Li, X.; Feng, Z. YOLOH: You Only Look One Hourglass for Real-time Object Detection. *IEEE Trans. Image Process.* **2024**, *33*, 2104–2115. [CrossRef]
30. Liu, Z.; Tan, Y.; Wu, W.; Tang, B. Dilated high-resolution network driven RGB-T multi-modal crowd counting. *Signal Process. Image Commun.* **2023**, *112*, 116915. [CrossRef]
31. Pandiyan, V.; Akeddar, M.; Prost, J.; Vorlaufer, G.; Varga, M.; Wasmer, K. Long short-term memory based semi-supervised encoder—Decoder for early prediction of failures in self-lubricating bearings. *Friction* **2023**, *11*, 109–124. [CrossRef]
32. Kong, S.; Fowlkes, C.C. Recurrent pixel embedding for instance grouping. In Proceedings of the IEEE Conference on Computer Vision and Pattern Recognition, Salt Lake City, UT, USA, 18–23 June 2018; pp. 9018–9028.
33. Gao, P.; Zheng, M.; Wang, X.; Dai, J.; Li, H. Fast convergence of detr with spatially modulated co-attention. In Proceedings of the IEEE/CVF International Conference on Computer Vision, Montreal, QC, Canada, 11–17 October 2021; pp. 3621–3630.
34. Zhu, X.; Su, W.; Lu, L.; Li, B.; Wang, X.; Dai, J. Deformable detr: Deformable transformers for end-to-end object detection. *arXiv* **2020**, arXiv:2010.04159.
35. Wu, H.; Lin, C.; Liu, J.; Song, Y.; Wen, Z.; Qin, J. Feature masking on non-overlapping regions for detecting dense cells in blood smear image. *IEEE Trans. Med. Imaging* **2023**, *42*, 1668–1680.
36. Lin, T.-Y.; Goyal, P.; Girshick, R.; He, K.; Dollár, P. Focal loss for dense object detection. In Proceedings of the IEEE International Conference on Computer Vision, Venice, Italy, 22–29 October 2017; pp. 2980–2988.
37. Sun, C.; Shrivastava, A.; Singh, S.; Gupta, A. Revisiting unreasonable effectiveness of data in deep learning era. In Proceedings of the IEEE International Conference on Computer Vision, Venice, Italy, 22–29 October 2017; pp. 843–852.
38. Mahajan, D.; Girshick, R.; Ramanathan, V.; He, K.; Paluri, M.; Li, Y.; Bharambe, A.; Van Der Maaten, L. Exploring the limits of weakly supervised pretraining. In Proceedings of the European Conference on Computer Vision (ECCV), Munich, Germany, 8–14 September 2018; pp. 181–196.
39. Kolesnikov, A.; Beyer, L.; Zhai, X.; Puigcerver, J.; Yung, J.; Gelly, S.; Houlsby, N. Big transfer (bit): General visual representation learning. In Proceedings of the Computer Vision—ECCV 2020: 16th European Conference, Glasgow, UK, 23–28 August 2020; Proceedings, Part V 16. Springer: Berlin/Heidelberg, Germany; pp. 491–507.
40. He, K.; Girshick, R.; Dollár, P. Rethinking imagenet pre-training. In Proceedings of the IEEE/CVF International Conference on Computer Vision, Seoul, Republic of Korea, 27 October–2 November 2019; pp. 4918–4927.
41. Chatterjee, A.; Mukherjee, J.; Das, P.P. ImageNet Classification using WordNet Hierarchy. *IEEE Trans. Artif. Intell.* **2023**, *5*, 1718–1727. [CrossRef]
42. Yalniz, I.Z.; Jégou, H.; Chen, K.; Paluri, M.; Mahajan, D. Billion-scale semi-supervised learning for image classification. *arXiv* **2019**, arXiv:1905.00546.

43. Ma, C.; Pan, X.; Ye, Q.; Tang, F.; Dong, W.; Xu, C. CrossRectify: Leveraging disagreement for semi-supervised object detection. *Pattern Recognit.* **2023**, *137*, 109280. [CrossRef]
44. Sarkar, H.; Chudasama, V.; Onoe, N.; Wasnik, P.; Balasubramanian, V.N. Open-Set Object Detection By Aligning Known Class Representations. In Proceedings of the IEEE/CVF Winter Conference on Applications of Computer Vision, Waikoloa, HI, USA, 1–6 January 2024; pp. 219–228.
45. He, J.; Zhang, S.; Yang, M.; Shan, Y.; Huang, T. Bi-directional cascade network for perceptual edge detection. In Proceedings of the IEEE/CVF Conference on Computer Vision and Pattern Recognition, Long Beach, CA, USA, 15–20 June 2019; pp. 3828–3837.
46. Ren, X.; Bo, L. Discriminatively trained sparse code gradients for contour detection. In Proceedings of the 25th International Conference on Neural Information Processing Systems, Red Hook, NY, USA, 3–6 December 2012; Volume 1, pp. 584–592.
47. Krizhevsky, A.; Sutskever, I.; Hinton, G.E. Imagenet classification with deep convolutional neural networks. *Commun. ACM* **2017**, *60*, 84–90. [CrossRef]
48. Sironi, A.; Lepetit, V.; Fua, P. Projection onto the manifold of elongated structures for accurate extraction. In Proceedings of the IEEE International Conference on Computer Vision, Santiago, Chile, 7–13 December 2015; pp. 316–324.
49. Ren, S.; He, K.; Girshick, R.; Sun, J. Faster r-cnn: Towards real-time object detection with region proposal networks. In Proceedings of the Advances in Neural Information Processing Systems, Montreal, QC, Canada, 7–12 December 2015; Volume 28.
50. Zheng, M.; Gao, P.; Zhang, R.; Li, K.; Wang, X.; Li, H.; Dong, H. End-to-end object detection with adaptive clustering transformer. *arXiv* **2020**, arXiv:2011.09315.
51. Wang, Y.; Zhao, X.; Li, Y.; Huang, K. Deep crisp boundaries: From boundaries to higher-level tasks. *IEEE Trans. Image Process.* **2018**, *28*, 1285–1298. [CrossRef]
52. Deng, R.; Shen, C.; Liu, S.; Wang, H.; Liu, X. Learning to predict crisp boundaries. In Proceedings of the European Conference on Computer Vision (ECCV), Munich, Germany, 8–14 September 2018; pp. 562–578.
53. Poma, X.S.; Riba, E.; Sappa, A. Dense extreme inception network: Towards a robust cnn model for edge detection. In Proceedings of the IEEE/CVF Winter Conference on Applications of Computer Vision, Snowmass Village, CO, USA, 1–5 March 2020; pp. 1923–1932.
54. Su, Z.; Liu, W.; Yu, Z.; Hu, D.; Liao, Q.; Tian, Q.; Pietikäinen, M.; Liu, L. Pixel difference networks for efficient edge detection. In Proceedings of the IEEE/CVF International Conference on Computer Vision, Montreal, QC, Canada, 11–17 October 2021; pp. 5117–5127.
55. Pu, M.; Huang, Y.; Liu, Y.; Guan, Q.; Ling, H. Edter: Edge detection with transformer. In Proceedings of the IEEE/CVF Conference on Computer Vision and Pattern Recognition, New Orleans, LA, USA, 18–24 June 2022; pp. 1402–1412.
56. Gupta, S.; Arbelaez, P.; Malik, J. Perceptual organization and recognition of indoor scenes from RGB-D images. In Proceedings of the IEEE Conference on Computer Vision and Pattern Recognition, Portland, OR, USA, 23–28 June 2013; pp. 564–571.
57. Gupta, S.; Girshick, R.; Arbeláez, P.; Malik, J. Learning rich features from RGB-D images for object detection and segmentation. In Proceedings of the Computer Vision—ECCV 2014: 13th European Conference, Zurich, Switzerland, 6–12 September 2014; Proceedings, Part VII 13. Springer: Berlin/Heidelberg, Germany; pp. 345–360.
58. Hallman, S.; Fowlkes, C.C. Oriented edge forests for boundary detection. In Proceedings of the IEEE Conference on Computer Vision and Pattern Recognition, Boston, MA, USA, 7–12 June 2015; pp. 1732–1740.
59. Zhang, Z.; Xing, F.; Shi, X.; Yang, L. Semicontour: A semi-supervised learning approach for contour detection. In Proceedings of the IEEE Conference on Computer Vision and Pattern Recognition, Las Vegas, NV, USA, 27–30 June 2016; pp. 251–259.
60. Xie, S.; Tu, Z. Holistically-nested edge detection. In Proceedings of the IEEE International Conference on Computer Vision, Santiago, Chile, 7–13 December 2015; pp. 1395–1403.
61. Liu, Y.; Cheng, M.-M.; Hu, X.; Wang, K.; Bai, X. Richer convolutional features for edge detection. In Proceedings of the IEEE Conference on Computer Vision and Pattern Recognition, Honolulu, HI, USA, 21–26 July 2017; pp. 3000–3009.
62. Xu, D.; Ouyang, W.; Alameda-Pineda, X.; Ricci, E.; Wang, X.; Sebe, N. Learning deep structured multi-scale features using attention-gated crfs for contour prediction. In Proceedings of the Advances in Neural Information Processing Systems, Long Beach, CA, USA, 4–9 December 2017; Volume 30.
63. Lim, J.J.; Zitnick, C.L.; Dollár, P. Sketch tokens: A learned mid-level representation for contour and object detection. In Proceedings of the IEEE Conference on Computer Vision and Pattern Recognition, Portland, OR, USA, 23–28 June 2013; pp. 3158–3165.
64. Dollár, P.; Zitnick, C.L. Fast edge detection using structured forests. *IEEE Trans. Pattern Anal. Mach. Intell.* **2014**, *37*, 1558–1570. [CrossRef]
65. Kokkinos, I. Pushing the boundaries of boundary detection using deep learning. *arXiv* **2015**, arXiv:1511.07386.

*algorithms*

MDPI

*Article*

# Measuring Student Engagement through Behavioral and Emotional Features Using Deep-Learning Models

**Nasir Mahmood [1,2], Sohail Masood Bhatti [1], Hussain Dawood [3], Manas Ranjan Pradhan [3] and Haseeb Ahmad [2,*]**

1 Department of Computer Science, Superior University, Lahore 54000, Pakistan; sohailmasood@superior.edu.pk (S.M.B.)
2 Department of Computer Science, National Textile University, Faisalabad 37610, Pakistan
3 School of Computing, Skyline University College, Sharjah 1797, United Arab Emirates; dawood.hussain@skylineuniversity.ac.ae (H.D.); manas.pradhan@skylineuniversity.ac.ae (M.R.P.)
* Correspondence: haseeb_ad@hotmail.com

**Abstract:** Students' behavioral and emotional engagement in the classroom environment may reflect the students' learning experience and subsequent educational outcomes. The existing research has overlooked the measurement of behavioral and emotional engagement in an offline classroom environment with more students, and it has not measured the student engagement level in an objective sense. This work aims to address the limitations of the existing research and presents an effective approach to measure students' behavioral and emotional engagement and the student engagement level in an offline classroom environment during a lecture. More precisely, video data of 100 students during lectures in different offline classes were recorded and pre-processed to extract frames with individual students. For classification, convolutional-neural-network- and transfer-learning-based models including ResNet50, VGG16, and Inception V3 were trained, validated, and tested. First, behavioral engagement was computed using salient features, for which the self-trained CNN classifier outperformed with a 97%, 91%, and 83% training, validation, and testing accuracy, respectively. Subsequently, the emotional engagement of the behaviorally engaged students was computed, for which the ResNet50 model surpassed the others with a 95%, 90%, and 82% training, validation, and testing accuracy, respectively. Finally, a novel student engagement level metric is proposed that incorporates behavioral and emotional engagement. The proposed approach may provide support for improving students' learning in an offline classroom environment and devising effective pedagogical policies.

**Keywords:** convolutional neural networks; Inception V3; ResNet50; student engagement; transfer learning; VGG16

## 1. Introduction

Student engagement in the classroom environment refers to a student's involvement, interest, and participation during a lecture. Student engagement may be further categorized in terms of cognitive, emotional, and behavioral contexts [1]. More precisely, cognitive engagement relates to the mental efforts that students make in the learning process in class. Emotional engagement refers to students' emotional responses toward learning, whereas behavioral engagement is inferred from the student's actions such as paying attention, completing tasks, and following instructions. Since behavioral and emotional engagements are interrelated, and behavioral engagement influences cognitive engagement positively, behavioral engagement should be precisely assessed to improve the learning experience of students [2].

To improve learning and the subsequent academic progress, students' engagement in the classroom environment is necessary. However, students may lose interest in the content delivered during a lecture due to a lack of relevance, a lack of interaction, a lack of variety, the teaching style, distractions, personal reasons, the lack of a challenge, and complex or overloaded information. Such issues are mostly observed during lectures in a traditional offline classroom environment (OCE) [3]. However, measuring students' engagement in comparatively large classes (more than 30 students) becomes difficult [4]. Moreover, the limited teaching resources, the limited time, the difficulty in observing non-verbal cues, and the limited training of an instructor may also be other challenges in measuring student engagement. Thus, alternative methods may be incorporated for the measurement of student engagement in an OCE.

Thus, a computer-vision-based solution may be suggested as a more feasible solution for measuring student engagement. More precisely, non-verbal clues such as affective states, including being focused, feeling sleepy, yawning, and a skewed head pose (right or left), may be incorporated to monitor student engagement. When the students are found to be engaged, the level of focus through facial expressions may be used to measure the level of student engagement. It has been statistically proven in the prevalent work that students' facial expressions may reveal their behavioral engagement [5]. Most researchers have incorporated computer vision for student engagement monitoring in e-learning environments [6–18]. However, these proposals monitor engagement in a controlled environment with few students [19–21]. Moreover, e-learning or an online learning environment differs from an OCE. Some works have also been proposed for student engagement monitoring in an OCE or in similar settings [2,22–27]. However, these proposals utilize dedicated physical devices or sensors [6,22,24], incorporate only behavioral features [7,23,25], test on limited data [8,27], are prone to efficiency issues [26], or use only emotional features [2]. Moreover, some of these proposals utilize a single pretrained transfer-learning (TL) model [8,25,28] or train a machine-learning or convolutional neural network model [2,6,8,22–24,26,27]. These limitations show that more pretrained and self-trained models may be incorporated for measuring student engagement in order to compare the performance of the underlying models. Moreover, behavioral and emotional features may be simultaneously incorporated for measuring student engagement. Furthermore, the level of engagement may be revealed instead of only classifying the affective states.

The proposed work utilizes pretrained and self-trained models along with behavioral and emotional features to measure student engagement in an OCE. More precisely, along with other contributions, the underlying work aims to find the answers to the following research questions: Can TL be effectively used for measuring student engagement in an OCE? Which TL model surpasses the others for measuring student engagement in an OCE? Does a self-trained model outperform the TL-based model for measuring student engagement in an OCE? How can a student's engagement level be measured instead of just being classified into engaged or not-engaged states? The explicit contributions of the underlying work are listed as follows:

1. To generate behavioral- and emotional-feature-based student datasets in the offline classroom environment;
2. To compare the performance of TL algorithms in terms of the computation of student engagement in the offline classroom environment;
3. To propose an effective model for computing student engagement based on behavioral features and revealing the level of engagement based on emotional features in the offline classroom environment.

The remainder of this work proceeds as follows: Section 2 briefly presents the prevalent works related to student engagement, their limitations, and the gaps to be filled. Section 3 details the materials and methods from dataset acquisition to the experimental setup. Section 4 highlights the obtained results, while Section 5 discusses the outcomes, comparisons with earlier works, the implications of this work, and the limitations and future directions. Finaly, the conclusions are provided in Section 6.

## 2. Related Work

Intelligent systems have thrived with the rise of artificial intelligence (AI) [29]. AI-based robust solutions are now widely applied across various domains, including education [2,30], healthcare [31], agriculture [32], security [33], online social media [34,35], sports [36], and many others. In particular, AI has been increasingly adopted to provide more precise and effective solutions in the education sector. For instance, AI is used in decision-making processes for higher education [37], predicting student performance [38], developing computer-vision-based attendance systems [39], generating multiple-choice questions [30], and monitoring student engagement [2,6–9,22–27]. Such smart solutions not only enhance student engagement and learning experiences but also assist teachers in ensuring positive learning outcomes.

Student engagement is a multifaceted concept, typically classified into cognitive, behavioral, and emotional engagement [1]. However, the constructs within these categories often overlap [40]. To measure student engagement, researchers estimate the cognitive, behavioral, and emotional aspects through various modalities, such as affective cues, including speech, head movements, facial expressions, or body language. Similarly, emotional engagement is often assessed based on Ekman's model of emotions (e.g., surprise, happiness, fear, anger, sadness, disgust, or contempt) or Russell's model (e.g., astonishment, embarrassment, perplexity, contentment, relaxation, boredom, or unresponsiveness).

Other modalities used to estimate engagement include physiological signals (e.g., heart rate, blood pressure, respiration, electroencephalograms (EEG), facial electromyograms (EMG), functional magnetic resonance imaging (fMRI), galvanic skin responses, or body temperature) and log files (e.g., number of logins, content views, forum reads and posts, number of clicks, access duration, or scores).

Several publicly available datasets, such as NVIE [41], DAISEE [42], and EmotiW [43], have been instrumental in the study of student engagement. However, these datasets are often affected by challenges such as occlusion, background noise, and poor illumination. As a result, many researchers prefer to create customized datasets to address these issues. For example, studies [44–46] have utilized self-generated datasets, although the number of participants was limited to 61, 50, and 21, respectively. Given the advantages of self-generated datasets, our study is motivated to use a larger dataset involving more students compared to prior work.

Incorporating multiple engagement constructs can improve the accuracy of student engagement estimation. In this regard, Goldberg et al. estimated cognitive engagement using knowledge tests and behavioral engagement using facial features in an offline classroom setting [47]. The authors extracted facial features using OpenFace [48], measured the intraclass correlation to assign final labels, and used regression models to estimate engagement. Other studies [2,13,44,49] have also incorporated behavioral and emotional features, but with smaller datasets and limited accuracy. Additionally, most of these works do not propose methods for determining the level of engagement. To address these limitations, our work integrates both behavioral and emotional features, aiming to not only detect student engagement but also assess its level.

To compute student engagement, researchers have employed variants of convolutional neural network (CNN) and fine-tuning-based transfer learning (TL) techniques to detect behavioral and emotional features from image frames [40]. For example, Ashwin et al. used hybrid CNN models to detect students' affective states, achieving a 76% accuracy [45]. Similarly, Pabba and Kumar used CNNs to classify engagement levels as low, medium, or high, with a 76.9% testing accuracy [2]. Mehta et al. later proposed a 3D DenseNet self-attention model for computing student engagement, achieving a 63.59% accuracy on the DAISEE dataset [50]. Furthermore, Thomas et al. incorporated the VGG16 model and temporal convolutional network to compute student engagement, reaching a 76% accuracy at the segment level [51]. However, these studies primarily relied on limited e-learning or publicly available datasets, resulting in constrained accuracy, as shown in Table 1.

**Table 1.** Comparison with earlier works.

| References | Dataset | No. of Participants | Features | Input | Classification | Methodology | Student Engagement Level | Test Accuracy |
|---|---|---|---|---|---|---|---|---|
| [2] | Self-generated | 61 | Facial expression, eye-tracking, EDA data | Dedicated sensors | Emotional engagement, cognitive engagement | Linear mixed-effects model for facial, ANOVA for eye tracking | No | 51% |
| [13] | Self-generated, BAUM-1, DAiSEE, and YawDD | 50 | Bored, confused, focused, frustrated, yawning, sleepy | Images | Low, medium, and high engagement | CNN | No | 76.9% |
| [44] | DAiSEE | 112 | Eye-gaze, FAU, head pose, body pose | Images | Completely disengaged, barely engaged, engaged, and highly engaged | Neural Turing machine | No | 61% |
| [45] | Self-generated | 50 | Facial expressions, body postures | Images | Engaged, non-engaged, and neutral | Inception V3 | No | 86% |
| [46] | DAiSEE and EmotiW | 112 | Gaze direction and head pose | Images | Low- and high-level engagement | LSTM and TCN | No | 63% |
| [49] | Self-generated | 21 | EEG signals and performance tests | EEG Signal | Emotion level, cognitive level | SVM | No | 76.7% 76.9% |

In our work, we apply self-trained CNN and TL models, including ResNet50, VGG16, and Inception V3, to compute student engagement in a real offline classroom environment.

## 3. Materials and Methods

This section outlines the proposed methodology for processing video frames to analyze student engagement by assessing their behavioral features and, subsequently, calculating engagement levels based on their emotional states. First, video data are collected from OCE during the lecture sessions. Frames containing behavioral features (e.g., being focused, looking away, having closed eyes, and yawning) and emotional features (e.g., happy, sad, neutral, and angry) are extracted from the videos. Next, four models are trained to classify behavioral engagement, and the best-performing model is selected to compute behavioral engagement for the remaining data. Once the behaviorally engaged students are identified, emotional engagement is modeled using the same four algorithms, and the best-performing model is chosen. Finally, a student engagement level metric is calculated by combining the models' confidence scores for both behavioral and emotional classification, along with survey scores. The following sections provide a detailed explanation of each step. Figure 1 illustrates the proposed methodology.

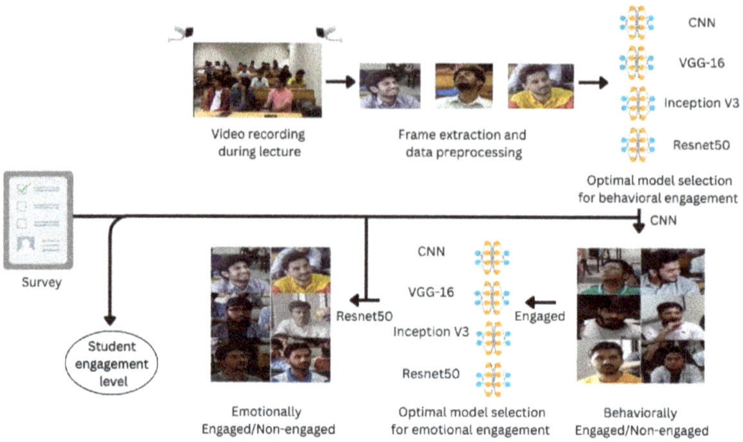


**Figure 1.** Proposed methodology.

### 3.1. *Dataset Acquisition*

Previous research suggests using self-generated datasets to compute student engagement levels by analyzing their behavior and expressions in the OCE environment [40]. In line with this approach, a dataset comprising 100 undergraduate and postgraduate students was recorded over various sessions, each lasting approximately 30 min. Two high-definition 1080p cameras, operating at 30 frames per second, were used for video recording. These cameras were strategically placed on the right and left sides of the lecture hall to capture the students' engagement in the OCE setting. Over the course of one month, a total of 40 videos were recorded in the OCE environment. The volunteer participants, both male and female, were between the ages of 19 and 25. All participants were informed about the study's objectives, and their consent was obtained for using their facial expressions in the experiment.

### 3.2. *Pre-Processing*

In the pre-processing phase, frames are extracted from the recorded videos and then augmented for training and testing purposes.

#### 3.2.1. Frame Extraction and Augmentation

Frames were extracted from the videos using Python's OpenCV and face-recognition libraries. Since each frame contained multiple students, it was necessary to isolate individual students from the entire frame. To achieve this, the Haar Cascade Frontal Face module from the OpenCV library was used to extract a $100 \times 100$ pixel frame of each student's face. In total, 10,000 frames were extracted, with blurred frames automatically rejected by the same module.

The extracted frames were then divided into two groups. While analyzing frames that reflected student behavior, various actions were observed, including looking/asking the teacher questions, talking with peers, using mobile phones, laughing, yawning, resting their heads, and sleeping. Due to the limited instances of some actions, these behaviors were grouped into four dominant categories: closed eyes (e.g., sleeping or using a mobile phone), focused (e.g., looking forward or asking the teacher questions), looking away (e.g., talking with a peer or looking away from the teacher/board), and yawning, as illustrated in Figure 2.

**Figure 2.** Behavioral reflecting frames.

The second group of extracted frames was categorized based on emotions using the DeepFace Python library. Several emotions were observed in the frames, including sadness, neutrality, frustration, fear, happiness, and anger. However, for analysis, the emotions selected were sadness, neutrality, happiness, and anger, as these were the most dominant. The emotion-reflecting frames are shown in Figure 3. Both datasets were split into 70% for training, 20% for validation, and 10% for testing. Each model was trained for 200 epochs following the same training steps. For model validation, the metrics used included Precision, Recall, F-measure, and Accuracy. Additionally, a survey was conducted to further validate the models.

**Figure 3.** Emotion-reflecting frames.

#### 3.2.2. Data Augmentation

Data augmentation is a pre-processing step that is used to extend the dataset for generating new set of frames. More precisely, the scaling parameter was set to 0.8 to 1.2 for both X and Y axes. The translation parameter was set to −0.2 to 0.2 for both X and Y axes. Rotation was set to −25 for X axis and 25 for the Y axis. Shear was set to −8 for the X axis and 8 for the Y axis. After data augmentation, the frame count of the training dataset for behavioral and emotion-based experiments is detailed in Table 2.

**Table 2.** Behavioral and emotional features' frame count.

| Dataset | Features | No. of Frames |
|---|---|---|
| Behavioral | Closed eyes | 648 |
| | Focused | 723 |
| | Looking away | 650 |
| | Yawning | 600 |
| Emotional | Happy | 710 |
| | Sad | 708 |
| | Angry | 500 |
| | Neutral | 550 |

### 3.3. *Survey Analysis*

A survey was conducted to gather responses from students regarding frames depicting engagement and non-engagement. Additionally, the level of engagement was assessed by 196 respondents (students and teachers) who were shown different frames. The survey consisted of 22 questions, each comprising three parts: (1) an image of a feature, (2) a question, and (3) a selection of either "engaged" or "non-engaged". Respondents were asked to determine whether the student in the image appeared engaged or not. After selecting "engaged" or "non-engaged", they were required to rate the level of engagement or non-engagement on a scale of 1 to 10. The results revealed that only students who appeared focused were categorized as engaged, while all other actions were rated as non-engaged. This survey was conducted for all seven emotions: angry, fearful, happy, sad, surprised, disgusted, and neutral. Table 3 presents the percentage of engaged and non-engaged responses across the engagement scale (1–10).

**Table 3.** Summary of the survey.

| | Features | Engaged | Non-Engaged | Scale (1–10) Average Score |
|---|---|---|---|---|
| Behavior reflecting features | Looking away | -- | 69% | 5.5 |
| | Yawning | -- | 71% | 5.5 |
| | Focused | 92% | -- | 7.7 |
| | Closed eyes | -- | 98% | 6.2 |
| Emotion reflecting feature | Sad | 69% | -- | 6.6 |
| | Happy | 88% | -- | 8 |
| | Angry | 75% | -- | 6.2 |
| | Neutral | 77% | -- | 6.8 |

### 3.4. *Experimental Setup*

The following models were trained on the pre-processed dataset, with all key training parameters detailed in Table 4.

**Table 4.** Training parameters.

| Parameters | Values |
|---|---|
| Epochs | 200 |
| Batch size | 16 |
| Activation function | ReLU |
| Learning rate | 0.0001 |
| Image size | 155 × 155 × 3 |
| Optimizer | Adam |
| Binary-class loss function | Binary cross-entropy |
| Multi-class loss function | Categorical cross-entropy |

The customized CNN model starts with an input layer, followed by several convolutional layers combined with batch normalization layers, which help stabilize and accelerate the training process. Max pooling layers are also included to reduce the spatial dimensions of the feature maps, improving model efficiency. To mitigate overfitting, dropout layers are incorporated, randomly deactivating units during training. The model includes four stages, each comprising a combination of the aforementioned layers. Finally, fully connected (dense) layers are used to connect all neurons from one layer to the next, leading to the output layer for classification.

ResNet50 is a deep convolutional neural network with 50 layers, utilizing residual learning to address the vanishing gradient issue, allowing for effective training of very deep networks. For fine-tuning, after freezing the top layers, we added four stages with combinations of dense and dropout layers. Various hyperparameters were tested to select the optimal configuration.

VGG16 consists of 16 layers in total, with 13 convolutional layers and 3 fully connected layers. It employs small 3 × 3 filters throughout the network. After freezing the top layers, we added six stages of dense and dropout layers. Multiple hyperparameters were explored to determine the best performing setup.

InceptionV3, developed by Google, is a deep convolutional neural network specifically designed for image analysis and object detection. It uses Inception modules, which apply convolutional filters of varying sizes simultaneously, helping to capture different levels of detail in images. The model incorporates techniques like factorized convolutions and label smoothing. We modified the network by adding four stages of dense and dropout layers. Various hyperparameters were evaluated, and the optimal ones were selected.

#### 3.4.1. Deep-Learning Models for Behavioral-Based Students' Engagement Level

In this work, transfer-learning (TL) models—VGG16, InceptionV3, and ResNet50—were customized by adding extra layers for binary classification. The performance of these models was then compared, and the best-performing model was selected for engagement computation. During training, all the pre-trained layers were frozen, and a flatten layer was added. Subsequently, six dense and dropout layers were introduced, followed by an output layer with a ReLU activation function. Additionally, a self-trained CNN model was proposed, incorporating extra layers to process the behavioral-reflecting dataset. Figure 4 illustrates the architecture of the proposed CNN model. An image of a student in the offline classroom environment (OCE) was provided as input to the customized CNN model, which processed the frame and detected the student's facial actions. If the model labeled the student as "focused", they were considered engaged; otherwise, they were classified as non-engaged. Among all the models tested, the customized CNN model demonstrated superior performance on the behavioral-reflecting dataset, outperforming VGG16, InceptionV3, and ResNet50.

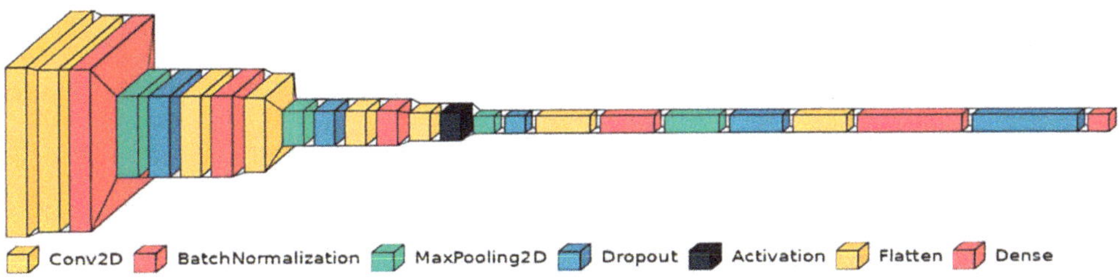


**Figure 4.** Proposed CNN architecture for measuring behavior level.

#### 3.4.2. Deep-Learning Models for Measuring Emotion-Based Engagement Level

For the detection of emotion-based features from the dataset, VGG16, Inception V3, and ResNet50 transfer-learning (TL) models were employed. These models were used with their basic architectures, enhanced by the addition of extra layers for multi-class classification. During training, all pre-trained layers were frozen, and a flatten layer was added, followed by six dense and dropout layers. Finally, an output layer with the ReLU activation function was included. Figure 5 illustrates the enhanced layer structure incorporated into the basic ResNet50 architecture. Additionally, a self-trained CNN model was developed by adding extra layers, specifically designed to compute behavior-based features.

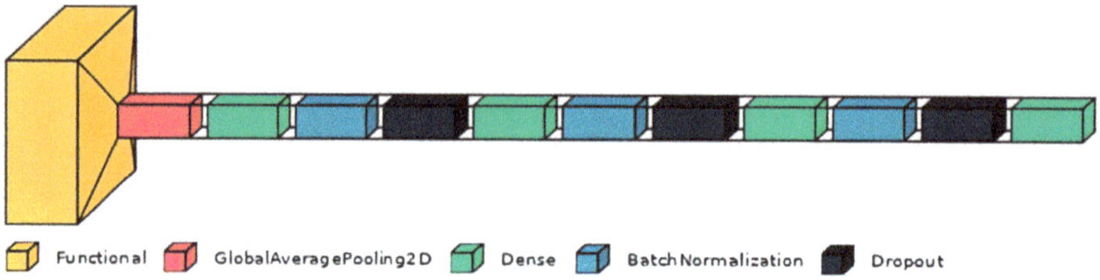


**Figure 5.** Proposed ResNet50 architecture for measuring emotion level.

## 4. Results

The evaluation results of the models are detailed as follows:

### 4.1. Evaluation of Behavior Detection Models

For detecting behavior-reflecting features, the customized CNN model outperformed the transfer-learning (TL) models. As shown in Table 5, the proposed CNN achieved a 97%, 91%, and 83% accuracy for training, validation, and testing, respectively, on the behavior-based dataset. Among the TL models, Inception V3 achieved the second-best performance for training, followed by VGG16 in third place and ResNet50 in fourth place. Notably, all models achieved a training accuracy of 90% or higher. For validation accuracy, VGG16 ranked second, followed by ResNet50 in third place and Inception V3 in fourth place, with all models achieving at least an 80% accuracy. During the testing phase, VGG16 again performed second-best, followed by ResNet50 in third place and Inception V3 in fourth place. Overall, all models attained a minimum of 69% accuracy during testing.

**Table 5.** Evaluation results for behavior detection.

| Model | Training Accuracy (%) | Validation Accuracy (%) | Training Loss | Validation Loss | Testing Accuracy (%) | Optimal Solution |
|---|---|---|---|---|---|---|
| CNN | 97 | 91 | 0.12 | 0.15 | 83 | Yes |
| VGG16 | 91 | 85 | 0.22 | 0.26 | 76 | No |
| Inception V3 | 93 | 80 | 0.28 | 0.46 | 69 | No |
| ResNet50 | 90 | 81 | 0.23 | 0.29 | 71 | No |

#### 4.1.1. Intra-Model Evaluations' Comparison of Behavior Detection Models

The detailed evaluation metrics for the behavior detection models are illustrated in Figure 6. It is evident that all models demonstrate promising results in terms of training and validation accuracies, as well as training and validation losses. Furthermore, there is an absence of underfitting and overfitting trends for all models throughout the 200 epochs, except for the Inception V3 model, which exhibits some variation after 125 epochs.

#### 4.1.2. Inter-Model Evaluations' Comparison of Behavior Detection Models

Figure 7 presents a comparative evaluation of the behavior detection models based on the respective dataset. It is clear that all models exhibit promising results; however, the proposed CNN model outperforms the others in terms of both training and validation accuracy, as well as loss.

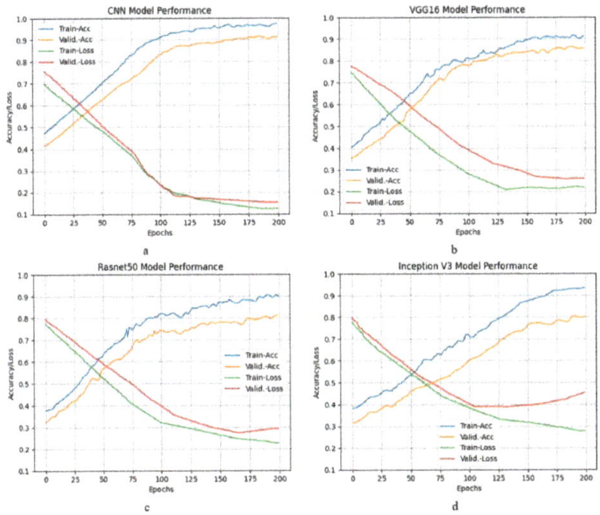


**Figure 6.** Intra-comparison of behavior detection models' training and validation accuracies and training and validation losses: (**a**) CNN; (**b**) VGG16; (**c**) ResNet50; and (**d**) Inception V3.

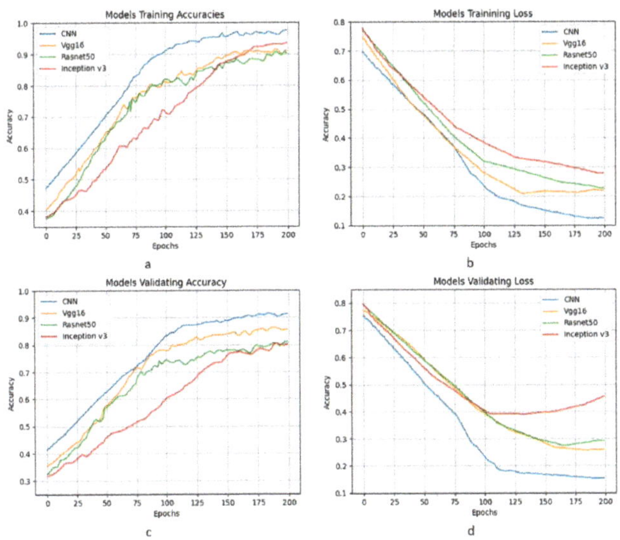


**Figure 7.** Inter-comparison of behavior detection models: (**a**) training accuracy; (**b**) training loss; (**c**) validation accuracy; and (**d**) validation loss.

## *4.2. Evaluation of Emotion Detection Models*

For the detection of emotion-reflecting features, ResNet50 outperformed the other models. As shown in Table 6, the ResNet50 achieved training, validation, and testing accuracies of 95%, 90%, and 82%, respectively, on the emotion-based dataset. Among the other models, the proposed CNN ranked second, followed by VGG16 in third place and Inception V3 in fourth during training. Overall, all models attained an accuracy of 85% or higher in the training phase. In terms of validation accuracy, the proposed CNN was in second place, with VGG16 in third and Inception V3 in fourth. All models achieved validation accuracies of 79% or greater. In the testing phase, the proposed CNN again performed second, followed by VGG16 in third place and Inception V3 in fourth place, with all models attaining at least a 58% accuracy. Notably, the testing accuracy for the emotion-based dataset is lower than that for the behavior-based dataset. This discrepancy arises because the behavior-based dataset addresses a binary classification problem, whereas the emotion-based dataset involves multiclass classification. Typically, binary classification problems yield better performance than multiclass classification problems.

**Table 6.** Evaluation results for emotion detection.

| Model | Training Accuracy (%) | Validation Accuracy (%) | Training Loss | Validation Loss | Testing Accuracy (%) | Optimal Solution |
|---|---|---|---|---|---|---|
| CNN | 92 | 86 | 0.14 | 0.26 | 70 | No |
| VGG16 | 91 | 80 | 0.21 | 0.26 | 62 | No |
| Inception V3 | 85 | 79 | 0.24 | 0.46 | 58 | No |
| ResNet50 | 95 | 90 | 0.15 | 0.19 | 82 | Yes |

#### 4.2.1. Intra-Model Evaluations' Comparison of Behavior Detection Models

The detailed evaluation metrics for the emotion detection models are illustrated in Figure 8. It is evident that all models demonstrate satisfactory results in terms of training and validation accuracies, as well as training and validation losses. Additionally, there are no signs of underfitting or overfitting trends for any of the models over the 200 epochs, with the exception of the Inception V3 model, which exhibits some variation after 100 epochs.

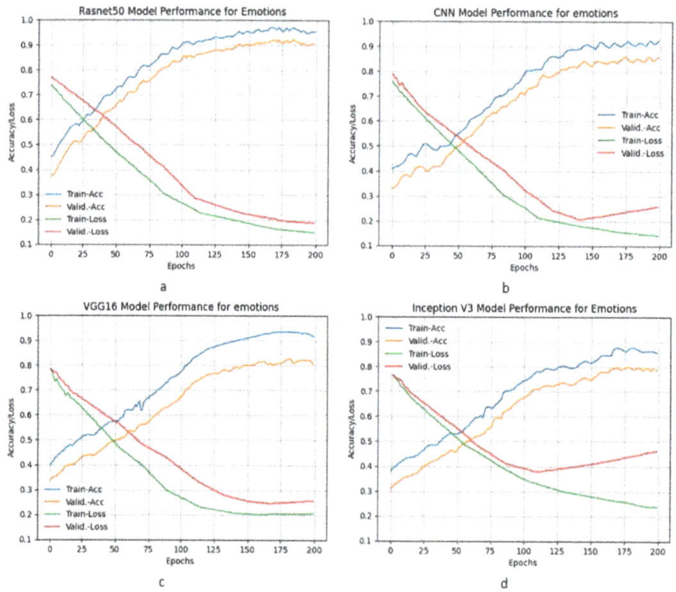


**Figure 8.** Intra-comparison of emotion detection models' training and validation accuracies and training and validation losses: (**a**) ResNet50; (**b**) CNN; (**c**) VGG16; and (**d**) Inception V3.

#### 4.2.2. Inter-Model Evaluations' Comparison of Emotion Detection Models

Figure 9 presents a comparative evaluation of the emotion detection models based on the respective dataset. It is clear that all models demonstrate satisfactory results; however, the ResNet50 model outperforms the others in terms of both training and validation accuracy, as well as loss.

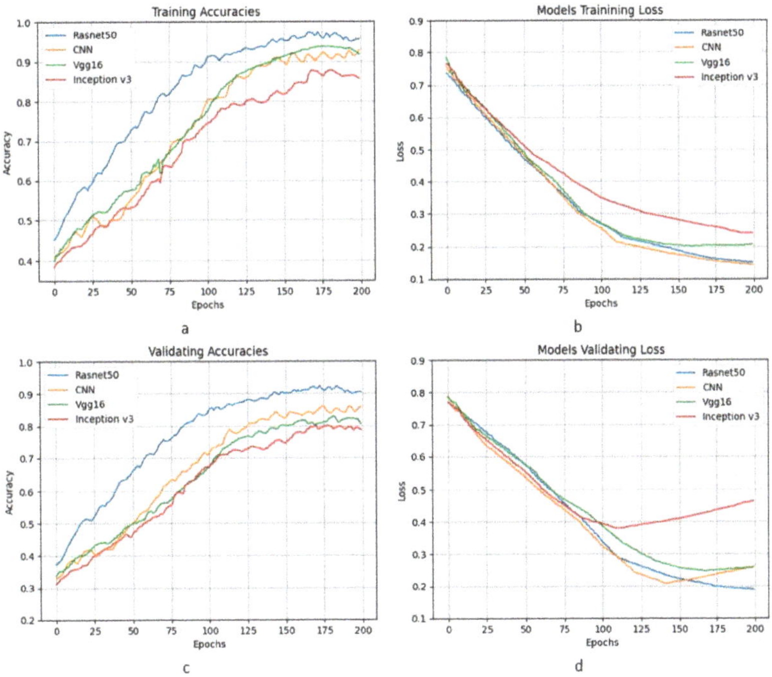


**Figure 9.** Inter-comparison of emotion detection models: (**a**) training accuracy; (**b**) training loss; (**c**) validation accuracy; and (**d**) validation loss.

### *4.3. Behavior and Emotion Detection Using Optimal Models*

The experimental results indicate that the proposed CNN model outperforms the other employed models in behavior detection. Similarly, ResNet50 excels in emotion detection, making these two models the preferred choices for detecting the respective underlying features from the testing data. Table 7 presents the evaluation results for behavior and emotion detection from the corresponding testing datasets, measured in terms of Precision, Recall, and F-measure. Behavior is classified as engaged or non-engaged using the binary CNN classifier, while emotions are classified as Happy, Sad, Angry, and Neutral using the multiclass ResNet50 classifier. The testing results reveal that the CNN achieves an F-measure of 83% for both categories of behavior detection. In the case of the four emotion categories, ResNet50 provides varying F-measure results: it achieves the highest F-measure of 86% for detecting the Neutral category, followed by the Sad category at 83%, the Angry category at 81%, and the Happy category at the lowest, at 79%.

**Table 7.** Evaluation metrics for behavior and emotion detection from testing dataset.

| Detection Type | Testing Accuracy | Mod | Precision | Recall | F-Measure |
|---|---|---|---|---|---|
| Behavior detection using CNN | 0.83 | Engaged | 0.84 | 0.82 | 0.83 |
| | | Non-Engaged | 0.82 | 0.84 | 0.83 |
| Emotion detection using ResNet50 | 0.82 | Happy | 0.80 | 0.78 | 0.79 |
| | | Sad | 0.85 | 0.82 | 0.83 |
| | | Angry | 0.82 | 0.80 | 0.81 |
| | | Neutral | 0.82 | 0.89 | 0.86 |

### 4.4. Computation of Student Engagement Level

After classifying the behavior and emotion, the Student Engagement Level (SEL) in the Online Classroom Environment (OCE) is computed. To achieve this, the confidence scores from the classification models, along with the survey scores for each engagement state, are integrated. Figure 10 illustrates the process of computing the SEL from the given input image frame.

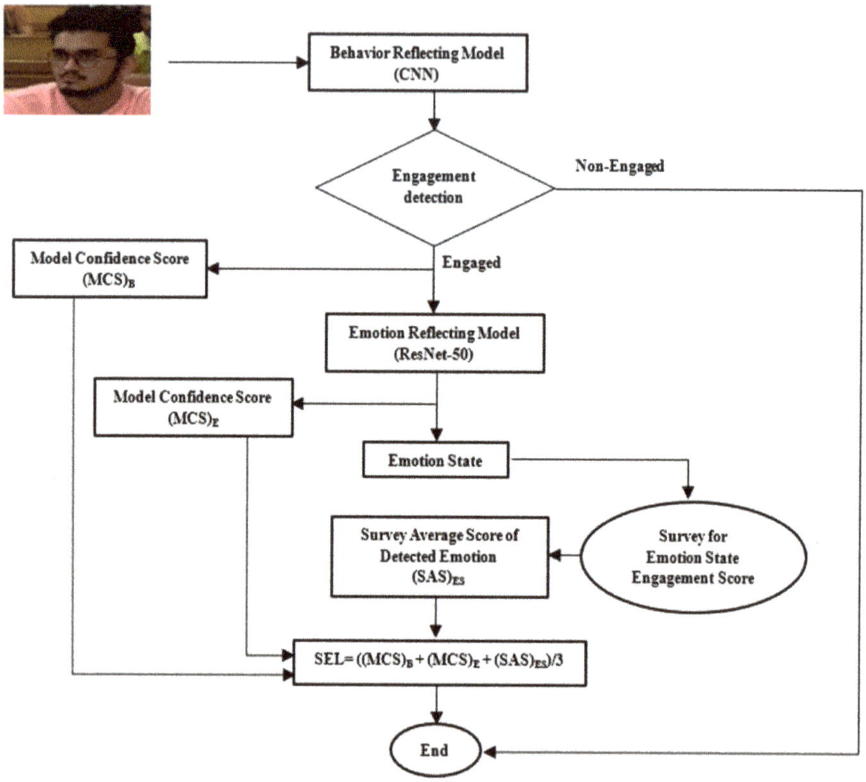


**Figure 10.** Student engagement level computation.

First, the CNN model classifies the student as engaged or non-engaged. In the case of engagement, the model's confidence score for the corresponding image frame is recorded. The same image is then sent to the ResNet50 model for emotional state classification, and the model's confidence score for the detected emotional state is also captured.

Next, the average survey score for the detected emotional state is obtained. Finally, the Student Engagement Level (SEL) is computed using the formulation provided in Equation (1):

$$SEL_i = \frac{(MCS_i)_B + (MCS_i)_E + (SAS)_{ES}}{3} \quad (1)$$

where $(MCS_i)_B$ refers to the model's confidence score for the classification of the behavior of the student in image *i*, $(MCS_i)_E$ presents the model's confidence score for the classification of the emotion of the student in image *i*, and $(SAS)_{ES}$ denotes the student's average survey score for that particular emotional state. Table 8 depicts some sample image frames and their corresponding SEL.

**Table 8.** Student engagement level.

| Sample Image Frame | $(MCS_i)_B$ | Detected Emotional State | $(MCS_i)_E$ | $(SAS)_{ES}$ | $SEL$ |
|---|---|---|---|---|---|
|  | 7.5 | Happy | 8.1 | 7.1 | 7.5 |
|  | NA | NA | NA | NA | Not engaged |
|  | 6.5 | Angry | 7.0 | 7 | 6.8 |
|  | 8.5 | Sad | 6 | 6 | 6.5 |
|  | 7 | Neutral | 8 | 6 | 6.9 |

## 5. Discussion

The underlying work presents a novel approach for computing students' engagement and the level of engagement in offline classroom environments (OCEs). While earlier studies have proposed methods for measuring students' engagement in an OCE or similar settings [2,22–27], these approaches often relied on dedicated physical devices or sensors [6,22,24], focused solely on behavioral features [7,23,25], tested limited datasets [8,27], encountered efficiency issues [26], or considered only emotional features [2].

To address these limitations, this study first generated data in the form of facial frames extracted from recorded videos during lectures in an OCE. A self-generated dataset comprising 100 students was utilized, as publicly available datasets [41–43] exhibited noise, occlusion, or illumination issues. Additionally, existing self-generated datasets [44–46] had a limited number of participants. Furthermore, using publicly available datasets to train models could introduce facial bias when measuring local students' engagement levels [52,53]. Following data generation, pre-processing was conducted, and four models—CNN, ResNet50, VGG16, and Inception V3—were trained, validated, and tested. Although some proposals have employed machine-learning or convolutional neural network models [2,6,8,22–24,26,27], or individual pre-trained transfer-learning models [8,25,28], these works often relied on limited e-learning datasets and achieved constrained accuracy compared to the results presented in this study.

To effectively measure students' engagement, behavior-reflecting feature frames were incorporated, including having closed eyes (indicating sleeping or using a mobile phone), being focused (looking forward or asking the teacher), looking away (talking to peers or diverting attention from the teacher/board), and yawning. These features were classified into the engaged and non-engaged categories, as seen in similar works [2,7,23,25,54]. The self-trained CNN demonstrated superior performance in the binary classification task, likely due to its inherent ability to learn hierarchical features, encompassing both low-level and high-level details [13]. Once engaged students were identified, their facial emotions—sad, neutral, happy, and angry—were classified, following methodologies established in previous studies [2,13,44,49,55]. Among the employed models, ResNet50 outperformed VGG16 and Inception V3 in this multiclassification task. ResNet50's effectiveness in multiclassification tasks can be attributed to its residual connections, which facilitate deeper networks in learning identity mappings more effectively, thus handling complex problems [56]. The model confidence scores from both binary and multiclass classification, alongside the average survey scores for the detected emotions, were utilized to compute the Student Engagement Level (SEL) in an OCE. This novel and practical metric holds potential for measuring individual students' engagement scores in real time during lectures.

Explicit Comparison: Existing works primarily measure students' engagement in online contexts or controlled offline environments with limited participant numbers and constrained accuracy. Moreover, the exploration of students' engagement levels remains underdeveloped. Thus, the proposed work offers a more practical solution by being implemented in a real OCE, incorporating 100 participants, achieving a higher accuracy, and computing students' engagement levels effectively.

Implications: The findings from this research may serve as valuable feedback for novice teachers, enhancing the teaching–learning process. Additionally, the proposed method can personalize education by providing affective content as feedback to both students and teachers. Furthermore, it may facilitate the exploration of the correlation between students' engagement levels and their performance assessments.

Limitations and Future Directions: While this work incorporates both behavioral and emotional features for measuring student engagement, cognitive features remain unexplored and should be investigated in future studies. Additionally, the introduction of an embedded system for the continuous monitoring of student engagement in real OCE settings could be beneficial. The data collected through this monitoring could provide insights for analytics and support data-driven decision-making in educational policy development.

## 6. Conclusions

This study presents an effective method for monitoring student engagement in real-time online classroom environments (OCEs). Specifically, it incorporates both behavioral and emotional features to compute student engagement using a self-trained convolutional neural network (CNN)- and transfer-learning models. In terms of behavioral indicators, students who are focused (looking forward or asking the teacher questions) are classified as engaged, which is supported by a 92% survey consensus. Conversely, behaviors such as looking away (talking to peers or avoiding the teacher/board) and yawning are categorized as non-engaged. Regarding emotional features, the survey shows that happiness, neutrality, sadness, and anger are associated with engagement at rates of 88%, 77%, 75%, and 69%, respectively. For detecting behavior-related features, the self-trained CNN classifier outperformed transfer-learning models, achieving training, validation, and testing accuracies of 97%, 91%, and 83%, respectively. On the other hand, for emotion-based feature detection, the ResNet50 model outperformed both the transfer learning-based models and the self-trained CNN, achieving training, validation, and testing accuracies of 95%, 90%, and 82%, respectively. In conclusion, both self-trained and transfer-learning-based models demonstrate efficacy in monitoring student engagement. The overall engagement level is computed using the models' confidence scores for behavior and emotion classification, combined with survey data.

**Author Contributions:** Conceptualization, N.M., S.M.B. and H.A.; methodology, N.M. and H.D.; software, N.M.; validation, S.M.B., H.A. and M.R.P.; formal analysis, H.A.; investigation, N.M.; resources, M.R.P.; data curation, N.M.; writing—original draft preparation, N.M., S.M.B. and H.A.; writing—review and editing, N.M.; visualization, N.M.; supervision, S.M.B.; project administration, H.D. All authors have read and agreed to the published version of the manuscript.

**Funding:** This research received no external funding.

**Data Availability Statement:** The data presented in this study are available upon request from the corresponding author by request of the volunteer participants (they requested only to share the data if demanded).

**Conflicts of Interest:** The authors declare no conflicts of interest.

## References


1. Fredricks, J.A.; Blumenfeld, P.C.; Paris, A.H. School engagement: Potential of the concept, state of the evidence. *Rev. Educ. Res.* **2004**, *74*, 59–109. [CrossRef]
2. Pabba, C.; Kumar, P. An intelligent system for monitoring students' engagement in large classroom teaching through facial expression recognition. *Expert Syst.* **2022**, *39*, e12839. [CrossRef]
3. Bradbury, N.A. Attention span during lectures: 8 seconds, 10 minutes, or more? *Adv. Physiol. Educ.* **2016**, *40*, 509–513. [CrossRef] [PubMed]
4. Exeter, D.J.; Ameratunga, S.; Ratima, M.; Morton, S.; Dickson, M.; Hsu, D.; Jackson, R. Student engagement in very large classes: The teachers' perspective. *Stud. High. Educ.* **2010**, *35*, 761–775. [CrossRef]
5. Sathik, M.; Jonathan, S.G. Effect of facial expressions on student's comprehension recognition in virtual educational environments. *SpringerPlus* **2013**, *2*, 455. [CrossRef]
6. Zaletelj, J.; Košir, A. Predicting students' attention in the classroom from Kinect facial and body features. *EURASIP J. Image Video Process.* **2017**, *2017*, 80. [CrossRef]
7. Klein, R.; Celik, T. The Wits Intelligent Teaching System: Detecting student engagement during lectures using convolutional neural networks. In Proceedings of the 2017 IEEE International Conference on Image Processing (ICIP), Beijing, China, 17–20 September 2017; IEEE: Piscataway, NJ, USA, 2017; pp. 2856–2860.
8. Thomas, C.; Jayagopi, D.B. Predicting student engagement in classrooms using facial behavioralal cues. In Proceedings of the 1st ACM SIGCHI International Workshop on Multimodal Interaction for Education, Glasgow, UK, 13 November 2017; pp. 33–40.
9. Hu, M.; Wei, Y.; Li, M.; Yao, H.; Deng, W.; Tong, M.; Liu, Q. Bimodal Learning Engagement Recognition from Videos in the Classroom. *Sensors* **2022**, *22*, 5932. [CrossRef] [PubMed]
10. Fredricks, J.A. The measurement of student engagement: Methodological advances and comparison of new self-report instruments. In *Handbook of Research on Student Engagement*; Springer International Publishing: Cham, Germany, 2022; pp. 597–616.
11. Dirican, A.C.; Göktürk, M. Psychophysiological measures of human cognitive states applied in human computer interaction. *Procedia Comput. Sci.* **2011**, *3*, 1361–1367. [CrossRef]
12. Murshed, M.; Dewan, M.A.A.; Lin, F.; Wen, D. Engagement detection in e-learning environments using convolutional neural networks. In Proceedings of the 2019 IEEE Intl Conf on Dependable, Autonomic and Secure Computing, Intl Conf on Pervasive Intelligence and Computing, Intl Conf on Cloud and Big Data Computing, Intl Conf on Cyber Science and Technology Congress (DASC/PiCom/CBDCom/CyberSciTech), Fukuoka, Japan, 5–8 August 2019; IEEE: Piscataway, NJ, USA, 2019; pp. 80–86.
13. Ma, X.; Xu, M.; Dong, Y.; Sun, Z. Automatic student engagement in online learning environment based on neural turing machine. *Int. J. Inf. Educ. Technol.* **2021**, *11*, 107–111. [CrossRef]
14. Bosch, N.; D'mello, S.K.; Ocumpaugh, J.; Baker, R.S.; Shute, V. Using video to automatically detect learner affect in computer-enabled classrooms. *ACM Trans. Interact. Intell. Syst. (TiiS)* **2016**, *6*, 1–26. [CrossRef]
15. Zhang, H.; Xiao, X.; Huang, T.; Liu, S.; Xia, Y.; Li, J. A novel end-to-end network for automatic student engagement recognition. In Proceedings of the 2019 IEEE 9th International Conference on Electronics Information and Emergency Communication (ICEIEC), Beijing, China, 12–14 July 2019; IEEE: Piscataway, NJ, USA; pp. 342–345.
16. Mukhopadhyay, M.; Pal, S.; Nayyar, A.; Pramanik, P.K.; Dasgupta, N.; Choudhury, P. Facial emotion detection to assess Learner's State of mind in an online learning system. In Proceedings of the 2020 5th International Conference on Intelligent Information Technology, Hanoi, Vietnam, 19–22 February 2020; pp. 107–115.
17. Bhardwaj, P.; Gupta, P.K.; Panwar, H.; Siddiqui, M.K.; Morales-Menendez, R.; Bhaik, A. Application of deep learning on student engagement in e-learning environments. *Comput. Electr. Eng.* **2021**, *93*, 107277. [CrossRef] [PubMed]
18. Yulina, S.; Elviyenti, M. An Exploratory Data Analysis for Synchronous Online Learning Based on AFEA Digital Images. *J. Nas. Tek. Elektro Dan Teknol. Inf.* **2022**, *11*, 114–120.
19. Altuwairqi, K.; Jarraya, S.K.; Allinjawi, A.; Hammami, M. Student behavior analysis to measure engagement levels in online learning environments. *Signal Image Video Process.* **2021**, *15*, 1387–1395. [CrossRef]
20. Kim, H.; Küster, D.; Girard, J.M.; Krumhuber, E.G. Human and machine recognition of dynamic and static facial expressions: Prototypicality, ambiguity, and complexity. *Front. Psychol.* **2023**, *14*, 1221081. [CrossRef] [PubMed]
21. Mastorogianni, M.E.; Konstanti, S.; Dratsiou, I.; Bamidis, P.D. Masked emotions: Does children's affective state influence emotion recognition? *Front. Psychol.* **2024**, *15*, 1329070. [CrossRef]
22. Peng, S.; Nagao, K. Recognition of students' mental states in discussion based on multimodal data and its application to educational support. *IEEE Access* **2021**, *9*, 18235–18250. [CrossRef]
23. Vanneste, P.; Oramas, J.; Verelst, T.; Tuytelaars, T.; Raes, A.; Depaepe, F.; Van den Noortgate, W. Computer vision and human behaviour, emotion and cognition detection: A use case on student engagement. *Mathematics* **2021**, *9*, 287. [CrossRef]

24. Luo, Z.; Chen, J.; Wang, G.; Liao, M. A three-dimensional model of student interest during learning using multimodal fusion with natural sensing technology. *Interact. Learn. Environ.* **2022**, *30*, 1117–1130. [CrossRef]
25. Zheng, R.; Jiang, F.; Shen, R. Intelligent student behavioral analysis system for real classrooms. In Proceedings of the ICASSP 2020–2020 IEEE International Conference on Acoustics, Speech, and Signal Processing (ICASSP), Barcelona, Spain, 4–8 May 2020; IEEE: Piscataway, NJ, USA, 2020; pp. 9244–9248.
26. Ashwin, T.S.; Guddeti, R.M. Unobtrusive behavioralal analysis of students in classroom environment using non-verbal cues. *IEEE Access* **2019**, *7*, 150693–150709. [CrossRef]
27. Soloviev, V. Machine learning approach for student engagement automatic recognition from facial expressions. *Sci. Publ. State Univ. Novi Pazar Ser. A Appl. Math. Inform. Mech.* **2018**, *10*, 79–86. [CrossRef]
28. Zhang, Z.; Fort, J.M.; Mateu, L.G. Facial expression recognition in virtual reality environments: Challenges and opportunities. *Front. Psychol.* **2023**, *14*, 1280136. [CrossRef]
29. Muarraf, A.; Ahmad, H.; Ahmad, W.; Faisal, N.; Ahmad, M. Research Trend Analysis of Artificial Intelligence. In Proceedings of the 2020 30th International Conference on Computer Theory and Applications (ICCTA), Alexandria, Egypt, 12–14 December 2020; IEEE: Piscataway, NJ, USA, 2020; pp. 49–53.
30. Maheen, F.; Asif, M.; Ahmad, H.; Ahmad, S.; Alturise, F.; Asiry, O.; Ghadi, Y.Y. Automatic computer science domain multiple-choice questions generation based on informative sentences. *PeerJ Comput. Sci.* **2022**, *8*, e1010. [CrossRef]
31. Rashid, H.U.; Ibrikci, T.; Paydaş, S.; Binokay, F.; Çevik, U. Analysis of breast cancer classification robustness with radiomics feature extraction and deep learning techniques. *Expert Syst.* **2022**, *39*, e13018. [CrossRef]
32. Thakur, A.; Aggarwal, P.; Dubey, A.K.; Abdelgawad, A.; Rocha, A. Design of decision model for sensitive crop irrigation system. *Expert Syst.* **2022**, *40*, e13119. [CrossRef]
33. Nyangaresi, V.O.; Ahmad, M.; Alkhayyat, A.; Feng, W. Artificial Neural Network and Symmetric Key Cryptography Based Verification Protocol for 5G Enabled Internet of Things. *Expert Syst.* **2022**, *39*, e13126. [CrossRef]
34. Asif, M.; Ishtiaq, A.; Ahmad, H.; Aljuaid, H.; Shah, J. Sentiment analysis of extremism in social media from textual information. *Telemat. Inform.* **2020**, *48*, 101345. [CrossRef]
35. Ahmad, H.; Nasir, F.; Faisal, C.M.N.; Ahmad, S. Depression Detection in Online Social Media Users Using Natural Language Processing Techniques. In *Handbook of Research on Opinion Mining and Text Analytics on Literary Works and Social Media*; IGI Global: Hershey, PA, USA, 2022; pp. 323–347.
36. Ahmad, H.; Ahmad, S.; Asif, M.; Rehman, M.; Alharbi, A.; Ullah, Z. Evolution-based performance prediction of star cricketers. *Comput. Mater. Contin.* **2021**, *69*, 1215–1232. [CrossRef]
37. Teng, Y.; Zhang, J.; Sun, T. Data-driven decision-making model based on artificial intelligence in higher education system of colleges and universities. *Expert Syst.* **2022**, *40*, e12820. [CrossRef]
38. Gamulin, J.; Gamulin, O.; Kermek, D. Using Fourier coefficients in time series analysis for student performance prediction in blended learning environments. *Expert Syst.* **2016**, *33*, 189–200. [CrossRef]
39. Sunaryono, D.; Siswantoro, J.; Anggoro, R. An android based course attendance system using face recognition. *J. King Saud Univ.-Comput. Inf. Sci.* **2021**, *33*, 304–312. [CrossRef]
40. Karimah, S.N.; Hasegawa, S. Automatic engagement estimation in smart education/learning settings: A systematic review of engagement definitions, datasets, and methods. *Smart Learn. Environ.* **2022**, *9*, 31. [CrossRef]
41. Wang, S.; Liu, Z.; Lv, S.; Lv, Y.; Wu, G.; Peng, P.; Chen, F.; Wang, X. A natural visible and infrared facial expression database for expression recognition and emotion inference. *IEEE Trans. Multimed.* **2010**, *12*, 682–691. [CrossRef]
42. Gupta, A.; D'Cunha, A.; Awasthi, K.; Balasubramanian, V. Daisee: Towards user engagement recognition in the wild. *arXiv* **2016**, arXiv:1609.01885.
43. Dhall, A.; Sharma, G.; Goecke, R.; Gedeon, T. Emotiw 2020: Driver gaze, group emotion, student engagement and physiological signal-based challenges. In Proceedings of the 2020 International Conference on Multimodal Interaction, Utrecht, The Netherlands, 25–29 October 2020; pp. 784–789.
44. Dubovi, I. Cognitive and emotional engagement while learning with VR: The perspective of multimodal methodology. *Comput. Educ.* **2022**, *183*, 104495. [CrossRef]
45. Ashwin, T.S.; Guddeti, R.M.R. Automatic detection of students' affective states in classroom environment using hybrid convolutional neural networks. *Educ. Inf. Technol.* **2020**, *25*, 1387–1415.
46. Apicella, A.; Arpaia, P.; Frosolone, M.; Improta, G.; Moccaldi, N.; Pollastro, A. EEG-based measurement system for monitoring student engagement in learning 4.0. *Sci. Rep.* **2022**, *12*, 5857. [CrossRef]
47. Goldberg, P.; Sümer, Ö.; Stürmer, K.; Wagner, W.; Göllner, R.; Gerjets, P.; Kasneci, E.; Trautwein, U. Attentive or not? Toward a machine learning approach to assessing students' visible engagement in classroom instruction. *Educ. Psychol. Rev.* **2021**, *33*, 27–49. [CrossRef]
48. Baltrušaitis, T.; Robinson, P.; Morency, L.-P. Openface: An open-source facial behavioural analysis toolkit. In Proceedings of the 2016 IEEE Winter Conference on Applications of Computer Vision (WACV), Lake Placid, NY, USA, 7–10 March 2016; IEEE: Piscataway, NJ, USA, 2016; pp. 1–10.
49. Abedi, A.; Khan, S. Affect-driven engagement measurement from videos. *Computer* **2021**, *11*, 12. [CrossRef]
50. Mehta, N.K.; Prasad, S.S.; Saurav, S.; Saini, R.; Singh, S. Three-dimensional DenseNet self-attention neural network for automatic detection of student's engagement. *Appl. Intell.* **2022**, *52*, 13803–13823. [CrossRef]

51. Thomas, C.; Sarma, K.A.P.; Gajula, S.S.; Jayagopi, D.B. Automatic prediction of presentation style and student engagement from videos. *Comput. Educ. Artif. Intell.* **2022**, *3*, 100079. [CrossRef]
52. Acharya, S.; Reza, M. Real-time emotion engagement tracking of students using human biometric emotion intensities. In *Machine Learning for Biometrics*; Academic Press: Cambridge, MA, USA, 2022; pp. 143–153.
53. Li, Y.-T.; Yeh, S.-L.; Huang, T.-R. The cross-race effect in automatic facial expression recognition violates measurement invariance. *Front. Psychol.* **2023**, *14*, 1201145. [CrossRef]
54. Ikram, S.; Ahmad, H.; Mahmood, N.; Faisal, C.M.N.; Abbas, Q.; Qureshi, I.; Hussain, A. Recognition of student engagement state in a classroom environment using deep and efficient transfer learning algorithm. *Appl. Sci.* **2023**, *13*, 8637. [CrossRef]
55. Pan, M.; Wang, J.; Luo, Z. Modelling study on learning affects for classroom teaching/learning auto-evaluation. *Sci. J. Educ.* **2018**, *6*, 81–86. [CrossRef]
56. Abedi, A.; Khan, S.S. Improving state-of-the-art in detecting student engagement with resnet and tcn hybrid network. In Proceedings of the 2021 18th Conference on Robots and Vision (CRV), Burnaby, BC, Canada, 26–28 May 2021; IEEE: Piscataway, NJ, USA, 2021; pp. 151–157.

algorithms

MDPI

Article

# Integrating Eye Movement, Finger Pressure, and Foot Pressure Information to Build an Intelligent Driving Fatigue Detection System

**Jong-Chen Chen * and Yin-Zhen Chen**

Information Management Department, National Yunlin University of Science and Technology, Douliu 640, Taiwan
* Correspondence: jcchen@yuntech.edu.tw

**Abstract:** Fatigued driving is a problem that every driver will face, and traffic accidents caused by drowsy driving often occur involuntarily. If there is a fatigue detection and warning system, it is generally believed that the occurrence of some incidents can be reduced. However, everyone's driving habits and methods may differ, so it is not easy to establish a suitable general detection system. If a customized intelligent fatigue detection system can be established, it may reduce unfortunate accidents. With its potential to mitigate unfortunate accidents, this study offers hope for a safer driving environment. Thus, on the one hand, this research hopes to integrate the information obtained from three different sensing devices (eye movement, finger pressure, and plantar pressure), which are chosen for their ability to provide comprehensive and reliable data on a driver's physical and mental state. On the other hand, it uses an autonomous learning architecture to integrate these three data types to build a customized fatigued driving detection system. This study used a system that simulated a car driving environment and then invited subjects to conduct tests on fixed driving routes. First, we demonstrated that the system established in this study could be used to learn and classify different driving clips. Then, we showed that it was possible to judge whether the driver was fatigued through a series of driving behaviors, such as lane drifting, sudden braking, and irregular acceleration, rather than a single momentary behavior. Finally, we tested the hypothesized situation in which drivers were experiencing three cases of different distractions. The results show that the entire system can establish a personal driving system through autonomous learning behavior and further detect whether fatigued driving abnormalities occur.

**Keywords:** intelligent system; fatigued driving; autonomous learning; distraction

## 1. Introduction

Car driving is indispensable in today's high-speed and highly mobile society, and driving safety is critical. However, safe driving must be achieved through constant eye, hand, and foot coordination. Of course, during this driving process, it may be acceptable if the eyes, hands, and feet do not cooperate for a short period, but it may also cause unimaginable consequences. Fatigued (or drowsy) driving is one of the above situations that may occur daily. Generally speaking, fatigued driving refers to slowness, blurring, weakness, dizziness, hallucinations, or even coma due to the driver's inability to control the driver's mind or body during driving. The usual reasons for this phenomenon are related to the driver's diseases, medications, physiological aging, and lack of sleep. Although everyone is aware of the dangers of fatigued driving, accidents caused by fatigue still occur from time to time. This is because most fatigued driving occurs unexpectedly when the driver thinks there will be no problem. Especially when micro-sleep occurs, most people will feel that they are awake. However, the scary thing is that even a few seconds of sleep may occur and cause an accident.

t is generally believed that some of the first signs of fatigued driving can be detected before a critical situation occurs. There are quite a few studies on drowsy driving. Related surveys can be found in [1–5]. Some scholars have proposed invasive physiological monitoring methods, such as electroencephalogram (EEG) [6], electrocardiogram (ECG) [7], and skin conductivity [8]. Intrusion detection generally affects humans. Overall, its acceptance is low. Therefore, some non-intrusive proposals have been made. Non-invasive methods use different algorithms to monitor drivers' facial features, eye signals, head movements, hand movements, and other physiological characteristics to infer driver fatigue [9–16]. There have been many improvements in artificial intelligence deep learning software and hardware in recent years. Therefore, some scholars advocate using these technologies to enhance fatigue judgment from the physiological characteristics of drivers [17–20].

People generally believe that most fatigued driving will cause symptoms such as blurred vision, red eyes, narrowed field of vision, unconscious nodding, frequent yawning, facial numbness, slow reaction, the inability to concentrate, decreased thinking ability, stiff and slow movements, loss of sense of direction, and speeding up and down. Therefore, in response to the above phenomenon, the method generally used by scholars to explore the problem of fatigue driving is to use face and eye image detection [21,22]. Some scholars have also suggested adding mouth shape changes, head movement, and eye information [23,24]. The above studies emphasize the fatigue phenomenon displayed by the head. Another group of scholars suggests judging fatigue phenomena such as slow response and stiff and slow movements by observing the position and posture changes of the driving hands [25]. The above methods are all started from the perspective of image processing. We know that image processing is generally affected by environmental factors (such as light, camera angle, etc.) but also varies significantly due to personal usage habits (such as wearing glasses, mouth photos, etc.). Therefore, another group of scholars emphasized the force exerted by the hand [26–28]. We know that fatigue driving presents many symptoms that vary from person to person and vary based on environmental conditions. While the studies mentioned above emphasize local fatigue detection, this study explores integrating information from three sources: eye movement and hand and foot force exertion.

Safe driving must rely on a high degree of coordination between the eyes, hands, feet, muscles, bones, ligaments, joints, etc., that control every movement. To achieve this goal, the human brain plays a vital role. Our brain is a highly developed organ, and its coordination with the human body's eyes, hands, and feet is an exquisite masterpiece. However, we must emphasize that sometimes, even though a driving control action is seen as simple (especially in an "unconscious state"), it is still highly contingent on the coordination of eyes, hands, and feet. Based on the above motivation, if a system that integrates eye movement, finger pressure, and foot pressure sensing information can be designed and controlled through an autonomous learning mechanism ("brain"), it is generally believed that the occurrence of accidents caused by fatigued driving can be reduced.

We plan to start with user behavior classification and train and learn each cluster, which is called customized learning. A customized detection system may be generated when driving data are considerably accumulated. Of course, the feasibility of using this customized intelligent system for fatigue detection will be significantly increased.

Previously, our team developed an intelligent learning system—an artificial neuromolecular system (ANM system) [29]. It is an information-processing architecture that captures biological structure/function relationships. In particular, in addition to information processing between neurons, it also emphasizes information processing within neurons. Because of this, it has sufficient system dynamics and can be transformed into a particular input/output information processor through evolutionary learning. Due to these features, it can perform specific functions according to the needs of the problem domain. It has been proven that it can be effectively applied in different fields, such as chopstick robot movement [29], finger motion control [30], and rehabilitation action control [31]. The entire system is implemented on a digital computer (program).

There were two differences between the ANM system currently developed in this study and the one from before 2015. The first is a classification system in terms of processing units, that is, the analysis of correctly classifying a series of time series input data [29]. The second change is that this research has added processing unit functions that can convert a series of sequential inputs into other sequential data [30,31]. We know that the functions of living things in nature result from the high interaction between some component molecular structures. Therefore, some scholars [32,33] have further proposed that it results from various weak interactions between constituent molecules. In other words, traditional learning algorithm research often needs to pay more attention to these interactive processes because they are too complex and unknown. In recent years, research on deep learning has shown rapid growth due to the acceleration of computer software and hardware, dramatically increasing its application scope. However, this line of study still falls into the style of Hebbian information processing, which still has the so-called problem of stagnating at the regional optimal solution. The most significant difference between this study and deep learning research is our hope to increase the dynamics of the processing unit of the ANM system, especially in adding weak interaction functions. Through this increase, we hope to make the system's learning curve show a smooth improvement method: continuous improvement (there is no complete stagnation of learning). When we allow the system to learn long enough, it can progress toward completely solving the problem.

We all know that collecting data on fatigued driving based on real-life driving conditions is very dangerous in a natural environment. Because of this, conducting it in a simulation is relatively appropriate. Instead, in this study, we use the City Car Driving (CCD) 1.5.9.2 simulation software to conduct driving tests and data collection. This simulation environment provides permutations and combinations of varying vehicle conditions, weather, and vehicles, allowing us to perform testing and data collection directly on specific situational settings through the driving simulator in a relatively simple and safe manner.

## 2. The System

The system will be described in three parts. The first part explains the experimental test bed of this study—the driving simulation environment. The second part describes the sensing system. The third part explains the learning mechanism of the ANM system.

### 2.1. Car Driving Environment

The CCD system provides different settings (including routes, road conditions, vehicle conditions, weather, and driving modes) that allow us to conduct driving tests in a specific environment. In addition, because it is a simulation system, we can conduct different tests under the same driving environment. Figure 1 shows the driver's field of vision in front of the vehicle. Figure 2 shows the steering wheel, accelerator pedal, and brake pedal. The steering wheel has a maximum rotation angle of 270 degrees and has an automatic return function.

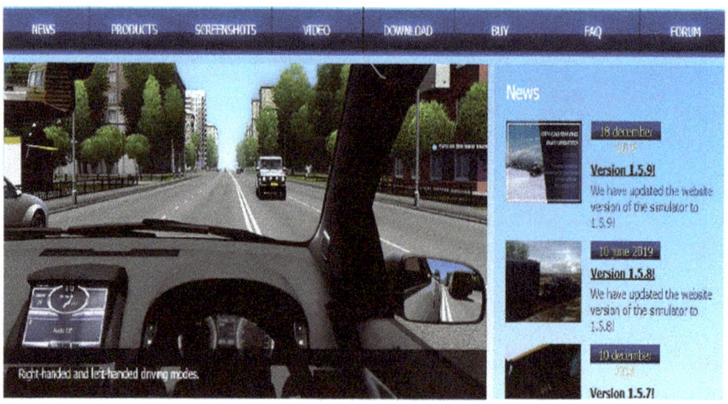


**Figure 1.** The simulation situation ahead of the vehicle.

**Figure 2.** The simulation system includes the steering wheel, accelerator, and brake pedal.

### *2.2. Sensing System*

#### 2.2.1. Eye Movement Tracking

Currently, four standard eye-tracking methods are used. Electro-oculography is the earliest tracking method used. This method is simple to use but has the disadvantage of poor accuracy. A scleral search coil method can improve accuracy, but its disadvantage is that it is invasive. The use of eye tracker technology improves the shortcomings of the above two methods. However, its disadvantage is that the user must wear the device on the head correctly and without deviation. Video-based pupil/corneal reflection combination is currently the most advanced and widely used method. The Tobii EyeX, which is the eye-tracking device used in this study, is one such device (Figure 3). It uses near-infrared light (800-1500 nanometers) to track the movement and gaze of the user's eyes. When the user's line of sight moves, the cursor will move to the corresponding position on the computer screen. A plug-and-play USB device records the subject's visual field and eye movements. The device only captures eye gaze data (not the user's face), so there are no privacy concerns. Figure 4 shows part of the user's captured gaze data (two-dimensional X- and Y-axes).

**Figure 3.** Tobii EyeX controller.

```
Left eye: X: 0, Y: 0	Right eye: X: 0, Y: 0
Left eye: X: 185.418748855591, Y: 822.814607620239	Right eye: X: 656.807956695557, Y: 809.192698001862
Left eye: X: 234.248886108398, Y: 656.742074489594	Right eye: X: 609.182395935059, Y: 737.344172000885
Left eye: X: 273.759956359863, Y: 647.866387367249	Right eye: X: 632.223701477051, Y: 684.242613315582
Left eye: X: 203.636498451233, Y: 628.911881446838	Right eye: X: 618.01305770874, Y: 686.151530742645
Left eye: X: 0, Y: 0	Right eye: X: 597.904472351074, Y: 653.754844665527
Left eye: X: 0, Y: 0	Right eye: X: 590.025787353516, Y: 691.850023269653
Left eye: X: 161.196842193604, Y: 823.150763511658	Right eye: X: 649.869575500488, Y: 881.644077301025
Left eye: X: 199.342489242554, Y: 668.64960193634	Right eye: X: 650.038890838623, Y: 719.35024023056
Left eye: X: 160.340938568115, Y: 672.112612724304	Right eye: X: 622.238330841064, Y: 687.769289016724
Left eye: X: 178.456792831421, Y: 666.586961746216	Right eye: X: 647.786464691162, Y: 695.382363796234
Left eye: X: 0, Y: 0	Right eye: X: 648.522148132324, Y: 697.413911819458
Left eye: X: 169.565877914429, Y: 632.60219335556	Right eye: X: 643.965682983398, Y: 702.633082866669
Left eye: X: 0, Y: 0	Right eye: X: 594.761352539063, Y: 696.117310523987
Left eye: X: 175.755586624146, Y: 600.161926746368	Right eye: X: 643.53630065918, Y: 697.451505661011
Left eye: X: 144.477310180664, Y: 602.33206987381	Right eye: X: 623.092746734619, Y: 701.203680038452
Left eye: X: 169.915523529053, Y: 613.903441429138	Right eye: X: 636.109256744385, Y: 677.113044261932
Left eye: X: 172.171139717102, Y: 613.52415561676	Right eye: X: 637.572498321533, Y: 674.150469303131
Left eye: X: 291.966133117676, Y: 641.710073947906	Right eye: X: 719.741477966309, Y: 724.831538200378
Left eye: X: 669.776744842529, Y: 608.613781929016	Right eye: X: 733.789672851563, Y: 633.967158794403
Left eye: X: 704.45686340332, Y: 787.916321754456	Right eye: X: 561.855010986328, Y: 903.137583732605
Left eye: X: 838.006439208984, Y: 641.400632858276	Right eye: X: 621.68529510498, Y: 757.792840003967
Left eye: X: 843.534679412842, Y: 529.694555997849	Right eye: X: 659.915828704834, Y: 652.42354631424
Left eye: X: 0, Y: 0	Right eye: X: 352.509155273438, Y: 657.92248249054
Left eye: X: 690.153694152832, Y: 504.847151041031	Right eye: X: 486.039047241211, Y: 610.382430553436
Left eye: X: 636.283836364746, Y: 472.188885211945	Right eye: X: 491.666450500488, Y: 595.051867961884
Left eye: X: 656.16886138916, Y: 491.267727613449	Right eye: X: 470.615816116333, Y: 605.531988143921
Left eye: X: 659.72225189209, Y: 488.368141651154	Right eye: X: 0, Y: 0
Left eye: X: 0, Y: 0	Right eye: X: 437.534093856812, Y: 578.163800239563
Left eye: X: 646.472110748291, Y: 518.342278003693	Right eye: X: 398.421192169189, Y: 566.114587783813
Left eye: X: 542.552604675293, Y: 549.990692138672	Right eye: X: 466.124296188354, Y: 608.164715766907
Left eye: X: 612.484531402588, Y: 820.082874298096	Right eye: X: 0, Y: 0
Left eye: X: 1612.16514587402, Y: 1061.56852483749	Right eye: X: 1466.84303283691, Y: 1282.09599494934
```

**Figure 4.** Part of the user's captured gaze data (two-dimensional X- and Y-axes).

2.2.2. Finger Pressure Sensing and Plantar Pressure Sensing

Eight piezoresistive pressure sensors were used in this study. Three relate to the brake pedal, three to the gas pedal, and two to the steering wheel. The brake and oil pedal are placed at the pedal's front, middle, and rear, respectively. The steering wheel is installed at both ends where people usually use the steering wheel. Although the brake and gas pedals are each equipped with three sensors, we will add up the three values and take the average when collecting data due to the different methods of use. All of the piezoresistive pressure sensors mentioned above will be connected to an Arduino board to collect the subject's finger pressure data and transmit it to the computer. Figure 5 is a simple schematic diagram without further processing. After testing its accuracy, this study further strengthened the closeness of the sensor to these devices.

**Figure 5.** (**a**) Two piezoresistive pressure sensors were installed on the simulated driving steering wheel. (**b**) Three piezoresistive pressure sensors were installed on the simulated pedal.

*2.3. The ANM System*

Generally speaking, computer programs using symbolic design methods are unsuitable for evolutionary autonomous learning. A slight change in a program may result in a malfunctioning program. This is because the fitness curve between the structure of the entire program and the functions represents a peak and valley full of distinct highs and lows. In other words, the feasible paths between mountain peaks are steep, which is unsuitable for evolutionary autonomous learning. Using the evolutionary learning method, the final result may lead to learning stagnation, falling into the so-called local optimal solution.

In response to the problems faced by symbolic programs, traditional neural networks use the connection relationship between neurons (including the strength of the connection) to store (or express) information to deal with this problem. When inputs and outputs change, the connections between neurons in the network must also be adjusted accordingly. In other words, the system's function entirely relies on the different link relationships on the network to express. Unfortunately, the processing of neurons' molecular and chemical messages has been completely ignored. In recent years, the information-processing function of neurons has been gradually discovered. For example, the second type of transmitter (cAMP) may play a role in controlling the firing of neurons in the central nervous system. These theories propose that some information transmitters and regulators on the cell membrane are converted into signals of the second type of transmitter. Then, this cAMP acts on some proteins (kinases), which control some reactor proteins that regulate ion channels or connect microtubules. These proteins directly or indirectly affect the opening of ion channels; that is, they directly or indirectly affect the potential or firing of neurons. Some other researchers believe the cytoskeleton plays the role of integrating signals (information) or memory functions. It is known that the cytoskeleton of neurons is a multi-molecular network of microtubules, microfilaments, and neurofilaments and some proteins (MAPs) that connect these molecules. These MAPs may coordinate other information-processing behaviors within neurons.

In addition to using the relationship between network neurons to express information, the ANM system also adds information processing within the neurons. However, a detailed simulation of intraneuronal dynamics would require significant computational cost (computer time). Therefore, we only consider modeling this neural information processing relatively abstractly. Even so, the fitness curve presented by the structure–function relationships represented by the internal dynamics of the entire neuron must be rich enough to be suitable for evolutionary learning. We would use the adjective "multidimensional bypass" to describe the curve between this structure and the function it represents. Intuitively, this kind of curve is due to adding extra spatial degrees, which increases the chance of saddle points. The theoretical basis is that when the number of constituent elements increases, the interaction between them increases, thereby increasing the opportunities for saddle points. In addition to adding more interactive elements, two features (redundancy and weak interactions) that facilitate evolutionary learning also play a crucial role. In simulating the internal dynamics of neurons, the ANM system uses evolutionary learning inside the neurons to place the above three factors.

### 2.3.1. Neuromolecular Information Processing

The ANM system assumes that information processing occurs in the cytoskeleton of neurons, which we call neuromolecular information processing. This study used a two-dimensional space cellular automata (CA) to simulate the information-processing method on the cytoskeleton. We call these types of neurons information-processing (IP) neurons. Figure 6 illustrates the molecular structure of an information-processing neuron, where each grid represents a unit molecule of the cytoskeleton. This study assumed three types of molecules (represented by C1, C2, and C3). Each molecule type is responsible for signal transmission and has different transmission characteristics. For example, the transmission speed of the C1 type of elements is the slowest, but the influence of the signal transmission is the strongest. In contrast, the signal transmission influence of the C3 type of elements is the weakest but has the fastest transmission speed. Among the three, the transfer speed and influence of the C2 element type are between C1 and C3.

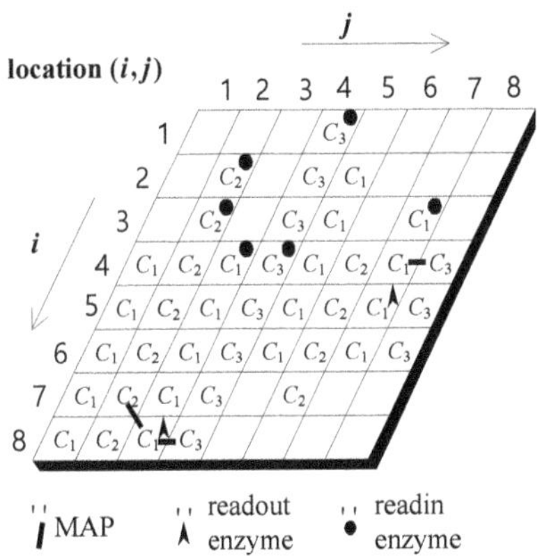


**Figure 6.** The molecular structure of an information-processing neuron is represented as a two-dimensional grid.

In the cytoskeleton, each component unit can act as a signal input and output site. The input site is called a readin enzyme, whereas the output site is a readout enzyme. The readin enzymes receive signals from outside the neuron and convert them into signals that flow through the molecular structure, while readout enzymes play a role in controlling whether neurons fire. The neuron fires when a specific combination of signals reaches a location with readout enzymes and the total signal kinetic state reaches a certain level. However, this model has some limitations: the readin enzyme can be configured on any element, but the readout enzyme can only be configured on the C1 element. This is based on the hypothesis in this study that only certain combinations of signals will cause neurons to fire.

When a signal from outside the cell is sent to the cell membrane, it causes the reader enzyme to activate and further turn on elements in their exact location. Each enabled piece will affect adjacent aspects of the same type in turn. As described above, it initiates a specific signal flow in the cytoskeleton. For example, as shown in Figure 6, when the read enzyme at the (2, 2) position receives a signal, it will activate the C2 element and generate a signal that moves along the C2 element, moving from (2, 2) to (8, 2). To form a unidirectional signal flow during the process, the aspect turned on will enter a very short backlash period after transmitting the signal. During the backlash period, the element can no longer be activated and must wait until the backlash period ends, which ensures unidirectional transmission.

Signals on different types of components can also affect each other through the MAP between them (of course, these effects are asymmetric). When a signal from one end reaches a place with a MAP, it will affect the kinetic state of different types of elements at the other end through the MAP (or even prompt the other end to generate new signal flows). The neuron triggers when a specific combination of signals reaches a location with a readout enzyme. The firing time of the neuron depends on how the cytoskeleton in the neuron integrates and processes these messages.

The two-dimensional cytoskeleton in the ANM system is arranged in a wrap-around manner. There will be no boundary restrictions when moving within the cytoskeleton. Each basic unit has eight possible directions to move and might form a circular path. Figure 7 shows a schematic diagram of the signal movement path. For example, in Figure 7a, the signal starting at location (3, 3) will move along (2,3), (1,3), and (8,3) and finally stop at (7,3). The other example, as shown in Figure 7b, is that the signal starting at location (5,2) will follow (4,1), (3,8), (2,7), and (1,6) and finally stop at (8,5).

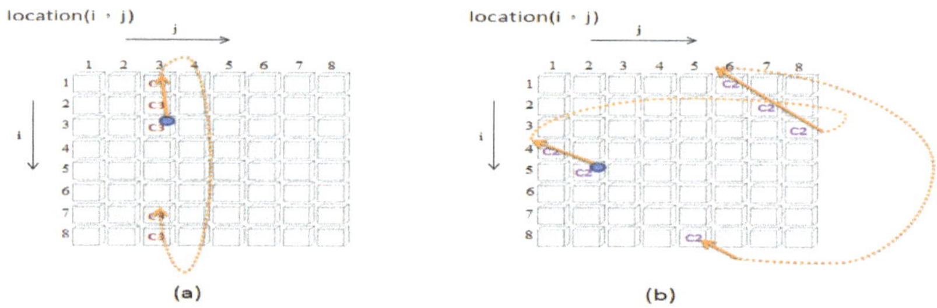


**Figure 7.** (**a**) A signal flows in an upward direction. (**b**) A signal flows in a left-upward direction.

Currently, the ANM system has 576 information-processing neurons (called cytoskeletal neurons). Each neuron has a different cytoskeletal structure when the system is initially designed. Figure 8 shows a hierarchical structure diagram of all information-processing neurons, from the population to the molecule level. Each neuron has different information-processing capabilities. To allow them to learn autonomously, they are divided into eight competitive subnetworks (each subnetwork has 72 information-processing neurons). The competitive learning approach used in this study allows each sub-network to have an "information processing neuron" with a very similar cytoskeletal structure (in the following, we refer to information-processing neurons with very similar cytoskeletal structures in different subnetworks as the same bundle of neurons). Given the same input data for the neurons in the same bundle, the output behavior of these neurons with similar cytoskeletons will be very similar (but not exactly equal). Furthermore, for the entire subnetwork group, the structure of the neurons in each subnetwork is also very similar. Through the characteristics of this similar structure, we can allow these different subnetworks to compete. First, we evaluate the performance of each subnet then select the better-performing subnet and copy it to the less-performing subnet (assuming that a slight error occurs during the copying process, a so-called mutation). The learning process described above is similar to Darwinian evolution, which will train these subnetworks to achieve the intended purpose of this study.

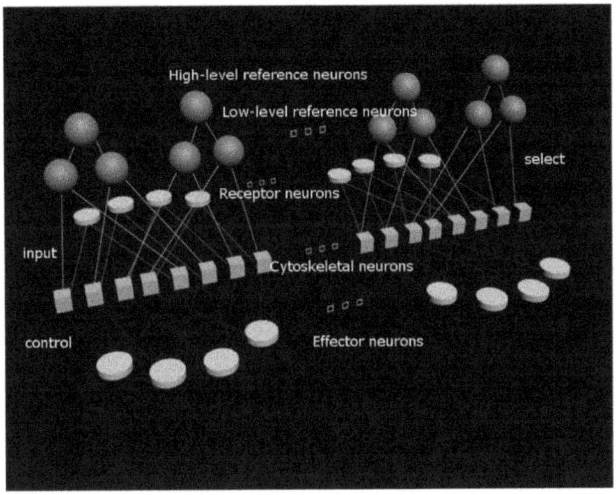


**Figure 8.** A hierarchical structure diagram of all information-processing neurons (cytoskeletal neurons).

Evolutionary learning uses a Darwinian evolutionary search method, which can be roughly divided into three steps (Figure 9).

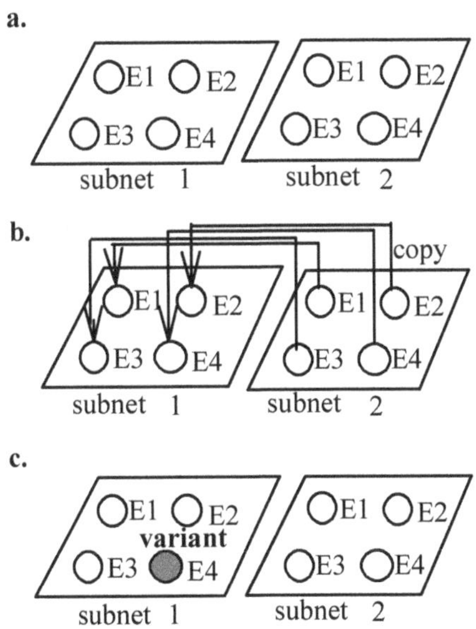


**Figure 9.** Evolutionary learning process at the level of information-processing neurons. (**a**) Evaluate the performance of each subnet and select a few subnets with better performance; (**b**) Copying occurs from better-performing subnets to worse-performing subnets (copying occurs in the same bundle of neurons with a similar cytoskeletal structure); and (**c**) Change the subnets with poor performance.

2.3.2. Manipulation Network

As mentioned, the learning algorithm used in this study produces something similar to competitive learning by allowing each subnetwork to change its cytoskeletal structure. Changing the cytoskeletal structure shapes the ANM system with gradual structure/function switching properties. This feature helps generate paths in multi-dimensional spaces (please refer to Section 2.1), and the system thus has a relatively high chance of escaping from the regional optimal solution when searching. However, this kind of change is a gradual fine-tuning, which improves slowly and takes a long time. The difficulty is relatively high if the goal is to train a large group of neurons to complete a specified task. From another perspective, it may not be necessary to use this approach because it may be possible to train a small group of suitable neurons to perform the same task. To deal with this problem, this study uses another type of neuron, whose task is to select appropriate information-processing neurons to achieve it (that is, only the chosen neurons will participate in information processing and fitness evaluation). This type of neuron is called a control neuron (CN). This study assumes that control neurons have hierarchical control (selection) functions. This hierarchical control method controls a group of information-processing neurons (selected) to achieve the task. This way of selecting neurons is called orchestration. The current operation method uses two layers of control neurons, as shown in Figure 10, to find suitable neurons through the Darwinian variation–selection method.

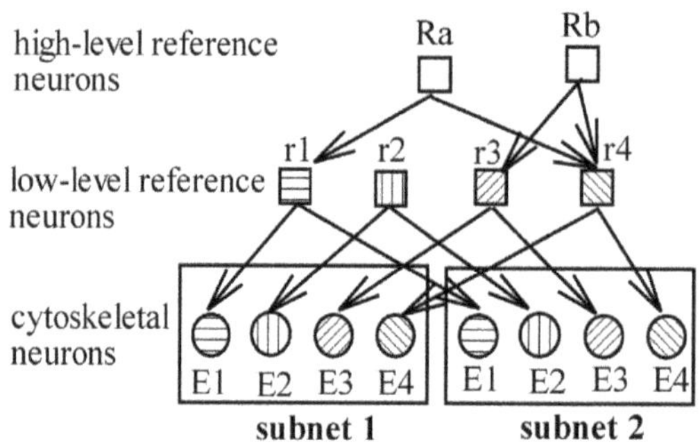


**Figure 10.** Two layers of control neurons control information-processing neurons.

As mentioned, the current ANM system has 576 information-processing neurons (or 72 bundles of neurons). A lower-level control neuron controls each bundle. Therefore, there are a total of 72 low-level control neurons. This study utilizes another layer of neurons, high-level control neurons, to control the firing of lower-level control neurons. Learning of control neurons occurs only between higher and lower layers. In other words, each high-level control neuron can select different low-level control neurons and change along with the learning process. However, the information-processing neurons controlled by low-level control neurons do not change with the learning process. The entire evolutionary learning step is first to evaluate the performance of each high-level control neuron and select the better-performing high-level control neuron. Then, the better-performing higher-level control neurons are copied to the worse-performing higher-level control neurons. It is assumed that there are slight errors during the copying process, which results in the low-level control neurons controlled by the replicator and the copied being different (Figure 11).

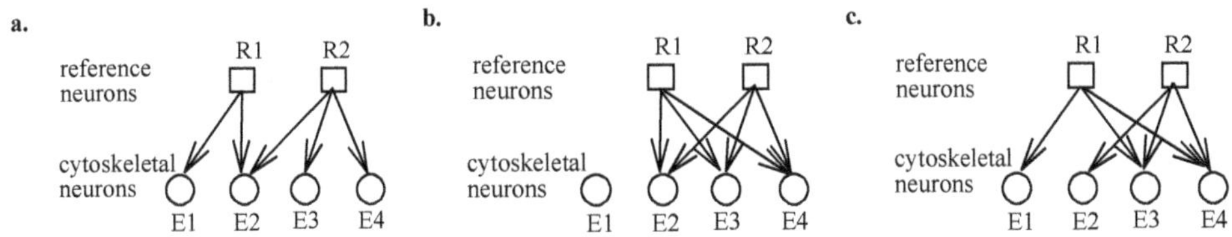


**Figure 11.** Evolutionary learning process at the level of control neurons. (**a**) Cytoskeletal neurons controlled by each reference neuron are activated sequentially to evaluate their performance. (**b**) Assume the cytoskeletal neurons controlled by R2 achieve better performance. The pattern of neural activities controlled by R2 is copied to R1. (**c**) R1 controls a slight variation of the neural grouping controlled by R2, assuming some errors occur during the copy process.

Evolutionary learning is implemented by allowing alternating learning between control and information-processing neurons. The current approach is to allow the system to learn at the control neuron level for a while and then allow the system to learn at the information-processing neuron level for another period. This cycle allows each level to learn sequentially until the system is stopped or the assigned task is completed.

## 3. Application Domain

The following will first explain how to collect driving data. We then explain how to preprocess the collected data. The last part describes how to connect these data to the system.

### 3.1. Driving Data Collection

Figure 12 shows our settings for the CCD system. We selected a U-shaped route with light traffic and good weather conditions, with average driving patterns for general roads. We selected a straight highway route, with 10% light and 80% heavy traffic. The details of data collection are explained below. We first connected the Tobii eye tracker to the computer, then used Open Broadcaster Software (OBS) 29.0.2 to record the coordinate information of the eye tracker through the computer screen, and finally turned on the CCD system to determine whether the eye tracker was correctly displayed on the screen. When all of the above equipment and subjects are ready, we further confirm whether the data collection of the eye tracker and hand and foot pressure are synchronized. Finally, data collection was officially carried out. The entire process was screen-recorded, and the time was recorded until the simulation ended.

The following explains how to synchronize the data collected through eye, hand, and foot sensors. We note that the data collection of hands and feet was performed through Arduino. These two data were synchronized. The main problem is synchronizing eye movement and hand and foot data. The current approach was to find the screen recording data based on when the hand and foot pressure values were obtained. When the image data were found, the HoughCircles function provided by the open-source computer vision library was used to find the coordinate values displayed by the eye tracker, which completed the integration of specific eye, hand, and foot data at a particular time.

To maintain the consistency of data collection, this study invited the same subjects to collect data ten times in the same driving environment. Each time, the driver drove on the entire route. The data on eye movements, braking, finger pressure, and accelerator were collected at intervals of 0.5 s. The subject was asked to drive the same route every time, but the traffic conditions varied (due to different traffic lights, pedestrians, and traffic volume). It took about three to five minutes from the beginning to the end for a drive test. In terms of driver behavior, this study assumed two types of driving: everyday driving and distracted driving. The former means the driver is relatively focused, while the latter means the driver has wandering eyes and changes lanes at will.

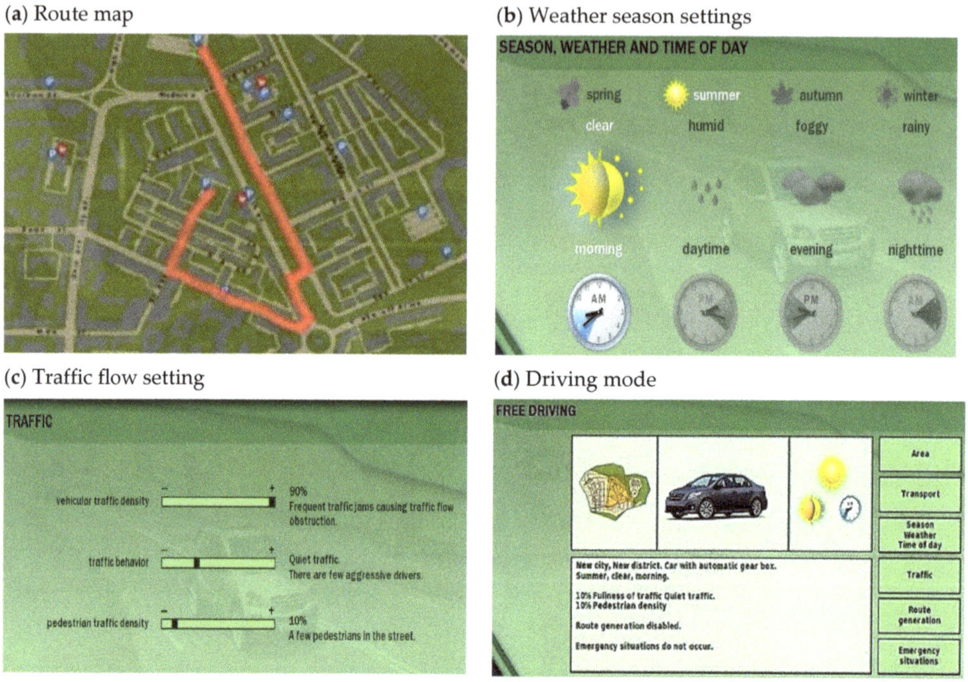


**Figure 12.** A schematic diagram of the driving environment setting for this study.

### *3.2. Data Preprocessing*

In this study, three participants were invited for data collection. All three collected data on general roads, while two also collected data on highways. Taking the first participant as an example, using the sliding window method (with a sliding speed of five time series points), all of the collected time series data were divided into 567 driving segments. The driving duration varied among participants, resulting in a different number of final driving segments. Each clip has 100 timing points (approximately 50 s of driving time). The clustering method used in this study is described below. The first step is to set a threshold. The dynamic timing warping (DTW) method is then used to compare two driving clips. When the difference between two driving clips is within the threshold, they belong to the same cluster. A new data cluster will be created when the newly-added clip does not belong to any cluster. This study followed the above method and organized the 567 driving clips into 73 clusters. The setting of this threshold is arbitrary and has no substantive significance. When this value is set too high, the number of clusters generated will be relatively small (relatively, it means that the difference within the cluster is more significant). On the contrary, relatively more clusters will be generated when set too low. When there is relatively enough data on subjects in the future, the choice of this value will have more substantial significance.

### *3.3. Connecting Driving Data with the I/O Interface of the ANM System*

As mentioned above, the length of each driving clip is 100 time series points, which is approximately 50 s of driving time. Each time series point has six values, including eye movement x- and y-axis data (represented by eye-x and eye-y), left and proper finger pressure on the steering wheel (represented by hand-left and hand-right), the average foot pressure of the brake pedal (expressed as foot-brake), and the average pressure of the accelerator pedal (expressed as foot-gas). This study assumes that during each driving clip, the behavior in the first 25 s will affect the behavior in the next 25 s. The method of this study is to use the movements, finger pressure, and accelerator foot pressure (including accelerator and brake) in the first 25 s as the input data of the system, and then the eye movements, finger pressure, and accelerator foot pressure in the next 25 s as the system's output data. For each data set, the smaller the difference between the outputs generated by the ANM system and the expected output, the better its learning performance is. Figure 13 gives an example of timing data 25 s before and 25 s after a specific time. In other words, we hope to convert the input data of Figure 13a into the waveform of Figure 13b through the ANM system.

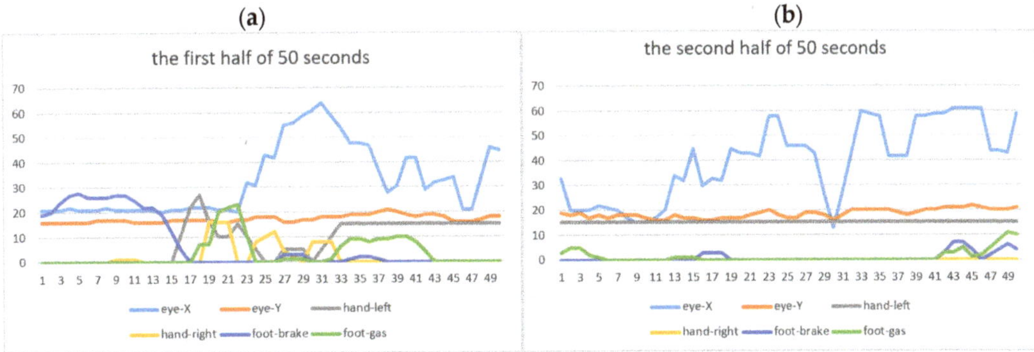


**Figure 13.** (**a**) An example of timing data 25 s before a specific time (**b**) An example of timing data 25 s after a particular time.

All information-processing neurons of the ANM system are divided into six groups, corresponding to the above six categories of data (eye-x, eye-y, hand-left, hand-right, foot-brake, foot-gas) (Figure 14). The firing behavior of each group of information-processing neurons represents the data conversion of specific output data. In the current implementation, we use the time difference between two adjacent firing neurons of the same group to describe the degree of data conversion. This study assumes that the relationship between the time difference and the degree of conversion is similar to a sigmoid-like waveform (Equation (1)). For a particular group of outputs, the waveforms generated by all of the same group of neurons that produce firing behavior will be superimposed in series to form a specific output waveform. Loss is the absolute difference between the waveform generated by the ANM system and the expected waveform. The smaller the loss value, the better the fitness of the system.

$$\text{Degree of transformation} = \left(\frac{1}{1+e(-2\times\Delta t)} - 0.5\right)\times 2\times 90 \quad (1)$$

$$\text{Loss} = \sum\nolimits_i \left|\sum\nolimits_{j=1}^{50} (E_{ij} - A_{ij})\right| \quad (2)$$

where $E_{ij}$ and $A_{ij}$ represent the expected trajectory and the trajectory generated by the ANM system, respectively; $i$ = eye-x, eye-y, hand-left, hand-right, foot-brake, and foot-gas.

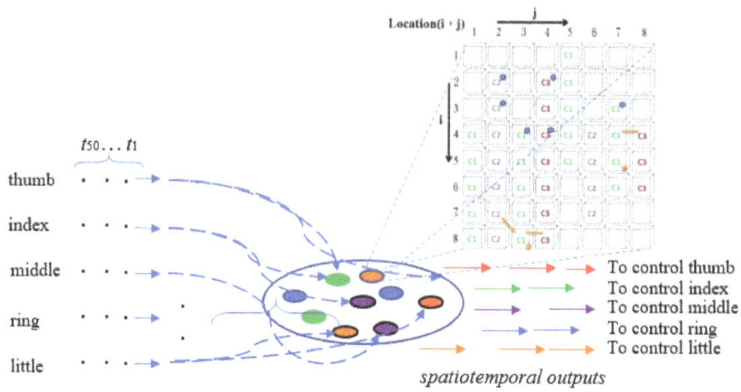


**Figure 14.** Input/Output interface of the ANM system.

## 4. Experiments

Six experiments were conducted in this study. The first part focuses on the learning ability of the system, exploring whether the ANM system can be used to learn each driving clip. The second part examines the relationship between a series of driving clips. If there is some correlation, we can judge whether the driver is fatigued through a series of driving behaviors (rather than a single momentary behavior). The third part is performed to classify different driving behaviors. The fourth part is based on the learning experiment from the first part, followed by adaptive experiments using the obtained information. It investigates whether the ANM system can be trained to apply one person's system to different people. The fifth part introduces driving segments with varying noise levels to explore whether the ANM system can detect abnormal behavior in drivers while the vehicle is in motion. The final experiment tests whether the driver has distracted (fatigued) driving.

### *4.1. Learning Capability*

As mentioned earlier, in this study, the data collected by the first participant on general roads were divided into 73 clusters, the second participant's data into 62 clusters, and the third participant's data into 67 clusters. For highway driving, the first participant's data were divided into 58 clusters and the second into 56. This experiment hopes to understand whether the ANM system has considerable learning capabilities for each data cluster. In other words, can we use the ANM system for judgment learning for each type of driving behavior? That is to say, we can use the driving behavior of the first 25 s to judge the reaction behavior of the next 25 s. If the preliminary experimental results prove that the above inference is feasible, we can gradually increase the driver's behavior. On the other hand, we can gradually increase the system's complexity according to the needs of the problem domain (for example, different weather, traffic flow, and road conditions). In this experiment, we randomly selected 20 clusters from the 73 clusters of the first participant in a general road environment. Additionally, nine clusters were selected from the other two participants in a general road environment. For the highway data, nine clusters were selected from the two participants in a heavy and light traffic environment. Each cluster also randomly selected a driving clip to test whether the relationship between the first 25 s and the last 25 s of driving behavior can be established. The results showed that the degree of learning improvement was relatively rapid in the early stages of learning but slowed down in the later stages. The degree of improvement became smaller and smaller in the last stages. Most importantly, however, the system showed continued improvement, even in the later stages of learning.

We allowed the ANM system's learning to terminate when the learning improvement was relatively slow. The results show (Tables 1–7) that the learning results in each cluster are above 75%. We add here that if the system can continue learning, there is still room for continuous improvement (i.e., higher accuracy). However, the experimental results in this part of the article were suspended at appropriate times to explore the different information processing of ANM systems more broadly.

**Table 1.** Participant A's performance during the first cycle and at termination while driving in a general road environment.

| Cluster | Run | Loss at Cycle 1 | Loss at Termination | Improvement Rate | Run | Loss at Cycle 1 | Loss at Termination | Improvement Rate |
|---|---|---|---|---|---|---|---|---|
| 1 | 3 | 3933.0 | 948.0 | 75.9% | 33 | 3161.0 | 559.0 | 82.3% |
| 2 | 6 | 4082.4 | 863.3 | 78.9% | 36 | 3410.0 | 744.0 | 78.2% |
| 3 | 9 | 3289.0 | 756.0 | 77.0% | 39 | 2937.0 | 739.0 | 75.0% |
| 4 | 12 | 4139.1 | 848.4 | 79.5% | 42 | 2933.0 | 975.0 | 66.8% |
| 5 | 15 | 3979.0 | 956.0 | 76.0% | 45 | 3104.0 | 730.0 | 76.5% |
| 6 | 18 | 4676.1 | 864.5 | 81.5% | 48 | 3057.6 | 537.9 | 82.4% |
| 7 | 21 | 4316.0 | 661.0 | 84.7% | 51 | 3039.0 | 290.0 | 90.5% |
| 8 | 24 | 4759.3 | 772.0 | 83.8% | 54 | 2866.2 | 460.3 | 83.9% |
| 9 | 27 | 5792.0 | 879.0 | 84.8% | 57 | 3425.0 | 1068.0 | 68.8% |
| 10 | 30 | 4230.6 | 537.4 | 87.3% | 60 | 4132.0 | 957.0 | 76.8% |

**Table 2.** Participant B's performance during the first cycle and at termination while driving in a general road environment.

| Cluster | Run | Loss at Cycle 1 | Loss at Termination | Improvement Rate |
|---|---|---|---|---|
| 1 | 6 | 3699.2 | 991.4 | 73.2% |
| 2 | 12 | 3392.5 | 712.2 | 79.0% |
| 3 | 18 | 4220.0 | 823.3 | 80.5% |
| 4 | 24 | 4346.3 | 783.2 | 82.0% |
| 5 | 30 | 4276.7 | 1035.0 | 75.8% |
| 6 | 36 | 4738.4 | 850.7 | 82.0% |
| 7 | 42 | 3563.8 | 888.9 | 75.1% |
| 8 | 48 | 3599.1 | 918.3 | 74.5% |
| 9 | 54 | 3211.7 | 1222.7 | 61.9% |

**Table 3.** Participant C's performance during the first cycle and termination while driving in a general road environment.

| Cluster | Run | Loss at Cycle 1 | Loss at Termination | Improvement Rate |
|---|---|---|---|---|
| 1 | 6 | 3604.2 | 944.7 | 73.8% |
| 2 | 12 | 3712.4 | 1207.6 | 67.5% |
| 3 | 18 | 4202.0 | 1303.2 | 69.0% |
| 4 | 24 | 4693.6 | 1199.5 | 74.4% |
| 5 | 30 | 4034.1 | 1307.7 | 67.6% |
| 6 | 36 | 3665.6 | 959.5 | 73.8% |

**Table 3.** *Cont.*

| Cluster | Run | Loss at Cycle 1 | Loss at Termination | Improvement Rate |
|---|---|---|---|---|
| 7 | 42 | 3229.5 | 898.6 | 72.2% |
| 8 | 48 | 3638.0 | 1146.3 | 68.5% |
| 9 | 54 | 2787.7 | 743.6 | 73.3% |

**Table 4.** Participant B's performance during the first cycle and termination time while driving on highways with a light traffic environment.

| Cluster | Run | Loss at Cycle 1 | Loss at Termination | Improvement Rate |
|---|---|---|---|---|
| 1 | 6 | 2822.4 | 710.9 | 74.8% |
| 2 | 12 | 2977.7 | 800.2 | 73.1% |
| 3 | 18 | 2830.0 | 605.1 | 78.6% |
| 4 | 24 | 2927.1 | 620.1 | 78.8% |
| 5 | 30 | 3057.8 | 563.0 | 81.6% |
| 6 | 36 | 3016.9 | 618.3 | 79.5% |
| 7 | 42 | 3032.6 | 592.8 | 80.5% |
| 8 | 48 | 4410.4 | 743.4 | 83.1% |
| 9 | 54 | 3716.0 | 879.6 | 76.3% |

**Table 5.** Participant B's performance during the first cycle and termination time while driving on highways in a heavy traffic environment.

| Cluster | Run | Loss at Cycle 1 | Loss at Termination | Improvement Rate |
|---|---|---|---|---|
| 1 | 6 | 3206.2 | 973.3 | 69.6% |
| 2 | 12 | 2769.2 | 784.1 | 71.7% |
| 3 | 18 | 2859.1 | 513.1 | 82.1% |
| 4 | 24 | 3075.1 | 740.1 | 75.9% |
| 5 | 30 | 2783.0 | 601.8 | 78.4% |
| 6 | 36 | 3002.4 | 619.9 | 79.4% |
| 7 | 42 | 2863.0 | 723.3 | 74.7% |
| 8 | 48 | 3837.9 | 917.4 | 76.1% |
| 9 | 6 | 3206.2 | 973.3 | 69.6% |

**Table 6.** Participant C's performance during the first cycle and termination time while driving on highways with a light traffic environment.

| Cluster | Run | Loss at Cycle 1 | Loss at Termination | Improvement Rate |
|---|---|---|---|---|
| 1 | 6 | 3965.3 | 982.6 | 75.2% |
| 2 | 12 | 2698.2 | 913.0 | 66.2% |
| 3 | 18 | 2576.9 | 882.4 | 65.8% |
| 4 | 24 | 2871.1 | 660.1 | 77.0% |
| 5 | 30 | 2901.4 | 917.0 | 68.4% |

**Table 6.** *Cont.*

| Cluster | Run | Loss at Cycle 1 | Loss at Termination | Improvement Rate |
|---|---|---|---|---|
| 6 | 36 | 2692.3 | 774.4 | 71.2% |
| 7 | 42 | 2844.9 | 722.6 | 74.6% |
| 8 | 48 | 4427.9 | 706.0 | 84.1% |
| 9 | 54 | 4836.1 | 580.6 | 88.0% |

**Table 7.** Participant C's performance during the first cycle and termination time while driving on highways in a heavy traffic environment.

| Cluster | Run | Loss at Cycle 1 | Loss at Termination | Improvement Rate |
|---|---|---|---|---|
| 1 | 6 | 2768.5 | 709.2 | 74.4% |
| 2 | 12 | 2659.0 | 729.5 | 72.6% |
| 3 | 18 | 2570.7 | 743.3 | 71.1% |
| 4 | 24 | 3157.3 | 665.0 | 78.9% |
| 5 | 30 | 2628.6 | 688.1 | 73.8% |
| 6 | 36 | 2770.8 | 769.7 | 72.2% |
| 7 | 42 | 3034.5 | 756.8 | 75.1% |
| 8 | 48 | 3885.2 | 724.8 | 81.3% |
| 9 | 54 | 2726.7 | 657.3 | 75.9% |

### 4.2. Correlation Analysis before and after Driving Clips

In the previous part of the experiment, we randomly selected 20 driving clips for learning. For each clip, this experiment wants to explore whether there is some correlation between the clips before and after the clip. In other words, if so, we can use different driving clips continuously (rather than just relying on a single driving segment) to determine whether the driver is driving fatigued. The testing method of this experiment is to use the ANM system that has been trained for a long time in the previous experiment and conduct individual tests on each of the first one to four driving clips and the last one to four driving clips used in the training period.

This experiment randomly selected 6 of the 20 learned systems from the first experiment. The correlation between a specific driving clip's first and last four driving clips is tested for each learned system. If their loss values are not much different from each other (compared with the loss value that the system has not learned; please refer to Table 1), it means that there is some correlation between adjacent driving clips. In other words, driver behavior changes step by step rather than in leaps and bounds. The results (Figure 15) show that driver behavior is highly similar when the gap between two driving clips is relatively tiny. As the gap gradually increases, so does the difference in driver behavior. The important thing is that there is some U-shaped relationship between them. This relationship represents two meanings. The first is that it again shows that the ANM system has a gradual transformation capability when the system's performance function will slowly change due to changes in the input data. The second is in driving fatigue detection; we can verify whether the driver is fatigued through a series of driving behaviors (clips).

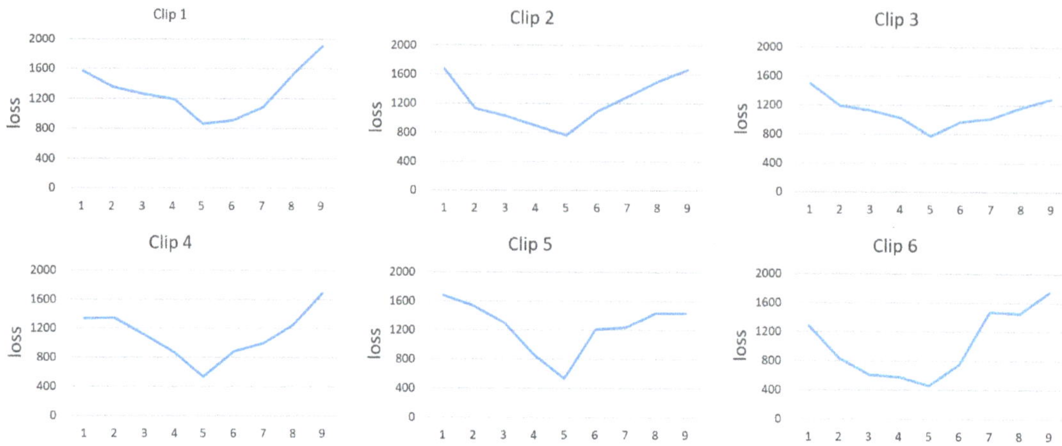


**Figure 15.** The correlation between a specific driving clip's first and last four driving clips. Annotation 5 on the x-axis is the loss value of a specific driving segment. On the x-axis, the numbers 1 to 4 are the first 4 driving segments of the driving segment, while 6 to 9 are the loss values of the last 4 driving segments.

### *4.3. Cluster Analysis*

The test data of the second experiment were related to driving clips before and after a specific driving clip. In other words, this is a driving segment of continuous driving before and after a certain driving period. This experiment's test data are driving clips from different periods. As mentioned before, during the data collection phase of this study, subjects were invited to drive the same route ten times. The test data of this experiment are similar driving clips of these ten drives at different periods. We interpret the former as the same type of driving segments, while the latter refers to utterly different driving segments. Simply put, the second experiment was a test during the same driving period, while this experiment was a driving test across various periods.

This experiment uses the 20 learning systems from the first experiment and finds all similar driving clips at different periods. Table 8 shows the number of similar clips between each driving clip and other clips in different periods. Figure 16 further organizes the data in Table 2. The results show that among the 20 groups, 10 (more than 50%) have loss values between 1022.2 and 1442.2. These values are not much different from the learned values in Table 1. The loss values of the other eight groups are between 1442.2 and 1862.2. These values are slightly higher than those learned in Table 1 but differ considerably. From the above results, we can roughly say that drivers' behavior is similar to a certain extent. In other words, we can perform classification to some extent from the driver's fragmentary behavior.

**Table 8.** Average loss and number of clips within a cluster.

| Cluster | Average Loss | No. of Clips | Cluster | Average Loss | No. of Clips |
|---|---|---|---|---|---|
| 1 | 2244.1 | 48 | 11 | 1142.3 | 76 |
| 2 | 1275.6 | 76 | 12 | 1823.7 | 77 |
| 3 | 1467.2 | 58 | 13 | 1076.7 | 76 |
| 4 | 1304.3 | 66 | 14 | 1549.5 | 75 |

Table 8. *Cont.*

| Cluster | Average Loss | No. of Clips | Cluster | Average Loss | No. of Clips |
|---|---|---|---|---|---|
| 5 | 2191.2 | 64 | 15 | 1434.1 | 86 |
| 6 | 1401.1 | 83 | 16 | 1365.4 | 108 |
| 7 | 1700.0 | 74 | 17 | 1022.2 | 74 |
| 8 | 1199.9 | 81 | 18 | 1239.1 | 137 |
| 9 | 1550.5 | 54 | 19 | 1719.6 | 70 |
| 10 | 1487.5 | 83 | 20 | 1543.9 | 65 |

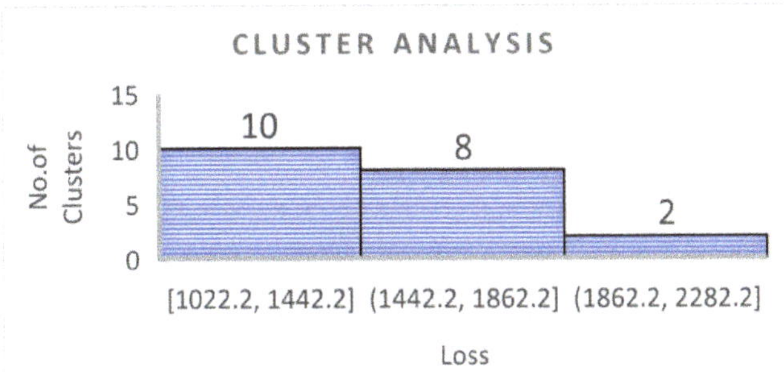


**Figure 16.** Analysis of loss data of 20 clusters.

### 4.4. Adaptability

#### 4.4.1. Different Participants Driving the General Road Environment

Based on the learning capability, subsequent adaptive experiments were conducted to explore whether the ANM system could further train and apply the system of one individual to others. Our approach is to test whether different subjects perform similarly in similar driving environments. The approach adopted is to use a system trained on one user's driving data to be tested on another user's driving data. This may be an assessment of the effectiveness of applying driving skills or knowledge learned through one participant to another participant in a particular driving scenario. It is a type of stress test. This study interprets it as adaptive capacity. The trained system was tested using nine driving segments from another participant with similar driving patterns. For each test, the system's loss values were initially recorded when encountering different drivers, followed by observing the outcomes after running for 500 iterations. Results from Tables 9–14 indicated that some driving segments achieved improvement rates of over 75% after just 500 training iterations, while others showed around 40% improvement. Even with relatively brief training periods, achieving 40% improvement demonstrates the adaptability of the ANM system. These data suggest that there is still room for learning. Moreover, using training data from the same individual may better suit drivers with similar habits; for example, Participant One and Participant Three share similar driving habits, as do Participant Two and Participant Three. In the future, systems trained on Participants One and Two could be applied to Participant Three.

**Table 9.** Participant A's data were tested with Participant B's learned system in a general road environment.

| Cluster | Run | Loss at Cycle 1 | Loss at Termination | Improvement Rate |
|---|---|---|---|---|
| 1 | 6 | 2723.2 | 1443.2 | 47.0% |
| 2 | 12 | 1838.0 | 1095.5 | 40.4% |
| 3 | 18 | 2829.4 | 1573.5 | 44.4% |
| 4 | 24 | 2052.0 | 1140.7 | 44.4% |
| 5 | 30 | 2517.2 | 1438.6 | 42.8% |
| 6 | 36 | 2080.3 | 906 | 56.4% |
| 7 | 42 | 2131.8 | 1069.9 | 49.8% |
| 8 | 48 | 1755.1 | 1149.5 | 34.5% |
| 9 | 54 | 1222.7 | 1219.9 | 0.2% |

**Table 10.** Participant A's data were tested with Participant C's learned system in a general road environment.

| Cluster | Run | Loss at Cycle 1 | Loss at Termination | Improvement Rate |
|---|---|---|---|---|
| 1 | 6 | 4517.7 | 1721.9 | 61.9% |
| 2 | 12 | 3799.8 | 1039.6 | 72.6% |
| 3 | 18 | 3854.7 | 2119.6 | 45.0% |
| 4 | 24 | 4077.3 | 1144.5 | 71.9% |
| 5 | 30 | 4263.1 | 1559.3 | 63.4% |
| 6 | 36 | 3620.8 | 1175.2 | 67.5% |
| 7 | 42 | 3855.0 | 1166 | 69.8% |
| 8 | 48 | 4339.0 | 1372.3 | 68.4% |
| 9 | 54 | 3955.4 | 1002.8 | 74.6% |

**Table 11.** Participant B's data were tested with Participant A's learned system in a general road environment.

| Cluster | Run | Loss at Cycle 1 | Loss at Termination | Improvement Rate |
|---|---|---|---|---|
| 1 | 6 | 1989.1 | 980.2 | 50.7% |
| 2 | 12 | 1147.3 | 812.5 | 29.2% |
| 3 | 18 | 2745.4 | 800.7 | 70.8% |
| 4 | 24 | 1986.3 | 892.4 | 55.1% |
| 5 | 30 | 1590.3 | 949.5 | 40.3% |
| 6 | 36 | 2599.2 | 719.5 | 72.3% |
| 7 | 42 | 1507.3 | 784.7 | 47.9% |
| 8 | 48 | 1807.8 | 965.6 | 46.6% |
| 9 | 54 | 1708.7 | 1291.9 | 24.4% |

**Table 12.** Participant B's data were tested with Participant C's learned system in a general road environment.

| Cluster | Run | Loss at Cycle 1 | Loss at Termination | Improvement Rate |
|---|---|---|---|---|
| 1 | 6 | 4639.9 | 2029.1 | 56.3% |
| 2 | 12 | 3487.7 | 1038.5 | 70.2% |
| 3 | 18 | 4939.2 | 2148.1 | 56.5% |
| 4 | 24 | 4896.9 | 1176.0 | 76.0% |
| 5 | 30 | 4295.0 | 1500.2 | 65.1% |
| 6 | 36 | 4164.1 | 1338.6 | 67.9% |
| 7 | 42 | 3208.1 | 1257.7 | 60.8% |
| 8 | 48 | 3888.7 | 1511.3 | 61.1% |
| 9 | 54 | 3880.1 | 1133.9 | 70.8% |

**Table 13.** Participant C's data was tested using Participant A's learned system in a general road environment.

| Cluster | Run | Loss at Cycle 1 | Loss at Termination | Improvement Rate |
|---|---|---|---|---|
| 1 | 6 | 4735.4 | 1102.6 | 76.7% |
| 2 | 12 | 5003.5 | 1676.1 | 66.5% |
| 3 | 18 | 5240.0 | 864.5 | 83.5% |
| 4 | 24 | 4386.8 | 1158.5 | 73.6% |
| 5 | 30 | 5040.4 | 1364.9 | 72.9% |
| 6 | 36 | 5215.3 | 891.3 | 82.9% |
| 7 | 42 | 4759.3 | 773.8 | 83.7% |
| 8 | 48 | 4716.2 | 1099.5 | 76.7% |
| 9 | 54 | 6275.7 | 1768.2 | 71.8% |

**Table 14.** Participant C's data were tested on a general road environment with Participant B's learned system.

| Cluster | Run | Loss at Cycle 1 | Loss at Termination | Improvement Rate |
|---|---|---|---|---|
| 1 | 6 | 4583.8 | 1271.8 | 72.3% |
| 2 | 12 | 5558.3 | 1572.7 | 71.7% |
| 3 | 18 | 6050.3 | 1784.3 | 70.5% |
| 4 | 24 | 5058.9 | 1169.7 | 76.9% |
| 5 | 30 | 6005.6 | 1030.3 | 82.8% |
| 6 | 36 | 6015.4 | 1451.7 | 75.9% |
| 7 | 42 | 4716.2 | 1099.5 | 76.7% |
| 8 | 48 | 4287.0 | 1225.9 | 71.4% |
| 9 | 54 | 5126.3 | 1370.1 | 73.3% |

#### 4.4.2. Different Participants Driving on the Highway

Like the previous experiment, the driver routes were changed to highway driving. We selected nine driving segments from both heavy and light traffic to observe the results of the system running 500 iterations on different drivers' driving segments. From Tables 15–18, it can be observed that the improvement rate on highways is generally lower than that on general roads. This suggests that driving behavior on highways differs from that on general roads. The traffic conditions on the road also influence driving behavior. It was also noted that the initial loss values for highway driving are at least one or two thousand units lower than those for general roads, indicating that highway driving behavior is more straightforward from the beginning and can be adequately handled using the system trained on general road driving.

**Table 15.** Participant A's data in a light traffic environment were tested with Participant B's learned system.

| Cluster | Run | Loss at Cycle 1 | Loss at Termination | Improvement Rate |
|---|---|---|---|---|
| 1 | 6 | 1337.9 | 543.3 | 59.4% |
| 2 | 12 | 968.2 | 823.3 | 15.0% |
| 3 | 18 | 989.4 | 581.4 | 41.2% |
| 4 | 24 | 1144.8 | 701.3 | 38.7% |
| 5 | 30 | 762.5 | 603.3 | 20.9% |
| 6 | 36 | 1541.7 | 783.5 | 49.2% |
| 7 | 42 | 1182.0 | 936.1 | 20.8% |
| 8 | 48 | 1626.5 | 684.8 | 57.9% |
| 9 | 54 | 1656.6 | 684.7 | 58.7% |

**Table 16.** Participant A's data in a heavy traffic environment were tested with Participant B's learned system.

| Cluster | Run | Loss at Cycle 1 | Loss at Termination | Improvement Rate |
|---|---|---|---|---|
| 1 | 6 | 1574.5 | 523.3 | 66.8% |
| 2 | 12 | 972.3 | 687.7 | 29.3% |
| 3 | 18 | 1013.6 | 543.7 | 46.4% |
| 4 | 24 | 1040.0 | 382.0 | 63.3% |
| 5 | 30 | 1196.3 | 842.3 | 29.6% |
| 6 | 36 | 1581.0 | 861.1 | 45.5% |
| 7 | 42 | 1710.5 | 1066.3 | 37.7% |
| 8 | 48 | 2630.3 | 923.4 | 64.9% |
| 9 | 54 | 1529.3 | 864.2 | 43.5% |

**Table 17.** Participant B's data in a light traffic environment were tested with Participant A's learned system.

| Cluster | Run | Loss at Cycle 1 | Loss at Termination | Improvement Rate |
|---|---|---|---|---|
| 1 | 6 | 1316.2 | 672.2 | 48.9% |
| 2 | 12 | 1169.8 | 858.7 | 26.6% |
| 3 | 18 | 1014.8 | 604.2 | 40.5% |
| 4 | 24 | 1337.9 | 378.6 | 71.7% |

Table 17. Cont.

| Cluster | Run | Loss at Cycle 1 | Loss at Termination | Improvement Rate |
|---|---|---|---|---|
| 5 | 30 | 1081.9 | 584.3 | 46.0% |
| 6 | 36 | 951.2 | 567.6 | 40.3% |
| 7 | 42 | 1156.4 | 489.2 | 57.7% |
| 8 | 48 | 1257.6 | 792.2 | 37.0% |
| 9 | 54 | 1697.7 | 750.6 | 55.8% |

Table 18. Participant B's data in a heavy traffic environment were tested with Participant A's learned system.

| Cluster | Run | Loss at Cycle 1 | Loss at Termination | Improvement Rate |
|---|---|---|---|---|
| 1 | 6 | 1214.6 | 877.5 | 27.8% |
| 2 | 12 | 1395.9 | 880.8 | 36.9% |
| 3 | 18 | 674.3 | 455.2 | 32.5% |
| 4 | 24 | 1461.4 | 839.0 | 42.6% |
| 5 | 30 | 1541.7 | 531.2 | 65.5% |
| 6 | 36 | 766.1 | 550.6 | 28.1% |
| 7 | 42 | 718.9 | 512.8 | 28.7% |
| 8 | 48 | 1351.0 | 906.1 | 32.9% |
| 9 | 54 | 1497.5 | 875.8 | 41.5% |

### 4.5. Noise

In this experiment, six driving segments from Participant One driving on general roads were selected, and different levels of noise (1%, 2%, 5%, and 10%) were added to each segment. The aim was to investigate whether the ANM system can detect abnormal behavior in drivers while the vehicle is in motion. As shown in Figure 17, even adding just 1% noise resulted in a significant increase in loss values, which increased further as the noise levels increased. The experimental results indicate that the ANM system can detect abnormal behavior in drivers while the vehicle is in motion.

$$\sigma_{noise} = k \times \sigma_{original} \quad (3)$$

### 4.6. Fatigued Driving

This study sorted out the possible symptoms of driver fatigue from relevant literature, including blurred vision, involuntary nodding, increasing eye closing frequency, longer eye closing time, continuous yawning, facial numbness, slow eye reaction, stiff movements, changing lanes at will, etc. Based on the current settings of this study, this experiment assumes that drivers are prone to three possible fatigue driving conditions: changing lanes at will, eyes wandering and closing, and slow reaction speed. The first case (eyes wandering and closing) tests eye movement information, while the last two instances (switching lanes at will and slow reaction speed) exist mainly to explore the effects caused by abnormal pressure on the hands and feet. The first case is to ask subjects to move and close their eyes while driving deliberately. The primary purpose of this experiment is to observe the impact of changes in eye movement. The second case (switching lanes at will) is simulated by asking the subjects to switch lanes at will many times while driving, while the third case (slow reaction speed) is simulated by asking the subjects to react with slow hand and foot reactions. As before, the settings for all driving environments are the same.

The driving clips collected in this experiment's first, second, and third cases are 40, 43, and 63, respectively. Each case is tested separately in this experiment, and the average value is taken. The average loss obtained in each case is relatively high (please refer to the loss value in Table 19).

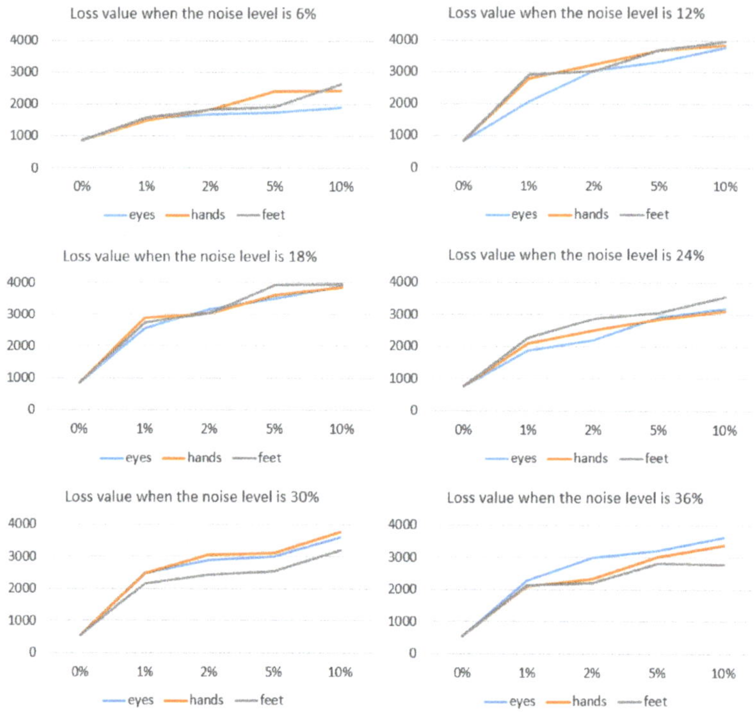


**Figure 17.** Loss values at different noise levels.

**Table 19.** The average loss of each distraction case.

| Distraction Case | No. of Clips | Average Loss |
|---|---|---|
| Eyes wandering and closing | 40 | 3293.1 |
| Switching lanes at will | 43 | 3452.3 |
| Slow reaction speed | 63 | 3457.7 |

In the following, we further explore whether these different distraction phenomena can be further trained through the ANM system. Similar to the second experiment, we took 6 of the 20 learned systems to conduct the above research. For each distraction case, five tests were performed. For each test, we first observed the loss values when the system faced driver distraction and then allowed the system to run for 500 generations to observe the final results. The results are shown in Table 20. After 500 generations of learning, some results can be good, while others still have considerable room for effort. However, looking at these data, there is still room for learning. However, the distraction test is a semi-random variation. There is still considerable room for discussion, or a certain degree of controversy, in trying to draw concrete conclusions from this approach.

**Table 20.** The improvement rate of loss at cycle 1 and cycle 500.

| | | Switching Lanes at Will | | | Eyes Wandering/Closing | | | Slow Reaction Speed | | |
|---|---|---|---|---|---|---|---|---|---|---|
| Clip | Run | Loss at Cycle 1 | Loss at Cycle 500 | Improvement Rate | Loss at Cycle 1 | Loss at Cycle 500 | Improvement Rate | Loss at Cycle 1 | Loss at Cycle 500 | Improvement Rate |
| 1 | 1 | 4232.9 | 795.7 | 81.2% | 3577.9 | 923.7 | 74.2% | 4310.0 | 1231.4 | 71.4% |
| | 2 | 4120.1 | 1020.7 | 75.2% | 3943.0 | 1578.7 | 60.0% | 4777.8 | 826.5 | 82.7% |
| | 3 | 3961.8 | 1549.6 | 60.9% | 3323.1 | 1387.2 | 58.3% | 5024.9 | 1377.2 | 72.6% |
| | 4 | 3657.5 | 1431.5 | 60.9% | 3323.1 | 1387.2 | 58.3% | 4664.9 | 1261.2 | 73.0% |
| | 5 | 4010.4 | 1145.7 | 71.4% | 3099.1 | 1475.3 | 52.4% | 3632.9 | 1009.5 | 72.2% |
| 2 | 1 | 4021.7 | 1001.4 | 75.1% | 3037.9 | 1130.0 | 62.8% | 3091.7 | 1340.9 | 56.6% |
| | 2 | 3919.3 | 1238.5 | 68.4% | 3523.6 | 1492.8 | 57.6% | 4548.3 | 930.1 | 79.6% |
| | 3 | 3331.8 | 1909.3 | 42.7% | 2952.4 | 1450.2 | 50.9% | 3834.2 | 1256.0 | 67.2% |
| | 4 | 2860.8 | 1437.4 | 49.8% | 2439.7 | 1150.1 | 52.9% | 3353.0 | 1513.1 | 54.9% |
| | 5 | 3007.4 | 1585.7 | 47.3% | 2881.3 | 1128.6 | 60.8% | 2617.0 | 991.7 | 62.1% |
| 3 | 1 | 3056.6 | 580.9 | 81.0% | 2468.9 | 864.8 | 65.0% | 3267.7 | 1264.7 | 61.3% |
| | 2 | 3416.3 | 883.8 | 74.1% | 3335.5 | 1423.6 | 57.3% | 4170.0 | 726.5 | 82.6% |
| | 3 | 3640.8 | 1450.1 | 60.2% | 2864.4 | 1564.0 | 45.4% | 4181.6 | 1183.2 | 71.7% |
| | 4 | 2944.6 | 1024.4 | 65.2% | 2791.0 | 1020.3 | 63.4% | 3462.9 | 1455.6 | 58.0% |
| | 5 | 3286.1 | 1068.8 | 67.5% | 2719.3 | 1445.5 | 46.8% | 3142.1 | 1032.5 | 67.1% |
| 4 | 1 | 3225.0 | 462.6 | 85.7% | 3092.1 | 889.9 | 71.2% | 3605.5 | 1228.1 | 65.9% |
| | 2 | 3660.5 | 1122.1 | 69.3% | 3345.9 | 1213.6 | 63.7% | 2969.0 | 965.7 | 67.5% |
| | 3 | 3517.0 | 1383.6 | 60.7% | 3536.9 | 1323.0 | 62.6% | 3791.0 | 1027.1 | 72.9% |
| | 4 | 3467.3 | 1065.5 | 69.3% | 3209.2 | 1093.2 | 65.9% | 3347.2 | 1377.5 | 58.8% |
| | 5 | 3684.7 | 1293.9 | 64.9% | 3186.8 | 1348.3 | 57.7% | 3446.5 | 1125.2 | 67.4% |
| 5 | 1 | 4054.9 | 763.6 | 81.2% | 4384.6 | 1273.8 | 70.9% | 3091.7 | 1340.9 | 56.6% |
| | 2 | 5115.5 | 1367.8 | 73.3% | 4838.1 | 1412.5 | 70.8% | 4548.3 | 930.1 | 79.6% |
| | 3 | 4268.9 | 1324.9 | 69.0% | 4124.7 | 1684.9 | 59.2% | 3834.2 | 1256.0 | 67.2% |
| | 4 | 4150.1 | 1524.5 | 63.3% | 3734.5 | 1173.7 | 68.6% | 3352.0 | 1513.1 | 54.9% |
| | 5 | 4181.0 | 1481.0 | 64.6% | 3445.8 | 1069.2 | 69.0% | 2617.0 | 991.7 | 62.1% |
| 6 | 1 | 2171.6 | 822.2 | 62.1% | 2769.2 | 968.5 | 65.0% | 2939.9 | 1095.4 | 62.7% |
| | 2 | 2616.2 | 1257.0 | 52.0% | 2884.0 | 1458.4 | 49.4% | 3663.4 | 785.0 | 78.6% |
| | 3 | 3182.4 | 1773.5 | 44.3% | 2596.0 | 1515.6 | 41.6% | 4206.4 | 1206.8 | 71.3% |
| | 4 | 2669.5 | 1067.9 | 60.0% | 3018.1 | 1177.5 | 61.0% | 3812.2 | 1082.2 | 71.6% |
| | 5 | 2932.5 | 1128.4 | 61.5% | 2662.9 | 1114.4 | 58.2% | 3126.1 | 816.9 | 73.9% |

## 5. Discussion

The computer industry is growing significantly as Moore's Law continues to ferment in recent years. However, the performance of the hardware could be improved by the functionality established by the original developers. In contrast, software systems can be used infinitely according to the user's imagination. The two play a complementary role, meaning they must complement each other for the entire computer system to achieve the state of truth, goodness, and beauty.

Unfortunately, current software design is geared towards programmable design. Under this premise, making programming more convenient is a goal people often consider, and structured design has become a method people usually use. The thinking of structured programming is to use appropriate symbols to represent the ideas people want to express and how to operate these designed symbols (so-called algorithms). When the entire system design moves towards programmable structural design, it will face a severe problem. When a specific function needs to be changed, even slightly, it may need to be significantly changed. From another perspective, when an existing system is created with minor changes, the entire system may become completely unsuitable (for example, modification of some initial settings). A feasible thinking is to put features conducive to malleability into software design thinking. We all know that biological systems are highly self-modifying. The ANM system used in this study captures some of the characteristics of organisms that are conducive to modification and implements them in the design of software systems.

From the perspective of building a customized intelligent fatigued driving detection system, biological-like adaptability is undoubtedly an ideal goal. This is because it must be able to meet different needs, such as various groups of people. Under this premise, an intelligent system must have rich learning capabilities, conduct long-term continuous problem solving of complex problems, and have a considerable degree of plasticity to adapt to different needs. The difficulty is that everyone's driving habits are entirely different. Therefore, establishing a fatigue detection system suitable for mass popularization is still a long way away. Customized design is an inevitable trend. Intelligent assistance systems must find the best answer and adjust at any time according to the user's needs in a self-corrective manner. In addition, the system must have a certain level of noise tolerance to cope with transient changes in user movements while operating in a disturbed environment.

This research integrates information obtained from three sensing devices: eye movement, finger pressure, and plantar pressure. It uses an autonomous learning architecture to build a customized fatigued driving detection system. Then, we explore its feasibility for fatigued driving detection through different experiments. First, we verified that the ANM system can be used to learn and classify driving clips. Then, we verified that we could judge whether the driver was fatigued by a series of driving behaviors (rather than a single momentary behavior). Finally, we verify the results under the assumption that drivers are experiencing three different distractions. The authors would like to add that the current stage of this research emphasizes functional exploration, that is, the feasibility of establishing an intelligent system that integrates eye, hand, and foot sensing. It is still different from the actual real driving situation.

The current research on intelligent fatigue driving detection includes two lines of directions. One is the fatigue driving sensor, and the other is the intelligent system. Regarding the studies on sensors, some studies focus on the judgment of the movements of the eyes, hands, and feet, while some focus on the analysis of the force of the hands and feet. However, whether the methods performed are action discrimination or force analysis, one of the limitations of research in this area is how to process sensor data from different sources in a timely or even synchronous manner, and another limitation is how to process sensor data from different sources appropriately. In the data synchronization processing part, this research is still at the stage of functional exploration. Therefore, the entire research is still limited to manual processing in the data collection part. However, the ANM system used in this study has an autonomous learning function in the information integration part. During the learning process, it can discover each information source's role in exploring different types of fatigue driving. However, this research still has limitations: it requires significant computer computing time to operate the entire ANM system with current computer hardware. Note that the concept of ANM system construction is a multi-layered competitive network. The information processing within each neuron can be comparable with that of the network architecture. We use discontinuous event processing to simulate such a multi-layer network architecture wherein each neural activity change is an event. In this way, we can make the system produce different timing processing dynamics (that is, converting from a series of time and space information to another series of time and space information). If we plan to use a sequential processing computer to simulate the entire system dynamics, it will require a lot of computing resources. Because of this, the information-processing capabilities that this study can present are also limited to some extent. In the future, when the hardware shows considerable growth, we can increase the dynamics within neurons (for example, by growing the essential components within the information-processing unit and the relationship between each other) or increase the processing methods of operating control neurons. Future research in this area can improve the integration of facial expressions and head information. Many scholars have made considerable research results in this area. In this way, we can make the system produce different timing processing dynamics.

On the other hand, this study considers further integrating the information of the electroencephalograph (this research team has obtained preliminary experimental results in this regard, but it has yet to be mature at this stage to the extent that it can be published publicly). In terms of algorithms, the system used in this study should make additional use of current deep learning technology (long- and short-term memory) to increase the system's functionality in a Hebbian manner (that is, converting a series of spatio-temporal information into another series of spatio-temporal information). If we plan to use a sequential processing computer to simulate the dynamics of the entire system, it will require a lot of computing resources. Because of this, the information-processing capabilities that this study can present are also limited. To a certain extent, in the future, when the hardware shows considerable growth, the limitation of information-processing capabilities that the ANM system can simulate will increase (for example, by increasing the essential components inside the information-processing unit and their relationship to each other); alternatively, increasing the processing methods of operating control neurons can improve the integration of facial outcomes.

## 6. Conclusions

Fatigued driving is a problem that most people will face, and this problem usually occurs without conscious awareness or through the driver not paying attention. If a customized intelligent assistance system can be built to assist driving from people's sensory systems, it is generally believed to help people drive more or less safely. Current development in this area is mainly accomplished by integrating deep learning, image processing, biomedicine, human factors engineering, and other technologies. In addition to driving fatigue, workplace fatigue caused by high-risk workplaces is similar. Most methods are to establish intelligent physiological fatigue detection systems based on physiological characteristics such as personal faces, eyes, mouth, and hand movements. However, everyone's driving behavior differs, and determining how to meet different customized needs is a severe issue. Intelligent systems play an essential bridge role in customization.

In response to the customization issue, the ANM system proposed in this study has more processing of the internal information of neurons than the general deep learning technology. The former emphasizes processing information within neurons, while the latter emphasizes processing information between neurons. Again, we emphasize that the ANM system can also include information processing between neurons. Under this premise, the ANM system in this study can also use the internal dynamics of a single neuron to express information processing between neurons. In other words, a single neuron in the ANM system is enough to handle the information processing that a traditional neural network can represent. Most importantly, we establish the information-processing activities inside neurons by capturing the characteristics of gradual changes in biological structure/function. The experimental results of this study prove its permanent learning ability and sufficient adaptability.

We indeed use simulations to generate distraction data. Undoubtedly, there is still a considerable difference between these data and the data generated by the driver's actual fatigue. In other words, the simulation data used in this study cannot accurately reflect the actual behavioral information of fatigue. However, this study emphasizes that collecting fatigue driving data from actual drivers is challenging. Undoubtedly, it is not only hazardous but also costly. Secondly, another insurmountable problem is sorting out the so-called "drowsy driving episodes" from a continuous period of driving behavior. It is a controversial issue, as judging "drowsy driving episodes could be subjective. In particular, it is more difficult for everyone to have different driving behaviors. Regarding this issue, the purpose of this study is not to immediately apply the entire system to fatigue driving detection but to prove whether the learning system used in this study has a self-correction mechanism for continuous learning. When the whole system matures, we can transplant it to actual driving situations and establish a personalized fatigue driving detection system through long-term personal use by drivers. In the current experimental stage, this study uses a series of simulation aspects to gradually fill the gap between simulated data and actual data during the experimental stage.

This study explores the establishment of a non-intrusive system. It allows us to research different topics without harming or affecting users. Although this study uses a simple information-processing system that integrates eye movement, finger bending/pressure, and plantar pressure sensing, the results obtained through this study can prove that in the future, through better eyes, hand, and foot sensing equipment, we can build a state-of-the-art, intelligent, customized fatigued driving detection system. It can even be developed into a simple and portable device or combined with a cloud server to calculate and analyze data, significantly increasing the possibility of creating a customized intelligent system.

**Author Contributions:** Conceptualization, J.-C.C. and Y.-Z.C.; methodology, J.-C.C.; software, J.-C.C.; validation, J.-C.C. and Y.-Z.C.; formal analysis, J.-C.C. and Y.-Z.C.; investigation, J.-C.C. and Y.-Z.C.; resources, J.-C.C.; data curation, J.-C.C. and Y.-Z.C.; writing—original draft preparation, J.-C.C. and Y.-Z.C.; writing—review and editing, J.-C.C.; visualization, J.-C.C.; supervision, J.-C.C.; project administration, J.-C.C.; funding acquisition, J.-C.C. All authors have read and agreed to the published version of the manuscript.

**Funding:** This study was partly funded by the Taiwan Ministry of Science and Technology (Grant MOST 110-2221-E-224-041-MY3).

**Institutional Review Board Statement:** This study was conducted according to the guidelines of the Declaration of Helsinki and approved by the Human Research Ethics Committee of the National Cheng Kung University (Approval No.: NCKU HREC-E-110-318-2; date: 9 August 2021).

**Informed Consent Statement:** Written informed consent has been obtained from the participants of the experiments to publish this paper.

**Data Availability Statement:** The data can be accessed found through the following link: https://drive.google.com/drive/folders/1Jlh9OHuIC5JzFMqda642x4fPdqdEYRJZ?usp=drive_link (accessed on 1 August 2024).

**Conflicts of Interest:** The authors have no conflicts of interest.

## References


1. Sikander, G.; Anwar, S. Driver Fatigue Detection Systems: A Review. *IEEE Trans. Intell. Transp. Syst.* **2019**, *20*, 2339–2352. [CrossRef]
2. Kamti, M.K.; Iqbal, R. Evolution of driver fatigue detection techniques—A review from 2007 to 2021. *Transp. Res. Record.* **2022**, *2676*, 485–507. [CrossRef]
3. Němcová, A.; Svozilová, V.; Bucsuházy, K.; Smíšek, R.; Mézl, M.; Hesko, B.; Belak, M.J.; Bilík, M.; Maxera, P.; Seitl, M.; et al. Multimodal features for detection of driver stress and Fatigue: Review. *IEEE Trans. Intell. Transp. Syst.* **2020**, *22*, 3214–3233. [CrossRef]
4. Kaplan, S.; Guvensan, M.A.; Yavuz, A.G.; Karalurt, Y. Driver behavior analysis for safe driving: A survey. *IEEE Trans. Intell. Transp. Systems.* **2015**, *16*, 3017–3032. [CrossRef]
5. Abbas, Q.; Alsheddy, A. Driver fatigue detection systems using multi-sensors, smartphone, and cloud-based computing platforms: A comparative analysis. *Sensors* **2020**, *21*, 56. [CrossRef]
6. Fu, R.; Wang, H.; Zhao, W. Dynamic driver fatigue detection using hidden Markov model in actual driving conditions. *Expert Syst. Appl.* **2016**, *63*, 397–411. [CrossRef]
7. Lee, B.G.; Park, J.; Pu, C.; Chung, W. Smart watch-based driver vigilance indicator with kernel-fuzzy-C-Means-Wavelet method. *IEEE Sens. J.* **2016**, *16*, 242–253. [CrossRef]
8. Foy, H.J.; Chapman, P. Mental workload is reflected in driver behavior, physiology, eye movements, and prefrontal cortex activation. *Appl. Ergon.* **2018**, *73*, 90–99. [CrossRef] [PubMed]
9. Kuwahara, A.; Nishikawa, K.; Hirakawa, R.; Kawano, H.; Nakatoh, Y. Eye fatigue estimation using blink detection based on eye aspect ratio mapping. *Cogn. Robot.* **2022**, *2*, 50–59. [CrossRef]
10. Yang, Z.; Ren, H. Feature extraction and simulation of EEG Signals during exercise-induced Fatigue. *IEEE Access* **2019**, *7*, 46389–46398. [CrossRef]
11. Chui, K.T.; Tsang, K.F.; Chi, H.R.; Ling, B.W.; Wu, C.K. An accurate ECG-based transportation safety drowsiness detection scheme. *IEEE Trans. Ind. Inform.* **2016**, *12*, 1438–1452. [CrossRef]
12. Balasubramanian, V.; Adalarasu, K. EMG-based analysis of change in muscle activity during simulated driving. *J. Bodyw. Mov. Ther.* **2007**, *11*, 151–158. [CrossRef]
13. Yi, Y.; Zhang, H.; Zhang, W.; Yuan, Y.; Li, C. Fatigue working detection based on facial multi-feature fusion. *IEEE Sens. J.* **2023**, *23*, 5956–5961. [CrossRef]
14. Yan, C.; Coenen, F.; Yue, Y.; Yang, X.; Zhang, B. Video-based classification of driving behavior using a hierarchical classification system with multiple features. *Int. J. Pattern Recognit. Artif. Intel.* **2016**, *30*, 1650010:1–1650010:33. [CrossRef]
15. Xiao, W.; Liu, H.; Ma, Z.; Chen, W.; Sun, C.; Shi, B. Fatigued driving recognition method based on multi-scale facial landmark detector. *Electronics* **2022**, *11*, 4103. [CrossRef]
16. Fang, H.; Li, J.; Tang, H.; Xu, C.; Zhu, H.; Xiu, Y.; Li, Y.; Lu, C. AlphaPose: Whole-body regional multi-person pose estimation and tracking in real-Time. *IEEE Trans. Pattern Anal. Mach. Intell.* **2022**, *45*, 7157–7173. [CrossRef]

17. Savaş, B.K.; Becerikli, Y. Real-time driver fatigue detection system based on multi-task ConNN. *IEEE Access* **2020**, *8*, 12491–12498. [CrossRef]
18. Ansari, S.; Du, H.; Naghdy, F.; Stirling, D. Automatic driver cognitive fatigue detection based on upper body posture variations. *Expert Syst. Appl.* **2022**, *203*, 117568. [CrossRef]
19. Chen, J.; Yan, M.; Zhu, F.; Xu, J.; Li, H.L.; Sun, X. Fatigued driving detection method based on combination of BP neural network and time cumulative effect. *Sensors* **2022**, *22*, 4717. [CrossRef]
20. Shulei, W.; Zihang, S.; Huandong, C.; Yuchen, Z.; Yang, Z.; Jinbiao, C.; Qiaona, M. The road rage detection algorithm is based on fatigued driving and facial feature point location. *Neural Comput. Appl.* **2022**, *34*, 12361–12371. [CrossRef]
21. Shi, L.-C.; Lu, B.-L. Eye-based vigilance estimation using extreme learning machines. *Neurocomputing* **2013**, *102*, 135–143. [CrossRef]
22. D'orazio, T.; Leo, M.; Distante, A. Eye detection in face images for a driver vigilance system. In Proceedings of the IEEE Intelligent Vehicles Symposium, Parma, Italy, 14–17 June 2004; pp. 95–98.
23. Cheng, W.; Wang, X.; Mao, B. A multi-feature fusion algorithm for driver fatigue detection based on a lightweight convolutional neural network. *Visual Comput.* **2024**, *40*, 2419–2441. [CrossRef]
24. Zhou, C.; Zhao, Y.; Liu, S.; Zhao, Y.; Li, X.; Cheng, C. Research on driver facial fatigue detection based on Yolov8 model. In Proceedings of the 5th International Conference on Information Science, Parallel and Distributed Systems (ISPDS 2024), Guangzhou, China, 31 May–2 June 2024. [CrossRef]
25. Soulmana, B.; Boukebbab, S.; Boulahlib, M.S. Hand position on steering wheel during fatigue and sleepiness case: Driving simulator. *Adv. Transp. Stud.* **2021**, *53*, 68–84.
26. Desai, A.V.; Haque, M.A. Vigilance monitoring for operator safety: A simulation study on highway driving. *J. Saf. Res.* **2006**, *37*, 139–147. [CrossRef]
27. Chieh, T.C.; Mustafa, M.M.; Hussain, A.; Zahedi, E.; Majlis, B. Driver fatigue detection using steering grip force. In Proceedings of the IEEE Student Conference on Research and Development, Putrajaya, Malaysia, 25–26 August 2003; pp. 45–48.
28. Eskandarian, A.; Mortazavi, A. Evaluation of a smart algorithm for commercial vehicle driver drowsiness detection. In Proceedings of the 2007 IEEE Intelligent Vehicles Symposium, Istanbul, Turkey, 13–15 June 2007; pp. 553–559.
29. Chen, J.-C. A study of the continuous optimization problem using a wood robot controlled by a biologically motivated system. *J. Dyn. Syst. Meas. Control.* **2015**, *137*, 071008. [CrossRef]
30. Chen, J.-C. Bridging the finger-action gap between hand patients and healthy people in daily life with a biomimetic System. *Biomimetics* **2023**, *8*, 76. [CrossRef] [PubMed]
31. Chen, J.-C. Using artificial neuro-molecular system in robotic arm motion control—Taking simulation of rehabilitation as an example. *Sensors* **2022**, *22*, 2584. [CrossRef] [PubMed]
32. Conrad, M. *Adaptability, the Significance of Variability from Molecule to Ecosystem*; Plenum Press: New York, NY, USA, 1983.
33. Darzacq, X.; Tjian, R. Weak multivalent biomolecular interactions: A strength versus numbers tug of war with implications for phase partitioning. *RNA* **2022**, *28*, 48–51. [CrossRef]

algorithms

MDPI

Article

# Optimization of Gene Selection for Cancer Classification in High-Dimensional Data Using an Improved African Vultures Algorithm

**Mona G. Gafar [1,2,*], Amr A. Abohany [3,†], Ahmed E. Elkhouli [4,†] and Amr A. Abd El-Mageed [5,†]**

[1] Department of Computer Engineering and Information, College of Engineering in Wadi Alddawasir, Prince Sattam bin Abdulaziz University, Kharj 16278, Saudi Arabia
[2] Machine Learning and Information Retrieval Department, Artificial Intelligence, Kafrelsheikh University, Kafrelsheikh 33511, Egypt
[3] Faculty of Computers and Information, Kafrelsheikh University, Kafrelsheikh 33511, Egypt; amrabohany8@gmail.com
[4] Department of Biomedical Engineering, Faculty of Electrical Engineering, Menofia University, Menofia 32951, Egypt; eng.elkholy.ahmed@gmail.com
[5] Department of Information Systems, Sohag University, Sohag 82511, Egypt; amr.atef@commerce.sohag.edu.eg
* Correspondence: m.gafar@psau.edu.sa or dr.mona.gamal85@gmail.com
† These authors contributed equally to this work.

**Abstract:** This study presents a novel method, termed RBAVO-DE (Relief Binary African Vultures Optimization based on Differential Evolution), aimed at addressing the Gene Selection (GS) challenge in high-dimensional RNA-Seq data, specifically the rnaseqv2 lluminaHiSeq rnaseqv2 un edu Level 3 RSEM genes normalized dataset, which contains over 20,000 genes. RNA Sequencing (RNA-Seq) is a transformative approach that enables the comprehensive quantification and characterization of gene expressions, surpassing the capabilities of micro-array technologies by offering a more detailed view of RNA-Seq gene expression data. Quantitative gene expression analysis can be pivotal in identifying genes that differentiate normal from malignant tissues. However, managing these high-dimensional dense matrix data presents significant challenges. The RBAVO-DE algorithm is designed to meticulously select the most informative genes from a dataset comprising more than 20,000 genes and assess their relevance across twenty-two cancer datasets. To determine the effectiveness of the selected genes, this study employs the Support Vector Machine (SVM) and k-Nearest Neighbor (*k*-NN) classifiers. Compared to binary versions of widely recognized meta-heuristic algorithms, RBAVO-DE demonstrates superior performance. According to Wilcoxon's rank-sum test, with a 5% significance level, RBAVO-DE achieves up to 100% classification accuracy and reduces the feature size by up to 98% in most of the twenty-two cancer datasets examined. This advancement underscores the potential of RBAVO-DE to enhance the precision of gene selection for cancer research, thereby facilitating more accurate and efficient identification of key genetic markers.

**Keywords:** RNA sequencing; gene selection; high dimensionality; meta-heuristic algorithms; African vultures algorithm; differential evolution; relief technique

## 1. Introduction

Deoxyribonucleic Acid (DNA) makes up our genetic code, containing the recipe for our existence. Although every cell has the same DNA, each tissue structure is unique and serves a distinct purpose. The RNA transcription mechanism determines which genes in a cell are active, enabling RNA to be transformed into proteins responsible for the cell's structure and functionality [1]. We analyze RNA-Seq gene expression data (GED) to determine genetic changes and evaluate disease biomarkers. Differential expression analysis identifies quantitative distinctions in gene expression, allowing us to categorize genes whose expression changes under various conditions. This method helps us understand illnesses and find ways to manage them. Gene expression profiling technologies have significantly developed over the years [2].

Two popular techniques are micro-array, which uses a hybridization-based approach, and RNA-Seq, which is based on next-generation sequencing. These technologies have demonstrated their value in advancing our understanding of gene expression [3]. Notable studies, such as those by Chen et al. [4] and Nunez et al. [5], have highlighted the potential of these techniques, while Wang et al. [6] have provided valuable insights into the RNA-Seq approach.

The two methods under consideration serve the purpose of quantifying gene expression for classification and statistical investigation. This paper has chosen the quantification data obtained through the next-generation sequencing (NGS)-based RNA-Seq approach because it offers more accuracy in detecting RNA quantification levels compared to micro-array data [7]. RNA-Seq has overcome several limitations of micro-array analysis, such as dependence on prior sequencing knowledge, which restricted the detection range [8,9]. Unlike micro-arrays, RNA-Seq does not require any previous knowledge and significantly expands the dynamic detection range. This enhancement improves the accuracy of results and enables the identification of a comprehensive set of genes, providing a precise understanding of disease biomarkers. As a result, RNA-Seq has emerged as a potent tool for researchers, offering valuable insights into the underlying molecular mechanisms of various diseases [10].

The "dimensionality curse" [11] has become a common challenge in contemporary times owing to the abundance of available data. This has caused a surge in the development of feature selection (FS) techniques and algorithms. FS algorithms can be classified into four distinct methods: filter, wrapper, embedded, and hybrid [12,13]. These approaches aim to identify the most informative features that can distinguish between different classes. In our case, we are concerned with identifying the genes linked to tumors.

The filter approach is a widely used technique in FS that involves evaluating the relevance of individual genes based on statistical scores. This method is known for its high accuracy in selecting the most satisfactory group of genes. Nevertheless, the filter approach has some limitations, as functioning on each gene individually ignores the interrelationships between genes, which can result in a local optima issue [14]. It is worth noting that the filter approach can be categorized into two sub-types—univariate and multivariate—with the latter considering the correlations between genes. Some examples of the filter approach include Relief [15], Fisher score [16], *t*-test [17], and information gain [18].

The wrapper method investigates all feasible gene subsets to test and create a subset of genes to determine their implications. A specific classifier is employed to determine the outcome of each subset, and the categorization technique is used multiple times for each assessment. Compared to the filter approach, the wrapper approach delivers superior performance by using a categorization technique that directs the learning procedure. However, this method requires substantial time and computational resources, especially when dealing with large-scale data [19].

Meta-heuristic methods (MHMs) are high-level heuristics used in mathematical optimization and computer science to find satisfactory solutions to optimization problems when information is imperfect or resources are limited [20]. MHMs sample a subset of solutions, making them useful for various optimization issues due to their few assumptions about the problem [21]. However, they do not guarantee globally optimal solutions. Many MHMs employ stochastic optimization, meaning the solution is based on random variables generated during the process [22].

Meta-heuristic methods (MHMs) are more practical than traditional iterative methods and optimization algorithms because they can explore a broader range of possible solutions. Consequently, MHMs have become a preferred strategy for solving optimization problems [23]. Numerous research papers have demonstrated that among the different wrapper methods, MHMs are well suited to address the feature selection (FS) issue. Stochastic methods, including MHMs, can produce optimal or near-optimal results quickly. They offer benefits such as flexibility, self-management without detailed mathematical properties, and the ability to assess numerous outcomes simultaneously. Various MHMs have recently been developed to solve the FS problem, providing reliable near-optimal solutions at significantly reduced computational costs [24].

Embedded FS methods utilize a learning technique to select appropriate genes that interact with the classification process. This method combines the FS technique as part of the learning model. The learning algorithm is trained with an initial attribute subset to estimate a measure for evaluating the rank values of attributes [25]. The ultimate goal is to decrease the computation time for reclassifying different subsets by incorporating the FS stage into the training process. Some techniques in this approach perform feature weighting based on regularization models with objective functions that minimize fitting errors while enforcing feature coefficients to be small or precisely zero. Examples of embedded methods are the First-Order Inductive Learner (FOIL) rule-based feature subset selection algorithm and SVM based on Recursive Feature Elimination (SVM-RFE) [26].

The hybrid method is a well-crafted technique that amalgamates the filter and wrapper methods to leverage the strengths of each. This approach begins with a filter that reduces the feature space dimensionality, generating multiple subsets with intermediate complexity. Subsequently, a wrapper is employed as a learning technique to choose the most suitable candidate subset [27]. The hybrid approach integrates the accuracy of wrappers and the efficiency of filters, resulting in an optimal methodology [28,29].

### 1.1. Motivation and Contributions

An effective global meta-heuristic optimization algorithm is presented in this paper, which is called the African Vultures Optimization (AVO) algorithm [30], which imitates the living and eating habits of African vultures. The proposed algorithm consists of four basic phases: population division into three groups—the best solution, the second-best solution, and the remaining solutions; famine-level measurement to formulate a mathematical model for the vultures' exploitation, exploration, and transfer; exploration of vultures employing two strategies to allow vultures to cover large distances over extended periods to find food at random sites; and exploitation of vultures involving two sub-phases. Two distinct strategies are used in the first sub-phase: siege fight for strong vultures and rotational flight, which forms a spiral activity between the outstanding vulture and the rest. Two strategies are utilized in the second sub-phase: assembling vultures around the food source and a hostile siege fight, where vultures become more aggressive and attempt to steal food left behind by healthy vultures.

This study proposes an enhanced binary variant of the AVO technique, namely the RBAVO-DE technique, which is a productive approach that demonstrates accurate performance in handling the GS problem. At first, there is a high possibility that the recommended technique will steer clear of local optima and accomplish sufficient examination precision, quick convergence, and improved stability. Compared to recent MHMs, the proposed RBAVO-DE technique achieves enhanced efficacy by producing optimal or substantially optimal solutions for many of the analyzed situations. The Relief algorithm is utilized to identify only the related features to produce the final classification dataset. RBAVO-DE combines the Relief algorithm with the DE approach to increase exploration capability and obtain the best results within the solution space via repetitions. It also utilizes a transfer function to transform real position values into binary values. The RBAVO-DE approach makes sense in GS because it is simple to comprehend and implement, can deal with various optimization problems, produces valuable results in an acceptable amount of time, requires less computing power, and uses a small number of control parameters. This paper's primary contributions are as follows:

- Level 3 data based on next-generation sequencing (RNA-Seq) have been pre-processed.

- The ability of the proposed AVO meta-heuristic algorithm to address the GS problem has not been investigated, as RNA-Seq GED has never been used with the AVO algorithm.
- To construct a binary version known as the RBAVO-DE algorithm, the AVO algorithm is altered and recreated.
- The proposed RBAVO-DE algorithm combines the binary variant of the AVO with a Relief approach and DE to improve the exploration ability of the search space and enhance the achieved optimal results.
- The proposed RBAVO-DE algorithm is applied to RNA-Seq GED for the first time.
- Several performance indicators, including average fitness, classification accuracy, number of selected genes, precision, recall, and F1-score, are used to assess the outcomes.
- A comparison is made between the impact of the presented RBAVO-DE algorithm, employing the two recommended ML classifiers (SVM and *k*-NN), and other algorithms in the literature.
- Twenty-two distinct cancer datasets are used to assess the proposed RBAVO-DE method, and the results are shown.
- The chosen genes are investigated using biomarkers associated with cancer.

### 1.2. Structure

This paper is structured into five main sections. Section 2 reviews previous research on FS using RNA-Seq GED. This is followed by Section 3, which offers an in-depth discussion of the RBAVO-DE algorithm, an enhanced version of AVO, including its parameters for addressing GS. Section 4 showcases the experimental findings compared to several recent MHMs. Lastly, Section 6 concludes this study and proposes avenues for future investigation.

## 2. Related Works

In this section, we discuss the literature that focuses on the methods researchers use to classify RNA-Seq GED, which typically has high dimensionality. To achieve optimal performance of classification methods, it is crucial to disregard irrelevant and unrelated genes; hence, selecting appropriate genes is a vital stage before utilizing ML and deep learning (DL) techniques [31] or any other classification techniques. In this regard, we have explored some relevant papers in this domain to accomplish the objective of RNA-Seq categorization for cancer identification.

Yaqoob et al. [32] introduced a cutting-edge technique for GS known as the Sine-Cosine–Cuckoo Search Algorithm (SCCSA), a hybrid method tailored to function alongside established ML models such as SVM. This innovative GS algorithm was evaluated using a breast cancer benchmark dataset, where its performance was meticulously analyzed and compared with other GS methodologies. To refine the selection of features, the minimum Redundancy Maximum Relevance method was initially applied as a preliminary filtering step. Subsequently, the hybrid SCCSA approach was deployed to further improve and fine-tune the GS process. The final stage involved using the SVM classifier to classify the dataset based on the selected genes. Considering the critical importance of GS in decoding complex biological datasets, SCCSA emerges as a crucial asset for the classification of cancer-related datasets.

Joshi et al. [33] introduced an innovative optimization strategy named PSO-CS integrated with DL for brain tumor classification. This method enhances the efficiency of the Particle Swarm Optimization (PSO) technique by incorporating the Cuckoo Search (CS) algorithm, optimizing the classification process. Following this optimization, PSO-CS utilizes DL to classify GED related to brain tumors, identifying various classes associated with specific tumors alongside the PSO-CS optimization method. By integrating the PSO-CS technique with DL, it significantly outperformed other DL and ML models regarding classification accuracy, as evidenced by various performance measures.

Mahto et al. [34] unveiled a groundbreaking approach for cancer classification through an integrated method based on CS-SMO (CS and Spider Monkey Optimization) for GS. Initially, the fitness function of the Spider Monkey Optimization (SMO) algorithm is modified using the CS algorithm. This modification leverages the strengths of both MHMs to identify a subset of genes capable of predicting cancer at an early stage. To further refine the accuracy of the CS-SMO algorithm, a pre-processing step, MRMR, is employed to reduce the complexity of cancer gene expression datasets. Subsequently, these gene subsets are processed using DL to classify different cancer types. The efficacy of the CS-SMO approach coupled with DL was evaluated using eight benchmark micro-array gene expression datasets for cancer, examining its performance across various measures. The CS-SMO method integrated with DL demonstrated superior classification accuracy across all examined large-scale gene expression datasets for cancer, outperforming existing DL and ML models.

Neggaz et al. [35] introduced an improved version of the manta ray foraging optimization, called MRFO-SC, which used trigonometric operators inspired by the sine-cosine (SC) algorithm to handle the GS issue. The $k$-NN model was used for gene-set selection. In addition, the statistical significance of the MRFO-SC was evaluated using Wilcoxon's rank-sum test at a 5% significance level. The results were evaluated and compared with some recent MHMs. The comparison and experimental results confirmed the effective performance of the proposed MRFO-SC on high- and low-dimensional benchmark datasets by obtaining the greatest classification accuracy on 85% of the GS benchmark datasets.

Lyu et al. [36] explored cancer biomarkers by focusing on genes' significance in their impact on classification. They followed a two-phase approach—data pre-processing and utilizing a convolutional neural network—to classify the type of tumor. In the second phase, they created heat maps for each category to identify genes related to pixels with the highest intensities in the heat maps. They then evaluated the selected genes' pathways. During pre-processing, they removed the levels of gene expression that had not been modified during the GS phase, using a variance threshold of 1.19, which decreased the number of genes from 19,531 to 10,381. The final classification accuracy obtained was 95.59, which is good but could still be improved using a more effective FS methodology to further decrease data dimensionality.

Khalifa et al. [37] built on the aforementioned paper [36]. The focus of their study was on five types of cancer data: Uterine Corpus Endometrial Carcinoma (UCEC), Lung Squamous Cell Carcinoma (LUSC), Lung Adenocarcinoma (LUAD), Kidney Renal Clear Cell Carcinoma (KIRC), and Breast Invasive Carcinoma (BRCA). The benchmark dataset used for the study comprised 2086 records and 972 attributes. Each record provided detailed sample information, while each attribute included the RNA-Seq values for a specific gene, represented as RPKM (Reads Per Kilobase per Million) [38]. The researchers employed a mixed approach using binary PSO with the decision trees (BPSO-DT) method to pre-process the data. Out of 971 attributes, 615 were selected as the best attributes of RNA-SEquation The proposed method achieved an overall testing classification accuracy of 96.90%, as demonstrated by the suggested outcomes and evaluation measures used.

Xiao et al. [39] assessed their methodology using three RNA-Seq datasets: Stomach Adenocarcinoma (STAD), BRCA, and LUAD. Their approach relied on DL techniques, wherein they employed five classifiers and subsequently utilized the DL technique to ensemble each output of the five classifiers. This led to an improvement in the classification accuracy of all the predictions, with the BRCA dataset achieving 98.4% accuracy, STAD achieving 98.78% accuracy, and LUAD achieving 99.20% accuracy.

Liu et al. [40] used micro-array data and a hybrid approach to address the problem. Unlike the previously mentioned papers, they studied each cancer class separately. To assess performance, they employed four gene benchmarks related to small round blue cell tumors, colon cancer, lung cancer, and leukemia. Their proposed method used Relief as the pre-processing technique to eliminate genes with a lower correlation with the specific cancer class, followed by PSO as the search technique. Finally, they employed the SVM model to evaluate the classification accuracy of the selected subset of genes and obtain the conclusive optimum gene subset for each cancer type.

Based on the existing research, it seems that most studies using RNA-Seq GED are still in their early stages, with researchers attempting to implement and test various ideas in this promising area. While the literature contains a plethora of experiments employing multiple techniques, such as FS and DL recent methods, no single technique is perfect due to the high dimensionality of RNA-Seq GED. FS of RNA-Seq GED plays a crucial role in determining the relationship between a gene and its category. It is a critical pre-processing task for validating gene biomarkers of cancer and overcoming the dimensionality curse. Consequently, this study aims to introduce a new wrapper approach, the RBAVO-DE algorithm, and apply it to RNA-Seq data for the first time. It also compares the proposed algorithm's effectiveness with that of other FS techniques.

## 3. Proposed RBAVO-DE for GS

An improved variant of AVO known as RBAVO-DE is proposed in this paper to discover the smallest relevant gene subsets from the classification process and to disregard irrelevant genes. RBAVO-DE utilizes a Relief-based binary AVO algorithm combined with the DE technique. RBAVO-DE's primary feature is its ability to maximize accuracy while utilizing the fewest features possible. The proposed RBAVO-DE consists of two primary steps. First, there is a pre-processing step in which the Relief algorithm is used to determine which features are significant by assigning each feature a weight and then removing the features that are irrelevant and have the lowest weights. In the second step, the binary AVO algorithm and the DE technique are applied to identify the more pertinent and unique features. The AVO algorithm is prone to the local optimum trap when handling large-scale problems. The AVO algorithm incorporates the DE technique to prevent this.

The proposed RBAVO-DE algorithm for tackling the GS strategy requires applying the Relief algorithm, initializing, position boosting using the AVO algorithm, binary conversion, fitness appraisal, and integration with DE. The following subsections explain these steps.

### *3.1. Applying the Relief Algorithm for Feature Filtration*

This step aims to pre-process the population using the Relief algorithm [41], which is considered a fast, easy, and efficient filtering technique for finding features related to one another. This algorithm's primary goal is to find characteristics that differentiate sample values and group similar samples close together. As a result, the method depends on the weighted ranking of features, where a feature with a higher weight indicates better classification performance.

After choosing a sample randomly, the Relief algorithm examines two different kinds of closest samples: near-hit samples, which are associated with samples from the same class, and near-miss samples, which are associated with samples from other classes. The near-hit and near-miss values can be used to determine the features' weights. To assess the importance in the classification process, the features' weights are arranged from most significant to least significant. Finally, the features with the most significant weights are selected. The following formula can be used to determine the weight $W$ for feature $A$:

$$W_A = \sum_{j=1}^{N} \left(x_A^j - NM(x^j)_A\right)^2 - \left(x_A^j - NH(x^j)_A\right)^2. \tag{1}$$

where $W_A$ denotes the weight of feature $A$, $x_A^j$ denotes the value of feature $A$ for data $x^j$, and N denotes the number of samples. The nearest data points to $x^j$ in the same or different classes are $NH(x^j)$ and $NM(x^j)$.

The Relief algorithm narrows its focus to only the necessary features and minimizes the search area to help the AVO algorithm find better features more quickly.

### 3.2. Initializing the Population

The proposed BAVO algorithm starts by randomly generating a population of $N$ positions. A vector of dimensions $D$ equivalent to the number of features in the original dataset describes each position as a possible solution at its constrained lower and upper bounds. This randomly initialized step, bounded within the $[-1, 1]$ range for each position vector's variable, uses the randomly produced position.

### 3.3. Boosting Positions via the AVO Algorithm

This paper presents the AVO algorithm [30], a meta-heuristic optimization algorithm inspired by vultures in Africa and their living and feeding behaviors. Based on fundamental ideas about vultures, the AVO algorithm is configured as follows: The African vulture population size is initially presumed by the AVO algorithm to consist of $N$ vultures. The population of African vultures is then divided into three groups to reflect the primary natural function of vultures, based on the computed fitness function. The first group consists of the strongest vulture, which is the best solution; the second group contains a vulture weaker than the first, which is the second-best solution; and the final group encompasses the remaining weaker vultures, which are the worst solutions.

Based on the above, the proposed AVO algorithm is composed of four fundamental phases to simulate the behavior of different types of vultures. The following subsections clarify these phases.

#### 3.3.1. Phase of Dividing the Population

The initial population is split into groups by assessing the solution's fitness function. The best solution is chosen as the best vulture in the first group, while the second group contains the second-best solution. The third group contains the remaining solutions. As the solutions constantly strive to approach the best and second-best solutions, the population needs to be re-evaluated for each iteration, as follows:

$$R^g = \begin{cases} BestVulture_1^g, & \text{if } pr^g = L_1, \\ SecondBestVulture_2^g, & \text{if } pr^g = L_2, \end{cases} \tag{2}$$

$$pr^g = \frac{v^g}{\sum_{g=1}^{N} v^g}. \tag{3}$$

The best vulture in the first group and the second-best vulture in the second group at the $g^{th}$ iteration are denoted by the expressions $BestVulture_1^g$ and $SecondBestVulture_2^g$, respectively. The probability of selecting the best solution for each group at the $g^{th}$ iteration is defined using the roulette wheel approach, as shown in Equation (3), $pr^g$. Two random parameters within the range $[0, 1]$ are $L_1$ and $L_2$.

#### 3.3.2. Phase of Measuring the Famine Level

This phase is utilized to formulate a mathematical model for the exploitation, exploration, and transfer among the vultures. When they are not famished, the vultures have a greater ability to search for food and can fly further. Furthermore, when famished, vultures cannot fly long distances in search of food and may become violent. The $i^{th}$ vulture's famine level ($F_i^g$) during the $g^{th}$ iteration can be written as follows, which is used to develop a mathematical model for the vultures' exploitation, exploration, and transfer:

$$F_i^g = (2 \times rand + 1) \times z \times \left(1 - \frac{g_i}{G_{max}}\right) + t, \tag{4}$$

$$t = h \times \left(\sin^w\left(\frac{\pi}{2} \times \frac{g_i}{G_{max}}\right) + \cos\left(\frac{\pi}{2} \times \frac{g_i}{G_{max}}\right) - 1\right). \tag{5}$$

The vultures are presumably full since the variable $F_i^g$ shows the vultures' shift from exploration to exploitation. A random number between 0 and 1 is called a $rand$. $z$ denotes a random value within the interval $[-1,1]$. The current iteration number is denoted by $g_i$, while the maximum iteration number is denoted by $G_{max}$. Equation (5) calculates the $t$ value to help solve complicated optimization problems more effectively and prevent reaching a local optimum. An arbitrary value within the interval $[-2,2]$ is represented by $h$. The probability of carrying out the exploration process is regulated by the predefined constant parameter $w$; the exploration likelihood grows as its value increases. Exploration is less probable as its value declines.

Equation (4) states that as the number of iterations increases, $F_i^g$ gradually lessens. As a result, the next step in the proposed AVO algorithm can be defined as follows:

$$\begin{cases} \textit{Exploration phase (Search food in diverse areas)}, & \textit{if } |F_i^g| \geq 1, \\ \textit{Exploitation phase (Search food in surrounding area)}, & \textit{if } |F_i^g| < 1. \end{cases} \tag{6}$$

3.3.3. Phase of Exploration

The vultures are characterized by their great ocular ability to locate appropriate food during this phase. There are two different strategies used in this phase to enable vultures to travel great distances for lengthy periods to search for food in random locations. These locations are selected using a random number $rand_{P_1}$ and a preset parameter $P_1$, both of which have values within the range $[0,1]$. In the exploration phase, the famine level $|F_i^g|$ is greater than or equal to 1. The exploration techniques are described as follows:

$$X_i^{g+1} = \left\{ \begin{array}{ll} R^g - D_i^g \times F_i^g, & \textit{if } rand_{P_1} \leq P_1, \\ R^g - F_i^g + rand \times ((UB - LB) \times rand + LB), & \textit{if } rand_{P_1} > P_1, \end{array} \right\} \textit{if } |F_i^g| \geq 1, \tag{7}$$

$$D_i^g = |(2 \times rand) \times R^g - X_i^g|. \tag{8}$$

where the upcoming updated position at the next $(g+1)^{th}$ iteration is denoted by $X_i^{g+1}$. The best vulture chosen for the current iteration $g$ is denoted by $R^g$. This is determined using Equation (2). The vultures move randomly to protect the food from other vultures and to provide a high degree of randomness in their search behavior. $rand$ is a random value between zero and one. The variables' upper bound is denoted by $UB$; their lower bound by $LB$; and the current position at the $g^{th}$ iteration is $X_i^g$.

3.3.4. Phase of Exploitation

In this phase, $|F_i^g|$ is less than 1. The proposed AVO algorithm's efficacy is evaluated in two sub-phases that comprise the exploitation phase. Each of these sub-phases uses two different strategies. For each internal sub-phase, the appropriate strategy is chosen using two predefined parameters: $P_2$ for the first sub-phase and $P_3$ for the second, with values ranging from 0 to 1. These two internal sub-phases are explained as follows:

- **First sub-phase of exploitation:** This sub-phase applies two different strategies when $|F_i^g|$ is less than 1 and greater than or equal to 0.5. The selection of one of these two strategies is made using a random value $rand_{P_2}$ within the range $[0,1]$ and a specified parameter $P_2$.
The initial strategy of this sub-phase is called **siege fight**, which involves sufficiently powerful and somewhat satiated vultures. More robust and healthier vultures try not to share food with others because they convene around a single food source. By swarming near the healthy vultures and engaging in small fights, the weaker vultures try to take food from them. Conversely, the second strategy is called **rotational flight**; it creates a spiral movement between a superior vulture and the others. The following illustrates the strategies for the first exploitation sub-phase:

$$X_i^{g+1} = \left\{ \begin{array}{ll} D_i^g \times (F_i^g + rand) - d_t^g, & \textit{if } rand_{P_2} \leq P_2, \\ R^g - (S_1^g + S_2^g), & \textit{if } rand_{P_2} > P_2, \end{array} \right\} \textit{if } 1 > |F_i^g| \geq 0.5, \tag{9}$$

$$d_t^g = R^g - X_i^g, \tag{10}$$

$$S_1^g = R^g \times \left(\frac{rand \times X_i^g}{2\pi}\right) \times \cos(X_i^g), \tag{11}$$

$$S_2^g = R^g \times \left(\frac{rand \times X_i^g}{2\pi}\right) \times \sin(X_i^g). \tag{12}$$

where the vulture's next updated position at the next $(g+1)^{th}$ iteration is denoted by $X_i^{g+1}$, $D_i^g$ is defined using Equation (8), and *rand* is an arbitrary value between 0 and 1. The distance $d_t^g$ between the vulture and one of the best two vultures is estimated using Equation (10); $R^g$ denotes the appropriate best vulture in the current $g^{th}$ iteration, which is computed using Equation (2); $S_1^g$ and $S_2^g$ are computed employing Equations (11) and (12), respectively; and $X_i^g$ denotes the current position at the $g^{th}$ iteration.

- **Second sub-phase of exploitation:** This sub-phase is carried out when $|F_i^g|$ is less than 0.5. Various vulture species gather around the food supply and engage in many sieges and brawls during this sub-phase. This sub-phase employs two different strategies. A predefined parameter $P_3$ and an arbitrary value $rand_{P_3}$, with values ranging from 0 to 1, are used to decide which of these two strategies to use.
This sub-phase's initial strategy is called **assemble vultures around the food source**. In this strategy, different kinds of vultures search for food and may compete near a single source. The second strategy is known as **hostile siege fight**. In this strategy, the vultures become more aggressive and try to plunder the leftover food from the healthy vultures by flocking around them in different ways. The healthy vultures, on the other hand, deteriorate and are unable to fend off the other vultures. The following illustrates the strategies for the second exploitation sub-phase:

$$X_i^{g+1} = \left\{ \begin{array}{ll} \frac{A_1^g + A_2^g}{2}, & if\ rand_{P_3} \leq P_3, \\ R^g - |d_t^g| \times F_i^g \times Levy_d, & if\ rand_{P_3} > P_3, \end{array} \right\} if\ |F_i^g| < 0.5, \tag{13}$$

$$A_1^g = BestVulture_1^g - \frac{BestVulture_1^g \times X_i^g}{BestVulture_1^g - (X_i^g)^2} \times F_i^g, \tag{14}$$

$$A_2^g = SecondBestVulture_2^g - \frac{SecondBestVulture_2^g \times X_i^g}{SecondBestVulture_2^g - (X_i^g)^2} \times F_i^g, \tag{15}$$

$$Levy_d = 0.01 \times \frac{\mu \times \sigma}{|v|^{\frac{1}{\beta}}}, \tag{16}$$

$$sigma = \left(\frac{\Gamma(1+\beta) \times \sin(\frac{\Pi\beta}{2})}{\Gamma(1+\beta 2) \times \beta \times 2^{(\frac{\beta-1}{2})}}\right)^{\frac{1}{\beta}}. \tag{17}$$

where the next updated position of the vulture at the next $(g+1)^{th}$ iteration, reflecting the assembly of vultures, is denoted by $X_i^{g+1}$. $A_1^g$ and $A_2^g$ are evaluated using, respectively, Equations (14) and (15). To increase the effectiveness of the AVO algorithm, $Levy_d$ is the levy flight distribution function obtained using Equation (16). $d$ is the dimensional space; $\sigma$ is defined by Equation (17), where $\beta = 1.5$ is a constant value; and $\mu$ and $v$ are random numbers distributed equally within the range $[0, 1]$.

### 3.4. Converting to Binary Nature

In the presented AVO algorithm, the positions are shown as real values. As such, they are not immediately applicable to the GS binary issue. Therefore, there is a need to convert these real position values into binary values to conform to GS's binary nature and maintain the original algorithm's structure. In this conversion, 1s represent the real values of the pertinent selected genes in the binarization vector, whereas 0s represent the real values of the unselected genes, which are not pertinent. At each iteration $g$, the following mathematical expression can be used to convert the real position $X_i^g$ to a binary position $(X_i^g)_{bin}$:

$$(X_i^g)_{bin} = \begin{cases} 1 & \text{if } \mathbf{X}_i^g > \delta, \\ 0 & \text{otherwise.} \end{cases} \tag{18}$$

where an arbitrary threshold point within $[0,1]$ is represented by $\delta$. According to this fundamental binary conversion approach, the binary "1" (selected feature) replaces its real value if $(X_i^g)_{bin}$ is greater than $\delta$. On the other hand, if $(X_i^g)_{bin}$ is smaller than $delta$, its real value is set to the binary "0" (a feature that was not chosen).

### 3.5. Appraising the Fitness Function Value

Finding the fewest number of selected features and optimizing the classification accuracy of the available classifiers ($k$-NN and SVM models) are two conflicting objectives that should be balanced to achieve the best solution and determine its quality. Since the $k$-NN and SVM classifiers' accuracies might be hampered if the number of selected features is lower than the optimal, the fitness function balances the selected features' size and accuracy. The fitness function concentrates on lowering the classification error rate rather than accuracy, as follows:

$$fit = w_1 \times Err_{rate} + w_2 \times \frac{|feat_{picked}|}{|D|}, \quad w_1 \in [0,1], w_2 = 1 - w_1. \tag{19}$$

where $feat_{picked}$ denotes the number of selected features, $D$ denotes the total number of features in the dataset, and $Err_{rate}$ represents the classification error rate from the $k$-NN and SVM classifiers. The classification accuracy importance and the number of selected features are denoted by the weight parameters $w_1$ and $w_2$, respectively. The values of $w_1$ (0.99) and $w_2$ (0.01) are determined through extensive trials conducted in previous studies [21,42,43].

### 3.6. Incorporating the DE Technique

DE [44] is characterized by its high efficiency and simplicity in finding a suitable solution for complex optimization problems. It can quickly produce value-added results. Three main processes—mutation, crossover, and selection—are necessary for DE. The differential mutation process seeks to produce a modified vector $v_i$ for each iteration's solution vector. This can be computed mathematically as follows:

$$\vec{v}_i = \vec{X}_{r_1} + W_M(\vec{X}_{r_2} - \vec{X}_{r_3}) \tag{20}$$

Within the range [1, population size], three randomly selected asymmetric vectors are denoted by the symbols $X_{r_1}$, $X_{r_2}$, and $X_{r_3}$. $W_M$ denotes the mutation weighting factor within the interval $[0,1]$.

After the mutation operation, DE performs a crossover operation to increase the population's variety. An offspring vector $u_i$ is produced by combining values from the target vector $X_i$ and the altered vector $v_i$. The most commonly used and basic factor of crossover search is binary crossover, which has the following mathematical expression:

$$u_{i,d} = \begin{cases} v_{i,d}, & \text{if } rand \leq C_R \quad or \quad d = j_{rand}, \\ X_{i,d}, & \text{otherwise.} \end{cases} \tag{21}$$

where a uniformly distributed random number $j_{rand} \in [1, 2, ..., D_X]$ is used to ensure that the mutated vector has at least one dimension. The possibility of crossing each element is calculated using the crossover rate $C_R$, frequently determined to be a big amount ($C_R$ = 0.9).

The selection operation is then carried out, as shown in Equation (22). Here, a comparison between the fitness function $f(X_i)$ of the target vector and the corresponding offspring vector $f(u_i)$ is performed, and the lowest-valued fitness function is kept for the upcoming iteration.

$$X_i = \begin{cases} u_i, & \text{if } f(u_i) < f(X_i) \\ X_i, & \text{otherwise.} \end{cases} \tag{22}$$

### 3.7. The Complete RBAVO-DE Algorithm

To handle the GS strategy, the steps of the recommended RBAVO-DE algorithm are described in the following subsections. The pseudo-code for the proposed RBAVO-DE algorithm is provided in Algorithm 1. A flowchart of the proposed RBAVO-DE algorithm is shown in Figure 1, illustrating its main steps.

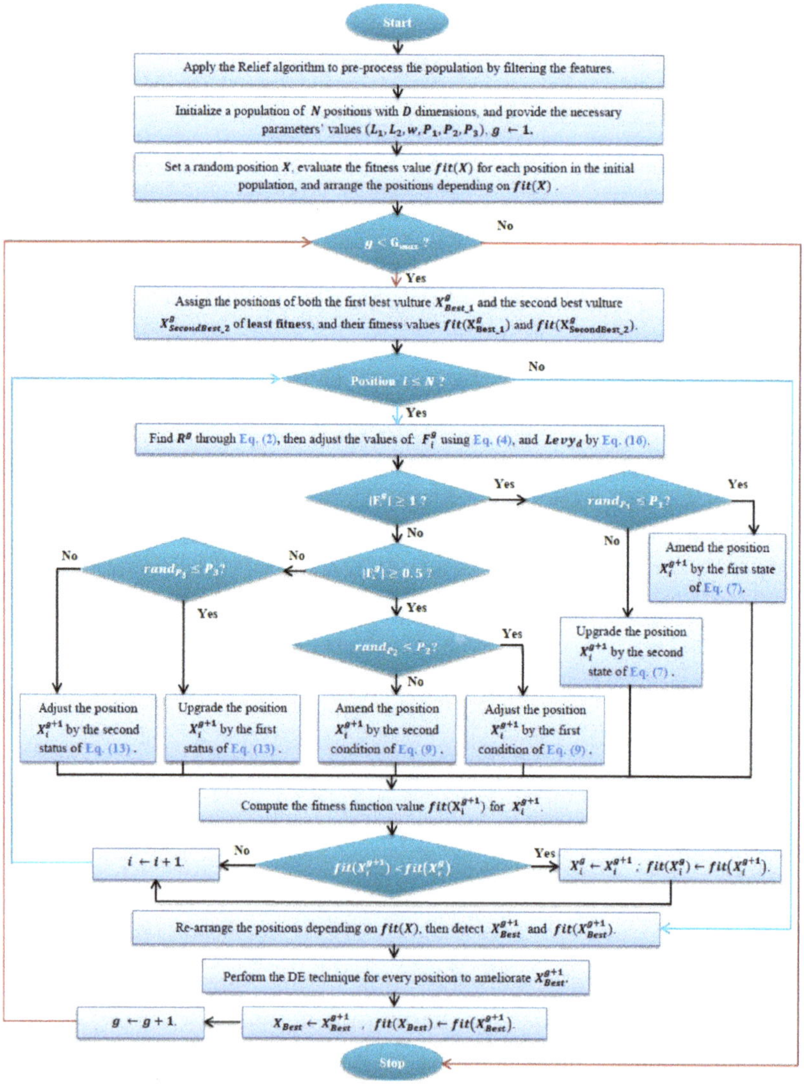


**Figure 1.** Flowchart of the RBAVO-DE algorithm.

**Algorithm 1** The proposed RBAVO-DE algorithm.

**Input:**
$N$—total number of positions (size of population)
$G_{max}$—maximum number of permitted iterations
$D$—problem's dimensional space
$LB$—lower bounds of variables
$UB$—upper bounds of variables
$C_R$—crossover rate
$W_M$—mutation weighting factor
**Output:**
$X_{Best}$—the global best vulture's position found while searching
$fit(X_{Best})$—the global best fitness function value found, which should be lessened

**Start**
  Apply the Relief approach for selecting the related features and filtering them, as demonstrated in Section 3.1;
  Initialize a population of $N$ positions, and provide the values of the necessary parameters ($L_1$, $L_2$, $w$, $P_1$, $P_2$, and $P_3$);
  Set a random position $X$ in the initial population;
  Evaluate the fitness values $fit(X)$ for each position in the initial population;
  Arrange the positions in ascending order depending on their fitness function $fit(X)$;
  $g \leftarrow 1$; ▷ Current number of iterations
  **while** $g < G_{max}$ **do**
    Assign the positions of both the first-best vulture $X^g_{Best_1}$ and the second-best vulture $X^g_{SecondBest_2}$, as well as their fitness values $fit(X^g_{Best_1})$ and $fit(X^g_{SecondBest_2})$, among all positions in the population;
    **for** vulture's position $i = 1 : N$ **do**
      Find the best vulture $R^g$ using Equation (2);
      Adjust the vulture's famine level $F^g_i$ using Equation (4);
      Modify the levy flight distribution function $Levy_d$ using Equation (16);
      **if** $|F^g_i| \geq 1$ **then**
        **if** $rand_{P_1} \leq P_1$ **then**
          Amend the vulture's position $X^{g+1}_i$ based on the first stage of the exploration phase using Equation (7);
        **else if** $rand_{P_1} > P_1$ **then**
          Upgrade the vulture's position $X^{g+1}_i$ based on the second stage of the exploration phase using Equation (7);
        **end if**
      **else if** $|F^g_i| < 1$ **then**
        **if** $|F^g_i| \geq 0.5$ **then**
          **if** $rand_{P_2} \leq P_2$ **then**
            Adjust the vulture's position $X^{g+1}_i$ based on the first condition of the first exploitation sub-phase using Equation (9);
          **else if** $rand_{P_2} > P_2$ **then**
            Amend the vulture's position $X^{g+1}_i$ based on the second condition of the first exploitation sub-phase using Equation (9);
          **end if**
        **else if** $|F^g_i| < 0.5$ **then**
          **if** $rand_{P_3} \leq P_3$ **then**
            Upgrade the vulture's position $X^{g+1}_i$ based on the first status of the second exploitation sub-phase using Equation (13);
          **else if** $rand_{P_3} > P_3$ **then**
            Adjust the vulture's position $X^{g+1}_i$ based on the second status of the second exploitation sub-phase using Equation (13);
          **end if**
        **end if**
      **end if**
      $fit(X^{g+1}_i) \leftarrow$ Compute the fitness function value for $X^{g+1}_i$;
      **if** $fit(X^{g+1}_i) < fit(X^g_i)$ **then**
        $X^g_i \leftarrow X^{g+1}_i$;
        $fit(X^g_i) \leftarrow fit(X^{g+1}_i)$;
      **end if**
    **end for**
    Re-arrange the positions in ascending order depending on their fitness function $fit(X)$;
    Detect the global best position $X^{g+1}_{Best}$ and its global best fitness value $fit(X^{g+1}_{Best})$ when the current iteration $g+1$ is over;
    Perform the DE technique for every position to ameliorate $X^{g+1}_{Best}$, as shown in Section 3.6;
    $X_{Best} \leftarrow X^{g+1}_{Best}$;
    $fit(X_{Best}) \leftarrow fit(X^{g+1}_{Best})$;
    $g \leftarrow g + 1$;
  **end while**
**End**

## 4. Experimental Results and Discussion

This section presents the empirical findings of the proposed RBAVO-DE and its counterparts: Binary Artificial Bee Colony (BABC) [45], Binary Salp Swarm Algorithm (BSSA) [46], Binary PSO (BPSO) [47], Binary Bat Algorithm (BBA) [48], Binary Grey-Wolf Optimization (BGWO) [49], Binary Grasshopper Optimization Algorithm (BGOA) [50], Binary Whale Optimization Algorithm (BWOA) [51], Binary ASO (BASO) [52], Binary Bird Swarm Algorithm (BBSA) [53], Binary HGSO (BHGSO) [54], and Binary Harris Hawks

Optimization (BHHO) [55]. The optimizers undergo evaluation through training and testing benchmarks, with conclusive results derived from the average values of the evaluation metrics. The benchmarks employed for assessing the performance of the proposed model are detailed in Section 4.1. The parameters used in the operational environments are outlined in Section 4.2. The metrics used for evaluation are described in Section 4.3. The analysis of the experimental outcomes is discussed in Section 4.4.

### 4.1. Dataset Description

In-depth experimental approaches and various wrapper algorithms were applied to twenty-two datasets of gene descriptions; the data comprise normalized Level 3 RNA-Seq gene expression data for twenty-two kinds of tumors from the Broad Institute. These data are publicly accessible and can be found in [56]. We adhered to the methodology described in [36] and observed discrepancies between the data referenced from GitHub in the paper and the figures reported within the document, which were sourced from the website. The website's data included a mix of tumor and standard samples, whereas the paper treated the data uniformly as tumor samples. Consequently, we conducted a detailed examination of the data. Initially, the website offered various formats of the identical dataset we intended to analyze. Upon delving into the data, we encountered the following challenges:

- Certain genes are identified by ID but lack an associated symbol.
- Some genes are absent from the annotation file.
- There is a mix-up of samples, including both normal and tumor types.

Consequently, pre-processing was necessary to segregate and identify samples, distinguish between normal and tumor samples for use in binary classification, and streamline the GS process. We addressed the challenges above in the following manner:

- We looked up the corresponding gene symbol for each ID found in the annotation file.
- After cross-referencing with the annotating file, over one hundred genes were eliminated.
- Based on the sample report, every Excel sheet's row was organized according to the kind of sample for binary classification.

Moreover, the Relief approach, as detailed in Section 3.1, was utilized in the pre-processing stage to calculate the weight of each gene within the benchmark. These weights were subsequently ordered from highest to lowest. Genes with lower weights were then removed. The Relief approach was useful for discarding genes that do not contribute to classification.

Following the pre-processing phase, the data were refined and ready for the GS process. Contrary to the approach used in [36], which tackled the multi-classification of all types of cancer together, we opted to analyze every cancer type individually for greater specificity. Table 1 [57] presents a comprehensive overview of all twenty-two tumor types and their respective sample counts. The number of features utilized in the benchmark datasets is 32,000 features (genes).

**Table 1.** Datasets employed in this paper [57].

| # | Cancer | Normal Records | Tumor Records |
|---|---|---|---|
| 1 | Bladder Urothelial Carcinoma (BLCA) | 19 | 408 |
| 2 | Thyroid Cancer (THCA) | 59 | 501 |
| 3 | Cervical and Endocervical Cancers (CESCs) | 3 | 304 |
| 4 | Cholangiocarcinoma (CHOL) | 9 | 36 |
| 5 | Colon Adenocarcinoma (COAD) | 41 | 458 |
| 6 | Esophageal Cancer (ESCA) | 13 | 184 |
| 7 | Glioblastoma Multiforme (GBM) | 5 | 153 |

**Table 1.** *Cont.*

| # | Cancer | Normal Records | Tumor Records |
|---|---|---|---|
| 8 | Thymoma (THYM) | 2 | 120 |
| 9 | Head and Neck Squamous Cell Carcinoma (HNSC) | 44 | 520 |
| 10 | Kidney Chromophobe (KICH) | 25 | 66 |
| 11 | KIRC | 72 | 533 |
| 12 | Kidney Renal Papillary (KIRP) | 32 | 290 |
| 13 | Liver Hepatocellular Carcinoma (LIHC) | 50 | 371 |
| 14 | LUAD | 59 | 515 |
| 15 | LUSC | 51 | 501 |
| 16 | Pancreatic Adenocarcinoma (PAAD) | 4 | 178 |
| 17 | UCEC | 35 | 176 |
| 18 | Pheochromocytoma and Paraganglioma (PCPG) | 3 | 179 |
| 19 | Rectum adenocarcinoma (READ) | 10 | 94 |
| 20 | Sarcoma (SARC) | 2 | 259 |
| 21 | Skin Cutaneous Melanoma (SKCM) | 1 | 103 |
| 22 | STAD | 37 | 415 |

### *4.2. Parameter Setting*

The proposed RBAVO-DE algorithm was compared against binary variants of different meta-heuristic optimizers, such as BABC, BSSA, BPSO, BBA, BGWO, BWOA, BBSA, BGOA, BHHO, BASO, and BHGSO. The critical parameters for the ML models employed in this study are detailed in Table 2.

**Table 2.** The key parameters of the employed ML models.

| Model | Parameters |
|---|---|
| SVM | Polynomial kernel = 2 |
| $k$-NN | Euclidean distance metric $k = 5$ [21,58,59] |

Within the proposed framework, the validity of the results was verified using a 10-fold cross-validation approach to ensure the reliability of the outcomes. This involved randomly dividing each dataset into two distinct subsets: 80% for training and the remaining 20% for testing. The training portion was employed to train the presented classifiers using optimization techniques, while the testing portion was used to evaluate the selected genes' effectiveness. The parameters most commonly applied across all compared algorithms are summarized in Table 3. To execute all experiments in this paper, Python was utilized in a computational environment with a Dual Intel® Xeon® Gold 5115 2.4 GHz CPU and 128 GB of RAM on the Microsoft Windows Server 2019 operating system.

**Table 3.** Parameter configurations of all utilized optimizers.

| Optimizer | Parameters |
|---|---|
| All optimizers | Execution count = 30<br>Maximum count of iterations $G_{max} = 100$<br>Size of population $N = 10$ |

**Table 3.** *Cont.*

| Optimizer | Parameters |
|---|---|
| Proposed RBAVO-DE | Dimensionality $D$ = The count of genes in the employed datasets<br>Upper boundaries $UB$<br>Lower boundaries $LB$<br>Parameter $L_1 = 0.7$<br>Parameter $L_2 = 0.2$<br>Parameter $w = 2$<br>Parameter $P_1 = 0.6$<br>Parameter $P_2 = 0.6$<br>Parameter $P_3 = 0.5$ |
| BSSA | Count of scroungers $SD = 0.1 \times N$<br>Count of producers $PD = 0.2 \times N$<br>Safety threshold $ST = 0.8$ |
| BABC | Count of employed bees $= 16$<br>Count of scout bees $= 3$<br>Count of onlooker bees $= 4$ |
| BPSO | Inertia weight $(\omega max = 0.9\omega min = 0.4)$<br>Acceleration coefficients $(c_2 = c_1 = 1.2)$ |
| BBA | Loudness $A = 0.8$<br>Pulse emission rate $r = 0.95$<br>Lower and upper pulse frequencies $= 0, 10$ |
| BWOA | $a$ is linearly decreased from 2 to 0<br>$p = 0.5$<br>$b = 1.0$ |
| BHHO | Rabbit energy $E \in [-1, 1]$ |
| BGWO | $a$ is linearly decreased from 2 to 0 |
| BGOA | $C_{\min} = 0.00004$ and $C_{\max} = 1$ |
| BBSA | Frequency of flight $ff = 10$<br>Effect on birds' vigilance<br>Followed coefficient $fl = 0.5$<br>Probability of foraging for food $p = 0.8$<br>Acceleration coefficients $(c_1 = c_2 = 1.5)$<br>behaviors $(a_1 = a_2 = 1.0)$ |
| BASO | Depth weight $\alpha = 50$<br>Multiplier weight $\beta = 0.2$ |
| BHGSO | Count of clusters $= 2$<br>$\alpha = \beta = 0.1$ $K = 1.0$, and $l_3 = 1E - 02$<br>$l_1 = 5E - 03$, $l_2 = 1E + 02$ |

### 4.3. Evaluation Criteria

To evaluate the proposed RBAVO-DE's effectiveness relative to other methods, each strategy was independently tested thirty times on each benchmark to ensure statistical validation of the results. For this purpose, the following established performance metrics for the GS issues were employed:

- **Mean classification accuracy** ($Mean_{AC}$): This measure represents the accuracy of correctly classifying data, calculated by running the algorithm independently thirty times. It is determined in the following way:

$$Mean_{AC} = \sum_{k=1}^{30} \sum_{r=1}^{m} match(PL_r, AL_r) \tag{23}$$

In this formula, $m$ denotes the number of samples in the test dataset, while $PL_r$ and $AL_r$ denote the predicted labels from the classifier and the actual class labels for sample $r$, respectively. The function $match(PL_r, AL_r)$ serves as a comparison mechanism, where if $PL_r$ is equal to $AL_r$, then $match(PL_r, AL_r)$ is assigned a value of 1; if they do not match, it is assigned a value of 0.

- **Mean fitness** $(Mean_{Fi})$: This measure calculates the average $meanFi$, achieved by running the proposed approach thirty times independently. It gauges the balance between lowering the classification error rate and minimizing the number of genes selected. A lower value indicates a superior solution, assessed based on fitness:

$$MeanFi = \frac{1}{30}\sum_{k=1}^{30} f_*^k \tag{24}$$

  where $f_*^k$ shows the optimum fitness value achieved in the $k-th$ execution.
- **Mean number of chosen genes** $(MeanGe)$: This metric calculates the average number of genes chosen (or GS ratio) by running the proposed approach thirty times independently, and it is defined as follows:

$$MeanFe = \frac{1}{30}\sum_{k=1}^{30} \frac{|d_*^k|}{|D|} \tag{25}$$

  Here, $|d_*^k|$ denotes the total count of genes chosen in the optimal solution for the $k^{th}$ execution, and $|D|$ represents the total number of genes present in the initial benchmark.
- **Standard Deviation** $(STDE)$: Based on the outcomes above, the overall average results derived from thirty separate executions of each optimizer on every benchmark were assessed for stability in the following manner:

$$STDE = \sqrt{\frac{1}{29}\sum_{k=1}^{30}(Y_*^k - Mean_Y)^2} \tag{26}$$

  where $Y$ shows the measure to be utilized, $Y * k$ denotes the measure value $Y$ in the $k_t h$ run, and $Mean_Y$ is the mean of the measure from thirty independent executions.

The data in the subsequent tables represent the mean values obtained from thirty independent executions, focusing on classification accuracy, the number of chosen genes, average fitness, precision, recall, and F1-score. The ensuing subsections thoroughly examine and discuss these experimental findings, with bold figures highlighting the optimal results.

### 4.4. *Results of Comparing the Proposed RBAVO-DE with Various Meta-Heuristic Algorithms*

The proposed RBAVO-DE approach with the SVM and $k$-NN models was compared with other recent meta-heuristic methods executed under the same conditions to show its superiority over its counterparts. The proposed RBAVO-DE algorithm was compared with binary variants of several optimizers, including BABC, BSSA, BPSO, BBA, BGWO, BWOA, BBSA, BGOA, BHHO, BASO, and BHGSO.

#### 4.4.1. Results Employing the $k$-NN Model

Table 4 shows the results of the proposed RBAVO-DE algorithm and other optimization techniques employing the $k$-NN model, based on accuracy metrics compared under similar conditions. The experimental outcomes reveal that the proposed RBAVO-DE achieved the most promising outcomes in four benchmarks. It is noteworthy that all competitive methods, including the proposed RBAVO-DE employing the $k$-NN model, produced comparable outcomes across eighteen benchmarks.

The rest of the metrics for the $k$-NN model are shown in Appendix A.1. In terms of the average fitness values, the proposed RBAVO-DE algorithm demonstrated higher efficiency compared to its counterparts using the $k$-NN model under similar conditions. The RBAVO-DE algorithm yielded the lowest fitness results and the most competitive STDE across all benchmarks. Also, all utilized benchmarks are high-dimensional, demonstrating that the proposed RBAVO-DE can run effectively on all benchmarks regardless of size. The RBAVO-DE algorithm shows promise by effectively balancing exploitation and exploration of the search space, avoiding becoming trapped in local optima during iterations. Unlike many other algorithms that tend to become trapped, it demonstrated the ability to escape such traps.

Regarding the mean results for the genes selected by the proposed RBAVO-DE algorithm and its counterparts employing *k*-NN, the proposed RBAVO-DE algorithm surpassed the other methods across all benchmarks concerning the number of chosen genes. Furthermore, the RBAVO-DE's capacity to identify significant genes is due to its effective exploration of possible areas while enhancing accuracy.

In terms of the mean precision of the proposed RBAVO-DE algorithm and its counterparts with *k*-NN, the proposed RBAVO-DE outperformed alternative approaches for three of the twenty-two datasets. For nineteen datasets, BWOA achieved similar results, while BABC, BPSO, BGWO, BGOA, and BHHO obtained results similar to those of the proposed RBAVO-DE. BASO and BHGSO, which produced the same outcomes as the proposed RBAVO-DE on seventeen datasets, ranked fourth. Ultimately, BBA ranked lowest among all approaches, producing similar outcomes to the proposed RBAVO-DE for fifteen datasets.

Regarding the mean recall of the proposed RBAVO-DE and its counterparts employing *k*-NN, RBAVO-DE outperformed the alternative approaches for three of the twenty-two datasets. On the other hand, BSSA, BABC, BPSO, BGWO, BWOA, BGOA, and BBSA produced the same outcomes as RBAVO-DE for 19 datasets, while BHHO achieved similar results for 18 datasets. BHGSO, which obtained the same outcomes as the proposed RBAVO-DE for seventeen datasets, ranked fourth. Ultimately, BASO and BBA ranked lowest among all approaches, producing similar results to RBAVO-DE for sixteen datasets.

With regard to the mean F1-score of the proposed RBAVO-DE and its counterparts employing *k*-NN, the proposed RBAVO-DE outperformed the alternative approaches for three of the twenty-two datasets. In contrast, for eighteen datasets, BSSA, BABC, BPSO, BGWO, BGOA, and BBSA produced the same outcomes as RBAVO-DE, while BWOA and BHHO produced comparable outcomes for seventeen datasets. BASO and BHGSO, which obtained the same outcomes for 16 datasets as the proposed RBAVO-DE, ranked fourth. Ultimately, BBA ranked lowest among all approaches, producing similar outcomes to the proposed RBAVO-DE for fourteen datasets.

**Table 4.** The results of the proposed RBAVO-DE algorithm and its counterparts using *k*-NN regarding average classification accuracy results.

| Dataset | Metric | RBAVO-DE | BSSA | BABC | BPSO | BBA | BGWO | BWOA | BGOA | BHHO | BBSA | BASO | BHGSO |
|---|---|---|---|---|---|---|---|---|---|---|---|---|---|
| BLCA | Average | **0.998** | 0.993 | 0.998 | 0.993 | 0.989 | 0.995 | 0.994 | 0.993 | 0.991 | 0.994 | 0.994 | 0.989 |
| | STDE | 0.004 | 0.006 | 0.005 | 0.006 | 0.003 | 0.006 | 0.006 | 0.006 | 0.005 | 0.006 | 0.006 | **0.002** |
| CESC | Average | **0.984** | **0.984** | **0.984** | **0.984** | **0.984** | **0.984** | **0.984** | **0.984** | **0.984** | **0.984** | **0.984** | **0.984** |
| | STDE | **0.000** | **0.000** | **0.000** | **0.000** | **0.000** | **0.000** | **0.000** | **0.000** | **0.000** | **0.000** | **0.000** | **0.000** |
| CHOL | Average | **1.000** | **1.000** | **1.000** | **1.000** | **1.000** | **1.000** | **1.000** | **1.000** | **1.000** | **1.000** | **1.000** | **1.000** |
| | STDE | **0.000** | **0.000** | **0.000** | **0.000** | **0.000** | **0.000** | **0.000** | **0.000** | **0.000** | **0.000** | **0.000** | **0.000** |
| COAD | Average | **1.000** | **1.000** | **1.000** | **1.000** | **1.000** | **1.000** | **1.000** | **1.000** | **1.000** | **1.000** | **1.000** | **1.000** |
| | STDE | **0.000** | **0.000** | **0.000** | **0.000** | **0.000** | **0.000** | **0.000** | **0.000** | **0.000** | **0.000** | **0.000** | **0.000** |
| ESCA | Average | **0.974** | **0.974** | **0.974** | **0.974** | **0.974** | **0.974** | **0.974** | **0.974** | **0.974** | **0.974** | **0.974** | **0.974** |
| | STDE | **0.000** | **0.000** | **0.000** | **0.000** | **0.000** | **0.000** | **0.000** | **0.000** | **0.000** | **0.000** | **0.000** | **0.000** |
| GBM | Average | **1.000** | **1.000** | **1.000** | **1.000** | **1.000** | **1.000** | **1.000** | **1.000** | **1.000** | **1.000** | **1.000** | **1.000** |
| | STDE | **0.000** | **0.000** | **0.000** | **0.000** | **0.000** | **0.000** | **0.000** | **0.000** | **0.000** | **0.000** | **0.000** | **0.000** |
| HNSC | Average | **0.993** | 0.991 | 0.991 | 0.991 | 0.991 | 0.992 | 0.991 | 0.991 | 0.991 | 0.991 | 0.991 | 0.991 |
| | STDE | 0.004 | 0.002 | 0.002 | **0.000** | **0.000** | 0.002 | **0.000** | **0.000** | **0.000** | 0.002 | **0.000** | **0.000** |
| KICH | Average | **1.000** | **1.000** | **1.000** | **1.000** | **1.000** | **1.000** | **1.000** | **1.000** | **1.000** | **1.000** | **1.000** | **1.000** |
| | STDE | **0.000** | **0.000** | **0.000** | **0.000** | **0.000** | **0.000** | **0.000** | **0.000** | **0.000** | **0.000** | **0.000** | **0.000** |
| KIRC | Average | **0.998** | 0.993 | 0.994 | 0.992 | 0.992 | 0.994 | 0.992 | 0.994 | 0.993 | 0.993 | 0.993 | 0.992 |
| | STDE | 0.003 | 0.003 | 0.004 | 0.002 | **0.000** | 0.004 | 0.002 | 0.004 | 0.003 | 0.003 | 0.003 | **0.000** |
| KIRP | Average | **1.000** | **1.000** | **1.000** | **1.000** | **1.000** | **1.000** | **1.000** | **1.000** | **1.000** | **1.000** | **1.000** | **1.000** |
| | STDE | **0.000** | **0.000** | **0.000** | **0.000** | **0.000** | **0.000** | **0.000** | **0.000** | **0.000** | **0.000** | **0.000** | **0.000** |
| LIHC | Average | **1.000** | **1.000** | **1.000** | **1.000** | **1.000** | **1.000** | **1.000** | **1.000** | **1.000** | **1.000** | **1.000** | **1.000** |
| | STDE | **0.000** | **0.000** | **0.000** | **0.000** | **0.000** | **0.000** | **0.000** | **0.000** | **0.000** | **0.000** | **0.000** | **0.000** |
| LUAD | Average | **0.991** | **0.991** | **0.991** | **0.991** | **0.991** | **0.991** | **0.991** | **0.991** | **0.991** | **0.991** | **0.991** | **0.991** |
| | STDE | **0.000** | **0.000** | **0.000** | **0.000** | **0.000** | **0.000** | **0.000** | **0.000** | **0.000** | **0.000** | **0.000** | **0.000** |
| LUSC | Average | **1.000** | **1.000** | **1.000** | **1.000** | **1.000** | **1.000** | **1.000** | **1.000** | **1.000** | **1.000** | **1.000** | **1.000** |
| | STDE | **0.000** | **0.000** | **0.000** | **0.000** | **0.000** | **0.000** | **0.000** | **0.000** | **0.000** | **0.000** | **0.000** | **0.000** |
| PAAD | Average | **1.000** | **1.000** | **1.000** | **1.000** | **1.000** | **1.000** | **1.000** | **1.000** | **1.000** | **1.000** | **1.000** | **1.000** |
| | STDE | **0.000** | **0.000** | **0.000** | **0.000** | **0.000** | **0.000** | **0.000** | **0.000** | **0.000** | **0.000** | **0.000** | **0.000** |

**Table 4.** *Cont.*

| Dataset | Metric | RBAVO-DE | BSSA | BABC | BPSO | BBA | BGWO | BWOA | BGOA | BHHO | BBSA | BASO | BHGSO |
|---|---|---|---|---|---|---|---|---|---|---|---|---|---|
| PCPG | Average | **1.000** | **1.000** | **1.000** | **1.000** | **1.000** | **1.000** | **1.000** | **1.000** | **1.000** | **1.000** | **1.000** | **1.000** |
| | STDE | **0.000** | **0.000** | **0.000** | **0.000** | **0.000** | **0.000** | **0.000** | **0.000** | **0.000** | **0.000** | **0.000** | **0.000** |
| READ | Average | **1.000** | **1.000** | **1.000** | **1.000** | **1.000** | **1.000** | **1.000** | **1.000** | **1.000** | **1.000** | **1.000** | **1.000** |
| | STDE | **0.000** | **0.000** | **0.000** | **0.000** | **0.000** | **0.000** | **0.000** | **0.000** | **0.000** | **0.000** | **0.000** | **0.000** |
| SARC | Average | **0.981** | **0.981** | **0.981** | **0.981** | **0.981** | **0.981** | **0.981** | **0.981** | **0.981** | **0.981** | **0.981** | **0.981** |
| | STDE | **0.000** | **0.000** | **0.000** | **0.000** | **0.000** | **0.000** | **0.000** | **0.000** | **0.000** | **0.000** | **0.000** | **0.000** |
| SKCM | Average | **1.000** | **1.000** | **1.000** | **1.000** | **1.000** | **1.000** | **1.000** | **1.000** | **1.000** | **1.000** | **1.000** | **1.000** |
| | STDE | **0.000** | **0.000** | **0.000** | **0.000** | **0.000** | **0.000** | **0.000** | **0.000** | **0.000** | **0.000** | **0.000** | **0.000** |
| STAD | Average | **0.999** | 0.996 | 0.999 | 0.996 | 0.989 | 0.996 | 0.995 | 0.997 | 0.992 | 0.995 | 0.996 | 0.989 |
| | STDE | 0.003 | 0.005 | 0.004 | 0.005 | **0.000** | 0.005 | 0.006 | 0.005 | 0.005 | 0.006 | 0.005 | **0.000** |
| THCA | Average | **1.000** | **1.000** | **1.000** | **1.000** | **1.000** | **1.000** | **1.000** | **1.000** | **1.000** | **1.000** | **1.000** | **1.000** |
| | STDE | **0.000** | **0.000** | **0.000** | **0.000** | **0.000** | **0.000** | **0.000** | **0.000** | **0.000** | **0.000** | **0.000** | **0.000** |
| THYM | Average | **1.000** | **1.000** | **1.000** | **1.000** | **1.000** | **1.000** | **1.000** | **1.000** | **1.000** | **1.000** | **1.000** | **1.000** |
| | STDE | **0.000** | **0.000** | **0.000** | **0.000** | **0.000** | **0.000** | **0.000** | **0.000** | **0.000** | **0.000** | **0.000** | **0.000** |
| UCEC | Average | **0.998** | 0.985 | 0.988 | 0.977 | 0.969 | 0.984 | 0.977 | 0.978 | 0.978 | 0.979 | 0.976 | 0.968 |
| | STDE | 0.008 | 0.012 | 0.013 | 0.006 | 0.011 | 0.012 | 0.006 | 0.008 | 0.009 | 0.009 | **0.005** | 0.011 |
| Ranking | W\|T\|L | **4\|18\|0** | 0\|18\|4 | 0\|18\|4 | 0\|18\|4 | 0\|18\|4 | 0\|18\|4 | 0\|18\|4 | 0\|18\|4 | 0\|18\|4 | 0\|18\|4 | 0\|18\|4 | 0\|18\|4 |

**Boldface** values denote the best results.

#### 4.4.2. Results Employing the SVM Model

Table 5 displays the outcomes of the proposed RBAVO-DE and various optimization techniques employing the SVM model concerning classification accuracy results assessed under identical running conditions. The experimental outcomes demonstrate that the proposed RBAVO-DE algorithm outperformed the other approaches by obtaining the most promising values for four datasets. All competitive methods, including the proposed RBAVO-DE employing SVM, obtained equivalent values across 18 benchmarks.

The rest of the metrics utilizing SVM are presented in Appendix A.2. Regarding the mean fitness values of the proposed RBAVO-DE and its counterparts employing the SVM model under equivalent running conditions, the proposed RBAVO-DE proved to be more efficient than the other methods. The proposed RBAVO-DE employing the SVM model yielded the lowest fitness values and the most competitive STDE across all benchmarks. Also, all utilized benchmarks are high-dimensional, demonstrating that the proposed RBAVO-DE can run effectively on all benchmarks regardless of size. The RBAVO-DE algorithm shows promise by effectively balancing exploitation and exploration of the search space, avoiding becoming trapped in local optima during iterations. Unlike many other algorithms that tend to become trapped, it demonstrated the ability to escape such traps.

Regarding the mean results for the genes selected by the proposed RBAVO-DE and its counterparts employing SVM, the proposed RBAVO-DE achieved more promising results than other techniques across all benchmarks utilized in this study. Also, the superiority of the proposed RBAVO-DE employing SVM in this context demonstrates its capability to effectively explore valuable regions of the search space while avoiding regions with non-feasible solutions.

With regard to the average precision values of the proposed RBAVO-DE and its counterparts employing SVM, the proposed RBAVO-DE outperformed the alternative approaches for three of the twenty-two datasets. On the other hand, for eighteen datasets, BABC, BGWO, BWOA, BBSA, and BASO yielded comparable results. For seventeen datasets, BSSA, BPSO, BGOA, and BHHO yielded results similar to those of RBAVO-DE, thereby ranking fourth. Ultimately, BBA ranked lowest among all approaches, producing similar outcomes to those of the proposed RBAVO-DE for twelve datasets.

In terms of the mean recall of the proposed RBAVO-DE method and its counterparts using SVM, the proposed RBAVO-DE outperformed the alternative approaches for three of the twenty-two datasets. In contrast, BPSO and BHHO performed similarly for eighteen datasets, while BSSA, BABC, BGWO, BWOA, BGOA, and BBSA produced the same results as the proposed RBAVO-DE for nineteen datasets. BHGSO, which obtained the same outcomes as RBAVO-DE for seventeen datasets, ranked fourth. In the end, BASO and BBA ranked lowest among all approaches, producing outcomes similar to those of RBAVO-DE for sixteen datasets.

Regarding the mean F1-score of the proposed RBAVO-DE algorithm and its counterparts employing SVM, the proposed RBAVO-DE outperformed the alternative approaches for five of the twenty-two datasets. On the other hand, BWOA produced outcomes similar to those of the proposed RBAVO-DE for seventeen datasets, while BSSA, BABC, BPSO, BGWO, BGOA, and BBSA produced comparable results for sixteen datasets. BHHO, which obtained the same outcomes as the proposed RBAVO-DE for fifteen datasets, ranked fourth. Ultimately, BBA ranked lowest among all approaches, producing similar outcomes to those of RBAVO-DE for 12 datasets.

**Table 5.** The results of the proposed RBAVO-DE algorithm and its counterparts employing SVM regarding average classification accuracy values.

| Dataset | Metric | RBAVO-DE | BSSA | BABC | BPSO | BBA | BGWO | BWOA | BGOA | BHHO | BBSA | BASO | BHGSO |
|---|---|---|---|---|---|---|---|---|---|---|---|---|---|
| BLCA | Average | 1.000 | 1.000 | 1.000 | 1.000 | 1.000 | 1.000 | 1.000 | 1.000 | 1.000 | 1.000 | 1.000 | 1.000 |
| | STDE | 0.000 | 0.000 | 0.000 | 0.000 | 0.000 | 0.000 | 0.000 | 0.000 | 0.000 | 0.000 | 0.000 | 0.000 |
| CESC | Average | 1.000 | 1.000 | 1.000 | 1.000 | 1.000 | 1.000 | 1.000 | 1.000 | 1.000 | 1.000 | 1.000 | 1.000 |
| | STDE | 0.000 | 0.000 | 0.000 | 0.000 | 0.000 | 0.000 | 0.000 | 0.000 | 0.000 | 0.000 | 0.000 | 0.000 |
| CHOL | Average | 1.000 | 1.000 | 1.000 | 1.000 | 1.000 | 1.000 | 1.000 | 1.000 | 1.000 | 1.000 | 1.000 | 1.000 |
| | STDE | 0.000 | 0.000 | 0.000 | 0.000 | 0.000 | 0.000 | 0.000 | 0.000 | 0.000 | 0.000 | 0.000 | 0.000 |
| COAD | Average | 1.000 | 1.000 | 1.000 | 1.000 | 1.000 | 1.000 | 1.000 | 1.000 | 1.000 | 1.000 | 1.000 | 1.000 |
| | STDE | 0.000 | 0.000 | 0.000 | 0.000 | 0.000 | 0.000 | 0.000 | 0.000 | 0.000 | 0.000 | 0.000 | 0.000 |
| ESCA | Average | **0.986** | 0.975 | 0.977 | 0.974 | 0.974 | 0.977 | 0.974 | 0.975 | 0.975 | 0.975 | 0.974 | 0.974 |
| | STDE | 0.013 | 0.004 | 0.008 | **0.000** | **0.000** | 0.008 | **0.000** | 0.005 | 0.005 | 0.005 | **0.000** | **0.000** |
| GBM | Average | 1.000 | 1.000 | 1.000 | 1.000 | 1.000 | 1.000 | 1.000 | 1.000 | 1.000 | 1.000 | 1.000 | 1.000 |
| | STDE | 0.000 | 0.000 | 0.000 | 0.000 | 0.000 | 0.000 | 0.000 | 0.000 | 0.000 | 0.000 | 0.000 | 0.000 |
| HNSC | Average | 1.000 | 1.000 | 1.000 | 1.000 | 1.000 | 1.000 | 1.000 | 1.000 | 1.000 | 1.000 | 1.000 | 1.000 |
| | STDE | 0.000 | 0.000 | 0.000 | 0.000 | 0.000 | 0.000 | 0.000 | 0.000 | 0.000 | 0.000 | 0.000 | 0.000 |
| KICH | Average | 1.000 | 1.000 | 1.000 | 1.000 | 1.000 | 1.000 | 1.000 | 1.000 | 1.000 | 1.000 | 1.000 | 1.000 |
| | STDE | 0.000 | 0.000 | 0.000 | 0.000 | 0.000 | 0.000 | 0.000 | 0.000 | 0.000 | 0.000 | 0.000 | 0.000 |
| KIRC | Average | 1.000 | 1.000 | 1.000 | 1.000 | 1.000 | 1.000 | 1.000 | 1.000 | 1.000 | 1.000 | 1.000 | 1.000 |
| | STDE | 0.000 | 0.000 | 0.000 | 0.000 | 0.000 | 0.000 | 0.000 | 0.000 | 0.000 | 0.000 | 0.000 | 0.000 |
| KIRP | Average | 1.000 | 1.000 | 1.000 | 1.000 | 1.000 | 1.000 | 1.000 | 1.000 | 1.000 | 1.000 | 1.000 | 1.000 |
| | STDE | 0.000 | 0.000 | 0.000 | 0.000 | 0.000 | 0.000 | 0.000 | 0.000 | 0.000 | 0.000 | 0.000 | 0.000 |
| LIHC | Average | 1.000 | 1.000 | 1.000 | 1.000 | 0.9992 | 1.000 | 1.000 | 1.000 | 1.000 | 1.000 | 1.000 | 1.000 |
| | STDE | 0.000 | 0.000 | 0.000 | 0.000 | 0.0029 | 0.000 | 0.000 | 0.000 | 0.000 | 0.000 | 0.000 | 0.000 |
| LUAD | Average | **0.993** | 0.991 | 0.991 | 0.991 | 0.991 | 0.991 | 0.991 | 0.991 | 0.991 | 0.991 | 0.992 | 0.991 |
| | STDE | 0.003 | **0.000** | **0.000** | **0.000** | **0.000** | **0.000** | **0.000** | **0.000** | **0.000** | **0.000** | 0.002 | **0.000** |
| LUSC | Average | 1.000 | 1.000 | 1.000 | 1.000 | 1.000 | 1.000 | 1.000 | 1.000 | 1.000 | 1.000 | 1.000 | 1.000 |
| | STDE | 0.000 | 0.000 | 0.000 | 0.000 | 0.000 | 0.000 | 0.000 | 0.000 | 0.000 | 0.000 | 0.000 | 0.000 |
| PAAD | Average | 1.000 | 1.000 | 1.000 | 1.000 | 1.000 | 1.000 | 1.000 | 1.000 | 1.000 | 1.000 | 1.000 | 1.000 |
| | STDE | 0.000 | 0.000 | 0.000 | 0.000 | 0.000 | 0.000 | 0.000 | 0.000 | 0.000 | 0.000 | 0.000 | 0.000 |
| PCPG | Average | 1.000 | 1.000 | 1.000 | 1.000 | 1.000 | 1.000 | 1.000 | 1.000 | 1.000 | 1.000 | 1.000 | 1.000 |
| | STDE | 0.000 | 0.000 | 0.000 | 0.000 | 0.000 | 0.000 | 0.000 | 0.000 | 0.000 | 0.000 | 0.000 | 0.000 |
| READ | Average | 1.000 | 1.000 | 1.000 | 1.000 | 1.000 | 1.000 | 1.000 | 1.000 | 1.000 | 1.000 | 1.000 | 1.000 |
| | STDE | 0.000 | 0.000 | 0.000 | 0.000 | 0.000 | 0.000 | 0.000 | 0.000 | 0.000 | 0.000 | 0.000 | 0.000 |
| SARC | Average | **0.994** | 0.986 | 0.989 | 0.986 | 0.981 | 0.989 | 0.987 | 0.986 | 0.984 | 0.986 | 0.984 | 0.981 |
| | STDE | 0.008 | 0.008 | 0.009 | 0.008 | **0.000** | 0.009 | 0.009 | 0.008 | 0.006 | 0.008 | 0.007 | **0.000** |
| SKCM | Average | 1.000 | 1.000 | 1.000 | 1.000 | 1.000 | 1.000 | 1.000 | 1.000 | 1.000 | 1.000 | 1.000 | 1.000 |
| | STDE | 0.000 | 0.000 | 0.000 | 0.000 | 0.000 | 0.000 | 0.000 | 0.000 | 0.000 | 0.000 | 0.000 | 0.000 |
| STAD | Average | **0.990** | 0.989 | 0.989 | 0.989 | 0.989 | 0.989 | 0.989 | 0.989 | 0.989 | 0.989 | 0.989 | 0.989 |
| | STDE | 0.003 | **0.000** | **0.000** | **0.000** | 0.002 | **0.000** | **0.000** | **0.000** | 0.002 | **0.000** | **0.000** | **0.000** |
| THCA | Average | 1.000 | 1.000 | 1.000 | 1.000 | 1.000 | 1.000 | 1.000 | 1.000 | 1.000 | 1.000 | 1.000 | 1.000 |
| | STDE | 0.000 | 0.000 | 0.000 | 0.000 | 0.000 | 0.000 | 0.000 | 0.000 | 0.000 | 0.000 | 0.000 | 0.000 |
| THYM | Average | 1.000 | 1.000 | 1.000 | 1.000 | 1.000 | 1.000 | 1.000 | 1.000 | 1.000 | 1.000 | 1.000 | 1.000 |
| | STDE | 0.000 | 0.000 | 0.000 | 0.000 | 0.000 | 0.000 | 0.000 | 0.000 | 0.000 | 0.000 | 0.000 | 0.000 |
| UCEC | Average | 1.000 | 1.000 | 1.000 | 1.000 | 1.000 | 1.000 | 1.000 | 1.000 | 1.000 | 1.000 | 1.000 | 1.000 |
| | STDE | 0.000 | 0.000 | 0.000 | 0.000 | 0.000 | 0.000 | 0.000 | 0.000 | 0.000 | 0.000 | 0.000 | 0.000 |
| Ranking | W\|T\|L | **4\|18\|0** | 0\|18\|4 | 0\|18\|4 | 0\|18\|4 | 0\|18\|4 | 0\|18\|4 | 0\|18\|4 | 0\|18\|4 | 0\|18\|4 | 0\|18\|4 | 0\|18\|4 | 0\|18\|4 |

**Boldface** numbers indicate the best results.

### 4.5. Convergence Analysis

It is evident in Appendix B [57] that the proposed RBAVO-DE employing the SVM and $k$-NN models attained optimum convergence behavior across all benchmarks. Therefore, the convergence performance of the proposed RBAVO-DE employing the SVM and $k$-NN models demonstrates its capability to reach optimal outcomes promptly while maintaining an efficient equilibrium between search and exploitation.

### 4.6. Wilcoxon's Rank-Sum Test

This paper compares the fitness values achieved by the proposed RBAVO-DE and its counterparts pairwise using the Wilcoxon rank-sum test [60], which aims to determine whether there is a statistically significant difference between the different approaches. This test is a crucial tool for evaluating the success of the proposed algorithm. The Wilcoxon test is employed in hypothesis testing to compare matched data. It involves sorting the absolute differences in the outcomes of paired procedures on the $j^{th}$ of $N$ issues. Next, the lowest value is found by summing the positive ($R^+$) and negative ($R^-$) rankings. The null hypothesis is rejected if the resultant significance level is less than 5%, and not rejected otherwise.

From examining the results of the comparison made between the RBAVO-DE and its counterparts pairwise using the Wilcoxon test, we found that all $R^+$ values equal 253, all $R^-$ values equal 0, and all $p$-values equal $4.768 \times 10^{-7}$ which are less than 0.05 (significance level of 5%). Hence, it can be concluded that the proposed RBAVO-DE employing SVM and $k$-NN performs better than any other algorithm in all cases. Therefore, all $p$-values less than 0.05 (significance level of 5%) offer compelling evidence that the outcomes of the proposed strategy are statistically significant and not just coincidental.

### 4.7. Computational Complexity of the RBAVO-DE Algorithm and Various Meta-Heuristic Algorithms

#### 4.7.1. Computational Complexity of the Execution Time of the RBAVO-DE Algorithm

Each of RBAVO-DE's five core steps can be analyzed separately to determine its computational complexity. These steps include filtering features, initializing the population, boosting and amending the position, appraising the fitness function, and using DE. Then, $O_{execute\_time}(RBAVO-DE)$ can be utilized to represent the overall computational complexity of the proposed RBAVO-DE algorithm. This can be computed using the following big-O notation formulas:

$$\begin{aligned} O_{execute\_time}(RBAVO-DE) = {} & O_{execute\_time}(\text{Filtering features})+ \\ & O_{execute\_time}(\text{Initializing population})+ \\ & O_{execute\_time}(\text{Boosting and amending position})+ \\ & O_{execute\_time}(\text{Appraising fitness function})+ \\ & O_{execute\_time}(\text{Incorporating DE technique}). \end{aligned} \tag{27}$$

Since $N$ determines the population size, $G_{max}$ is the maximum number of iterations allowed, and $D$ is the problem's dimensional space. Hence,

$O_{execute\_time}(\text{Filtering features}) = O_{execute\_time}(D)$.
$O_{execute\_time}(\text{Initializing population}) = O_{execute\_time}(N)$.
$O_{execute\_time}(\text{Boosting and amending position}) = O_{execute\_time}(G_{max} \times N \times D)$.
$O_{execute\_time}(\text{Appraising fitness function}) = O_{execute\_time}(G_{max} \times N)$.
$O_{execute\_time}(\text{Incorporating DE technique}) = O_{execute\_time}(N \times D)$.

For that,

$$\begin{aligned} O_{execute\_time}(RBAVO-DE) = {} & O_{execute\_time}(D)+ \\ & O_{execute\_time}(N) + O_{execute\_time}(G_{max} \times N \times D)+ \\ & O_{execute\_time}(G_{max} \times N) + O_{execute\_time}(N \times D) = \\ & O_{execute\_time}(G_{max} \times N \times D). \end{aligned}$$

4.7.2. Computational Complexity of the Memory Usage of the RBAVO-DE Algorithm

This involves measuring the amount of memory required by an algorithm to tackle a problem as the quantity of the input increases. It is frequently expressed as the additional memory needed by the algorithm beyond the input. It entails merging the following two primary elements:

1. **Memory usage of input variables**: This is the amount of memory required for the algorithm to store the input data. There are 13 input variables related to the proposed RBAVO-DE algorithm, as follows: $N$, $G_{max}$, $D$, $LB$, $UB$, $C_R$, $W_M$, $L_1$, $L_2$, $w$, $P_1$, $P_2$, and $P_3$. Since each variable stores numerical values, 4 bytes of memory are utilized by each one. Consequently, the total memory usage complexity of these 13 input variables is 52 bytes (13 × 4 bytes = 52 bytes). The memory usage complexity of the input values is constant.
2. **Additional memory usage**: This shows how much more memory the algorithm needs in addition to the input. It includes the memory required for data structures, internal variables, and other components of the algorithm. Regardless of the size of the input, the RBAVO-DE algorithm requires a specific amount of extra memory. The following variables are involved:
    - The memory usage complexity consumed by $X_{initial}$ is $(4 \times N \times D)$ bytes. This is because each position in the positions vector $X_{initial}$ requires 4 bytes of memory, and its size is $(N \times D)$, proportionate to the initial population of $N$ positions with dimension size $D$. Because the amount of memory required rises linearly with the value $(N \times D)$, its memory use complexity is linear.
    - The variables $pr$, $g$, $F_i$, $t$, $R$, $D_i$, $d_t$, $S_1$, $S_2$, $A_1$, $A_2$, $sigma$, $fit(X_i)$, $fit(X_{Best_1})$, $fit(X_{SecondBest_2})$, and $fit(X_{Best})$ require 4 bytes of memory space each since they only represent numerical values. As a result, the total memory usage complexity of these 16 variables is 64 bytes (16 × 4 bytes = 64 bytes). This memory usage complexity is constant.
    - The position vectors $BestVulture_1$, $SecondBestVulture_2$, $X_i$, $Levy_d$, $\mu$, $\sigma$, $X_i^{bin}$, $v_i$, $X_{r_1}$, $X_{r_2}$, $X_{r_3}$, $u_i$, and $X_{Best}$ each require 4 bytes of memory space, and the size of each vector is $D$, proportionate to the dimension size of the acquired positions. As a result, the vectors at these 13 points have a total memory usage complexity of $(52 \times D)$ bytes ($13 \times 4 \times D$ bytes). Since the memory needed grows linearly with the value $D$, its memory consumption complexity is linear.

   As a result, the overall memory usage complexity for all of the additional variables listed above is $(4 \times N \times D) + 64 + (52 \times D)$ bytes.

Lastly, the following formula can be used to determine the computational complexity of the overall memory usage of the proposed RBAVO-DE algorithm:

$$\text{Memory usage complexity(RBAVO-DE)} = \text{Input values memory usage} + \text{Additional memory usage} = 52 + \left((4 \times N \times D) + 64 + (52 \times D)\right) \text{ bytes.}$$

Keep in mind that there are constant bytes that are not taken into account. In big-O notation, the computational complexity of the total memory consumption of RBAVO-DE can be represented as $O_{memory\_usage}(RBAVO - DE)$. This can then be calculated in big-O notation after eliminating all constants in the following way:

$$O_{memory\_usage}(RBAVO - DE) = O_{memory\_usage}(\text{Input values memory usage}) + O_{memory\_usage}(\text{Additional memory usage}) = O_{memory\_usage}(1) + (O_{memory\_usage}(N \times D) + O_{memory\_usage}(1) + O_{memory\_usage}(D)) = O_{memory\_usage}(N \times D).$$

It can be difficult to compile a thorough comparison of the memory usage and execution time complexity of various meta-heuristic algorithms since these complexities might differ based on the particular implementation, size of the problem, and other operators. Furthermore, not all of the algorithms listed have comprehensive evaluations of the execution time and memory usage complexity available, and their properties may vary depending on the problem at hand.

## 5. Benefits and Drawbacks of the RBAVO-DE Algorithm

This part presents a balanced discussion of the benefits and drawbacks of the RBAVO-DE algorithm. The benefits of the RBAVO-DE algorithm can be listed as follows:

- **High Accuracy in Classification**: The RBAVO-DE algorithm has demonstrated high classification accuracy, achieving up to 100% in some cases. This is a noteworthy achievement, particularly regarding cancer datasets, as accurate gene selection can directly impact diagnostic and therapeutic outcomes.
- **Effective Feature Size Reduction**: The algorithm has shown remarkable capability in reducing the feature size by up to 98% while maintaining or improving classification accuracy. This dimensionality reduction is crucial for processing high-dimensional datasets efficiently.
- **Robustness Across Diverse Datasets**: The effectiveness of the RBAVO-DE algorithm across twenty-two cancer datasets indicates its robustness and adaptability to various genetic data characteristics. This versatility is beneficial for broader applications in genomics research.
- **Superior Performance Over Competitors**: When compared with binary variants of widely recognized meta-heuristic algorithms, RBAVO-DE stands out for its outstanding performance in accuracy and feature reduction, highlighting its innovative approach to gene selection.

On the other hand, the drawbacks of the proposed methodology can be listed as follows:

- **Computational Complexity**: The high dimensionality of the datasets and the iterative nature of meta-heuristic algorithms suggest that RBAVO-DE may have a significant computational cost. This aspect could limit its applicability in environments with constrained computational resources.
- **Generalizability Concerns**: Despite its success across various cancer datasets, the algorithm's generalizability to other types of biological data or diseases remains to be thoroughly investigated. It is crucial to test RBAVO-DE in broader contexts to confirm its applicability beyond the datasets examined.
- **Parameter Sensitivity**: Like many meta-heuristic algorithms, RBAVO-DE might be sensitive to its parameter settings, affecting performance and efficiency. Detailed studies on the impact of different parameter configurations and strategies for their optimization could enhance the algorithm's utility.

In summary, the RBAVO-DE algorithm represents a significant advancement in gene selection for cancer classification, with notable strengths in accuracy and efficiency. However, addressing its potential drawbacks through further research could broaden its applicability and improve its performance, making it an even more valuable tool in genomics and personalized medicine.

## 6. Conclusions and Future Directions

The RBAVO-DE approach proposed in this paper was the first to be implemented for handling GS issues in RNA-Seq gene expression data and determining potential biomarkers for different tumor classes to enhance the best solution discovered. The outcomes were promising, revealing that the proposed RBAVO-DE algorithm's effectiveness and capabilities were significantly improved. SVM and *k*-NN, two widely used classification models, were employed to evaluate the efficacy of each set of selected genes. The proposed RBAVO-DE algorithm's capability was compared to binary variants of eleven widely used meta-heuristic techniques to assess it on different tumor classes with various instances. The assessment was executed employing a combination of evaluation measures, such as average fitness, classification accuracy, the number of selected genes, precision, recall, and F1-score. The proposed RBAVO-DE algorithm using the SVM and *k*-NN classifiers achieved more promising results than other optimizers in handling GS issues. Despite the promising outcomes, this research opens several avenues for future exploration to further advance the field:

- Algorithmic Enhancements: Improving the algorithm's efficiency and reducing computational complexity.
- Cross-disease Applicability: Testing the proposed algorithm on genetic data from various diseases beyond cancer.
- Comparative Analyses with Deep Learning Models: Evaluating RBAVO-DE against advanced deep learning models for genetic data analysis.
- Real-world Clinical Validation: Collaborating with clinical experts to validate the practical utility of selected genes in cancer treatment.
- Scalability and Parallelization: Enhancing the algorithm's scalability through parallel computing to handle larger genetic datasets efficiently.
- Interdisciplinary Applications: Exploring the algorithm's potential in other fields dealing with high-dimensional data, such as finance and environmental modeling.

In conclusion, while the RBAVO-DE algorithm represents a significant step forward in the field of gene selection for cancer classification, the paths outlined for future research highlight the potential for further advancements and broader applications of this work. Continued interdisciplinary collaboration and innovation will be crucial for unlocking the full capacity of gene selection methodologies to enhance healthcare outcomes and advance our understanding of complex diseases.

**Author Contributions:** M.G.G.: Resources, Validation, and Writing—review and editing. A.A.A.: Resources, Formal analysis, Data Curation, Validation, Writing—original draft, and Writing—review and editing. A.E.E.: Investigation, Visualization, Data Curation, Validation, Writing—original draft, and Writing—review and editing. A.A.A.E.-M.: Conceptualization, Methodology, Software, Formal analysis, Investigation, Data Curation, Validation, Writing—original draft, and Writing—review and editing. All authors have read and agreed to the published version of the manuscript.

**Funding:** Prince Sattam bin Abdulaziz University funded this research work under project number PSAU/2023/01/25612.

**Data Availability Statement:** For enhancing the applicability and reproducibility of this research, the developed software and relevant Python code of this research are publicly available and obtainable in [61].

**Acknowledgments:** The authors express their gratitude to Prince Sattam bin Abdulaziz University for providing financial support for this research project.

**Conflicts of Interest:** The authors declare that they have no known competing financial interests or personal relationships that could have appeared to influence the work reported in this paper.

## Abbreviations

The following abbreviations are used in this research:

| | |
|---|---|
| AVO | African Vultures Optimization |
| HNSC | Head and Neck Squamous Cell Carcinoma |
| DE | Differential Evolution |
| KICH | Kidney Chromophobe |
| RBAVO-DE | Relief Binary African Vultures Optimization based on Differential Evolution |
| KIRP | Kidney Renal Papillary |
| GS | Gene Selection |
| LIHC | Liver Hepatocellular Carcinoma |
| RNA-Seq | RNA Sequencing |

| | |
|---|---|
| PAAD | Pancreatic Adenocarcinoma |
| DNA | Deoxyribonucleic Acid |
| PCPG | Pheochromocytoma and Paraganglioma |
| SVM | Support Vector Machine |
| READ | Rectum adenocarcinoma |
| $k$-NN | k-Nearest Neighbor |
| SARC | Sarcoma |
| FS | Feature Selection |
| SKCM | Skin Cutaneous Melanoma |
| MHMs | Meta-heuristic methods |
| $Mean_{Fi}$ | Mean fitness |
| ML | Machine Learning |
| $MeanGe$ | Mean size of chosen genes |
| DL | Deep learning |
| $STDE$ | Standard Deviation |
| SA | Simulated Annealing |
| RF | Random Forest |
| FOIL | First-Order Inductive Learner |
| GSO | Gravitational Optimizer |
| SCCSA | Sine-Cosine–Cuckoo Search Algorithm |
| SMO | Spider Monkey Optimization |
| BHGSO | Binary Henry Gas Solubility Optimization |
| BPSO | Binary Particle Swarm Optimization |
| BABC | Binary Artificial Bee Colony |
| BSSA | Binary Salp Swarm Algorithm |
| BBA | Binary Bat Algorithm |
| BGWO | Binary Grey-Wolf Optimization |
| BGOA | Binary Grasshopper Optimization Algorithm |
| BWOA | Binary Whale Optimization Algorithm |
| BASO | Binary Atom Search Optimization |
| BBSA | Binary Bird Swarm Algorithm |
| BHHO | Binary Harris Hawks Optimization |
| BBBO | Binary Brown-Bear Optimization |
| BAO | Binary Aquila Optimization |
| BMOA | Binary Meerkat Optimization Algorithm |
| LUAD | Lung Adenocarcinoma |
| LUSC | Lung Squamous Cell Carcinoma |
| BRCA | Breast Invasive Carcinoma |
| KIRC | Kidney Renal Clear Cell Carcinoma |
| UCEC | Uterine Corpus Endometrial Carcinoma |
| RPKM | Reads Per Kilobase per Million mapped reads |
| STAD | Stomach Adenocarcinoma |
| SDAE | Stacked Denoising Autoencoder |
| CGA | Cancer Genome Atlas |
| BLCA | Bladder Urothelial Carcinoma |
| THCA | Thyroid Cancer |
| CESC | Cervical and Endocervical Cancers |
| CHOL | Cholangiocarcinoma |
| COAD | Colon Adenocarcinoma |
| ESCA | Esophageal Cancer |
| GBM | Glioblastoma Multiforme |
| THYM | Thymoma |

## Appendix A. Comparison Results of the Proposed RBAVO-DE and Its Counterparts

### *Appendix A.1. Comparison Results Based on the k-NN Model*

**Table A1.** The results of the proposed RBAVO-DE algorithm and its counterparts employing *k*-NN regarding average fitness values.

| Dataset | Metric | RBAVO-DE | BSSA | BABC | BPSO | BBA | BGWO | BWOA | BGOA | BHHO | BBSA | BASO | BHGSO |
|---|---|---|---|---|---|---|---|---|---|---|---|---|---|
| BLCA | Average | **0.00190** | 0.01110 | 0.00710 | 0.01120 | 0.01470 | 0.00940 | 0.01070 | 0.01140 | 0.01310 | 0.01030 | 0.01080 | 0.01590 |
| | STDE | 0.00430 | 0.00530 | 0.00440 | 0.00540 | 0.00240 | 0.00550 | 0.00540 | 0.00540 | 0.00440 | 0.00550 | 0.00540 | 0.00180 |
| CESC | Average | **0.01610** | 0.01990 | 0.02020 | 0.02050 | 0.01980 | 0.02000 | 0.02020 | 0.02020 | 0.01970 | 0.02020 | 0.02030 | 0.02060 |
| | STDE | **0.00000** | 0.00020 | 0.00010 | 0.00010 | 0.00020 | 0.00020 | 0.00020 | 0.00010 | 0.00010 | 0.00010 | 0.00010 | 0.00010 |
| CHOL | Average | **0.00000** | 0.00390 | 0.00430 | 0.00450 | 0.00390 | 0.00400 | 0.00430 | 0.00430 | 0.00370 | 0.00420 | 0.00420 | 0.00470 |
| | STDE | **0.00000** | 0.00020 | 0.00010 | 0.00010 | 0.00020 | 0.00020 | 0.00020 | 0.00010 | 0.00010 | 0.00010 | 0.00010 | 0.00010 |
| COAD | Average | **0.00000** | 0.00390 | 0.00430 | 0.00450 | 0.00390 | 0.00400 | 0.00430 | 0.00430 | 0.00370 | 0.00420 | 0.00420 | 0.00470 |
| | STDE | **0.00000** | 0.00020 | 0.00010 | 0.00010 | 0.00020 | 0.00020 | 0.00020 | 0.00010 | 0.00010 | 0.00010 | 0.00010 | 0.00010 |
| ESCA | Average | **0.02560** | 0.02930 | 0.02960 | 0.02990 | 0.02930 | 0.02940 | 0.02970 | 0.02960 | 0.02910 | 0.02960 | 0.02980 | 0.03000 |
| | STDE | **0.00000** | 0.00020 | 0.00010 | 0.00010 | 0.00020 | 0.00020 | 0.00020 | 0.00010 | 0.00010 | 0.00010 | 0.00010 | 0.00020 |
| GBM | Average | **0.00000** | 0.00390 | 0.00430 | 0.00450 | 0.00390 | 0.00400 | 0.00430 | 0.00430 | 0.00370 | 0.00420 | 0.00420 | 0.00470 |
| | STDE | **0.00000** | 0.00020 | 0.00010 | 0.00010 | 0.00020 | 0.00020 | 0.00020 | 0.00010 | 0.00010 | 0.00010 | 0.00010 | 0.00010 |
| HNSC | Average | **0.00710** | 0.01250 | 0.01290 | 0.01330 | 0.01280 | 0.01240 | 0.01310 | 0.01320 | 0.01270 | 0.01290 | 0.01320 | 0.01360 |
| | STDE | 0.00350 | 0.00160 | 0.00140 | **0.00010** | 0.00030 | 0.00210 | **0.00010** | **0.00010** | 0.00020 | 0.00150 | **0.00010** | **0.00010** |
| KICH | Average | **0.00000** | 0.00390 | 0.00430 | 0.00450 | 0.00390 | 0.00400 | 0.00430 | 0.00430 | 0.00370 | 0.00420 | 0.00420 | 0.00470 |
| | STDE | **0.00000** | 0.00020 | 0.00010 | 0.00010 | 0.00020 | 0.00020 | 0.00020 | 0.00010 | 0.00010 | 0.00010 | 0.00010 | 0.00010 |
| KIRC | Average | **0.00250** | 0.01110 | 0.01040 | 0.01220 | 0.01200 | 0.01020 | 0.01200 | 0.01070 | 0.01040 | 0.01120 | 0.01170 | 0.01290 |
| | STDE | 0.00380 | 0.00270 | 0.00340 | 0.00190 | 0.00020 | 0.00340 | 0.00190 | 0.00320 | 0.00300 | 0.00280 | 0.00220 | **0.00010** |
| KIRP | Average | **0.00000** | 0.00390 | 0.00430 | 0.00450 | 0.00390 | 0.00400 | 0.00430 | 0.00430 | 0.00370 | 0.00420 | 0.00420 | 0.00470 |
| | STDE | **0.00000** | 0.00020 | 0.00010 | 0.00010 | 0.00020 | 0.00020 | 0.00020 | 0.00010 | 0.00010 | 0.00010 | 0.00010 | 0.00010 |
| LIHC | Average | **0.00000** | 0.00390 | 0.00430 | 0.00450 | 0.00390 | 0.00400 | 0.00420 | 0.00430 | 0.00380 | 0.00430 | 0.00420 | 0.00460 |
| | STDE | **0.00000** | 0.00020 | 0.00010 | 0.00010 | 0.00020 | 0.00020 | 0.00020 | 0.00010 | 0.00010 | 0.00010 | 0.00010 | 0.00010 |
| LUAD | Average | **0.00870** | 0.01260 | 0.01290 | 0.01310 | 0.01240 | 0.01270 | 0.01290 | 0.01290 | 0.01240 | 0.01290 | 0.01300 | 0.01340 |
| | STDE | **0.00000** | 0.00020 | 0.00010 | 0.00010 | 0.00020 | 0.00020 | 0.00010 | 0.00010 | 0.00020 | 0.00010 | 0.00010 | 0.00010 |
| LUSC | Average | **0.00000** | 0.00400 | 0.00430 | 0.00450 | 0.00380 | 0.00410 | 0.00430 | 0.00430 | 0.00390 | 0.00430 | 0.00430 | 0.00480 |
| | STDE | **0.00000** | 0.00020 | 0.00010 | 0.00010 | 0.00020 | 0.00010 | 0.00020 | 0.00010 | 0.00010 | 0.00010 | 0.00010 | 0.00010 |
| PAAD | Average | **0.00000** | 0.00390 | 0.00430 | 0.00450 | 0.00390 | 0.00400 | 0.00430 | 0.00430 | 0.00370 | 0.00420 | 0.00420 | 0.00470 |
| | STDE | **0.00000** | 0.00020 | 0.00010 | 0.00010 | 0.00020 | 0.00020 | 0.00020 | 0.00010 | 0.00010 | 0.00010 | 0.00010 | 0.00010 |
| PCPG | Average | **0.00000** | 0.00390 | 0.00430 | 0.00450 | 0.00390 | 0.00400 | 0.00430 | 0.00430 | 0.00370 | 0.00420 | 0.00420 | 0.00470 |
| | STDE | **0.00000** | 0.00020 | 0.00010 | 0.00010 | 0.00020 | 0.00020 | 0.00020 | 0.00010 | 0.00010 | 0.00010 | 0.00010 | 0.00010 |
| READ | Average | **0.00000** | 0.00390 | 0.00430 | 0.00450 | 0.00390 | 0.00400 | 0.00430 | 0.00430 | 0.00370 | 0.00420 | 0.00420 | 0.00470 |
| | STDE | **0.00000** | 0.00020 | 0.00010 | 0.00010 | 0.00020 | 0.00020 | 0.00020 | 0.00010 | 0.00010 | 0.00010 | 0.00010 | 0.00010 |
| SARC | Average | **0.01890** | 0.02260 | 0.02290 | 0.02320 | 0.02260 | 0.02270 | 0.02300 | 0.02290 | 0.02240 | 0.02290 | 0.02300 | 0.02330 |
| | STDE | **0.00000** | 0.00020 | 0.00010 | 0.00010 | 0.00020 | 0.00020 | 0.00020 | 0.00010 | 0.00010 | 0.00010 | 0.00010 | 0.00010 |
| SKCM | Average | **0.00000** | 0.00390 | 0.00430 | 0.00450 | 0.00390 | 0.00400 | 0.00430 | 0.00430 | 0.00370 | 0.00420 | 0.00420 | 0.00470 |
| | STDE | **0.00000** | 0.00020 | 0.00010 | 0.00010 | 0.00020 | 0.00020 | 0.00020 | 0.00010 | 0.00010 | 0.00010 | 0.00010 | 0.00010 |
| STAD | Average | **0.00070** | 0.00830 | 0.00620 | 0.00930 | 0.01470 | 0.00810 | 0.00950 | 0.00800 | 0.01170 | 0.00940 | 0.00840 | 0.01570 |
| | STDE | 0.00280 | 0.00500 | 0.00360 | 0.00510 | 0.00020 | 0.00500 | 0.00510 | 0.00480 | 0.00480 | 0.00520 | 0.00490 | **0.00010** |
| THCA | Average | **0.00000** | 0.00390 | 0.00430 | 0.00450 | 0.00390 | 0.00400 | 0.00430 | 0.00430 | 0.00370 | 0.00420 | 0.00420 | 0.00460 |
| | STDE | **0.00000** | 0.00020 | 0.00010 | 0.00010 | 0.00020 | 0.00020 | 0.00020 | 0.00010 | 0.00010 | 0.00010 | 0.00010 | 0.00010 |
| THYM | Average | **0.00000** | 0.00390 | 0.00430 | 0.00450 | 0.00390 | 0.00400 | 0.00430 | 0.00430 | 0.00370 | 0.00420 | 0.00420 | 0.00470 |
| | STDE | **0.00000** | 0.00020 | 0.00010 | 0.00010 | 0.00020 | 0.00020 | 0.00020 | 0.00010 | 0.00010 | 0.00010 | 0.00010 | 0.00010 |
| UCEC | Average | **0.00000** | 0.01920 | 0.01710 | 0.02780 | 0.03540 | 0.02010 | 0.02770 | 0.02690 | 0.02560 | 0.02520 | 0.02860 | 0.03670 |
| | STDE | **0.00250** | 0.01200 | 0.01220 | 0.00610 | 0.01000 | 0.01190 | 0.00620 | 0.00720 | 0.00830 | 0.00910 | 0.00450 | 0.01050 |
| Ranking | W\|T\|L | **22\|0\|0** | 0\|0\|22 | 0\|0\|22 | 0\|0\|22 | 0\|0\|22 | 0\|0\|22 | 0\|0\|22 | 0\|0\|22 | 0\|0\|22 | 0\|0\|22 | 0\|0\|22 | 0\|0\|22 |

**Boldface** values denote the best results.

**Table A2.** The results of the proposed RBAVO-DE algorithm and its counterparts employing *k*-NN regarding average values of selected genes.

| Dataset | Metric | RBAVO-DE | BSSA | BABC | BPSO | BBA | BGWO | BWOA | BGOA | BHHO | BBSA | BASO | BHGSO |
|---|---|---|---|---|---|---|---|---|---|---|---|---|---|
| BLCA | Average | **142.03** | 210.17 | 237.70 | 235.00 | 196.03 | 218.17 | 228.50 | 226.30 | 195.23 | 228.27 | 232.03 | 237.13 |
| | STDE | 017.18 | 020.50 | 019.07 | 017.12 | 023.83 | 018.27 | 019.43 | 014.81 | **013.17** | 014.60 | 018.90 | 014.14 |
| CESC | Average | **122.50** | 195.13 | 213.03 | 225.30 | 194.10 | 199.50 | 213.63 | 212.67 | 185.60 | 213.33 | 215.90 | 233.43 |
| | STDE | 005.45 | 011.17 | 005.31 | **003.11** | 009.66 | 009.30 | 008.35 | 005.66 | 006.49 | 005.88 | 006.02 | 005.64 |
| CHOL | Average | **122.13** | 195.13 | 213.03 | 225.30 | 194.10 | 199.50 | 213.63 | 212.67 | 185.60 | 211.00 | 211.57 | 232.63 |
| | STDE | 006.18 | 011.17 | 005.31 | **003.11** | 009.66 | 009.30 | 008.35 | 005.66 | 006.49 | 006.44 | 005.08 | 004.36 |
| COAD | Average | **120.30** | 195.13 | 213.03 | 225.30 | 194.10 | 199.50 | 213.63 | 212.67 | 185.60 | 211.00 | 211.57 | 232.63 |
| | STDE | 005.82 | 011.17 | 005.31 | **003.11** | 009.66 | 009.30 | 008.35 | 005.66 | 006.49 | 006.44 | 005.08 | 004.36 |
| ESCA | Average | **120.17** | 195.13 | 213.03 | 225.30 | 194.10 | 199.50 | 213.63 | 212.67 | 185.60 | 211.57 | 218.87 | 230.07 |
| | STDE | 006.81 | 011.17 | 005.31 | **003.11** | 009.66 | 009.30 | 008.35 | 005.66 | 006.49 | 006.94 | 004.68 | 007.64 |
| GBM | Average | **120.73** | 195.13 | 212.77 | 225.30 | 194.10 | 199.73 | 213.17 | 212.80 | 185.43 | 211.00 | 211.83 | 232.63 |
| | STDE | 006.54 | 011.17 | 005.40 | **003.11** | 009.66 | 009.05 | 008.51 | 005.72 | 006.40 | 006.44 | 004.99 | 004.39 |
| HNSC | Average | **133.43** | 202.87 | 222.67 | 227.43 | 203.00 | 211.37 | 217.97 | 220.87 | 195.93 | 219.83 | 223.63 | 241.27 |
| | STDE | 017.63 | 009.26 | 011.96 | **003.91** | 013.24 | 007.65 | 007.41 | 005.32 | 008.26 | 007.71 | 005.68 | 006.21 |
| KICH | Average | **121.43** | 195.13 | 213.03 | 225.30 | 194.10 | 199.50 | 213.63 | 212.67 | 185.60 | 211.00 | 211.57 | 232.63 |
| | STDE | 006.58 | 011.17 | 005.31 | **003.11** | 009.66 | 009.30 | 008.35 | 005.66 | 006.49 | 006.44 | 005.08 | 004.36 |

**Table A2.** *Cont.*

| Dataset | Metric | RBAVO-DE | BSSA | BABC | BPSO | BBA | BGWO | BWOA | BGOA | BHHO | BBSA | BASO | BHGSO |
|---|---|---|---|---|---|---|---|---|---|---|---|---|---|
| KIRC | Average | **137.57** | 200.83 | 220.17 | 227.70 | 192.17 | 209.87 | 216.13 | 222.30 | 193.27 | 218.73 | 218.60 | 234.10 |
| | STDE | 017.10 | 009.63 | 011.74 | 008.27 | 008.73 | 014.08 | 010.11 | 015.18 | 017.36 | 013.82 | 012.78 | **004.21** |
| KIRP | Average | **122.33** | 195.13 | 213.03 | 225.30 | 194.10 | 199.50 | 213.63 | 212.67 | 185.60 | 211.00 | 211.57 | 232.63 |
| | STDE | 009.08 | 011.17 | 005.31 | **003.11** | 009.66 | 009.30 | 008.35 | 005.66 | 006.49 | 006.44 | 005.08 | 004.36 |
| LIHC | Average | **123.40** | 197.00 | 214.03 | 225.67 | 193.33 | 200.63 | 212.33 | 213.63 | 189.30 | 213.10 | 212.03 | 232.43 |
| | STDE | 006.59 | 007.78 | 005.22 | **003.36** | 009.17 | 010.02 | 009.35 | 004.89 | 006.89 | 005.69 | 004.81 | 004.97 |
| LUAD | Average | **127.03** | 197.47 | 216.13 | 222.93 | 190.83 | 205.33 | 212.57 | 215.67 | 191.80 | 215.27 | 217.83 | 237.90 |
| | STDE | 008.62 | 008.98 | 004.74 | 006.16 | 008.61 | 010.57 | 006.15 | **004.43** | 008.50 | 006.13 | 004.71 | 004.94 |
| LUSC | Average | **125.73** | 198.87 | 215.63 | 223.00 | 189.13 | 203.60 | 213.23 | 216.37 | 194.67 | 215.53 | 215.23 | 241.23 |
| | STDE | 006.35 | 008.77 | 003.54 | 004.89 | 010.69 | 007.20 | 009.70 | **003.44** | 006.40 | 005.54 | 006.16 | 004.66 |
| PAAD | Average | **121.10** | 195.13 | 213.03 | 225.30 | 194.10 | 199.50 | 213.63 | 212.67 | 185.60 | 211.00 | 211.57 | 232.63 |
| | STDE | 007.71 | 011.17 | 005.31 | **003.11** | 009.66 | 009.30 | 008.35 | 005.66 | 006.49 | 006.44 | 005.08 | 004.36 |
| PCPG | Average | **122.17** | 195.13 | 213.03 | 225.30 | 194.10 | 199.50 | 213.63 | 212.67 | 185.60 | 211.00 | 211.57 | 232.63 |
| | STDE | 006.42 | 011.17 | 005.31 | **003.11** | 009.66 | 009.30 | 008.35 | 005.66 | 006.49 | 006.44 | 005.08 | 004.36 |
| READ | Average | **120.13** | 195.13 | 213.03 | 225.30 | 194.10 | 199.50 | 213.63 | 212.67 | 185.60 | 211.00 | 211.57 | 232.63 |
| | STDE | 007.72 | 011.17 | 005.31 | **003.11** | 009.66 | 009.30 | 008.35 | 005.66 | 006.49 | 006.44 | 005.08 | 004.36 |
| SARC | Average | **122.47** | 195.13 | 213.03 | 225.30 | 194.10 | 199.50 | 213.63 | 212.67 | 185.60 | 212.90 | 216.43 | 231.80 |
| | STDE | 005.79 | 011.17 | 005.31 | **003.11** | 009.66 | 009.30 | 008.35 | 005.66 | 006.49 | 006.30 | 004.98 | 003.40 |
| SKCM | Average | **123.03** | 195.13 | 213.03 | 225.30 | 194.10 | 199.50 | 213.63 | 212.67 | 185.60 | 211.00 | 211.57 | 232.63 |
| | STDE | 008.83 | 011.17 | 005.31 | **003.11** | 009.66 | 009.30 | 008.35 | 005.66 | 006.49 | 006.44 | 005.08 | 004.36 |
| STAD | Average | **142.60** | 215.00 | 236.17 | 243.33 | 187.50 | 221.17 | 234.87 | 232.77 | 201.73 | 231.13 | 237.10 | 236.97 |
| | STDE | 013.31 | 018.43 | 013.94 | 016.29 | 010.27 | 019.24 | 022.63 | 014.25 | 014.00 | 014.04 | 015.35 | **005.86** |
| THCA | Average | **117.97** | 195.43 | 213.40 | 225.13 | 194.10 | 199.63 | 214.13 | 212.80 | 186.53 | 211.00 | 211.57 | 231.90 |
| | STDE | 006.67 | 011.20 | 005.29 | **003.10** | 009.66 | 009.81 | 008.59 | 005.69 | 005.88 | 006.44 | 005.08 | 004.78 |
| THYM | Average | **120.37** | 195.13 | 213.03 | 225.30 | 194.10 | 199.50 | 213.63 | 212.67 | 185.60 | 211.00 | 211.57 | 232.63 |
| | STDE | 004.89 | 011.17 | 005.31 | **003.11** | 009.66 | 009.30 | 008.35 | 005.66 | 006.49 | 006.44 | 005.08 | 004.36 |
| UCEC | Average | **143.93** | 216.33 | 237.87 | 236.00 | 242.37 | 220.07 | 230.80 | 229.17 | 206.77 | 228.40 | 235.00 | 266.67 |
| | STDE | 013.18 | 015.41 | 015.82 | 010.11 | 034.13 | 011.26 | 011.27 | 011.66 | 010.84 | 010.32 | **006.14** | 030.55 |
| Ranking | W\|T\|L | **22\|0\|0** | 0\|0\|22 | 0\|0\|22 | 0\|0\|22 | 0\|0\|22 | 0\|0\|22 | 0\|0\|22 | 0\|0\|22 | 0\|0\|22 | 0\|0\|22 | 0\|0\|22 | 0\|0\|22 |

**Boldface** values denote the best results.

**Table A3.** The results of the proposed RBAVO-DE algorithm and its counterparts employing *k*-NN regarding average precision values.

| Dataset | RBAVO-DE | BSSA | BABC | BPSO | BBA | BGWO | BWOA | BGOA | BHHO | BBSA | BASO | BHGSO |
|---|---|---|---|---|---|---|---|---|---|---|---|---|
| BLCA | **1.00000** | **1.00000** | **1.00000** | **1.00000** | 0.99960 | **1.00000** | **1.00000** | **1.00000** | **1.00000** | **1.00000** | **1.00000** | **1.00000** |
| CESC | **0.98390** | **0.98390** | **0.98390** | **0.98390** | **0.98390** | **0.98390** | **0.98390** | **0.98390** | **0.98390** | **0.98390** | **0.98390** | **0.98390** |
| CHOL | **1.00000** | **1.00000** | **1.00000** | **1.00000** | **1.00000** | **1.00000** | **1.00000** | **1.00000** | **1.00000** | **1.00000** | **1.00000** | **1.00000** |
| COAD | **1.00000** | **1.00000** | **1.00000** | **1.00000** | 0.99890 | **1.00000** | **1.00000** | **1.00000** | **1.00000** | **1.00000** | **1.00000** | **1.00000** |
| ESCA | **0.97370** | **0.97370** | **0.97370** | **0.97370** | **0.97370** | **0.97370** | **0.97370** | **0.97370** | **0.97370** | **0.97370** | **0.97370** | **0.97370** |
| GBM | **1.00000** | **1.00000** | **1.00000** | **1.00000** | **1.00000** | **1.00000** | **1.00000** | **1.00000** | **1.00000** | **1.00000** | **1.00000** | **1.00000** |
| HNSC | **0.99180** | 0.96470 | 0.96540 | 0.96500 | 0.96350 | 0.96690 | 0.96660 | 0.96570 | 0.96540 | 0.96540 | 0.96100 | 0.96290 |
| KICH | **1.00000** | **1.00000** | **1.00000** | **1.00000** | **1.00000** | **1.00000** | **1.00000** | **1.00000** | **1.00000** | **1.00000** | **1.00000** | **1.00000** |
| KIRC | **1.00000** | **1.00000** | **1.00000** | **1.00000** | **1.00000** | **1.00000** | **1.00000** | **1.00000** | **1.00000** | **1.00000** | **1.00000** | **1.00000** |
| KIRP | **1.00000** | **1.00000** | **1.00000** | **1.00000** | **1.00000** | **1.00000** | **1.00000** | **1.00000** | **1.00000** | **1.00000** | **1.00000** | **1.00000** |
| LIHC | **1.00000** | **1.00000** | **1.00000** | **1.00000** | **1.00000** | **1.00000** | **1.00000** | **1.00000** | **1.00000** | **1.00000** | **1.00000** | **1.00000** |
| LUAD | **1.00000** | 0.99770 | 0.99740 | 0.99840 | 0.99870 | 0.99770 | 0.99800 | 0.99540 | 0.99710 | 0.99740 | 0.99670 | 0.99800 |
| LUSC | **1.00000** | **1.00000** | **1.00000** | **1.00000** | 0.99790 | **1.00000** | 0.99970 | **1.00000** | **1.00000** | **1.00000** | 0.97900 | 0.99930 |
| PAAD | **1.00000** | **1.00000** | **1.00000** | **1.00000** | **1.00000** | **1.00000** | **1.00000** | **1.00000** | **1.00000** | **1.00000** | **1.00000** | **1.00000** |
| PCPG | **1.00000** | **1.00000** | **1.00000** | **1.00000** | **1.00000** | **1.00000** | **1.00000** | **1.00000** | **1.00000** | **1.00000** | **1.00000** | **1.00000** |
| READ | **1.00000** | **1.00000** | **1.00000** | **1.00000** | **1.00000** | **1.00000** | **1.00000** | **1.00000** | **1.00000** | **1.00000** | **1.00000** | **1.00000** |
| SARC | **0.98110** | **0.98110** | **0.98110** | **0.98110** | **0.98110** | **0.98110** | **0.98110** | **0.98110** | **0.98110** | **0.98110** | **0.98110** | **0.98110** |
| SKCM | **1.00000** | **1.00000** | **1.00000** | **1.00000** | **1.00000** | **1.00000** | **1.00000** | **1.00000** | **1.00000** | **1.00000** | **1.00000** | **1.00000** |
| STAD | **0.99920** | 0.95180 | 0.95180 | 0.95180 | 0.94870 | 0.95180 | 0.95180 | 0.95180 | 0.95180 | 0.95180 | 0.99000 | 0.95090 |
| THCA | **1.00000** | **1.00000** | **1.00000** | **1.00000** | **1.00000** | **1.00000** | **1.00000** | **1.00000** | **1.00000** | **1.00000** | **1.00000** | **1.00000** |
| THYM | **1.00000** | **1.00000** | **1.00000** | **1.00000** | **1.00000** | **1.00000** | **1.00000** | **1.00000** | **1.00000** | **1.00000** | **1.00000** | **1.00000** |
| UCEC | **1.00000** | **1.00000** | **1.00000** | **1.00000** | 0.99910 | **1.00000** | **1.00000** | **1.00000** | **1.00000** | **1.00000** | 0.93330 | 0.99910 |
| Ranking (W\|T\|L) | **3\|19\|0** | 0\|19\|3 | 0\|19\|3 | 0\|19\|3 | 0\|15\|7 | 0\|19\|3 | 0\|18\|4 | 0\|19\|3 | 0\|19\|3 | 0\|19\|3 | 0\|17\|5 | 0\|17\|5 |

**Boldface** values denote the best results.

**Table A4.** The results of the proposed RBAVO-DE algorithm and its counterparts employing *k*-NN regarding average recall values.

| Dataset | RBAVO-DE | BSSA | BABC | BPSO | BBA | BGWO | BWOA | BGOA | BHHO | BBSA | BASO | BHGSO |
|---|---|---|---|---|---|---|---|---|---|---|---|---|
| BLCA | **1.00000** | **1.00000** | **1.00000** | **1.00000** | **1.00000** | **1.00000** | **1.00000** | **1.00000** | **1.00000** | **1.00000** | **1.00000** | **1.00000** |
| CESC | **1.00000** | **1.00000** | **1.00000** | **1.00000** | **1.00000** | **1.00000** | **1.00000** | **1.00000** | **1.00000** | **1.00000** | **1.00000** | **1.00000** |
| CHOL | **1.00000** | **1.00000** | **1.00000** | **1.00000** | **1.00000** | **1.00000** | **1.00000** | **1.00000** | **1.00000** | **1.00000** | **1.00000** | **1.00000** |
| COAD | **1.00000** | **1.00000** | **1.00000** | **1.00000** | **1.00000** | **1.00000** | **1.00000** | **1.00000** | **1.00000** | **1.00000** | **1.00000** | **1.00000** |
| ESCA | **1.00000** | **1.00000** | **1.00000** | **1.00000** | **1.00000** | **1.00000** | **1.00000** | **1.00000** | **1.00000** | **1.00000** | **1.00000** | **1.00000** |
| GBM | **1.00000** | **1.00000** | **1.00000** | **1.00000** | **1.00000** | **1.00000** | **1.00000** | **1.00000** | **1.00000** | **1.00000** | **1.00000** | **1.00000** |

**Table A4.** *Cont.*

| Dataset | RBAVO-DE | BSSA | BABC | BPSO | BBA | BGWO | BWOA | BGOA | BHHO | BBSA | BASO | BHGSO |
|---|---|---|---|---|---|---|---|---|---|---|---|---|
| HNSC | **1.00000** | 0.99520 | 0.99450 | 0.99480 | 0.99590 | 0.99280 | 0.99310 | 0.99420 | 0.99450 | 0.99450 | 0.99790 | 0.99730 |
| KICH | **1.00000** | **1.00000** | **1.00000** | **1.00000** | **1.00000** | **1.00000** | **1.00000** | **1.00000** | **1.00000** | **1.00000** | **1.00000** | **1.00000** |
| KIRC | **0.99710** | 0.99040 | 0.99040 | 0.99040 | 0.98970 | 0.99040 | 0.99040 | 0.99040 | 0.99040 | 0.99040 | 0.99010 | 0.99040 |
| KIRP | **1.00000** | **1.00000** | **1.00000** | **1.00000** | **1.00000** | **1.00000** | **1.00000** | **1.00000** | **1.00000** | **1.00000** | **1.00000** | **1.00000** |
| LIHC | **1.00000** | **1.00000** | **1.00000** | **1.00000** | **1.00000** | **1.00000** | **1.00000** | **1.00000** | **1.00000** | **1.00000** | **1.00000** | **1.00000** |
| LUAD | **1.00000** | 0.99240 | 0.99270 | 0.99170 | 0.99140 | 0.99240 | 0.99210 | 0.99470 | 0.99310 | 0.99270 | 0.99340 | 0.99210 |
| LUSC | **1.00000** | **1.00000** | **1.00000** | **1.00000** | 0.99580 | **1.00000** | **1.00000** | **1.00000** | 0.99930 | **1.00000** | 0.99310 | 0.99270 |
| PAAD | **1.00000** | **1.00000** | **1.00000** | **1.00000** | **1.00000** | **1.00000** | **1.00000** | **1.00000** | **1.00000** | **1.00000** | **1.00000** | **1.00000** |
| PCPG | **1.00000** | **1.00000** | **1.00000** | **1.00000** | **1.00000** | **1.00000** | **1.00000** | **1.00000** | **1.00000** | **1.00000** | **1.00000** | **1.00000** |
| READ | **1.00000** | **1.00000** | **1.00000** | **1.00000** | **1.00000** | **1.00000** | **1.00000** | **1.00000** | **1.00000** | **1.00000** | **1.00000** | **1.00000** |
| SARC | **1.00000** | **1.00000** | **1.00000** | **1.00000** | **1.00000** | **1.00000** | **1.00000** | **1.00000** | **1.00000** | **1.00000** | **1.00000** | **1.00000** |
| SKCM | **1.00000** | **1.00000** | **1.00000** | **1.00000** | **1.00000** | **1.00000** | **1.00000** | **1.00000** | **1.00000** | **1.00000** | **1.00000** | **1.00000** |
| STAD | **1.00000** | **1.00000** | **1.00000** | **1.00000** | 0.99750 | **1.00000** | **1.00000** | **1.00000** | **1.00000** | **1.00000** | 0.99620 | 0.99750 |
| THCA | **1.00000** | **1.00000** | **1.00000** | **1.00000** | **1.00000** | **1.00000** | **1.00000** | **1.00000** | **1.00000** | **1.00000** | **1.00000** | **1.00000** |
| THYM | **1.00000** | **1.00000** | **1.00000** | **1.00000** | **1.00000** | **1.00000** | **1.00000** | **1.00000** | **1.00000** | **1.00000** | **1.00000** | **1.00000** |
| UCEC | **1.00000** | **1.00000** | **1.00000** | **1.00000** | 0.99370 | **1.00000** | **1.00000** | **1.00000** | **1.00000** | **1.00000** | 0.99640 | **1.00000** |
| Ranking (W\|T\|L) | 3\|**19**\|0 | 0\|19\|3 | 0\|19\|3 | 0\|19\|3 | 0\|16\|6 | 0\|19\|3 | 0\|19\|3 | 0\|19\|3 | 0\|18\|4 | 0\|19\|3 | 0\|16\|6 | 0\|17\|5 |

**Boldface** values denote the best results.

**Table A5.** The results of the proposed RBAVO-DE algorithm and its counterparts employing *k*-NN regarding average F1-score values.

| Dataset | RBAVO-DE | BSSA | BABC | BPSO | BBA | BGWO | BWOA | BGOA | BHHO | BBSA | BASO | BHGSO |
|---|---|---|---|---|---|---|---|---|---|---|---|---|
| BLCA | **1.00000** | **1.00000** | **1.00000** | **1.00000** | 0.99980 | **1.00000** | **1.00000** | **1.00000** | **1.00000** | **1.00000** | **1.00000** | **1.00000** |
| CESC | **0.99190** | **0.99190** | **0.99190** | **0.99190** | **0.99190** | **0.99190** | **0.99190** | **0.99190** | **0.99190** | **0.99190** | **0.99190** | **0.99190** |
| CHOL | **1.00000** | **1.00000** | **1.00000** | **1.00000** | **1.00000** | **1.00000** | **1.00000** | **1.00000** | **1.00000** | **1.00000** | **1.00000** | **1.00000** |
| COAD | **1.00000** | **1.00000** | **1.00000** | **1.00000** | 0.99940 | **1.00000** | **1.00000** | **1.00000** | **1.00000** | **1.00000** | **1.00000** | **1.00000** |
| ESCA | **0.98670** | **0.98670** | **0.98670** | **0.98670** | **0.98670** | **0.98670** | **0.98670** | **0.98670** | **0.98670** | **0.98670** | **0.98670** | **0.98670** |
| GBM | **1.00000** | **1.00000** | **1.00000** | **1.00000** | **1.00000** | **1.00000** | **1.00000** | **1.00000** | **1.00000** | **1.00000** | **1.00000** | **1.00000** |
| HNSC | **0.99590** | 0.97970 | 0.97970 | 0.97970 | 0.97940 | 0.97970 | 0.97970 | 0.97970 | 0.97970 | 0.97970 | 0.97980 | 0.97970 |
| KICH | **1.00000** | **1.00000** | **1.00000** | **1.00000** | **1.00000** | **1.00000** | **1.00000** | **1.00000** | **1.00000** | **1.00000** | **1.00000** | **1.00000** |
| KIRC | **0.99860** | 0.99520 | 0.99520 | 0.99520 | 0.99480 | 0.99520 | 0.99520 | 0.99520 | 0.99520 | 0.99520 | 0.99500 | 0.99520 |
| KIRP | **1.00000** | **1.00000** | **1.00000** | **1.00000** | **1.00000** | **1.00000** | **1.00000** | **1.00000** | **1.00000** | **1.00000** | **1.00000** | **1.00000** |
| LIHC | **1.00000** | **1.00000** | **1.00000** | **1.00000** | **1.00000** | **1.00000** | **1.00000** | **1.00000** | **1.00000** | **1.00000** | **1.00000** | **1.00000** |
| LUAD | **0.99500** | **0.99500** | **0.99500** | **0.99500** | **0.99500** | **0.99500** | **0.99500** | **0.99500** | **0.99500** | **0.99500** | **0.99500** | **0.99500** |
| LUSC | **1.00000** | **1.00000** | **1.00000** | **1.00000** | 0.99690 | **1.00000** | 0.99980 | **1.00000** | 0.99970 | **1.00000** | 0.99630 | 0.99600 |
| PAAD | **1.00000** | **1.00000** | **1.00000** | **1.00000** | **1.00000** | **1.00000** | **1.00000** | **1.00000** | **1.00000** | **1.00000** | **1.00000** | **1.00000** |
| PCPG | **1.00000** | **1.00000** | **1.00000** | **1.00000** | **1.00000** | **1.00000** | **1.00000** | **1.00000** | **1.00000** | **1.00000** | **1.00000** | **1.00000** |
| READ | **1.00000** | **1.00000** | **1.00000** | **1.00000** | **1.00000** | **1.00000** | **1.00000** | **1.00000** | **1.00000** | **1.00000** | **1.00000** | **1.00000** |
| SARC | **0.99050** | **0.99050** | **0.99050** | **0.99050** | **0.99050** | **0.99050** | **0.99050** | **0.99050** | **0.99050** | **0.99050** | **0.99050** | **0.99050** |
| SKCM | **1.00000** | **1.00000** | **1.00000** | **1.00000** | **1.00000** | **1.00000** | **1.00000** | **1.00000** | **1.00000** | **1.00000** | **1.00000** | **1.00000** |
| STAD | **0.99960** | 0.97530 | 0.97530 | 0.97530 | 0.97240 | 0.97530 | 0.97530 | 0.97530 | 0.97530 | 0.97530 | 0.97180 | 0.97360 |
| THCA | **1.00000** | **1.00000** | **1.00000** | **1.00000** | **1.00000** | **1.00000** | **1.00000** | **1.00000** | **1.00000** | **1.00000** | **1.00000** | **1.00000** |
| THYM | **1.00000** | **1.00000** | **1.00000** | **1.00000** | **1.00000** | **1.00000** | **1.00000** | **1.00000** | **1.00000** | **1.00000** | **1.00000** | **1.00000** |
| UCEC | **1.00000** | **1.00000** | **1.00000** | **1.00000** | 0.99640 | **1.00000** | **1.00000** | **1.00000** | **1.00000** | **1.00000** | 0.99640 | 0.99960 |
| Ranking (W\|T\|L) | 3\|**19**\|0 | 0\|18\|4 | 0\|18\|4 | 0\|18\|4 | 0\|14\|8 | 0\|18\|4 | 0\|17\|5 | 0\|18\|4 | 0\|17\|5 | 0\|18\|4 | 0\|16\|6 | 0\|16\|6 |

**Boldface** values denote the best results.

*Appendix A.2. Comparison Results Based on the SVM Model*

**Table A6.** The results of the proposed RBAVO-DE algorithm and its counterparts employing SVM regarding average fitness values.

| Dataset | Metric | RBAVO-DE | BSSA | BABC | BPSO | BBA | BGWO | BWOA | BGOA | BHHO | BBSA | BASO | BHGSO |
|---|---|---|---|---|---|---|---|---|---|---|---|---|---|
| BLCA | Average | **0.00000** | 0.00390 | 0.00430 | 0.00450 | 0.00390 | 0.00400 | 0.00430 | 0.00430 | 0.00370 | 0.00420 | 0.00420 | 0.00460 |
| | STDE | **0.00000** | 0.00020 | 0.00010 | 0.00010 | 0.00020 | 0.00020 | 0.00020 | 0.00010 | 0.00010 | 0.00010 | 0.00010 | 0.00010 |
| CESC | Average | **0.00000** | 0.00390 | 0.00430 | 0.00450 | 0.00390 | 0.00400 | 0.00430 | 0.00430 | 0.00370 | 0.00420 | 0.00420 | 0.00470 |
| | STDE | **0.00000** | 0.00020 | 0.00010 | 0.00010 | 0.00020 | 0.00020 | 0.00020 | 0.00010 | 0.00010 | 0.00010 | 0.00010 | 0.00010 |
| CHOL | Average | **0.00000** | 0.00390 | 0.00430 | 0.00450 | 0.00390 | 0.00400 | 0.00430 | 0.00430 | 0.00370 | 0.00420 | 0.00420 | 0.00470 |
| | STDE | **0.00000** | 0.00020 | 0.00010 | 0.00010 | 0.00020 | 0.00020 | 0.00020 | 0.00010 | 0.00010 | 0.00010 | 0.00010 | 0.00010 |
| COAD | Average | **0.00000** | 0.00390 | 0.00430 | 0.00450 | 0.00390 | 0.00400 | 0.00430 | 0.00430 | 0.00370 | 0.00420 | 0.00420 | 0.00470 |
| | STDE | **0.00000** | 0.00020 | 0.00010 | 0.00010 | 0.00020 | 0.00020 | 0.00020 | 0.00010 | 0.00010 | 0.00010 | 0.00010 | 0.00010 |
| ESCA | Average | **0.01370** | 0.02840 | 0.02720 | 0.02990 | 0.02930 | 0.02690 | 0.02970 | 0.02880 | 0.02830 | 0.02880 | 0.02980 | 0.03000 |
| | STDE | **0.01280** | 0.00460 | 0.00750 | **0.00010** | 0.00020 | 0.00750 | 0.00020 | 0.00450 | 0.00460 | 0.00440 | **0.00010** | 0.00020 |
| GBM | Average | **0.00000** | 0.00390 | 0.00430 | 0.00450 | 0.00390 | 0.00400 | 0.00430 | 0.00430 | 0.00370 | 0.00420 | 0.00420 | 0.00460 |
| | STDE | **0.00000** | 0.00020 | 0.00010 | 0.00010 | 0.00020 | 0.00020 | 0.00020 | 0.00010 | 0.00010 | 0.00010 | 0.00010 | 0.00010 |
| HNSC | Average | **0.00000** | 0.00390 | 0.00430 | 0.00450 | 0.00390 | 0.00400 | 0.00430 | 0.00430 | 0.00370 | 0.00420 | 0.00420 | 0.00460 |
| | STDE | **0.00000** | 0.00020 | 0.00010 | 0.00010 | 0.00020 | 0.00020 | 0.00020 | 0.00010 | 0.00010 | 0.00010 | 0.00010 | 0.00010 |

**Table A6.** *Cont.*

| Dataset | Metric | RBAVO-DE | BSSA | BABC | BPSO | BBA | BGWO | BWOA | BGOA | BHHO | BBSA | BASO | BHGSO |
|---|---|---|---|---|---|---|---|---|---|---|---|---|---|
| KICH | Average | **0.00000** | 0.00390 | 0.00430 | 0.00450 | 0.00390 | 0.00400 | 0.00430 | 0.00430 | 0.00370 | 0.00420 | 0.00420 | 0.00470 |
| | STDE | **0.00000** | 0.00020 | 0.00010 | 0.00010 | 0.00020 | 0.00020 | 0.00020 | 0.00010 | 0.00010 | 0.00010 | 0.00010 | 0.00010 |
| KIRC | Average | **0.00000** | 0.00390 | 0.00430 | 0.00450 | 0.00380 | 0.00400 | 0.00430 | 0.00430 | 0.00380 | 0.00430 | 0.00430 | 0.00460 |
| | STDE | **0.00000** | 0.00020 | 0.00010 | 0.00010 | 0.00020 | 0.00020 | 0.00020 | 0.00010 | 0.00010 | 0.00010 | 0.00010 | 0.00020 |
| KIRP | Average | **0.00000** | 0.00390 | 0.00430 | 0.00450 | 0.00390 | 0.00400 | 0.00430 | 0.00430 | 0.00370 | 0.00420 | 0.00420 | 0.00470 |
| | STDE | **0.00000** | 0.00020 | 0.00010 | 0.00010 | 0.00020 | 0.00020 | 0.00020 | 0.00010 | 0.00010 | 0.00010 | 0.00010 | 0.00010 |
| LIHC | Average | **0.00000** | 0.00410 | 0.00440 | 0.00450 | 0.00500 | 0.00430 | 0.00440 | 0.00450 | 0.00400 | 0.00450 | 0.00450 | 0.00500 |
| | STDE | **0.00000** | 0.00010 | 0.00010 | 0.00010 | 0.00280 | 0.00010 | 0.00020 | 0.00010 | 0.00020 | 0.00010 | 0.00010 | 0.00020 |
| LUAD | Average | **0.00840** | 0.01250 | 0.01290 | 0.01310 | 0.01250 | 0.01260 | 0.01290 | 0.01290 | 0.01230 | 0.01290 | 0.01260 | 0.01330 |
| | STDE | **0.00160** | 0.00020 | **0.00010** | **0.00010** | 0.00020 | 0.00020 | 0.00020 | **0.00010** | **0.00010** | **0.00010** | 0.00150 | **0.00010** |
| LUSC | Average | **0.00000** | 0.00390 | 0.00430 | 0.00450 | 0.00390 | 0.00400 | 0.00430 | 0.00430 | 0.00370 | 0.00420 | 0.00420 | 0.00470 |
| | STDE | **0.00000** | 0.00020 | 0.00010 | 0.00010 | 0.00020 | 0.00020 | 0.00020 | 0.00010 | 0.00010 | 0.00010 | 0.00010 | 0.00010 |
| PAAD | Average | **0.00000** | 0.00390 | 0.00430 | 0.00450 | 0.00390 | 0.00400 | 0.00430 | 0.00430 | 0.00370 | 0.00420 | 0.00420 | 0.00470 |
| | STDE | **0.00000** | 0.00020 | 0.00010 | 0.00010 | 0.00020 | 0.00020 | 0.00020 | 0.00010 | 0.00010 | 0.00010 | 0.00010 | 0.00010 |
| PCPG | Average | **0.00000** | 0.00390 | 0.00430 | 0.00450 | 0.00390 | 0.00400 | 0.00430 | 0.00430 | 0.00370 | 0.00420 | 0.00420 | 0.00470 |
| | STDE | **0.00000** | 0.00020 | 0.00010 | 0.00010 | 0.00020 | 0.00020 | 0.00020 | 0.00010 | 0.00010 | 0.00010 | 0.00010 | 0.00010 |
| READ | Average | **0.00000** | 0.00390 | 0.00430 | 0.00450 | 0.00390 | 0.00400 | 0.00430 | 0.00430 | 0.00370 | 0.00420 | 0.00420 | 0.00470 |
| | STDE | **0.00000** | 0.00020 | 0.00010 | 0.00010 | 0.00020 | 0.00020 | 0.00020 | 0.00010 | 0.00010 | 0.00010 | 0.00010 | 0.00010 |
| SARC | Average | **0.00570** | 0.01780 | 0.01570 | 0.01840 | 0.02260 | 0.01480 | 0.01760 | 0.01870 | 0.02000 | 0.01870 | 0.02000 | 0.02330 |
| | STDE | **0.00860** | 0.00800 | 0.00880 | 0.00800 | 0.00020 | 0.00900 | 0.00820 | 0.00770 | 0.00610 | 0.00770 | 0.00670 | **0.00010** |
| SKCM | Average | **0.00000** | 0.00390 | 0.00430 | 0.00450 | 0.00390 | 0.00400 | 0.00430 | 0.00430 | 0.00370 | 0.00420 | 0.00420 | 0.00470 |
| | STDE | **0.00000** | 0.00020 | 0.00010 | 0.00010 | 0.00020 | 0.00020 | 0.00020 | 0.00010 | 0.00010 | 0.00010 | 0.00010 | 0.00010 |
| STAD | Average | **0.01040** | 0.01490 | 0.01530 | 0.01550 | 0.01450 | 0.01500 | 0.01530 | 0.01530 | 0.01470 | 0.01520 | 0.01530 | 0.01560 |
| | STDE | **0.00280** | 0.00020 | **0.00010** | **0.00010** | 0.00200 | 0.00020 | 0.00020 | **0.00010** | **0.00010** | **0.00010** | **0.00010** | **0.00010** |
| THCA | Average | **0.00000** | 0.00390 | 0.00430 | 0.00450 | 0.00390 | 0.00400 | 0.00430 | 0.00430 | 0.00370 | 0.00420 | 0.00420 | 0.00470 |
| | STDE | **0.00000** | 0.00020 | 0.00010 | 0.00010 | 0.00020 | 0.00020 | 0.00020 | 0.00010 | 0.00010 | 0.00010 | 0.00010 | 0.00010 |
| THYM | Average | **0.00000** | 0.00390 | 0.00430 | 0.00450 | 0.00390 | 0.00400 | 0.00430 | 0.00430 | 0.00370 | 0.00420 | 0.00420 | 0.00470 |
| | STDE | **0.00000** | 0.00020 | 0.00010 | 0.00010 | 0.00020 | 0.00020 | 0.00020 | 0.00010 | 0.00010 | 0.00010 | 0.00010 | 0.00010 |
| UCEC | Average | **0.00000** | 0.00390 | 0.00430 | 0.00450 | 0.00380 | 0.00400 | 0.00430 | 0.00430 | 0.00380 | 0.00420 | 0.00430 | 0.00470 |
| | STDE | **0.00000** | 0.00020 | 0.00010 | 0.00010 | 0.00020 | 0.00020 | 0.00020 | 0.00010 | 0.00020 | 0.00010 | 0.00010 | 0.00010 |
| Ranking | W\|T\|L | **22\|0\|0** | 0\|0\|22 | 0\|0\|22 | 0\|0\|22 | 0\|0\|22 | 0\|0\|22 | 0\|0\|22 | 0\|0\|22 | 0\|0\|22 | 0\|0\|22 | 0\|0\|22 | 0\|0\|22 |

**Boldface** values denote the best results.

**Table A7.** The results of the proposed RBAVO-DE algorithm and its counterparts employing SVM regarding average chosen gene values.

| Dataset | Metric | RBAVO-DE | BSSA | BABC | BPSO | BBA | BGWO | BWOA | BGOA | BHHO | BBSA | BASO | BHGSO |
|---|---|---|---|---|---|---|---|---|---|---|---|---|---|
| BLCA | Average | **121.37** | 194.70 | 213.03 | 225.30 | 194.10 | 199.50 | 213.40 | 212.67 | 186.27 | 211.00 | 211.83 | 232.37 |
| | STDE | 007.49 | 011.44 | 005.18 | **003.11** | 009.66 | 009.30 | 008.44 | 005.66 | 005.77 | 006.44 | 005.25 | 004.42 |
| CESC | Average | **119.83** | 195.13 | 213.03 | 225.30 | 194.10 | 199.50 | 213.63 | 212.67 | 185.60 | 211.00 | 211.57 | 232.63 |
| | STDE | 007.02 | 011.17 | 005.31 | **003.11** | 009.66 | 009.30 | 008.35 | 005.66 | 006.49 | 006.44 | 005.08 | 004.36 |
| CHOL | Average | **125.57** | 195.13 | 213.03 | 225.30 | 194.10 | 199.50 | 213.63 | 212.67 | 185.60 | 211.00 | 211.57 | 232.63 |
| | STDE | 007.14 | 011.17 | 005.31 | **003.11** | 009.66 | 009.30 | 008.35 | 005.66 | 006.49 | 006.44 | 005.08 | 004.36 |
| COAD | Average | **122.63** | 195.13 | 213.03 | 225.30 | 194.10 | 199.50 | 213.63 | 212.67 | 185.60 | 211.00 | 211.57 | 232.63 |
| | STDE | 007.73 | 011.17 | 005.31 | **003.11** | 009.66 | 009.30 | 008.35 | 005.66 | 006.49 | 006.44 | 005.08 | 004.36 |
| ESCA | Average | **125.50** | 195.13 | 215.40 | 225.30 | 194.10 | 201.77 | 213.63 | 213.13 | 185.70 | 212.40 | 218.87 | 230.07 |
| | STDE | 011.18 | 011.17 | 009.58 | **003.11** | 009.66 | 012.33 | 008.35 | 006.44 | 006.47 | 008.98 | 004.68 | 007.64 |
| GBM | Average | **119.73** | 194.93 | 213.03 | 225.30 | 193.90 | 198.77 | 213.70 | 212.83 | 185.50 | 211.00 | 211.00 | 232.33 |
| | STDE | 008.07 | 011.27 | 005.31 | **003.11** | 009.47 | 010.28 | 008.36 | 005.69 | 006.51 | 006.44 | 004.92 | 004.15 |
| HNSC | Average | **122.17** | 196.40 | 213.90 | 225.13 | 194.03 | 202.10 | 213.83 | 213.50 | 186.93 | 211.47 | 210.87 | 232.17 |
| | STDE | 008.29 | 008.49 | 005.22 | **003.19** | 009.56 | 010.76 | 009.34 | 005.22 | 005.74 | 005.66 | 004.79 | 005.02 |
| KICH | Average | **121.73** | 195.13 | 213.03 | 225.30 | 194.10 | 199.50 | 213.63 | 212.67 | 185.60 | 211.00 | 211.57 | 232.63 |
| | STDE | 008.49 | 011.17 | 005.31 | **003.11** | 009.66 | 009.30 | 008.35 | 005.66 | 006.49 | 006.44 | 005.08 | 004.36 |
| KIRC | Average | **123.87** | 197.10 | 214.70 | 225.00 | 191.93 | 200.30 | 212.97 | 213.13 | 187.57 | 213.83 | 214.63 | 231.27 |
| | STDE | 007.57 | 009.42 | 005.09 | 004.23 | 008.70 | 011.59 | 007.64 | 004.94 | 005.31 | 005.81 | **004.20** | 008.02 |
| KIRP | Average | **120.07** | 195.13 | 213.03 | 225.30 | 194.10 | 199.50 | 213.63 | 212.67 | 185.60 | 211.00 | 211.57 | 232.63 |
| | STDE | 007.87 | 011.17 | 005.31 | **003.11** | 009.66 | 009.30 | 008.35 | 005.66 | 006.49 | 006.44 | 005.08 | 004.36 |
| LIHC | Average | **122.63** | 204.27 | 220.37 | 226.40 | 212.83 | 214.07 | 219.07 | 223.70 | 200.60 | 223.03 | 225.17 | 249.90 |
| | STDE | 008.01 | 006.99 | 006.29 | 006.80 | 017.60 | 007.06 | 007.88 | **004.13** | 007.66 | 006.48 | 004.81 | 007.97 |
| LUAD | Average | **121.17** | 195.13 | 213.03 | 225.30 | 194.10 | 199.43 | 213.63 | 212.67 | 185.87 | 212.40 | 214.50 | 233.00 |
| | STDE | 007.56 | 011.17 | 005.31 | **003.11** | 009.66 | 009.37 | 008.35 | 005.66 | 006.40 | 006.10 | 005.98 | 004.34 |
| LUSC | Average | **122.67** | 195.13 | 213.03 | 225.30 | 194.10 | 199.50 | 213.63 | 212.67 | 185.60 | 211.00 | 211.57 | 232.63 |
| | STDE | 006.28 | 011.17 | 005.31 | **003.11** | 009.66 | 009.30 | 008.35 | 005.66 | 006.49 | 006.44 | 005.08 | 004.36 |
| PAAD | Average | **119.23** | 195.13 | 213.03 | 225.30 | 194.10 | 199.50 | 213.63 | 212.67 | 185.60 | 211.00 | 211.57 | 232.63 |
| | STDE | 006.90 | 011.17 | 005.31 | **003.11** | 009.66 | 009.30 | 008.35 | 005.66 | 006.49 | 006.44 | 005.08 | 004.36 |
| PCPG | Average | **122.43** | 195.13 | 213.03 | 225.30 | 194.10 | 199.50 | 213.63 | 212.67 | 185.60 | 211.00 | 211.57 | 232.63 |
| | STDE | 006.68 | 011.17 | 005.31 | **003.11** | 009.66 | 009.30 | 008.35 | 005.66 | 006.49 | 006.44 | 005.08 | 004.36 |
| READ | Average | **123.93** | 195.13 | 213.03 | 225.30 | 194.10 | 199.50 | 213.63 | 212.67 | 185.60 | 211.00 | 211.57 | 232.63 |
| | STDE | 007.45 | 011.17 | 005.31 | **003.11** | 009.66 | 009.30 | 008.35 | 005.66 | 006.49 | 006.44 | 005.08 | 004.36 |
| SARC | Average | **135.27** | 202.90 | 226.90 | 233.77 | 194.10 | 210.53 | 223.87 | 217.80 | 189.93 | 220.57 | 220.87 | 231.53 |
| | STDE | 018.57 | 020.86 | 020.25 | 014.44 | 009.66 | 017.74 | 017.39 | 013.90 | 013.41 | 016.40 | 011.76 | **003.70** |
| SKCM | Average | **122.47** | 195.13 | 213.03 | 225.30 | 194.10 | 199.50 | 213.63 | 212.67 | 185.60 | 211.00 | 211.57 | 232.63 |
| | STDE | 007.66 | 011.17 | 005.31 | **003.11** | 009.66 | 009.30 | 008.35 | 005.66 | 006.49 | 006.44 | 005.08 | 004.36 |

**Table A7.** *Cont.*

| Dataset | Metric | RBAVO-DE | BSSA | BABC | BPSO | BBA | BGWO | BWOA | BGOA | BHHO | BBSA | BASO | BHGSO |
|---|---|---|---|---|---|---|---|---|---|---|---|---|---|
| STAD | Average | **123.53** | 194.60 | 213.40 | 225.03 | 194.30 | 198.80 | 214.10 | 212.70 | 185.70 | 211.97 | 215.07 | 231.77 |
| | STDE | 010.65 | 010.22 | 005.38 | **003.29** | 009.79 | 009.09 | 008.68 | 005.54 | 006.92 | 005.88 | 005.12 | 004.58 |
| THCA | Average | **119.47** | 195.13 | 213.03 | 225.30 | 194.10 | 199.50 | 213.63 | 212.67 | 185.60 | 211.00 | 211.57 | 232.63 |
| | STDE | 005.58 | 011.17 | 005.31 | **003.11** | 009.66 | 009.30 | 008.35 | 005.66 | 006.49 | 006.44 | 005.08 | 004.36 |
| THYM | Average | **121.80** | 195.13 | 213.03 | 225.30 | 194.10 | 199.50 | 213.63 | 212.67 | 185.60 | 211.00 | 211.57 | 232.63 |
| | STDE | 007.21 | 011.17 | 005.31 | **003.11** | 009.66 | 009.30 | 008.35 | 005.66 | 006.49 | 006.44 | 005.08 | 004.36 |
| UCEC | Average | **122.23** | 196.00 | 213.27 | 224.83 | 192.03 | 200.97 | 212.60 | 213.03 | 189.23 | 212.23 | 212.93 | 233.93 |
| | STDE | 005.93 | 009.06 | 006.31 | 004.27 | 007.85 | 008.24 | 007.74 | 005.67 | 008.78 | 004.98 | 004.97 | **003.97** |
| Ranking | W\|T\|L | **22**\|**0**\|**0** | 0\|0\|22 | 0\|0\|22 | 0\|0\|22 | 0\|0\|22 | 0\|0\|22 | 0\|0\|22 | 0\|0\|22 | 0\|0\|22 | 0\|0\|22 | 0\|0\|22 | 0\|0\|22 |

**Boldface** values denote the best results.

**Table A8.** The results of the proposed RBAVO-DE algorithm and its counterparts employing SVM regarding average precision values.

| Dataset | RBAVO-DE | BSSA | BABC | BPSO | BBA | BGWO | BWOA | BGOA | BHHO | BBSA | BASO | BHGSO |
|---|---|---|---|---|---|---|---|---|---|---|---|---|
| BLCA | **1.00000** | **1.00000** | **1.00000** | **1.00000** | **1.00000** | **1.00000** | **1.00000** | **1.00000** | **1.00000** | **1.00000** | **1.00000** | **1.00000** |
| CESC | **1.00000** | **1.00000** | **1.00000** | **1.00000** | 0.99890 | **1.00000** | **1.00000** | **1.00000** | **1.00000** | **1.00000** | **1.00000** | **1.00000** |
| CHOL | **1.00000** | **1.00000** | **1.00000** | **1.00000** | **1.00000** | **1.00000** | **1.00000** | **1.00000** | **1.00000** | **1.00000** | **1.00000** | **1.00000** |
| COAD | **1.00000** | **1.00000** | **1.00000** | **1.00000** | 0.99890 | **1.00000** | **1.00000** | **1.00000** | **1.00000** | **1.00000** | **1.00000** | **1.00000** |
| ESCA | **1.00000** | **1.00000** | **1.00000** | **1.00000** | 0.99820 | **1.00000** | **1.00000** | **1.00000** | **1.00000** | **1.00000** | **1.00000** | 0.99210 |
| GBM | **1.00000** | **1.00000** | **1.00000** | **1.00000** | **1.00000** | **1.00000** | **1.00000** | **1.00000** | **1.00000** | **1.00000** | **1.00000** | **1.00000** |
| HNSC | **1.00000** | 0.94140 | 0.94170 | 0.93750 | 0.92840 | 0.94140 | 0.93990 | 0.94170 | 0.94110 | 0.94050 | 0.84550 | 0.93150 |
| KICH | **1.00000** | **1.00000** | **1.00000** | **1.00000** | **1.00000** | **1.00000** | **1.00000** | **1.00000** | **1.00000** | **1.00000** | **1.00000** | **1.00000** |
| KIRC | **1.00000** | **1.00000** | **1.00000** | **1.00000** | 0.99940 | **1.00000** | **1.00000** | **1.00000** | **1.00000** | **1.00000** | **1.00000** | **1.00000** |
| KIRP | **1.00000** | **1.00000** | **1.00000** | **1.00000** | **1.00000** | **1.00000** | **1.00000** | **1.00000** | **1.00000** | **1.00000** | **1.00000** | **1.00000** |
| LIHC | **1.00000** | **1.00000** | **1.00000** | **1.00000** | **1.00000** | **1.00000** | **1.00000** | **1.00000** | **1.00000** | **1.00000** | **1.00000** | **1.00000** |
| LUAD | **1.00000** | **1.00000** | **1.00000** | **1.00000** | 0.99870 | **1.00000** | **1.00000** | **1.00000** | **1.00000** | **1.00000** | **1.00000** | 0.99930 |
| LUSC | **1.00000** | 0.99860 | 0.99860 | 0.99860 | 0.99830 | 0.99660 | 0.99860 | 0.99900 | 0.99930 | 0.99860 | 0.81400 | 0.99970 |
| PAAD | **1.00000** | **1.00000** | **1.00000** | **1.00000** | **1.00000** | **1.00000** | **1.00000** | **1.00000** | **1.00000** | **1.00000** | **1.00000** | **1.00000** |
| PCPG | **1.00000** | **1.00000** | **1.00000** | **1.00000** | **1.00000** | **1.00000** | **1.00000** | **1.00000** | **1.00000** | **1.00000** | **1.00000** | **1.00000** |
| READ | **1.00000** | **1.00000** | **1.00000** | **1.00000** | **1.00000** | **1.00000** | **1.00000** | **1.00000** | **1.00000** | **1.00000** | **1.00000** | **1.00000** |
| SARC | **1.00000** | 0.99940 | **1.00000** | 0.99940 | 0.99500 | 0.99940 | **1.00000** | 0.99940 | 0.99620 | 0.99940 | **1.00000** | 0.99120 |
| SKCM | **1.00000** | **1.00000** | **1.00000** | **1.00000** | **1.00000** | **1.00000** | **1.00000** | **1.00000** | **1.00000** | **1.00000** | **1.00000** | **1.00000** |
| STAD | **0.98830** | 0.94840 | 0.95110 | 0.94170 | 0.93610 | 0.94730 | 0.94690 | 0.94690 | 0.93910 | 0.94650 | 0.95200 | 0.93500 |
| THCA | **1.00000** | **1.00000** | **1.00000** | **1.00000** | **1.00000** | **1.00000** | **1.00000** | **1.00000** | **1.00000** | **1.00000** | **1.00000** | **1.00000** |
| THYM | **1.00000** | **1.00000** | **1.00000** | **1.00000** | **1.00000** | **1.00000** | **1.00000** | **1.00000** | **1.00000** | **1.00000** | **1.00000** | **1.00000** |
| UCEC | **1.00000** | 0.99910 | 0.99820 | 0.99820 | 0.99300 | **1.00000** | 0.99820 | 0.99820 | 0.99910 | **1.00000** | **1.00000** | 0.99390 |
| Ranking (W\|T\|L) | **3**\|**19**\|**0** | 0\|17\|5 | 0\|18\|4 | 0\|17\|5 | 0\|12\|10 | 0\|18\|4 | 0\|18\|4 | 0\|17\|5 | 0\|17\|5 | 0\|18\|4 | 0\|19\|3 | 0\|15\|7 |

**Boldface** values denote the best results.

**Table A9.** The results of the proposed RBAVO-DE algorithm and its counterparts employing SVM regarding average recall values.

| Dataset | RBAVO-DE | BSSA | BABC | BPSO | BBA | BGWO | BWOA | BGOA | BHHO | BBSA | BASO | BHGSO |
|---|---|---|---|---|---|---|---|---|---|---|---|---|
| BLCA | **1.00000** | **1.00000** | **1.00000** | **1.00000** | **1.00000** | **1.00000** | **1.00000** | **1.00000** | **1.00000** | **1.00000** | **1.00000** | **1.00000** |
| CESC | **1.00000** | **1.00000** | **1.00000** | **1.00000** | **1.00000** | **1.00000** | **1.00000** | **1.00000** | **1.00000** | **1.00000** | **1.00000** | **1.00000** |
| CHOL | **1.00000** | **1.00000** | **1.00000** | **1.00000** | **1.00000** | **1.00000** | **1.00000** | **1.00000** | **1.00000** | **1.00000** | **1.00000** | **1.00000** |
| COAD | **1.00000** | **1.00000** | **1.00000** | **1.00000** | 0.99940 | **1.00000** | **1.00000** | **1.00000** | **1.00000** | **1.00000** | 0.99940 | **1.00000** |
| ESCA | **1.00000** | **1.00000** | **1.00000** | **1.00000** | **1.00000** | **1.00000** | **1.00000** | **1.00000** | **1.00000** | **1.00000** | **1.00000** | **1.00000** |
| GBM | **1.00000** | **1.00000** | **1.00000** | **1.00000** | **1.00000** | **1.00000** | **1.00000** | **1.00000** | **1.00000** | **1.00000** | **1.00000** | **1.00000** |
| HNSC | **1.00000** | **1.00000** | **1.00000** | 0.99970 | 0.99930 | **1.00000** | **1.00000** | **1.00000** | **1.00000** | **1.00000** | 0.99930 | 0.99930 |
| KICH | **1.00000** | **1.00000** | **1.00000** | **1.00000** | **1.00000** | **1.00000** | **1.00000** | **1.00000** | **1.00000** | **1.00000** | **1.00000** | **1.00000** |
| KIRC | **1.00000** | 0.99040 | 0.99040 | 0.99040 | 0.99010 | 0.99040 | 0.99040 | 0.99040 | 0.99040 | 0.99040 | 0.98780 | 0.99040 |
| KIRP | **1.00000** | **1.00000** | **1.00000** | **1.00000** | **1.00000** | **1.00000** | **1.00000** | **1.00000** | **1.00000** | **1.00000** | **1.00000** | **1.00000** |
| LIHC | **1.00000** | **1.00000** | **1.00000** | **1.00000** | **1.00000** | **1.00000** | **1.00000** | **1.00000** | **1.00000** | **1.00000** | **1.00000** | **1.00000** |
| LUAD | **1.00000** | **1.00000** | **1.00000** | **1.00000** | 0.99500 | **1.00000** | **1.00000** | **1.00000** | 0.99930 | **1.00000** | 0.99830 | 0.99770 |
| LUSC | **1.00000** | 0.99100 | 0.99100 | 0.99100 | 0.99130 | 0.98960 | 0.99100 | 0.99060 | 0.99030 | 0.99100 | 0.99100 | 0.98990 |
| PAAD | **1.00000** | **1.00000** | **1.00000** | **1.00000** | **1.00000** | **1.00000** | **1.00000** | **1.00000** | **1.00000** | **1.00000** | **1.00000** | **1.00000** |
| PCPG | **1.00000** | **1.00000** | **1.00000** | **1.00000** | **1.00000** | **1.00000** | **1.00000** | **1.00000** | **1.00000** | **1.00000** | **1.00000** | **1.00000** |
| READ | **1.00000** | **1.00000** | **1.00000** | **1.00000** | **1.00000** | **1.00000** | **1.00000** | **1.00000** | **1.00000** | **1.00000** | **1.00000** | **1.00000** |
| SARC | **1.00000** | **1.00000** | **1.00000** | **1.00000** | **1.00000** | **1.00000** | **1.00000** | **1.00000** | **1.00000** | **1.00000** | **1.00000** | **1.00000** |
| SKCM | **1.00000** | **1.00000** | **1.00000** | **1.00000** | **1.00000** | **1.00000** | **1.00000** | **1.00000** | **1.00000** | **1.00000** | **1.00000** | **1.00000** |
| STAD | **1.00000** | **1.00000** | **1.00000** | **1.00000** | **1.00000** | **1.00000** | **1.00000** | **1.00000** | **1.00000** | **1.00000** | **1.00000** | **1.00000** |
| THCA | **1.00000** | **1.00000** | **1.00000** | **1.00000** | **1.00000** | **1.00000** | **1.00000** | **1.00000** | **1.00000** | **1.00000** | **1.00000** | **1.00000** |
| THYM | **1.00000** | **1.00000** | **1.00000** | **1.00000** | **1.00000** | **1.00000** | **1.00000** | **1.00000** | **1.00000** | **1.00000** | **1.00000** | **1.00000** |
| UCEC | **1.00000** | 0.99550 | 0.99640 | 0.98380 | 0.98200 | 0.99460 | 0.99100 | 0.99010 | 0.98470 | 0.99370 | 0.97840 | 0.97930 |
| Ranking (W\|T\|L) | **3**\|**19**\|**0** | 0\|19\|3 | 0\|19\|3 | 0\|18\|4 | 0\|16\|6 | 0\|19\|3 | 0\|19\|3 | 0\|19\|3 | 0\|18\|4 | 0\|19\|3 | 0\|16\|6 | 0\|17\|5 |

**Boldface** values denote the best results.

**Table A10.** The results of the proposed RBAVO-DE algorithm and its counterparts employing SVM regarding average F1-score values.

| Dataset | RBAVO-DE | BSSA | BABC | BPSO | BBA | BGWO | BWOA | BGOA | BHHO | BBSA | BASO | BHGSO |
|---|---|---|---|---|---|---|---|---|---|---|---|---|
| BLCA | 1.00000 | 1.00000 | 1.00000 | 1.00000 | 1.00000 | 1.00000 | 1.00000 | 1.00000 | 1.00000 | 1.00000 | 1.00000 | 1.00000 |
| CESC | 1.00000 | 1.00000 | 1.00000 | 1.00000 | 0.99950 | 1.00000 | 1.00000 | 1.00000 | 1.00000 | 1.00000 | 1.00000 | 1.00000 |
| CHOL | 1.00000 | 1.00000 | 1.00000 | 1.00000 | 1.00000 | 1.00000 | 1.00000 | 1.00000 | 1.00000 | 1.00000 | 1.00000 | 1.00000 |
| COAD | 1.00000 | 1.00000 | 1.00000 | 1.00000 | 0.99910 | 1.00000 | 1.00000 | 1.00000 | 1.00000 | 1.00000 | 0.99970 | 1.00000 |
| ESCA | 1.00000 | 1.00000 | 1.00000 | 1.00000 | 0.99910 | 1.00000 | 1.00000 | 1.00000 | 1.00000 | 1.00000 | 0.99820 | 0.99600 |
| GBM | 1.00000 | 1.00000 | 1.00000 | 1.00000 | 1.00000 | 1.00000 | 1.00000 | 1.00000 | 1.00000 | 1.00000 | 1.00000 | 1.00000 |
| HNSC | 1.00000 | 0.96980 | 0.97000 | 0.96760 | 0.96250 | 0.96980 | 0.96900 | 0.96970 | 0.96970 | 0.96940 | 0.95730 | 0.96420 |
| KICH | 1.00000 | 1.00000 | 1.00000 | 1.00000 | 1.00000 | 1.00000 | 1.00000 | 1.00000 | 1.00000 | 1.00000 | 1.00000 | 1.00000 |
| KIRC | 1.00000 | 0.99520 | 0.99520 | 0.99520 | 0.99470 | 0.99520 | 0.99520 | 0.99520 | 0.99520 | 0.99520 | 0.99320 | 0.99520 |
| KIRP | 1.00000 | 1.00000 | 1.00000 | 1.00000 | 1.00000 | 1.00000 | 1.00000 | 1.00000 | 1.00000 | 1.00000 | 1.00000 | 1.00000 |
| LIHC | 1.00000 | 1.00000 | 1.00000 | 1.00000 | 1.00000 | 1.00000 | 1.00000 | 1.00000 | 1.00000 | 1.00000 | 1.00000 | 1.00000 |
| LUAD | 1.00000 | 1.00000 | 1.00000 | 1.00000 | 0.99690 | 1.00000 | 1.00000 | 1.00000 | 0.99970 | 1.00000 | 0.99880 | 0.99850 |
| LUSC | 1.00000 | 0.99480 | 0.99480 | 0.99480 | 0.99480 | 0.99480 | 0.99480 | 0.99480 | 0.99480 | 0.99480 | 0.99480 | 0.99480 |
| PAAD | 1.00000 | 1.00000 | 1.00000 | 1.00000 | 1.00000 | 1.00000 | 1.00000 | 1.00000 | 1.00000 | 1.00000 | 1.00000 | 1.00000 |
| PCPG | 1.00000 | 1.00000 | 1.00000 | 1.00000 | 1.00000 | 1.00000 | 1.00000 | 1.00000 | 1.00000 | 1.00000 | 1.00000 | 1.00000 |
| READ | 1.00000 | 1.00000 | 1.00000 | 1.00000 | 1.00000 | 1.00000 | 1.00000 | 1.00000 | 1.00000 | 1.00000 | 1.00000 | 1.00000 |
| SARC | 0.99900 | 0.99970 | 0.99810 | 0.99970 | 0.99750 | 0.99970 | 1.00000 | 0.99970 | 0.99810 | 0.99970 | 0.99710 | 0.99560 |
| SKCM | 1.00000 | 1.00000 | 1.00000 | 1.00000 | 1.00000 | 1.00000 | 1.00000 | 1.00000 | 1.00000 | 1.00000 | 1.00000 | 1.00000 |
| STAD | 0.99410 | 0.97350 | 0.97490 | 0.96990 | 0.96700 | 0.97290 | 0.97270 | 0.97270 | 0.96860 | 0.97250 | 0.96560 | 0.96640 |
| THCA | 1.00000 | 1.00000 | 1.00000 | 1.00000 | 1.00000 | 1.00000 | 1.00000 | 1.00000 | 1.00000 | 1.00000 | 1.00000 | 1.00000 |
| THYM | 1.00000 | 1.00000 | 1.00000 | 1.00000 | 1.00000 | 1.00000 | 1.00000 | 1.00000 | 1.00000 | 1.00000 | 1.00000 | 1.00000 |
| UCEC | 1.00000 | 0.99730 | 0.99730 | 0.99090 | 0.98730 | 0.99730 | 0.99450 | 0.99410 | 0.99180 | 0.99680 | 0.98680 | 0.98640 |
| Ranking (W\|T\|L) | 5\|17\|0 | 0\|16\|6 | 0\|16\|6 | 0\|16\|6 | 0\|12\|10 | 0\|16\|6 | 0\|17\|5 | 0\|16\|6 | 0\|15\|7 | 0\|16\|6 | 0\|13\|9 | 0\|14\|8 |

**Boldface** values denote the best results.

## Appendix B. Convergence Graphs of the Proposed RBAVO-DE and Competitive Methods

### *Appendix B.1. Convergence Graphs Employing the SVM Model*

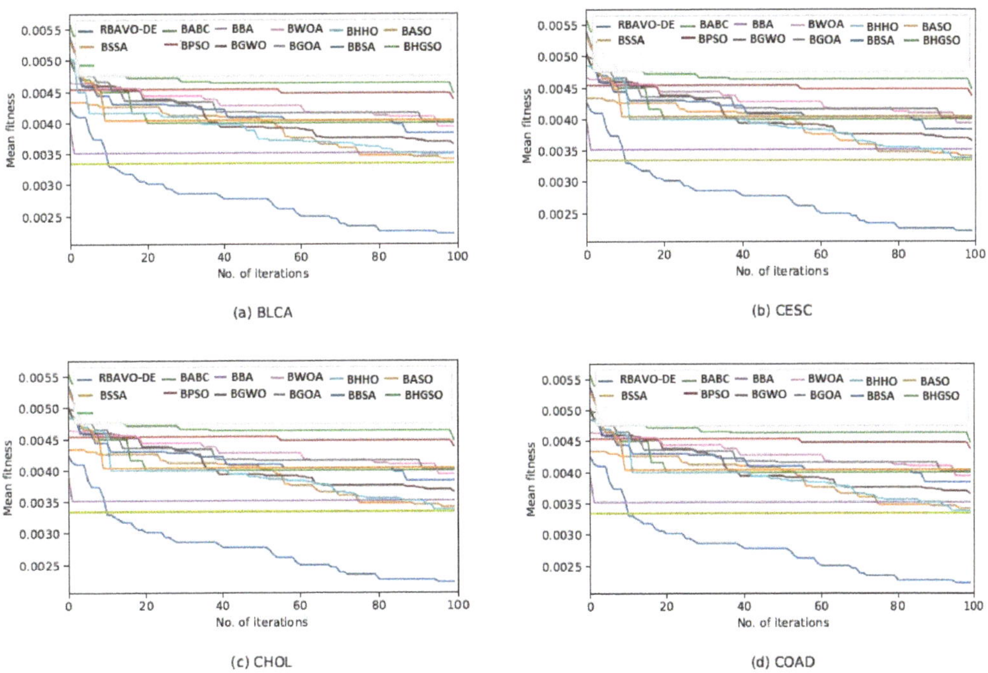


(a) BLCA (b) CESC

(c) CHOL (d) COAD

**Figure A1.** *Cont.*

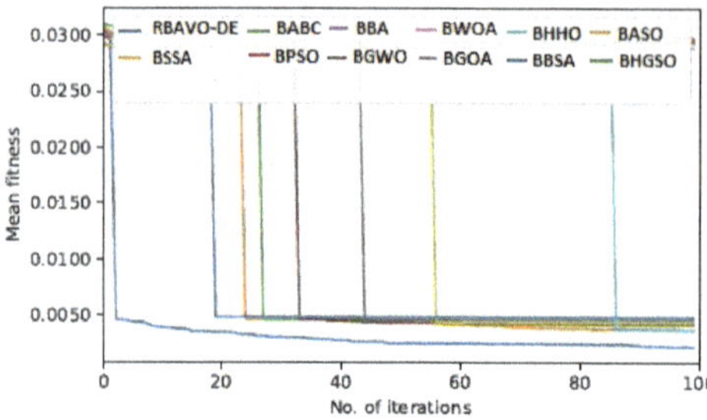


(e) ESCA

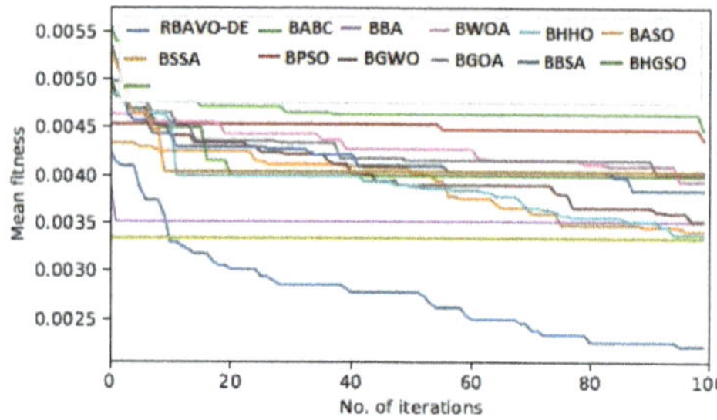


(f) GBM

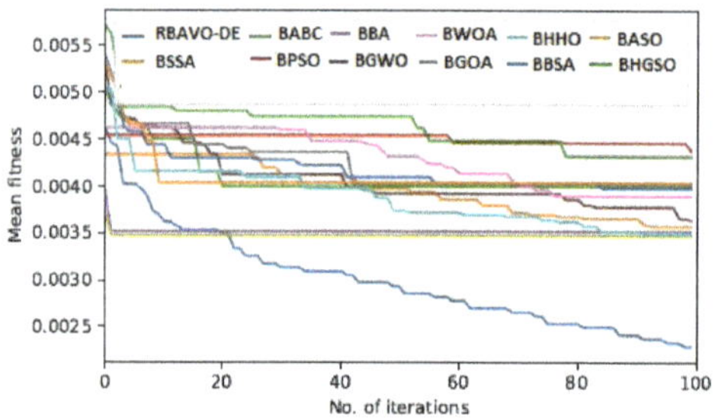


(g) HNSC

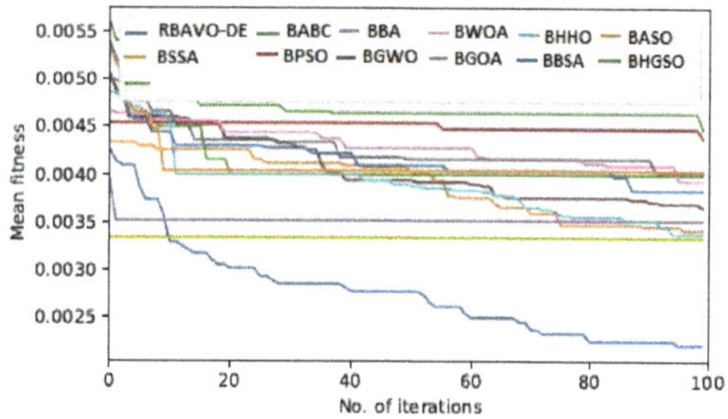


(h) KICH

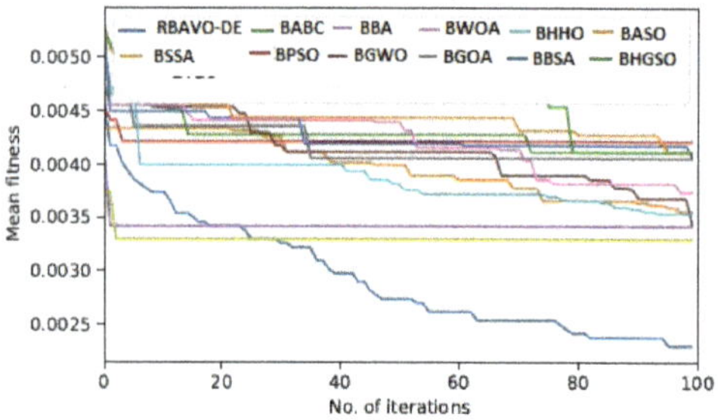


(i) KIRC

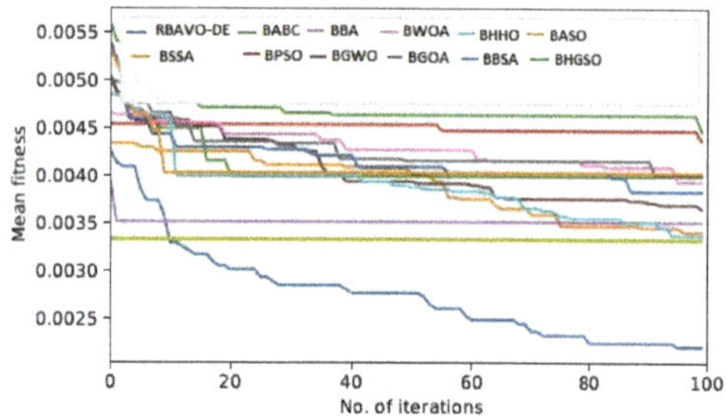


(j) KIRP

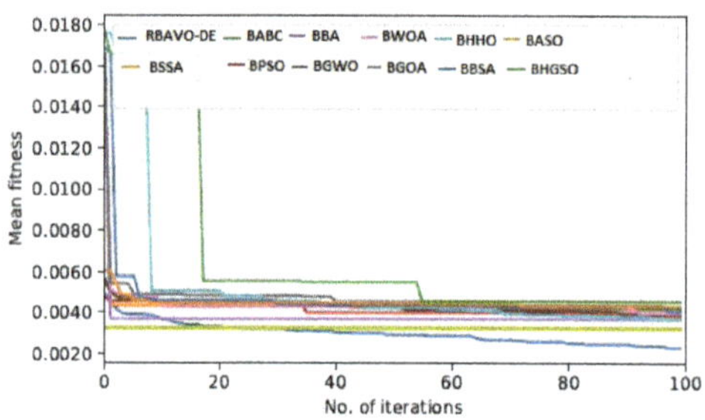


(k) LIHC

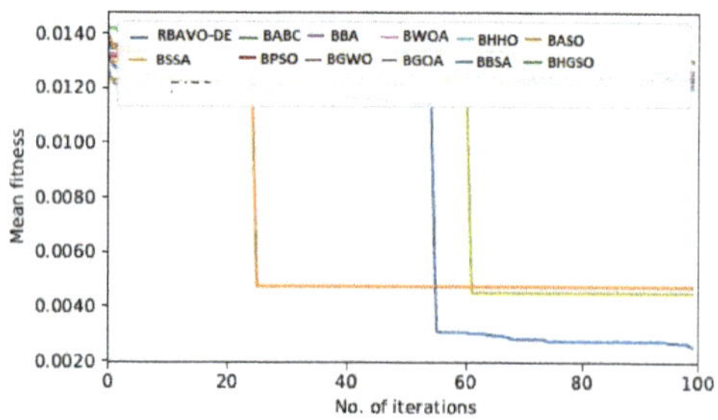


(l) LUAD

**Figure A1.** *Cont.*

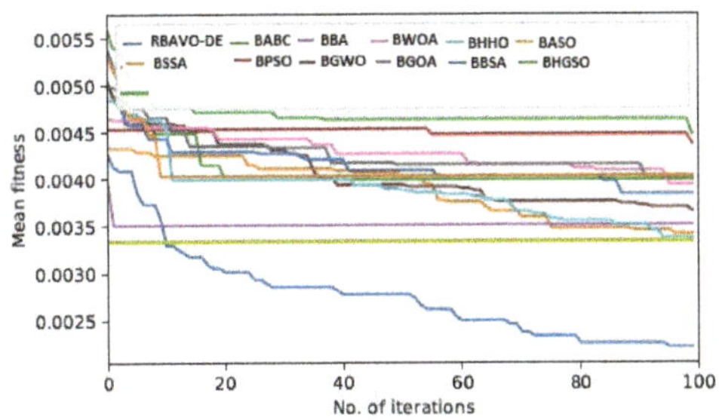


(m) LUSC

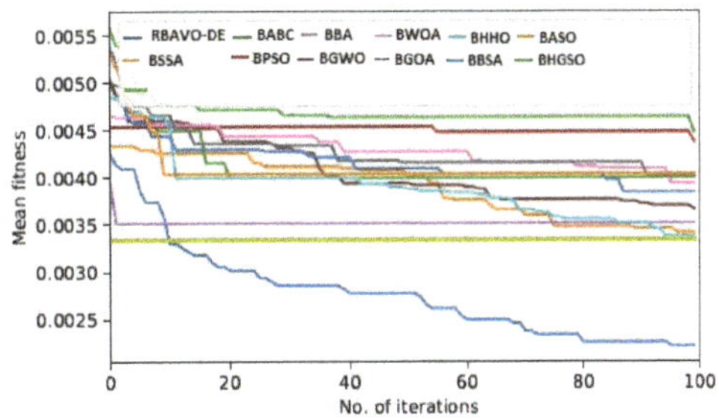


(n) PAAD

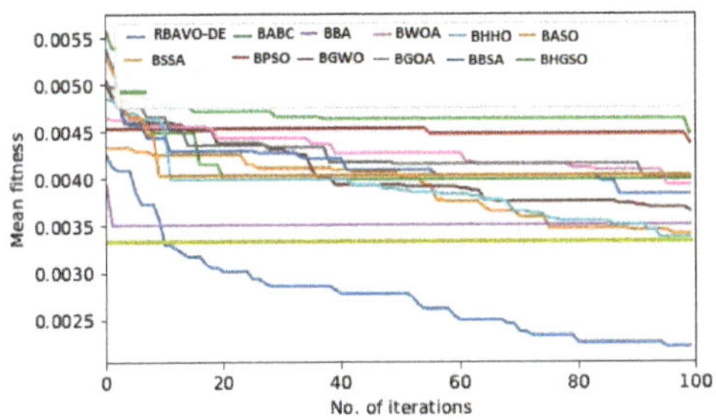


(o) PCPG

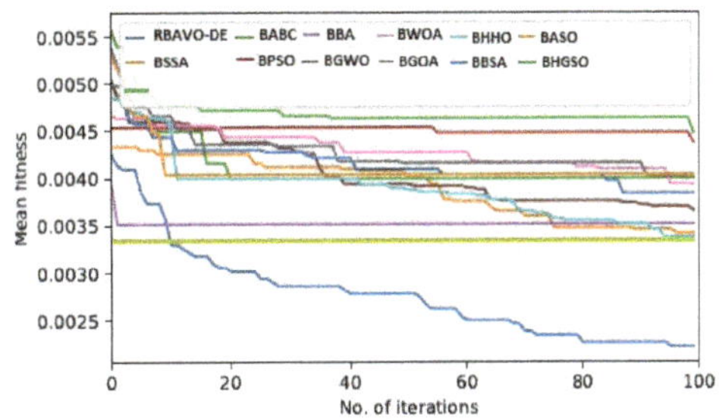


(p) READ

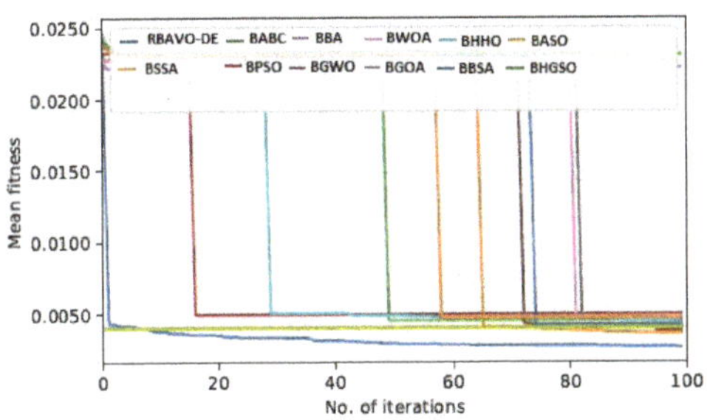


(q) SARC

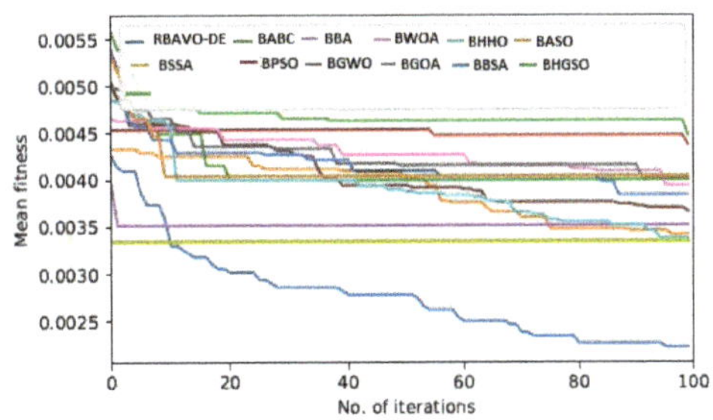


(r) SKCM

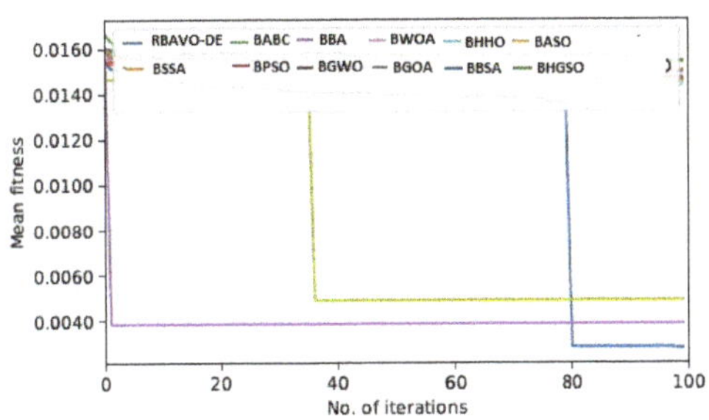


(s) STAD

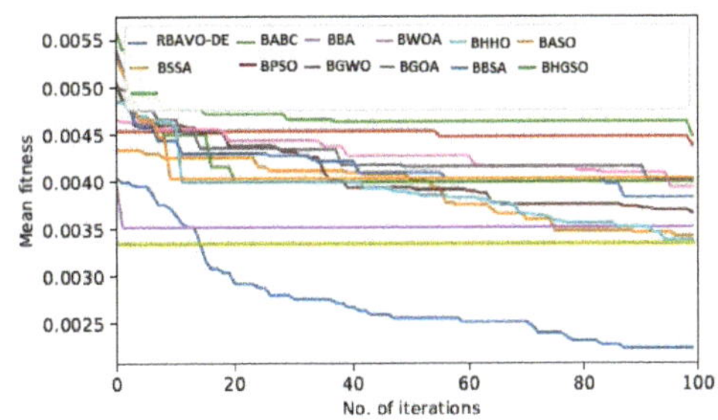


(t) THCA

**Figure A1.** *Cont.*

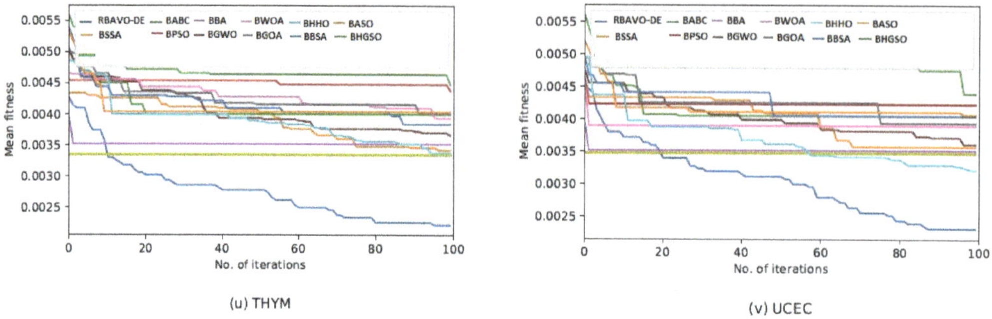


**Figure A1.** Convergence graphs of the proposed RBAVO-DE algorithm and competitive methods employing the SVM model on the overall benchmarks [57].

*Appendix B.2. Convergence Graphs Employing the k-NN Model*

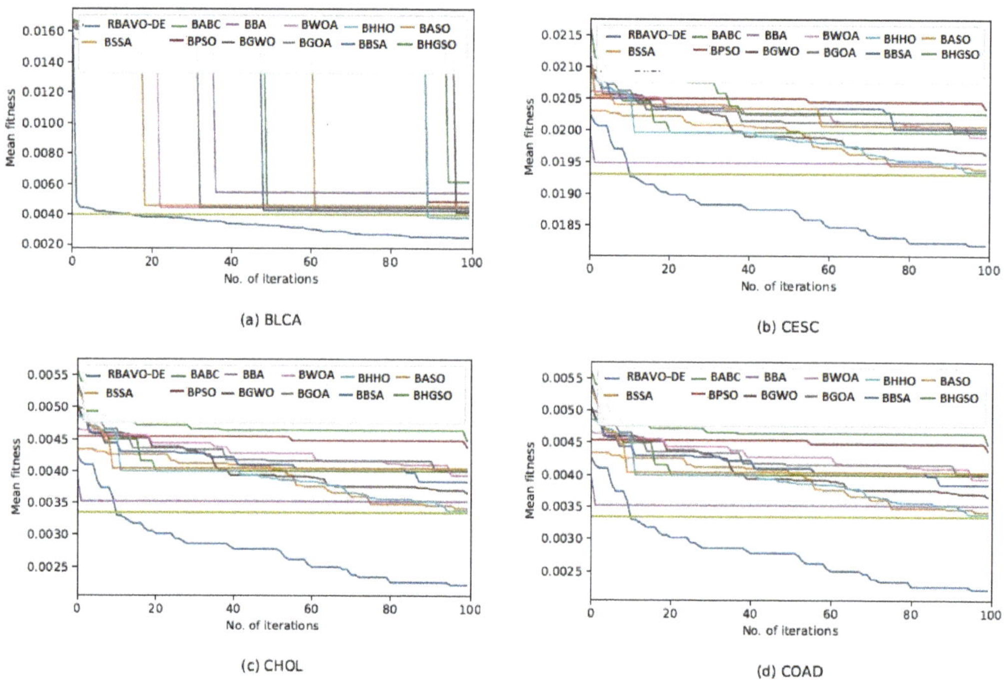


**Figure A2.** *Cont.*

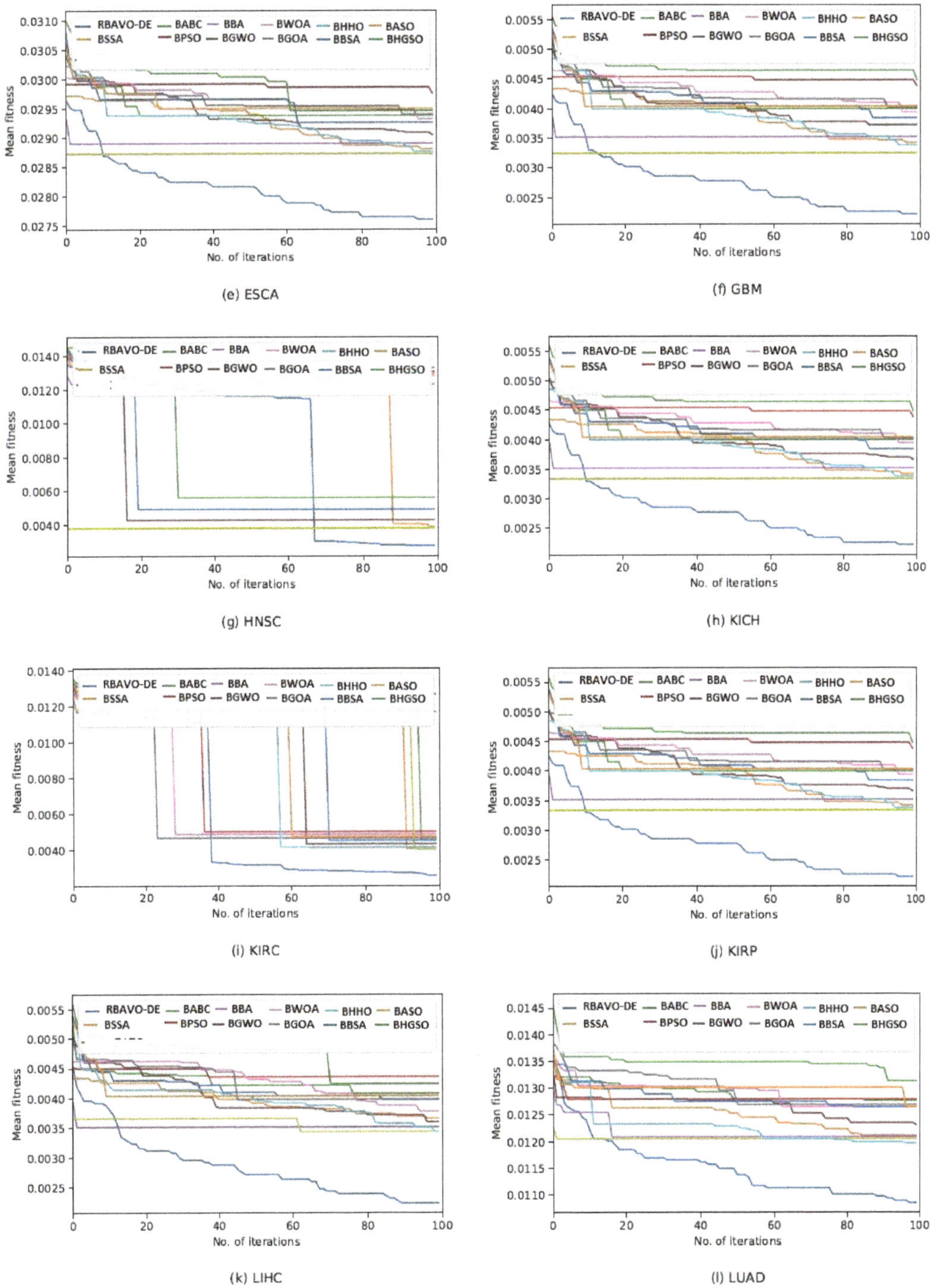


(e) ESCA (f) GBM (g) HNSC (h) KICH (i) KIRC (j) KIRP (k) LIHC (l) LUAD

**Figure A2.** *Cont.*

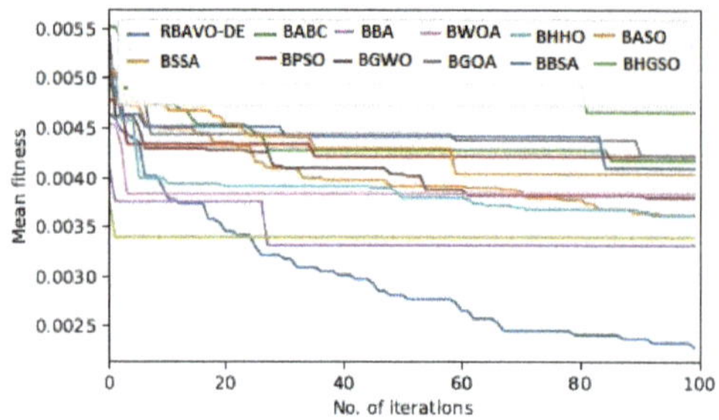


(m) LUSC

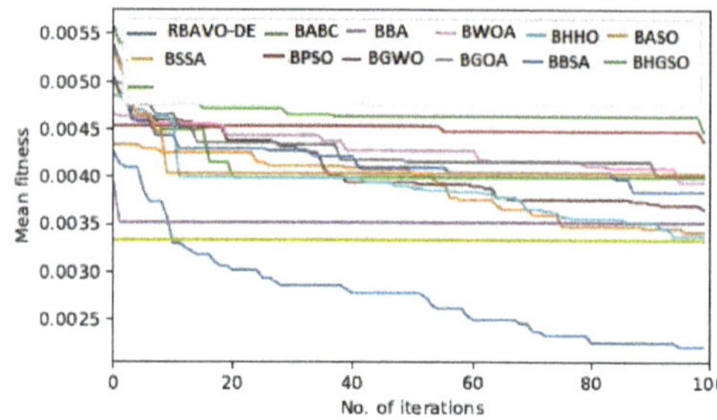


(n) PAAD

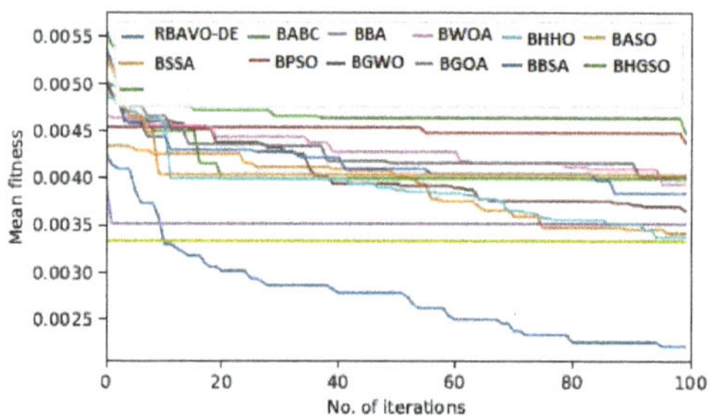


(o) PCPG

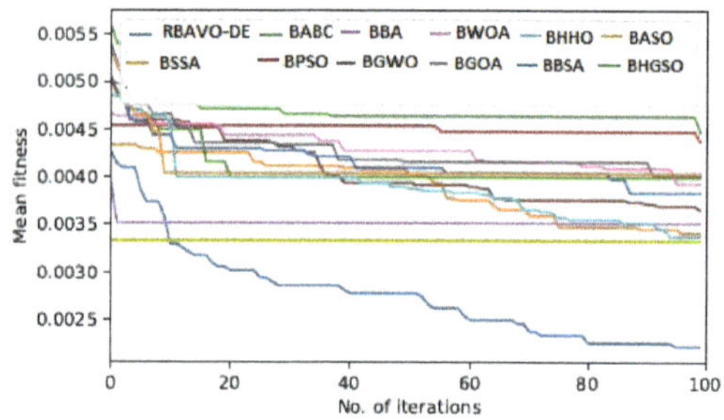


(p) READ

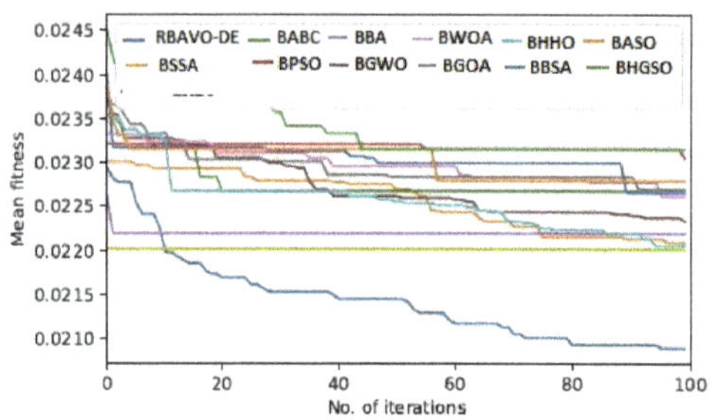


(q) SARC

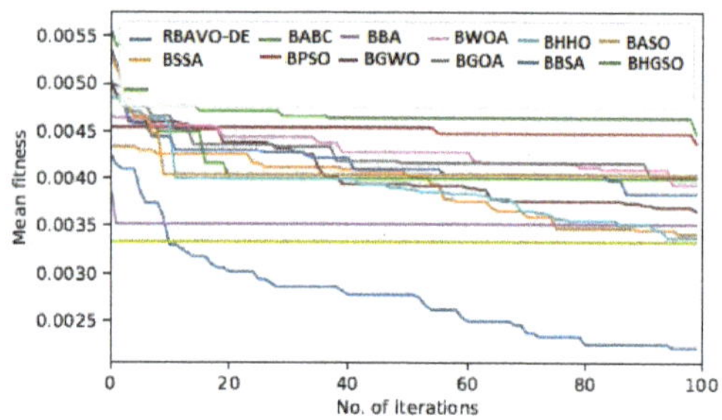


(r) SKCM

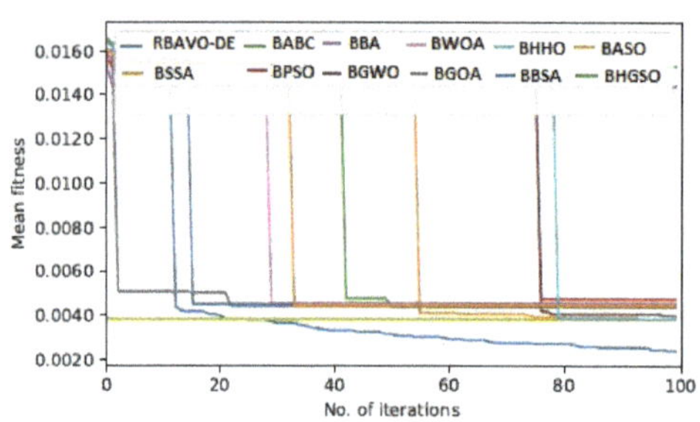


(s) STAD

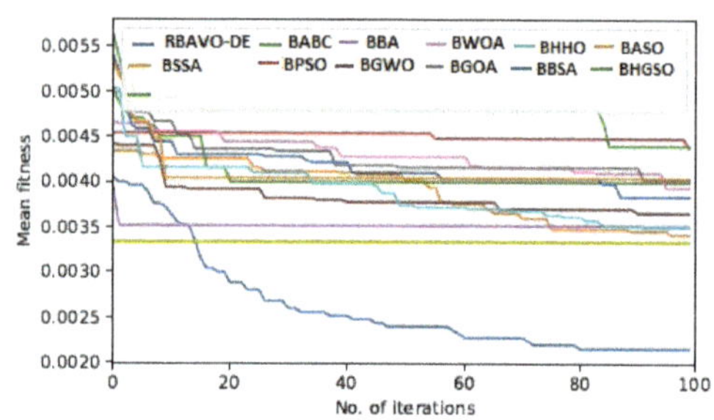


(t) THCA

**Figure A2.** *Cont.*

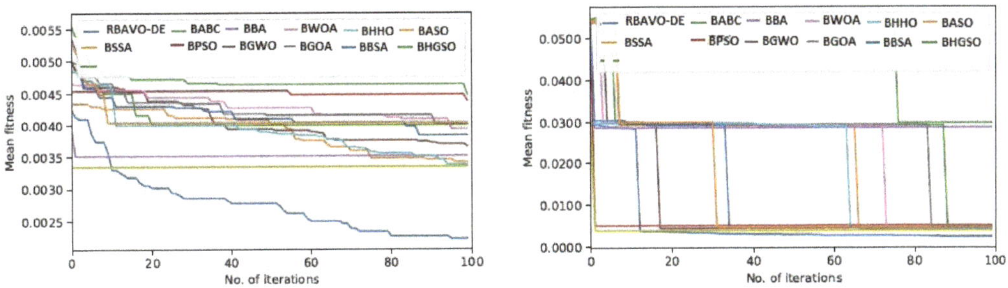


(u) THYM (v) UCEC

**Figure A2.** Convergence graphs of the proposed RBAVO-DE algorithm and competitive methods employing the *k*-NN model on the overall benchmarks (Cont.) [57].

## References


1. Estrada-Meza, C.; Torres-Copado, A.; Loreti González-Melgoza, L.; Ruiz-Manriquez, L.M.; De Donato, M.; Sharma, A.; Pathak, S.; Banerjee, A.; Paul, S. Recent insights into the microRNA and long non-coding RNA-mediated regulation of stem cell populations. *3 Biotech* **2022**, *12*, 270. [CrossRef] [PubMed]
2. Kakati, T.; Bhattacharyya, D.K.; Kalita, J.K.; Norden-Krichmar, T.M. DEGnext: Classification of differentially expressed genes from RNA-seq data using a convolutional neural network with transfer learning. *BMC Bioinform.* **2022**, *23*, 17. [CrossRef]
3. Zhao, S.; Fung-Leung, W.P.; Bittner, A.; Ngo, K.; Liu, X. Comparison of RNA-Seq and microarray in transcriptome profiling of activated T cells. *PLoS ONE* **2014**, *9*, e78644. [CrossRef]
4. Chen, Z.; Luo, Z.; Zhang, D.; Li, H.; Liu, X.; Zhu, K.; Zhang, H.; Wang, Z.; Zhou, P.; Ren, J.; et al. TIGER: A web portal of tumor immunotherapy gene expression resource. *Genom. Proteom. Bioinform.* **2023**, *21*, 337–348. [CrossRef] [PubMed]
5. Nunez-Garcia, J.; AbuOun, M.; Storey, N.; Brouwer, M.; Delgado-Blas, J.; Mo, S.S.; Ellaby, N.; Veldman, K.; Haenni, M.; Châtre, P.; et al. Harmonisation of in-silico next-generation sequencing based methods for diagnostics and surveillance. *Sci. Rep.* **2022**, *12*, 14372. [CrossRef]
6. Wang, Z.; Gerstein, M.; Snyder, M. RNA-Seq: A revolutionary tool for transcriptomics. *Nat. Rev. Genet.* **2009**, *10*, 57–63. [CrossRef]
7. Kim, W.J.; Choi, B.R.; Noh, J.J.; Lee, Y.Y.; Kim, T.J.; Lee, J.W.; Kim, B.G.; Choi, C.H. Comparison of RNA-Seq and microarray in the prediction of protein expression and survival prediction. *Front. Genet.* **2024**, *15*, 1342021. [CrossRef]
8. Wang, M.; Chen, X.; Dai, Y.; Wu, D.; Liu, F.; Yang, Z.; Song, B.; Xie, L.; Yang, L.; Zhao, W.; et al. Concordance study of a 520-gene next-generation sequencing-based genomic profiling assay of tissue and plasma samples. *Mol. Diagn. Ther.* **2022**, *26*, 309–322. [CrossRef]
9. Metzker, M.L. Sequencing technologies—The next generation. *Nat. Rev. Genet.* **2010**, *11*, 31–46. [CrossRef] [PubMed]
10. Pandey, D.; Onkara Perumal, P. A scoping review on deep learning for next-generation RNA-Seq. data analysis. *Funct. Integr. Genom.* **2023**, *23*, 134. [CrossRef]
11. Liu, S.; Yao, W. Prediction of lung cancer using gene expression and deep learning with KL divergence gene selection. *BMC Bioinform.* **2022**, *23*, 175. [CrossRef] [PubMed]
12. Houssein, E.H.; Oliva, D.; Celik, E.; Emam, M.M.; Ghoniem, R.M. Boosted sooty tern optimization algorithm for global optimization and feature selection. *Expert Syst. Appl.* **2023**, *213*, 119015. [CrossRef]
13. Joshi, A.A.; Aziz, R.M. A two-phase cuckoo search based approach for gene selection and deep learning classification of cancer disease using gene expression data with a novel fitness function. *Multimed. Tools Appl.* **2024**, *83*, 71721–71752. [CrossRef]
14. Ramaswamy, R.; Kandhasamy, P.; Palaniswamy, S. Feature selection for Alzheimer's gene expression data using modified binary particle swarm optimization. *IETE J. Res.* **2023**, *69*, 9–20. [CrossRef]
15. Cui, X.; Li, Y.; Fan, J.; Wang, T. A novel filter feature selection algorithm based on relief. *Appl. Intell.* **2022**, *52*, 5063–5081. [CrossRef]
16. Alhenawi, E.; Al-Sayyed, R.; Hudaib, A.; Mirjalili, S. Feature selection methods on gene expression microarray data for cancer classification: A systematic review. *Comput. Biol. Med.* **2022**, *140*, 105051. [CrossRef] [PubMed]
17. Parlak, B.; Uysal, A.K. A novel filter feature selection method for text classification: Extensive Feature Selector. *J. Inf. Sci.* **2023**, *49*, 59–78. [CrossRef]
18. Albulayhi, K.; Abu Al-Haija, Q.; Alsuhibany, S.A.; Jillepalli, A.A.; Ashrafuzzaman, M.; Sheldon, F.T. IoT intrusion detection using machine learning with a novel high performing feature selection method. *Appl. Sci.* **2022**, *12*, 5015. [CrossRef]
19. Fatima, A.; Nazir, T.; Nazir, A.K.; Din, A.M.U. An efficient Incremental Wrapper-based Information Gain Gene Subset Selection (IG based on IWSSr) method for Tumor Discernment. *Multimed. Tools Appl.* **2024**, *83*, 64741–64766. [CrossRef]
20. Kaur, S.; Kumar, Y.; Koul, A.; Kumar Kamboj, S. A systematic review on metaheuristic optimization techniques for feature selections in disease diagnosis: Open issues and challenges. *Arch. Comput. Methods Eng.* **2023**, *30*, 1863–1895. [CrossRef]

21. Abd El-Mageed, A.A.; Gad, A.G.; Sallam, K.M.; Munasinghe, K.; Abohany, A.A. Improved Binary Adaptive Wind Driven Optimization Algorithm-Based Dimensionality Reduction for Supervised Classification. *Comput. Ind. Eng.* **2022**, *167*, 107904. [CrossRef]
22. Gad, A.G.; Sallam, K.M.; Chakrabortty, R.K.; Ryan, M.J.; Abohany, A.A. An improved binary sparrow search algorithm for feature selection in data classification. *Neural Comput. Appl.* **2022**, *34*, 15705–15752. [CrossRef]
23. Hussien, R.M.; Abohany, A.A.; Abd El-Mageed, A.A.; Hosny, K.M. Improved Binary Meerkat Optimization Algorithm for efficient feature selection of supervised learning classification. *Knowl.-Based Syst.* **2024**, *292*, 111616. [CrossRef]
24. Abd El-Mageed, A.A.; Abohany, A.A.; Elashry, A. Effective Feature Selection Strategy for Supervised Classification based on an Improved Binary Aquila Optimization Algorithm. *Comput. Ind. Eng.* **2023**, *181*, 109300. [CrossRef]
25. Yin, Y.; Jang-Jaccard, J.; Xu, W.; Singh, A.; Zhu, J.; Sabrina, F.; Kwak, J. IGRF-RFE: A hybrid feature selection method for MLP-based network intrusion detection on UNSW-NB15 dataset. *J. Big Data* **2023**, *10*, 15. [CrossRef]
26. Nakao, H.; Imaoka, M.; Hida, M.; Imai, R.; Nakamura, M.; Matsumoto, K.; Kita, K. Determination of individual factors associated with hallux valgus using SVM-RFE. *BMC Musculoskelet. Disord.* **2023**, *24*, 534. [CrossRef] [PubMed]
27. Sarafrazi, S.; Nezamabadi-Pour, H. Facing the classification of binary problems with a GSA-SVM hybrid system. *Math. Comput. Model.* **2013**, *57*, 270–278. [CrossRef]
28. Cadenas, J.M.; Garrido, M.C.; MartíNez, R. Feature subset selection filter–wrapper based on low quality data. *Expert Syst. Appl.* **2013**, *40*, 6241–6252. [CrossRef]
29. Oh, I.S.; Lee, J.S.; Moon, B.R. Hybrid genetic algorithms for feature selection. *IEEE Trans. Pattern Anal. Mach. Intell.* **2004**, *26*, 1424–1437.
30. Abdollahzadeh, B.; Gharehchopogh, F.S.; Mirjalili, S. African vultures optimization algorithm: A new nature-inspired metaheuristic algorithm for global optimization problems. *Comput. Ind. Eng.* **2021**, *158*, 107408. [CrossRef]
31. El-Shafeiy, E.; Hassanien, A.E.; Sallam, K.M.; Abohany, A. Approach for training quantum neural network to predict severity of COVID-19 in patients. *Comput. Mater. Contin.* **2020**, *66*, 1745–1755. [CrossRef]
32. Yaqoob, A.; Verma, N.K.; Aziz, R.M. Optimizing gene selection and cancer classification with hybrid sine cosine and cuckoo search algorithm. *J. Med. Syst.* **2024**, *48*, 10. [CrossRef]
33. Joshi, A.A.; Aziz, R.M. Deep learning approach for brain tumor classification using metaheuristic optimization with gene expression data. *Int. J. Imaging Syst. Technol.* **2023**, *34*, e23007. [CrossRef]
34. Mahto, R.; Ahmed, S.U.; Rahman, R.u.; Aziz, R.M.; Roy, P.; Mallik, S.; Li, A.; Shah, M.A. A novel and innovative cancer classification framework through a consecutive utilization of hybrid feature selection. *BMC Bioinform.* **2023**, *24*, 479. [CrossRef] [PubMed]
35. Neggaz, N.; Neggaz, I.; Abd Elaziz, M.; Hussien, A.G.; Abulaigh, L.; Damaševičius, R.; Hu, G. Boosting manta rays foraging optimizer by trigonometry operators: A case study on medical dataset. *Neural Comput. Appl.* **2024**, *36*, 9405–9436. [CrossRef]
36. Lyu, B.; Haque, A. Deep learning based tumor type classification using gene expression data. In Proceedings of the 2018 ACM International Conference on Bioinformatics, Computational Biology, and Health Informatics, Washington, DC, USA, 29 August–1 September 2018; pp. 89–96.
37. Khalifa, N.E.M.; Taha, M.H.N.; Ali, D.E.; Slowik, A.; Hassanien, A.E. Artificial intelligence technique for gene expression by tumor RNA-Seq data: A novel optimized deep learning approach. *IEEE Access* **2020**, *8*, 22874–22883. [CrossRef]
38. Dillies, M.A.; Rau, A.; Aubert, J.; Hennequet-Antier, C.; Jeanmougin, M.; Servant, N.; Keime, C.; Marot, G.; Castel, D.; Estelle, J.; et al. A comprehensive evaluation of normalization methods for Illumina high-throughput RNA sequencing data analysis. *Briefings Bioinform.* **2013**, *14*, 671–683. [CrossRef]
39. Xiao, Y.; Wu, J.; Lin, Z.; Zhao, X. A deep learning-based multi-model ensemble method for cancer prediction. *Comput. Methods Programs Biomed.* **2018**, *153*, 1–9. [CrossRef]
40. Liu, M.; Xu, L.; Yi, J.; Huang, J. A feature gene selection method based on ReliefF and PSO. In Proceedings of the 2018 10th International Conference on Measuring Technology and Mechatronics Automation (ICMTMA), Changsha, China, 7–8 January 2018; IEEE: New York, NY, USA, 2018; pp. 298–301.
41. Kononenko, I. Estimating attributes: Analysis and extensions of RELIEF. In Proceedings of the European Conference on Machine Learning, Catania, Italy, 6–8 April 1994; Springer: Berlin/Heidelberg, Germany, 1994; pp. 171–182.
42. Faris, H.; Mafarja, M.M.; Heidari, A.A.; Aljarah, I.; Ala'M, A.Z.; Mirjalili, S.; Fujita, H. An efficient binary salp swarm algorithm with crossover scheme for feature selection problems. *Knowl.-Based Syst.* **2018**, *154*, 43–67. [CrossRef]
43. Abdel-Basset, M.; Ding, W.; El-Shahat, D. A hybrid Harris Hawks optimization algorithm with simulated annealing for feature selection. *Artif. Intell. Rev.* **2020**, *54*, 593–637. [CrossRef]
44. Storn, R.; Price, K. Differential evolution—A simple and efficient heuristic for global optimization over continuous spaces. *J. Glob. Optim.* **1997**, *11*, 341–359. [CrossRef]
45. Karaboga, D.; Basturk, B. A powerful and efficient algorithm for numerical function optimization: Artificial bee colony (ABC) algorithm. *J. Glob. Optim.* **2007**, *39*, 459–471. [CrossRef]
46. Mirjalili, S.; Gandomi, A.H.; Mirjalili, S.Z.; Saremi, S.; Faris, H.; Mirjalili, S.M. Salp Swarm Algorithm: A bio-inspired optimizer for engineering design problems. *Adv. Eng. Softw.* **2017**, *114*, 163–191. [CrossRef]
47. Khanesar, M.A.; Teshnehlab, M.; Shoorehdeli, M.A. A novel binary particle swarm optimization. In Proceedings of the 2007 Mediterranean Conference on Control & Automation, Athens, Greece, 27–29 June 2007; IEEE: New York, NY, USA, 2007; pp. 1–6.

48. Mirjalili, S.; Mirjalili, S.M.; Yang, X.S. Binary bat algorithm. *Neural Comput. Appl.* **2014**, *25*, 663–681. [CrossRef]
49. Emary, E.; Zawbaa, H.M.; Hassanien, A.E. Binary grey wolf optimization approaches for feature selection. *Neurocomputing* **2016**, *172*, 371–381. [CrossRef]
50. Hichem, H.; Elkamel, M.; Rafik, M.; Mesaaoud, M.T.; Ouahiba, C. A new binary grasshopper optimization algorithm for feature selection problem. *J. King Saud Univ. Comput. Inf. Sci.* **2022**, *34*, 316–328. [CrossRef]
51. Hussien, A.G.; Hassanien, A.E.; Houssein, E.H.; Bhattacharyya, S.; Amin, M. S-shaped binary whale optimization algorithm for feature selection. In *Recent Trends in Signal and Image Processing: ISSIP 2017*; Springer: Berlin/Heidelberg, Germany, 2019; pp. 79–87.
52. Zhao, W.; Wang, L.; Zhang, Z. Atom search optimization and its application to solve a hydrogeologic parameter estimation problem. *Knowl.-Based Syst.* **2019**, *163*, 283–304. [CrossRef]
53. Meng, X.B.; Gao, X.Z.; Lu, L.; Liu, Y.; Zhang, H. A new bio-inspired optimisation algorithm: Bird Swarm Algorithm. *J. Exp. Theor. Artif. Intell.* **2016**, *28*, 673–687. [CrossRef]
54. Hashim, F.A.; Houssein, E.H.; Mabrouk, M.S.; Al-Atabany, W.; Mirjalili, S. Henry gas solubility optimization: A novel physics-based algorithm. *Future Gener. Comput. Syst.* **2019**, *101*, 646–667. [CrossRef]
55. Heidari, A.A.; Mirjalili, S.; Faris, H.; Aljarah, I.; Mafarja, M.; Chen, H. Harris hawks optimization: Algorithm and applications. *Future Gener. Comput. Syst.* **2019**, *97*, 849–872. [CrossRef]
56. Normalized-level3 RNA-Seq Gene Expression Dataset. Available online: https://gdac.broadinstitute.org/ (accessed on 20 December 2023).
57. El-Mageed, A.A.A.; Elkhouli, A.E.; Abohany, A.A.; Gafar, M. Gene selection via improved nuclear reaction optimization algorithm for cancer classification in high-dimensional data. *J. Big Data* **2024**, *11*, 46. [CrossRef]
58. Mafarja, M.; Mirjalili, S. Whale optimization approaches for wrapper feature selection. *Appl. Soft Comput.* **2018**, *62*, 441–453. [CrossRef]
59. Thaher, T.; Heidari, A.A.; Mafarja, M.; Dong, J.S.; Mirjalili, S. Binary Harris Hawks optimizer for high-dimensional, low sample size feature selection. In *Evolutionary Machine Learning Techniques*; Springer: Berlin/Heidelberg, Germany, 2020; pp. 251–272.
60. Derrac, J.; García, S.; Molina, D.; Herrera, F. A practical tutorial on the use of nonparametric statistical tests as a methodology for comparing evolutionary and swarm intelligence algorithms. *Swarm Evol. Comput.* **2011**, *1*, 3–18. [CrossRef]
61. Python Code for Gene Selection via Relief Binary African Vultures Optimization Integrated with Differential Evolution. Available online: https://github.com/D-Amr-Atef/Gene_Selection_RBAVO-DE.git (accessed on 18 May 2024).

algorithms

MDPI

*Article*

# New Multi-View Feature Learning Method for Accurate Antifungal Peptide Detection

**Sayeda Muntaha Ferdous [1], Shafayat Bin Shabbir Mugdha [1] and Iman Dehzangi [2,3,*]**

1 Department of Computer Science & Engineering, United International University, Dhaka 1212, Bangladesh; smugdha161190@bscse.uiu.ac.bd (S.M.F.); sferdous181279@bscse.uiu.ac.bd (S.B.S.M.)
2 Department of Computer Science, Rutgers University, Camden, NJ 08854, USA
3 Center for Computational and Integrative Biology, Rutgers University, Camden, NJ 08103, USA
* Correspondence: i.dehzangi@rutgers.edu

**Abstract:** Antimicrobial resistance, particularly the emergence of resistant strains in fungal pathogens, has become a pressing global health concern. Antifungal peptides (AFPs) have shown great potential as a promising alternative therapeutic strategy due to their inherent antimicrobial properties and potential application in combating fungal infections. However, the identification of antifungal peptides using experimental approaches is time-consuming and costly. Hence, there is a demand to propose fast and accurate computational approaches to identifying AFPs. This paper introduces a novel multi-view feature learning (MVFL) model, called AFP-MVFL, for accurate AFP identification, utilizing multi-view feature learning. By integrating the sequential and physicochemical properties of amino acids and employing a multi-view approach, the AFP-MVFL model significantly enhances prediction accuracy. It achieves 97.9%, 98.4%, 0.98, and 0.96 in terms of accuracy, precision, F1 score, and Matthews correlation coefficient (MCC), respectively, outperforming previous studies found in the literature.

**Keywords:** AFP-MVFL; peptide; multi-view feature learning; iFeature; random forest

## 1. Introduction

Fungal infections pose a significant threat to human health, affecting over one billion people worldwide annually [1]. Unlike bacteria, fungi share similar biological characteristics with mammalian cells as eukaryotes, making it challenging to develop antifungal drugs [2]. Currently, the clinical treatment options for fungal infections are limited to polyenes, azoles, echinocandins, and a few auxiliary drugs like flucytosine, which are constrained by fungal resistance and have drug toxicity side effects [3]. Therefore, there is a critical need to expand the repertoire of antifungal drugs [4].

Antifungal peptides (AFPs) represent a class of naturally occurring peptides produced by organisms as a defense mechanism against fungal pathogens [5]. Typically consisting of 10–100 amino acids, AFPs are amphipathic. AFPs have low toxicity and high efficiency. Due to these favorable characteristics, they have emerged as promising alternatives to chemical antifungal agents [6]. In contrast to traditional antifungal drugs, AFPs exhibit diverse modes of action, such as disrupting fungal cell membranes or inducing the production of reactive oxygen species (ROS) [7]. Identifying AFPs experimentally is time-consuming and costly, especially for the pre-screening of a large number of AFP candidates. Therefore, there is a pressing need for computational models that can rapidly and accurately predict AFPs [8].

In recent years, a wide range of machine-learning-based approaches have been proposed to predict antifungal peptides (AFPs). For instance, Leyi Wei et al. introduced a novel computational model called AFP-MFL (multi-view feature learning) for accurately identifying antifungal peptides (AFPs) by integrating different feature groups [9]. Later,

Agrawal et al. [10] employed a combination of amino acid composition (AAC), dipeptide composition (DPC), split amino acid composition, and binary profiles to characterize peptides, subsequently utilizing support vector machine (SVM) classifier to construct prediction models [11].

More recently, Ahmad et al. introduced a feature fusion scheme to integrate diverse peptide features, which were then used to train a deep neural network (DNN) for prediction purposes [12]. Later, Ahmad et al. proposed another innovative computational model for AFP prediction using sequential and evolutionary information extracted from peptides and employing a minimum redundancy and maximum relevance (mRMR) based method for feature extraction [13]. Most recently, Zhang et al. proposed a machine-learning-based approach for accurately identifying and classifying AFPs by developing a comprehensive dataset of known AFPs and applying various feature extraction techniques to represent peptide sequences [14].

Most existing studies heavily rely on expert-knowledge-based handcrafted features to characterize intrinsic peptide properties [15]. These approaches need help with handling short peptide sequences. For instance, descriptors such as AAC, DPC, and reduced amino acid alphabet composition (RAAAC) only consider the frequency of individual amino acid residues, overlooking the sequential order of amino acids in the peptide sequence. The integration of different feature vectors into a high-dimensional feature space has been used to achieve a more expressive feature representation [16]. Nevertheless, this often leads to the curse of dimensionality, introducing redundant information and resulting in heightened computational complexity [17].

To address these issues, we present AFP_MVFL, a new machine learning model based on multi-view feature learning (MVFL) aimed at accurately identifying AFPs. The AFP-MVFL model leverages a diverse range of sequence-based information and physicochemical properties to comprehensively represent peptide characteristics [10]. By incorporating multiple properties of peptides, our model enhances its ability to capture patterns underlying antifungal activity. AFP-MVFL achieves 97.9%, 98.4%, 0.98, and 0.96 in terms of accuracy, precision, F1 score, and Matthews correlation coefficient (MCC), respectively, outperforming previous studies found in the literature. The AFP-MVFL model and its source code are publicly available at https://github.com/MuntahaMim/AFP-MVFL.git (accessed on 1 May 2024).

## 2. Materials and Methods

The initial steps include importing necessary libraries, loading training and test datasets, and converting labels into binary values (0 for the negative and 1 for the positive classes). The training data are then preprocessed via scaling to ensure uniformity. Next, a random forest classifier with 100 estimators is initialized and fitted to the scaled training data to determine feature importance. At this stage, features with an importance level above the mean are selected and extracted. For evaluating classifier performance, stratified 10-fold cross-validation is employed. The general architecture of our model is presented in Figure 1. This section elaborates on the materials and methods used to build AFP_MVFL.

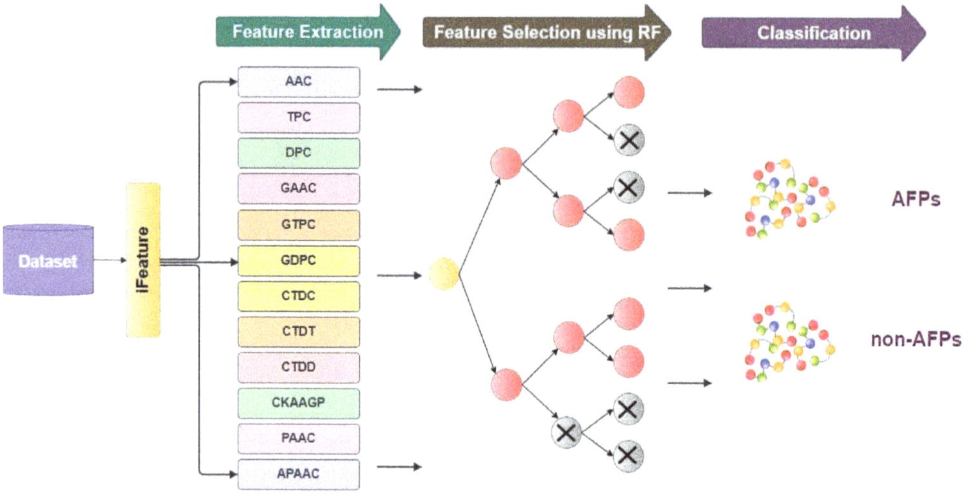


**Figure 1.** The overall architecture of AFP-MVFL. The AFPs prediction pipeline consists of three modules: (i) feature extraction module using iFeature; (ii) feature selection using random forest; (iii) classification module for the prediction task.

## 2.1. Dataset

To ensure a comprehensive evaluation and proper comparison with previous studies, this study leverages three benchmark datasets, namely, Antifp_DS1, Antifp_DS2, and Antifp_DS3, which have been widely used in the literature [17–21]. These datasets, outlined in Table 1, encompass distinct characteristics and composition. In Antifp_DS1, Antifp_DS2, and Antifp_DS3, the positive samples originate from the data repository of antimicrobial peptides (DRAMP) [20], while excluding sequences containing unnatural amino acids (BIJOUX). However, the negative samples in each dataset differ. Antifp_DS1 negatives comprise active antimicrobial peptides, while Antifp_DS2 negatives are randomly generated from SwissProt. Notably, the maximum peptide length in these three datasets is 100. On the other hand, Antifp_DS3 encompasses peptides with lengths ranging from 5 to 30. Positive samples in Antifp_DS3 were collected from CAMP [21], DRAMP [22], and StarPep [23,24] databases, whereas negatives were randomly generated from the Swiss-Prot database. As shown in Table 1, all three datasets are balanced (equal number of positive and negative samples). They are also normally distributed.

**Table 1.** Statistics and properties of the datasets employed in this study, namely, Antifp-DS1, Antifp-DS2, and Antifp-DS3.

| Dataset | | AFPs | Non-AFPs | Description of AFPs and Non-AFPs |
|---|---|---|---|---|
| Antifp_DS1 | Train<br>Test | 1168<br>291 | 1168<br>291 | The non-AFPs were chosen at random from the Swiss-Prot database, and antimicrobial peptides other than antifungals were obtained from the DRAMA database. |
| Antifp_DS2 | Train<br>Test | 1168<br>291 | 1168<br>291 | The non-AFPs were antimicrobial peptides other than antifungal peptides. |
| Antifp_DS3 | Train<br>Test | 1168<br>291 | 1168<br>291 | The non-AFPs were chosen at random from the Swiss-Prot database. |

### 2.2. Classifiers

To test the efficiency of our extracted features and identify the best classifier to build our model, we investigated eight different classifiers, most of which have been effectively used for similar studies [25]. These eight classifiers are support vector machine (SVM), logistic regression (LR), decision tree (DT), rotation forest (RT), stochastic gradient descent (SGD), AdaBoost, naive Bayes (NB), and random forest (RF).

#### 2.2.1. Support Vector Machine (SVM)

SVM is one of the most extensively used machine learning techniques in this field. It has been shown to outperform other classifiers for similar tasks [26–28]. SVM aims to identify the biggest marginal hyperplane across classes to decrease prediction errors and improve classification task generality. In the case of linearly separable data, it generates a hyperplane with a maximum margin to distinguish two distinct classes. The SVM technique employs many kernel functions, such as linear, nonlinear, polynomial, radial basis function (RBF), and sigmoid [29]. In this study, we have used the linear kernel for the SVM and "C = 1" as a regularization parameter to influence the trade-off between having a smooth decision boundary and classifying the training points correctly.

#### 2.2.2. Logistic Regression (LR)

The probability is estimated using log odds in logistic regression. It has been frequently employed for a variety of tasks with promising outcomes [30]. It is also an excellent model for estimating the likelihood of a linear solution to a problem [31]. In this study, we have used the default random state "0" to ensure the reproducibility of this method in the future.

#### 2.2.3. Naive Bayes (NB)

In the field of machine learning and data mining, naive Bayes is regarded as one of the most prevalent types of classifiers [32]. It is based on the assumption of conditional independence between features. This model creates a Gaussian naive Bayes classifier, and the instance is created with default parameters so that it represents the prior probabilities of the classes.

#### 2.2.4. AdaBoost

AdaBoost is a booting-based approach that employs a basic classifier, also known as a weak learner, and improves its performance iteratively. It raises the cost of misclassified samples in each iteration to ensure they are correctly classified in the following iterations [33]. Adaboost's performance strongly depends on its weak learner's performance in each iteration. We implemented the AdaBoost classifier using a decision tree as weak learners with 50 n_estimators to shrink the contribution of each classifier.

#### 2.2.5. Random Forest (RF)

Proposed by Breiman in 2001 [34], random forest aims at building a powerful and divergent decision boundary by employing decision trees on numerous random subsets of data collected using the bagging technique [34]. Random forest is a flexible technique for large-scale problems and has yielded promising results for various challenges [35].

#### 2.2.6. Stochastic Gradient Descent (SGT)

Stochastic gradient descent (SGD) is a robust optimization algorithm widely used in machine learning and deep learning. It is a variant of the gradient descent method that is particularly well-suited for large datasets and complex models and has obtained promising results for similar studies [36,37].

2.2.7. Decision Tree (DT)

A decision tree is a non-parametric supervised learning approach for classification and regression applications. It has a hierarchical tree structure consisting of a root node, branches, internal nodes, and leaf nodes [38].

## 2.3. *Feature Extraction*

In this study, we employed iFeature, a widely used feature extraction tool, to extract informative features from the input data [39]. iFeature provides a comprehensive set of feature descriptors that capture diverse aspects of the data, enabling a more comprehensive analysis. iFeature possesses the ability to compute and derive an extensive array of 18 primary sequence encoding schemes that cover 53 diverse feature descriptors. Within various feature categories, users are also able to extract distinct physiochemical properties of amino acids from the AAindex database [40]. The following commonly used feature descriptors are calculated and extracted using iFeature.

2.3.1. Amino Acid Composition (AAC)

AAC presents the frequency or occurrence of each amino acid residue in the protein sequence. It provides insights into the overall amino acid distribution, which can be indicative of certain functional properties [41]. The frequencies are computed for all 20 natural amino acids, denoted as "ACDEFGHIKLMNPQRSTVWY".

There are 20 elements in the amino acid composition (AAC) feature vector, each corresponding to one of the 20 standard amino acids. These elements indicate the percentage or frequency of each amino acid in the protein sequence.

2.3.2. Composition of Tripeptide (CTDC, CTDT, CTDD)

Tripeptide composition descriptors capture the occurrence frequencies of different combinations of three adjacent amino acids in the protein sequence. CTDC focuses on the composition of tripeptides in the C-terminus, CTDT in the middle, and CTDD in the N-terminus.

The composition of the tripeptide feature vector is an 8000-dimensional vector, with each dimension representing the frequency or occurrence of a specific tripeptide in the protein sequence. Each element in this vector corresponds to a unique tripeptide combination, capturing the information about the presence and distribution of these tripeptides in the protein sequence.

2.3.3. Dipeptide Composition (DPC)

DPC quantifies the occurrence frequencies of different combinations of two adjacent amino acids in the protein sequence. It provides information about local structural patterns and short-range interactions.

The dipeptide composition (DPC) is a 400-dimensional feature vector [42], with each dimension representing the frequency of a specific dipeptide in the protein sequence.

2.3.4. Grouped Amino Acid Composition (GAAC)

The "Grouped Amino Acid Composition" (GAAC) feature in iFeature involves grouping amino acids into predefined categories or classes and then computing the composition of these groups. We have used the basic grouping scheme that divides amino acids into four categories (e.g., hydrophobic, polar, charged, and aromatic). This GAAC feature vector has four features, each representing the composition of one of these groups in the protein sequence.

2.3.5. Global Descriptors of Protein Composition (GDPC)

GDPC captures the overall composition and properties of the protein by considering various physicochemical properties of the constituent amino acids. It provides a holistic view of the protein's chemical characteristics.

The "Grouped Diamino Acid Composition" (GDAC) feature in iFeature involves grouping dipeptides (two consecutive amino acids) into predefined categories or classes and then computing the composition of these groups. The GDPC is a 25-dimensional feature vector, with each dimension representing how dipeptides are grouped and the chosen classification scheme.

2.3.6. Grouped Tripeptide Composition (GTPC)

GTPC extends the tripeptide composition by grouping tripeptides with similar physicochemical properties. This allows for capturing higher-level structural and functional patterns in the protein sequence.

The GTPC is a 125-dimensional feature vector. Each feature vector represents the frequency or composition of tripeptides grouped into predefined categories or classes based on their physicochemical properties or structural similarities.

2.3.7. Tripeptide Position-Specific Composition (TPC)

TPC captures the position-specific occurrence frequencies of tripeptides in the protein sequence. It provides insights into the specific arrangement and distribution of tripeptides, which can be relevant for understanding functional motifs.

For a protein sequence of length L and using a standard scheme where the tripeptide composition is encoded at each position, the TPC feature vector will be L $\times$ 8000 (where 8000 represents the number of possible tripeptides).

*2.4. Feature Selection*

As is explained in Section 2.3, using iFeature, we extract over 20,000 features. This number of features exceeds the number of samples in our employed datasets by a 1:20 ratio (less than 1200 training samples and over 20,000 features). Hence, reducing the number of features is necessary to avoid under-training. In this study, after extracting the features using iFeature, we performed feature selection on our extracted features to identify the most effective features and filter out redundant features or those with limited discriminatory information. In this way, we aim to use a shortened input feature vector, which consequently enables us to build a more generalizable model. The significance of each feature in the training data is assessed using a random forest with 100 estimators. We have investigated several feature selection techniques. Among them, RF demonstrated the best performance. RF is considered an effective model for feature selection and classification. Feature importance is calculated, and features with importance surpassing the mean importance are selected for further analysis. These selected features are then extracted from both the training and test datasets to focus on the most informative aspects of the data [34,35].

The Gini index, widely employed in decision tree-based algorithms such as RF, is a metric to evaluate impurity or purity within a dataset [43]. Specifically, it quantifies the likelihood that a randomly selected element would be misclassified, reflecting the overall impurity of a set of data points. In the context of the RF method, which is an ensemble of decision trees, the Gini index plays a crucial role in assessing the importance of each feature in contributing to the model's predictive accuracy. Features that lead to nodes with lower impurity are considered more important, as they contribute to more accurate classifications [44].

Here, we focused on the most important features to reduce the model's dimensionality, which improved computational efficiency. Features with higher Gini importance scores are indicative of their greater contribution to the overall predictive power of the model. This process aided in selecting a subset of features that are not only relevant but also collectively provide meaningful information for the given prediction task.

### 2.5. Performance Evaluation

To assess the performance and generalization capability of different classifiers, stratified 10-fold cross-validation and independent test sets are used. To report the results, we run our experiments 10 times and then report the average.

### 2.6. Evaluation Metrics

For the evaluation of our model's performance, various metrics, including accuracy (ACC), precision (PRE), the area under the precision–recall curve (AUPRC), the area under the receiver–operating characteristic curve (AUC), Matthews correlation coefficient (MCC), and F1-score are used. These metrics serve as reliable measures to assess the effectiveness and robustness of the model. The calculations for each metric are defined as follows:

$$ACC = \frac{TP + TN}{TP + TN + FP + FN},$$

$$SN = \frac{TP}{TP + FN},$$

$$SP = \frac{TN}{TN + FP},$$

$$Pre = \frac{TP}{TP + FP},$$

$$MCC = \frac{TP \times TN - FP \times FN}{\sqrt{(TP + FP) \times (TP + FN) \times (TN + FP) \times (TN + FN)}},$$

$$F1 - score = 2 \times \frac{Pre \times SN}{Pre + SN},$$

where TP represents the count of true positives, TN represents the count of true negatives, FP represents the count of false positives, and FN represents the count of false negatives.

## 3. Results and Discussion

This section showcases the experimental outcomes of multiple models employed for AFP prediction, utilizing diverse sequence encoding techniques and machine learning frameworks. A comprehensive comparison between our proposed model and state-of-the-art AFP classifiers is also provided.

### 3.1. Performance of the Model for Different Classifiers

We conducted a comprehensive comparison using different classifiers to identify the best classifier to build AFP_MVLF. The results of the comparison between the classifiers for 10-fold cross-validation and the independent test set are presented in Tables 2 and 3 for the dataset Antifp_DS1, respectively. Note that for this comparison, we used all the extracted features using iFeature (no feature extraction). As shown in these tables, RF performs better than other classifiers used in this study. Using RF, we achieve an accuracy of 93.5%, F1 score of 0.92, precision of 91.2%, and MCC of 0.89 for the 10-fold cross-validation. RF also stands out with the highest accuracy of 93.8%, F1 score of 0.93, precision of 96.6%, and MCC of 0.80 for the independent test dataset.

As shown in Tables 4 and 5, again, RF consistently delivered the top performance among all classifiers for the Antifp_DS2 dataset using a 10-fold cross-validation and independent test set, respectively. It achieves remarkable accuracy of (93.5% and 93.1%), F1 scores of (0.93 and 0.93), MCC scores of (0.87 and 0.86), and precision scores of (92.6% and 92.3%), respectively, using 10-fold cross-validation and the independent test dataset.

**Table 2.** The results of comparing machine learning algorithms based on various performance metrics using 10-fold cross-validation for the Antifp_DS1 dataset.

| Algo | Acc (%) | F1 | MCC | Precision (%) | SN (%) | SE (%) |
|---|---|---|---|---|---|---|
| SVM | 91.5 | 0.91 | 0.83 | 91.2 | 90.5 | 91.4 |
| **RF** | **93.5** | **0.92** | **0.89** | **93.1** | **93.2** | **93.8** |
| AdaBoost | 91.2 | 0.93 | 0.90 | 90.2 | 89.5 | 91.1 |
| NB | 78.4 | 0.77 | 0.57 | 81.4 | 80.2 | 78.8 |
| LR | 90.9 | 0.90 | 0.81 | 90.5 | 90.1 | 90.5 |
| SGD | 89.3 | 0.88 | 0.80 | 89.1 | 88.3 | 86.1 |
| Bernoulli NB | 87.4 | 0.87 | 0.74 | 88.7 | 88.3 | 87.6 |
| DT | 91.7 | 0.91 | 0.83 | 90.8 | 89.5 | 90.0 |
| RT | 91.7 | 0.90 | 0.91 | 92.4 | 92.3 | 91.7 |

**Table 3.** The results of comparing machine learning algorithms based on various performance metrics using an independent test set for the Antifp_DS1 dataset.

| Algo | Acc (%) | F1 | MCC | Pre(%) | SN (%) | SE (%) |
|---|---|---|---|---|---|---|
| SVM | 91.4 | 0.91 | 0.82 | 91.1 | 90.5 | 91.5 |
| **RF** | **93.8** | **0.93** | **0.80** | **96.6** | **93.2** | **93.5** |
| AdaBoost | 91.7 | 0.92 | 0.89 | 90.8 | 89.5 | 91.2 |
| NB | 78.8 | 0.78 | 0.57 | 79.7 | 80.2 | 78.4 |
| LR | 90.5 | 0.90 | 0.81 | 90.4 | 90.1 | 90.9 |
| SGD | 86.1 | 0.85 | 0.71 | 86.7 | 88.3 | 89.3 |
| Bernoulli NB | 87.6 | 0.87 | 0.75 | 90.1 | 88.3 | 87.4 |
| DT | 90.0 | 0.90 | 0.80 | 89.1 | 89.5 | 91.7 |
| RT | 91.7 | 0.91 | 0.90 | 92.5 | 92.3 | 91.7 |

**Table 4.** The results of comparing machine learning algorithms based on various performance metrics using 10-fold cross-validation for the Antifp_DS2 dataset.

| Algo | Acc (%) | F1 | MCC | Precision (%) | SN (%) | SE (%) |
|---|---|---|---|---|---|---|
| SVM | 93.5 | 0.93 | 0.87 | 92.6 | 90.5 | 91.4 |
| **RF** | **96.4** | **0.95** | **0.92** | **97.7** | **93.2** | **93.8** |
| AdaBoost | 92.6 | 0.91 | 0.90 | 89.0 | 89.5 | 91.1 |
| NB | 88.9 | 0.89 | 0.82 | 86.3 | 80.2 | 78.8 |
| LR | 92.5 | 0.91 | 0.85 | 92.8 | 90.1 | 90.5 |
| SGD | 90.9 | 0.91 | 0.81 | 90.9 | 88.3 | 86.1 |
| Bernoulli NB | 91.1 | 0.90 | 0.82 | 93.9 | 88.3 | 87.6 |
| DT | 91.6 | 0.91 | 0.83 | 90.8 | 89.5 | 90.0 |
| RT | 92.5 | 0.92 | 0.92 | 92.2 | 92.3 | 91.7 |

We also conducted the comparison for the Antifp_DS3 dataset and the summarized result in Tables 6 and 7 for a 10-fold cross-validation and independent test set, respectively. As shown in these tables, the model constructed with the RF performs the best among all the other classifiers. The model outperformed, resulting in ACC values of 93.7% and 94.1%, F1 scores of 0.93 and 0.92, MCC scores of 0.82 and 0.87, and precision scores of 94.3% and 95.1%, respectively.

**Table 5.** The results of comparing machine learning algorithms based on various performance metrics using an independent test set for the Antifp_DS2 dataset.

| Algo | Acc (%) | F1 | MCC | Precision (%) | SN (%) | SE (%) |
|---|---|---|---|---|---|---|
| SVM | 93.1% | 0.93 | 0.86 | 92.3 | 93.5 | 91.4 |
| **RF** | **96.2** | **0.96** | **0.92** | **96.8** | **96.4** | **93.8** |
| AdaBoost | 92.3 | 0.91 | 0.90 | 91.4 | 92.6 | 91.1 |
| NB | 85.6 | 0.89 | 0.86 | 80.5 | 88.9 | 78.8 |
| LR | 93.6 | 0.94 | 0.87 | 92.9 | 92.5 | 90.5 |
| SGD | 91.4 | 0.91 | 0.83 | 91.4 | 90.9 | 86.1 |
| Bernoulli NB | 90.4 | 0.90 | 0.80 | 92.1 | 91.1 | 87.6 |
| DT | 90.4 | 0.90 | 0.80 | 89.2 | 91.6 | 90.0 |
| RT | 91.1 | 0.91 | 0.92 | 91.2 | 92.5 | 91.7 |

**Table 6.** Results of the comparison of machine learning algorithms based on various performance metrics using 10-fold cross-validation for the Antifp_DS3 dataset.

| Algo | Acc (%) | F1 | MCC | Precision (%) | SN (%) | SE (%) |
|---|---|---|---|---|---|---|
| SVM | 91.4 | 0.91 | 0.82 | 90.9 | 90.5 | 92.3 |
| RF | 93.7 | 0.92 | 0.86 | 94.3 | 93.2 | 96.8 |
| AdaBoost | 88.3 | 0.87 | 0.85 | 85.2 | 89.5 | 87.2 |
| NB | 77.2 | 0.74 | 0.55 | 84.2 | 80.2 | 80.6 |
| LR | 91.7 | 0.91 | 0.83 | 90.8 | 90.1 | 92.9 |
| SGD | 88.1 | 0.88 | 0.88 | 86.8 | 88.3 | 91.4 |
| Bernoulli NB | 86.1 | 0.86 | 0.72 | 86.4 | 88.3 | 92.1 |
| DT | 87.3 | 0.87 | 0.74 | 88.7 | 89.5 | 89.2 |
| RT | 91.2 | 0.92 | 0.90 | 92.6 | 92.3 | 91.3 |

**Table 7.** The results of comparing machine learning algorithms based on various performance metrics using an independent test set for the Antifp_DS3 dataset.

| Algo | Acc (%) | F1 | MCC | Precision (%) | SN (%) | SE (%) |
|---|---|---|---|---|---|---|
| SVM | 90.8 | 0.91 | 0.81 | 89.9 | 90.5 | 92.3 |
| **RF** | **94.1** | **0.93** | **0.87** | **95.1** | **93.2** | **96.8** |
| AdaBoost | 83.4 | 0.82 | 0.81 | 82.1 | 89.5 | 82.0 |
| NB | 78.0 | 0.75 | 0.57 | 85.5 | 80.2 | 80.5 |
| LR | 90.1 | 0.90 | 0.80 | 89.3 | 90.1 | 92.9 |
| SGD | 88.3 | 0.88 | 0.76 | 89.6 | 88.3 | 91.4 |
| Bernoulli NB | 86.9 | 0.86 | 0.73 | 89.6 | 88.3 | 92.1 |
| DT | 87.6 | 0.87 | 0.75 | 90.1 | 89.5 | 89.2 |
| RT | 92.2 | 0.90 | 0.92 | 91.8 | 92.3 | 91.2 |

The ROC curves of all models on the independent test datasets—Antifp_DS1, Antifp_DS2, and Antifp_DS3—are displayed in Figures 2–4, respectively. As shown in these figures, RF demonstrates better results compared to other classifiers.

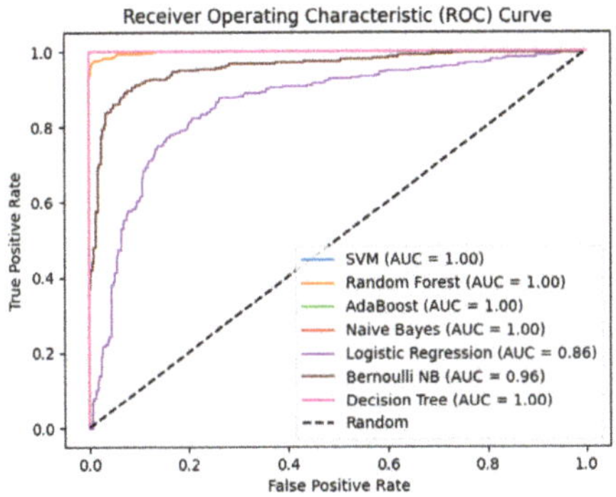


**Figure 2.** ROC curve of the results for various classification models on the independent test of the Antifp_DS1 dataset.

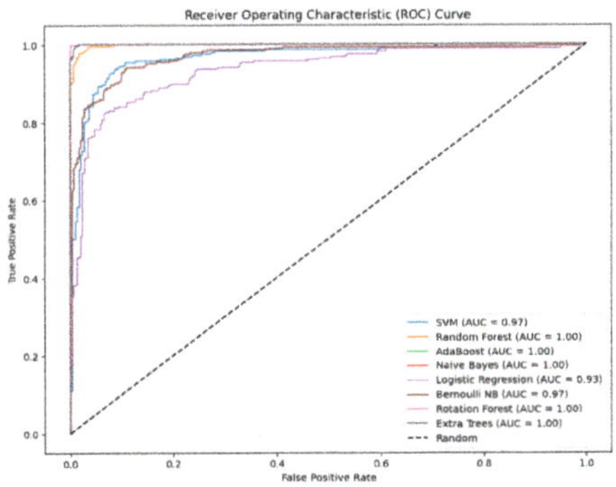


**Figure 3.** ROC curve of the results for various classification models on the independent test of the Antifp_DS2 dataset.

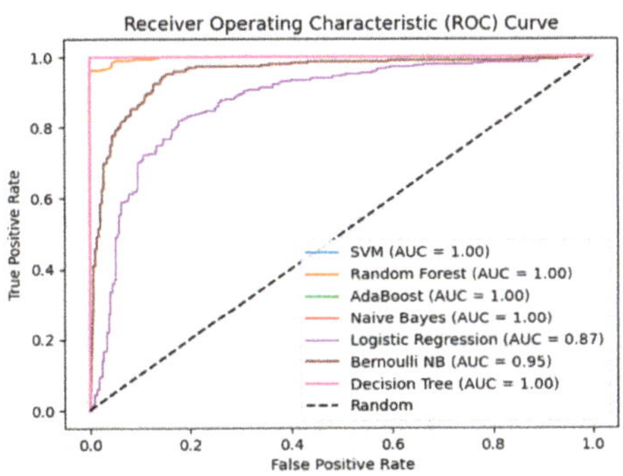


**Figure 4.** ROC curve of the results for various classification models on the independent test of the Antifp_DS3 dataset.

### *3.2. Results Achieved on the Selected Feature Set*

As a result of our comparison study, we use RF as the main classifier to build AFP_MVLF. Next, we use our feature extraction model and compare the results of using RF with and without feature extraction. The results of this comparison for Antifp_DS1 are presented in Table 8. As shown in this table, the models constructed with feature selection consistently outperform the alternative model (RF and the whole feature set without using feature selection) in terms of accuracy (ACC), precision (PRE), F1 score, and MCC.

**Table 8.** Comparison of the AFP-MVFL model with and without feature selection of Antifp_DS1.

| Datasets | Model | ACC (%) | PRE(%) | F1 Score | MCC |
|---|---|---|---|---|---|
| Antifp_DS1 | Without Feature Selection | 93.5 | 93.1 | 0.92 | 0.89 |
| | With Feature Selection | 97.9 | 98.4 | 0.98 | 0.96 |

Specifically, employing the random forest algorithm with 100 n_estimators in conjunction with the feature selection model yielded superior predictive capabilities, resulting in ACC values of 97.9% and 97.6%, F1 scores of 0.98 and 0.75, and MCC scores of 0.95 and 0.95 for the Antifp_DS1 dataset, respectively. These results substantiate the advantage of employing feature selection in improving the overall performance of the predictive models.

### 3.3. Comparison of the Proposed Model with Existing Models

Next, to investigate the effectiveness of our proposed model (AFP_MVLF), we compare its results against other state-of-the-art models found in the literature. The results achieved for AFP_MVLF compared to previous studies for Antifp_DS1 are presented in Table 9. As demonstrated in this table, AFP_MVLF outperforms previous studies, including [9,10,12,14,19,21,23,45] across all evaluation metrics. When compared to AFP-MFL, AFP-MVFL represents relative improvements of 2.1%, 2.4%, 1.3%, and 0.04 in terms of ACC, F1 score, precision, and MCC, respectively, for the Antifp_DS1 dataset.

**Table 9.** Comparison of AFP-MVFL with other antifungal peptide predictors on the independent test dataset of Antifp_DS1.

| Datasets | Model | ACC (%) | PRE(%) | F1 score | MCC |
|---|---|---|---|---|---|
| Antifp_DS1 | MIMML [23] | 91.3 | - | - | 0.83 |
| | AntiMF [45] | 90.2 | - | - | 0.80 |
| | Antifp [10] | 86.3 | - | - | 0.73 |
| | AFPDeep [19] | 90.2 | - | - | - |
| | Deep-AntiFP [12] | 89.1 | - | - | 0.78 |
| | iAFPs-EnC-GA [21] | 93.9 | - | - | 0.90 |
| | AFP-MFL [9] | 95.8 | 97.1 | 0.96 | 0.92 |
| | AFP-MVFL | 97.9 | 98.4 | 0.98 | 0.96 |

We also compare AFP_MVLF's performance to the state-of-the-art methods found in the literature for the Antifp_DS2 and Antifp_DS3 datasets. The experimental results obtained from these different datasets are presented in Table 10. AFP_MVLF consistently outperforms the competitive approaches across all evaluation metrics in each dataset.

Specifically, when tested on the Antifp_DS2 dataset, the AFP-MVFL achieves improved prediction rates with an accuracy of 98.3%, precision of 99.1%, F1 score of 0.98, and MCC of 0.97. A relative increase is observed compared to the AFP-MFL model. On the Antifp_DS3 dataset, the AFP-MVFL achieves an accuracy of 97.4%, precision of 98.4%, F1 score of 0.97, and MCC of 0.95, representing a relative improvement over the previous three models. These results establish that the AFP-MVFL consistently outperforms other methods in distinguishing AFPs from non-AFPs across all evaluated datasets.

We also generated t-SNE graphs in Figures 5–7 for the Antifp_DS1, Antifp_DS2, and Antifp_DS3 datasets to explore the importance and contribution of different features. Here we choose t-SNE to investigate feature importance since it was demonstrated as a better candidate than principal component analysis (PCA) in similar studies [46]. By plotting the t-SNE, we can visualize the data in a reduced space, which helps us to identify which features are most relevant for distinguishing between different data points [47]. By visualizing the distribution of instances in the reduced space, we can also assess the quality of the feature selection process [48].

**Table 10.** Comparison of AFP-MVFL with other antifungal peptide predictors on Antifp_DS2 and Antifp_DS3 datasets.

| Datasets | Model | ACC (%) | PRE(%) | F1 score | MCC |
|---|---|---|---|---|---|
| Antifp_DS2 | AFPDeep | 93.5 | - | - | - |
| | Antifp | 85.9 | - | - | 0.72 |
| | AFP-MFL | 94.4 | 95.9 | 0.94 | 0.88 |
| | AFP-MVFL | **98.3** | **99.1** | **0.98** | **0.97** |
| Antifp_DS3 | AFPDeep | 88.7 | - | - | - |
| | Antifp | 90.4 | - | - | 0.81 |
| | AFP-MFL | 96.8 | 97.6 | 0.96 | 0.93 |
| | AFP-MVFL | **97.4** | **98.3** | **0.97** | **0.95** |

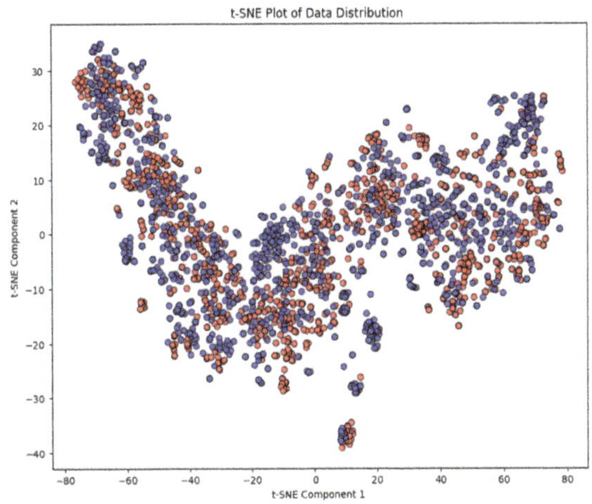


**Figure 5.** Feature visualization of AFP-MVFL on the AntiFP_DS1 dataset. Blue dots correspond to instances where the label negative equals 0 and red dots correspond to instances where the label positive equals 1.

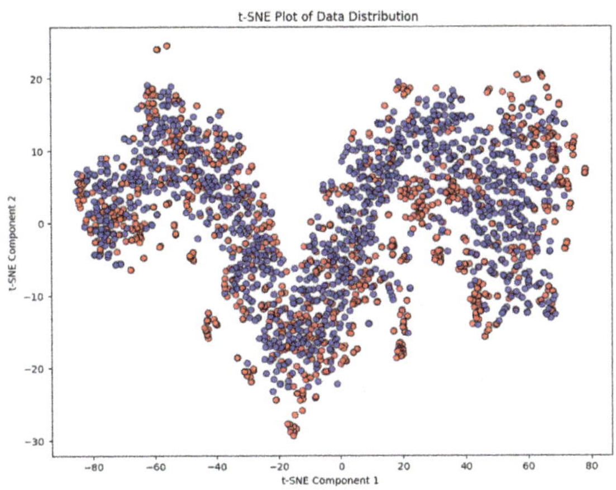


**Figure 6.** Feature visualization of random forest on the AntiFP_DS2 dataset. Blue dots correspond to instances where the label negative equals 0 and red dots correspond to instances where the label positive equals 1.

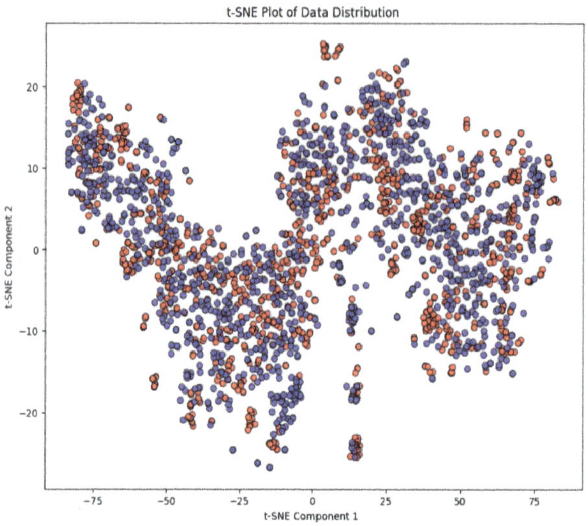


**Figure 7.** Feature visualization of random forest on the AntiFP_DS3 dataset. Blue dots correspond to instances where the label negative equals 0 and red dots correspond to instances where the label positive equals 1.

The results above highlight the robustness and generalizability of AFP-MVFL. By integrating a co-attention mechanism to fuse semantic information, evolutionary information, and physicochemical properties, AFP-MVFL effectively generates more informative features. Consequently, AFP-MVFL exhibits superior performance compared to alternative methods, positioning it as a reliable tool for AFP prediction. The AFP-MVFL model and its source code are publicly available at https://github.com/MuntahaMim/AFP-MVFL.git (accessed on 1 May 2024).

## 4. Conclusions

The accurate prediction of antifungal peptides is crucial for the advancement of therapeutic peptide design. In this study, we proposed a new machine learning framework called AFP_MVLF to predict AFPs accurately. Our approach employed a multi-view feature learning strategy to extract informative features from diverse perspectives, encompassing semantic information, evolutionary patterns, and physicochemical properties.

AFP-MVFL initially generated comprehensive profiles of peptide features by incorporating a set of sequence-based descriptors. AFP-MVFL achieved accurate AFP prediction based solely on sequence-based input features using the multi-view approach. Through rigorous cross-validation experiments conducted on three benchmark datasets, we demonstrated the superior performance of the AFP-MVFL compared to state-of-the-art methods in AFP prediction. Overall, AFP-MVFL presented a robust tool for accurate AFP prediction based solely on sequence-based information. The AFP-MVFL model and its source code are publicly available at https://github.com/MuntahaMim/AFP-MVFL.git (accessed on 1 May 2024).

One of the main limitations of this study is having a limited number of samples with which to train our model. As shown in the Section 3, the results on the independent test set are similar or slightly better than those reported using 10-fold cross-validation. It means that when we use all the training data to build our model, we can achieve better performance. Hence, if we have more samples, we are likely to achieve better results. Therefore, for our future direction, we aim to build larger benchmarks to train more complex models and possibly enhance prediction performance. We also aim to investigate more complex classification models to enhance the prediction performance even further to correctly determine unknown antifungal peptides.

**Author Contributions:** Conceptualization, S.M.F. and I.D.; methodology, S.M.F. and S.B.S.M.; software, S.M.F. and S.B.S.M.; validation, S.M.F. and S.B.S.M.; formal analysis, S.M.F., I.D. and S.B.S.M.; investigation, S.M.F., I.D. and S.B.S.M.; resources, S.M.F., I.D. and S.B.S.M.; data curation, I.D.; writing—original draft preparation, S.M.F., I.D. and S.B.S.M.; writing—review and editing, S.M.F., I.D. and S.B.S.M.; visualization, S.M.F. and S.B.S.M.; supervision, I.D. All authors have read and agreed to the published version of the manuscript.

**Funding:** This research received no external funding.

**Data Availability Statement:** The datasets used in this study are publicly available in the AFP-MVFL model, and its source code is publicly available at https://github.com/MuntahaMim/AFP-MVFL.git (accessed on 1 May 2024).

**Conflicts of Interest:** The authors declare no conflicts of interest.

## References

1. Bongomin, F.; Gago, S.; Oladele, R.O.; Denning, D.W. Global and Multi-National Prevalence of Fungal Diseases—Estimate Precision. *J. Fungi* **2017**, *3*, 57. [CrossRef] [PubMed]
2. Richardson, M.D. Changing patterns and trends in systemic fungal infections. *J. Antimicrob. Chemother.* **2005**, *56*, i5–i11. [CrossRef] [PubMed]
3. Miceli, M.H.; Diaz, J.A.; Lee, S.A. Emerging opportunistic yeast infections. *Lancet Infect. Dis.* **2011**, *11*, 142–151. [CrossRef] [PubMed]
4. Brown, G.D.; Denning, D.W.; Gow, N.A.R.; Levitz, S.M.; Netea, M.G.; White, T.C. Hidden Killers: Human Fungal Infections. *Sci. Transl. Med.* **2012**, *4*, 165rv13. [CrossRef] [PubMed]
5. Perfect, J.R. The antifungal pipeline: A reality check. *Nat. Rev. Drug Discov.* **2017**, *16*, 603–616. [CrossRef] [PubMed]
6. Butts, A.; Krysan, D.J. Antifungal Drug Discovery: Something Old and Something New. *PLOS Pathog.* **2012**, *8*, e1002870. [CrossRef]
7. Dhama, K.; Chakrabort, S.; Verma, A.K.; Tiwari, R.; Barathidas, R.; Kumar, A.; Singh, S.D. Fungal/mycotic diseases of poultry-diagnosis, treatment and control: A review. *Pak. J. Biol. Sci.* **2013**, *16*, 1626–1640. [CrossRef] [PubMed]
8. Lestrade, P.P.; Bentvelsen, R.G.; Schauwvlieghe, A.F.; Schalekamp, S.; van der Velden, W.J.; Kuiper, E.J.; van Paassen, J.; van der Hoven, B.; van der Lee, H.A.; Melchers, W.J.; et al. Voricona-zole resistance and mortality in invasive aspergillosis: A multi-center retrospective cohort study. *Clin. Infect. Dis.* **2019**, *68*, 1463–1471. [CrossRef]
9. Fang, Y.; Xu, F.; Wei, L.; Jiang, Y.; Chen, J.; Wei, L.; Wei, D.-Q. AFP-MFL: Accurate identification of antifungal peptides using multi-view feature learning. *Brief. Bioinform.* **2023**, *24*, bbac606. [CrossRef]
10. Agrawal, P.; Bhalla, S.; Chaudhary, K.; Kumar, R.; Sharma, M.; Raghava, G.P. In silico approach for prediction of antifungal peptides. *Front. Microbiol.* **2018**, *9*, 323. [CrossRef]
11. Fisher, M.C.; Hawkins, N.J.; Sanglard, D.; Gurr, S.J. Worldwide emergence of resistance to antifungal drugs challenges human health and food security. *Science* **2018**, *360*, 739–742. [CrossRef] [PubMed]
12. Ahmad, A.; Akbar, S.; Khan, S.; Hayat, M.; Ali, F.; Ahmed, A.; Tahir, M. Deep-AntiFP: Prediction of antifungal peptides using distanct multi-informative features incorporating with deep neural networks. *Chemom. Intell. Lab. Syst.* **2021**, *208*, 104214. [CrossRef]
13. Akbar, S.; Mohamed, H.G.; Ali, H.; Saeed, A.; Khan, A.A.; Gul, S.; Ahmad, A.; Ali, F.; Ghadi, Y.Y.; Assam, M. Identifying Neuropeptides via Evolutionary and Sequential Based Multi-Perspective Descriptors by Incorporation With Ensemble Classification Strategy. *IEEE Access* **2023**, *11*, 49024–49034. [CrossRef]
14. Yao, L.; Zhang, Y.; Li, W.; Chung, C.; Guan, J.; Zhang, W.; Chiang, Y.; Lee, T. DeepAFP: An effective computational framework for identifying antifungal peptides based on deep learning. *Protein Sci.* **2023**, *32*, e4758. [CrossRef] [PubMed]
15. Wang, K.; Dang, W.; Xie, J.; Zhu, R.; Sun, M.; Jia, F.; Zhao, Y.; An, X.; Qiu, S.; Li, X.; et al. Antimicrobial peptide protonectin disturbs the membrane integrity and induces ROS production in yeast cells. *Biochim. Biophys. Acta (BBA)-Biomembr.* **2015**, *1848*, 2365–2373. [CrossRef]
16. Landon, C.; Meudal, H.; Boulanger, N.; Bulet, P.; Vovelle, F. Solution structures of stomoxyn and spinigerin, two insect antimicrobial peptides with an α-helical conformation. *Biopolym. Orig. Res. Biomol.* **2006**, *81*, 92–103. [CrossRef]
17. Mousavizadegan, M.; Mohabatkar, H. Computational prediction of antifungal peptides via Chou's PseAAC and SVM. *J. Bioinform. Comput. Biol.* **2018**, *16*, 1850016. [CrossRef] [PubMed]
18. Ahmed, S.; Muhammod, R.; Khan, Z.H.; Adilina, S.; Sharma, A.; Shatabda, S.; Dehzangi, A. ACP-MHCNN: An accurate multi-headed deep-convolutional neural network to predict anticancer peptides. *Sci. Rep.* **2021**, *11*, 23676. [CrossRef] [PubMed]
19. Fang, C.; Moriwaki, Y.; Li, C.; Shimizu, K. Prediction of antifungal peptides by deep learning with character embedding. *IPSJ Trans. Bioinform.* **2019**, *12*, 21–299. [CrossRef]

20. Fan, L.; Sun, J.; Zhou, M.; Zhou, J.; Lao, X.; Zheng, H.; Xu, H. DRAMP: A comprehensive data repository of antimicrobial peptides. *Sci. Rep.* **2016**, *6*, 24482. [CrossRef]
21. Ahmad, A.; Akbar, S.; Tahir, M.; Hayat, M.; Ali, F. iAFPs-EnC-GA: Identifying antifungal peptides using sequential and evolutionary descrip-tors based multi-information fusion and ensemble learning approach. *Chemom. Intell. Lab. Syst.* **2022**, *222*, 104516. [CrossRef]
22. Sharma, R.; Shrivastava, S.; Kumar Singh, S.; Kumar, A.; Saxena, S.; Kumar Singh, R. Deep-AFPpred: Identifying novel antifungal peptides using pretrained embeddings from seq2vec with 1DCNN-BiLSTM. *Brief. Bioinform.* **2022**, *3*, bbab422. [CrossRef] [PubMed]
23. He, W.; Jiang, Y.; Jin, J.; Li, Z.; Zhao, J.; Manavalan, B.; Su, R.; Gao, X.; Wei, L. Accelerating bioactive peptide discovery via mutual information-based meta-learning. *Brief. Bioinform.* **2022**, *23*, bbab499. [CrossRef] [PubMed]
24. Lv, Z.; Ao, C.; Zou, Q. Protein function prediction: From traditional classifier to deep learning. *Proteomics* **2019**, *19*, e1900119. [CrossRef] [PubMed]
25. Vaswani, A.; Shazeer, N.; Parmar, N.; Uszkoreit, J.; Jones, L.; Gomez, A.N.; Kaiser, Ł.; Polosukhin, I. Attention Is All You Need. Available online: https://proceedings.neurips.cc/paper_files/paper/2017/hash/3f5ee243547dee91fbd053c1c4a845aa-Abstract.html (accessed on 1 May 2024).
26. Bhasin, M.; Raghava, G.P.S. SVM based method for predicting HLA-DRB1* 0401 binding peptides in an antigen sequence. *Bioinformatics* **2004**, *20*, 421–423. [CrossRef] [PubMed]
27. Zhang, Y. Support vector machine classification algorithm and its application. In *Information Computing and Applications: Proceedings of the Third International Conference, ICICA 2012, Chengde, China, 14–16 September 2012*; Part II 3; Springer: Berlin/Heidelberg, Germany, 2012; pp. 179–186.
28. Lata, S.; Mishra, N.K.; Raghava, G.P. AntiBP2: Improved version of antibacterial peptide prediction. *BMC Bioinform.* **2010**, *11*, S19. [CrossRef] [PubMed]
29. Ding, X.; Liu, J.; Yang, F.; Cao, J. Random radial basis function kernel-based support vector machine. *J. Frankl. Inst.* **2021**, *358*, 10121–10140. [CrossRef]
30. Westreich, D.; Lessler, J.; Funk, M.J. Propensity score estimation: Neural networks, support vector machines, decision trees (CART), and meta-classifiers as alternatives to logistic regression. *J. Clin. Epidemiol.* **2010**, *63*, 826–833. [CrossRef] [PubMed]
31. Heinze, G.; Schemper, M. A solution to the problem of separation in logistic regression. *Stat. Med.* **2002**, *21*, 2409–2419. [CrossRef]
32. Rish, I. An empirical study of the naive Bayes classifier. In Proceedings of the IJCAI 2001 Workshop on Empirical Methods in Artificial Intelligence, Seattle, WA, USA, 4 August 2001; Volume 3, pp. 41–46.
33. Cao, J.; Kwong, S.; Wang, R. A noise-detection based AdaBoost algorithm for mislabeled data. *Pattern Recognit.* **2012**, *45*, 4451–4465. [CrossRef]
34. Breiman, L. Random forests. *Mach. Learn.* **2001**, *45*, 5–32. [CrossRef]
35. Kirasich, K.; Smith, T.; Sadler, B. Random forest vs logistic regression: Binary classification for heterogeneous datasets. *SMU Data Sci. Rev.* **2018**, *1*, 9.
36. Haji, S.H.; Abdulazeez, A.M. Comparison of optimization techniques based on gradient descent algorithm: A review. *PalArch's J. Archaeol. Egypt/Egyptol.* **2021**, *18*, 2715–2743.
37. Bottou, L. Large-scale machine learning with stochastic gradient descent. In Proceedings of the COMPSTAT'2010: 19th International Conference on Computational Statistics, Paris, France, 22–27 August 2010.
38. Wu, C.-C.; Chen, Y.-L.; Liu, Y.-H.; Yang, X.-Y. Decision tree induction with a constrained number of leaf nodes. *Appl. Intell.* **2016**, *45*, 673–685. [CrossRef]
39. Chen, Z.; Zhao, P.; Li, F.; Leier, A.; Marquez-Lago, T.T.; Wang, Y.; Webb, G.I.; Smith, A.I.; Daly, R.J.; Chou, K.C.; et al. iFeature: A python package and web server for features extraction and selection from protein and peptide sequences. *Bioinformatics* **2018**, *34*, 2499–2502. [CrossRef] [PubMed]
40. Kawashima, S.; Pokarowski, P.; Pokarowska, M.; Kolinski, A.; Katayama, T.; Kanehisa, M. AAindex: Amino acid index database, progress report 2008. *Nucleic Acids Res.* **2007**, *36*, D202–D205. [CrossRef] [PubMed]
41. Bhasin, M.; Raghava, G.P. Classification of nuclear receptors based on amino acid composition and dipeptide composition. *J. Biol. Chem.* **2004**, *279*, 23262–23266. [CrossRef]
42. Saravanan, V.; Gautham, N. Harnessing computational biology for exact linear b-cell epitope prediction: A novel amino acid composition-based feature descriptor. *OMICS J. Integr. Biol.* **2015**, *19*, 648–658. [CrossRef] [PubMed]
43. Chang, K.Y.; Yang, J.-R. Analysis and prediction of highly effective antiviral peptides based on random forests. *PLoS ONE* **2013**, *8*, e70166. [CrossRef]
44. Schaduangrat, N.; Nantasenamat, C.; Prachayasittikul, V.; Shoombuatong, W. ACPred: A computational tool for the prediction and analysis of anticancer peptides. *Molecules* **2019**, *24*, 1973. [CrossRef]
45. Liu, J.; Li, M.; Chen, X. AntiMF: A deep learning framework for predicting anticancer peptides based on multi-view feature extraction. *Methods* **2022**, *207*, 38–43. [CrossRef] [PubMed]
46. Pareek, J.; Jacob, J. Data compression and visualization using PCA and T-SNE. In *Advances in Information Communication Technology and Computing: Proceedings of AICTC 2019*; Springer: Singapore, 2021; pp. 327–337.

47. Charoenkwan, P.; Schaduangrat, N.; Moni, M.A.; Manavalan, B.; Shoombuatong, W. SAPPHIRE: A stacking-based ensemble learning framework for accurate prediction of thermophilic proteins. *Comput. Biol. Med.* **2022**, *146*, 105704. [CrossRef] [PubMed]
48. Charoenkwan, P.; Ahmed, S.; Nantasenamat, C.; Quinn, J.M.; Moni, M.A.; Lio', P.; Shoombuatong, W. AMYPred-FRL is a novel approach for accurate prediction of amyloid proteins by using feature representation learning. *Sci. Rep.* **2022**, *12*, 7697. [CrossRef] [PubMed]

*algorithms*

*Article*

# A Comparative Study of Machine Learning Methods and Text Features for Text Authorship Recognition in the Example of Azerbaijani Language Texts

**Rustam Azimov [1] and Efthimios Providas [2,*]**

[1] Laboratory of Recognition, Identification and Methods of Optimal Solutions, Institute of Control Systems, Baku AZ1141, Azerbaijan; rustemazimov1999@gmail.com
[2] Department of Environmental Sciences, University of Thessaly, 415 00 Larissa, Greece
* Correspondence: providas@uth.gr; Tel.: +30-2410-684331

**Abstract:** This paper presents various machine learning methods with different text features that are explored and evaluated to determine the authorship of the texts in the example of the Azerbaijani language. We consider techniques like artificial neural network, convolutional neural network, random forest, and support vector machine. These techniques are used with different text features like word length, sentence length, combined word length and sentence length, n-grams, and word frequencies. The models were trained and tested on the works of many famous Azerbaijani writers. The results of computer experiments obtained by utilizing a comparison of various techniques and text features were analyzed. The cases where the usage of text features allowed better results were determined.

**Keywords:** authorship recognition of literary works; authorship attribution; author identification; text feature engineering; machine learning

**MSC:** 68Q32; 68T20

## 1. Introduction

Authorship analysis is widely used to identify the author of an anonymous or disputed literary work, especially in a copyright dispute, to verify the authorship of suicide letters, for information to determine whether an anonymous message or statement was written by a known terrorist, to identify the author of malicious computer programs, for example, computer viruses and malware, and to identify the authors of certain Internet texts, such as e-mails, blog posts, and texts on Internet forum pages [1,2].

One of the important classes of problems in the authorship analysis of texts is authorship recognition of texts. Studies in the direction of text authorship recognition differ in the types of the text features, i.e., stylistic characteristics of the authors in the texts, genre and size characteristics of texts, the language, authorship identification approach used, etc. Among the scientific studies carried out on the identification of the author of texts, several works can be found related to the identification of the author of texts in newspapers [3–10] and the identification of the author of literary works [11–15].

Machine learning methods and models are widely used in text author recognition. Among these methods and models are support vector machine [4–6,11,16–18], naive Bayes [7,8,16], random forest [5,6,8,19], k-nearest neighbors [5–7], and artificial neural network [15,20,21]. The recognition of the author of the text can be considered in the example of texts in different languages, e.g., Arabic, Chinese, Dutch, English, German, Greek, Russian, Spanish, Turkish, and Ukrainian [3–17,22–26]. Different types of text features, for example, frequencies of selected words or frequencies of some tags/signs that replace words (e.g., part-of-speech tags) and frequencies of their n-grams [3,4,6,8,14,16,22,23,27], frequencies of character n-grams [5,7,9,10,12,17,24,25,28], and frequencies of word lengths [13], can be used in author identification.

In the present study, a comparative analysis of the effectiveness of the use of different methods and models of machine learning with different feature groups consisting of different types of text features to recognize the authorship of texts was carried out based on the results of computer experiments in the example of large and small literary works of some Azerbaijani writers.

The rest of this article is structured as follows: In Section 2, the considered authorship recognition problem is discussed. In Section 3, various text feature types used in the study are given. In Section 4, feature selection procedures used in the study are described. In Section 5, feature groups used in the study are depicted. In Section 6, the dataset and characteristics of the recognition methods are given. In Section 7, analysis and discussion of the results of computer experiments are carried out. Finally, we draw our conclusions in Section 8 and provide several ideas for future work.

## 2. Purpose of the Study

There are certain categories of problems in the direction of authorship analysis of texts, namely:

- authorship verification of texts—determination of whether a given text was written by a certain person.
- authorship attribution of texts, author recognition of texts, or authorship identification—determination of the author of a given text from predetermined, suspected candidate authors.
- plagiarism detection—detection of similarities between two given texts.
- author profiling—detection of author's characteristics or building author profile consisting of some characteristics—age, gender, education level, etc. based on the given text.
- detection of stylistic inconsistencies within a text—detection of text parts that do not correspond to the general writing style of the text that is written by more than one author.

The purpose of the study is to solve the problem of determining the authors of texts. The problem arises in relation to the author of a given text among a priori well-known authors. It is possible that the author of the text is not among these candidates. In the considered research study, there is a set of texts written by candidate authors. The author of a text is determined using computer models that use assessments of the stylistic quantitative characteristics of the texts of this author and the stylistic quantitative characteristics of the texts of candidate authors.

This evaluation can be performed with the help of machine learning methods. Each machine learning method can be used with different sets of text features. In the present study, frequencies of word lengths, frequencies of sentence lengths, frequencies of character n-grams, statistical characteristics of character n-grams frequencies in the text, and frequencies of selected words were used, where a word length, sentence length, and character n-gram refer to the number of letters in a word, the number of words in a sentence, and a given combination of $n = 1, 2, \ldots$ given characters, respectively. Also, in addition to the frequencies of the selected words in a given text whose author is to be determined, the frequencies of the words in the candidate authors' texts in the training set were also used in some feature groups as text features. The generated feature sets were used with artificial neural network, support vector machine, and random forest methods, and machine learning models. In addition, an n-gram frequency character group was also used with a convolutional neural network in the form of a two-dimensional matrix.

A comparative analysis of different feature sets with different machine learning methods and models was performed based on the results of computer experiments conducted on the example of works of literary fiction in the Azerbaijani language by eleven Azerbaijani authors.

The results of the conducted research study on feature types, feature selection procedures, and machine learning techniques can be used for author recognition in many other languages.

## 3. Types of Text Features

Below, it is assumed that the author of a given text is one of a certain limited number of candidate authors, and some other texts written by these candidate authors are known in advance. Let us adopt the following notation.

Consider the set of given candidate authors $A = \{A^i : i = 1, 2, \ldots, L\}$, where $L$ is the number of the candidate authors, and let us denote the set of texts of author $A^i$ by $T^i = \{T^i_j : j = 1, 2, \ldots, l_i\}$, where $l_i$ is the number of texts of the author $A^i$, $i = 1, 2, \ldots, L$.

The set of all texts with known authors $T$ is divided into two non-intersecting subsets $T = \overline{T} \cup \widetilde{T}$, $\overline{T} \cap \widetilde{T} = \varnothing$ where $\overline{T}$ is the training set and $\widetilde{T}$ is the test set.

Text feature groups consist of the following text characteristics, which are considered by many researchers to be important features and have a distinctive character among authors.

### 3.1. Sentence Length Frequency

By sentence length, we mean the number of words in a sentence [29]. The frequency of sentences of a certain length in a given text is calculated by dividing the number of sentences of that length by the total number of sentences in the text [30].

### 3.2. Word Length Frequency

By word length, we mean the number of letters in a word [13]. The frequency of words of a given length in a given text is calculated by dividing the number of words of that length by the total number of words in the text.

### 3.3. Character n-Gram Frequency

In the scientific literature, a character n-gram is considered to mean any given combination of the given $n = 1, 2, \ldots$ characters [12,17,24,25].

For a given $n$, let us denote the character alphabet set, i.e., the set of all character 1-grams from which characters in any character n-gram are selected as follows:

$$\alpha^1 = \left\{\alpha_k : k = 1, 2, \ldots, \left|\alpha^1\right|\right\}.$$

Hereafter in the article, $\hat{i}^n_m = (i_1, \ldots, i_n)$ notation will be used for $n$ dimensional multi-index $\hat{i}^n_m$. Here, each of the $i_v$, $v = 1, 2, \ldots, n$, indices can take a value in the given set $\{1, 2, \ldots, m\}$, hence $1 \le i_v \le m$, $v = 1, 2, \ldots, n$.

After that, we will use n-grams and character n-grams interchangeably. An n-gram with an arbitrary multi-index $\hat{i}^n_m$ whose characters are chosen from the character alphabet set $\alpha^1$ will be used as $\alpha_{\hat{i}^n_m} = \left(\alpha_{i_1}, \ldots, \alpha_{i_n}\right)$, where $m = \left|\alpha^1\right|$.

Let us denote the set of all character n-grams as follows:

$$\alpha^n = \left\{\alpha_{\hat{i}^n_m} : 1 \le i_v \le m, \quad v = 1, 2, \ldots, n, \quad m = \left|\alpha^1\right|\right\}.$$

The frequency of any arbitrary character n-gram $\alpha_{\hat{i}^n_m} \in \alpha^n$ with $n$ characters in a given text is calculated by dividing the number of times that $\alpha_{\hat{i}^n_m}$ is used by the total number of character n-grams in the text.

### 3.4. Variance of Character n-Gram Frequencies

Statistical characteristics (e.g., variances) of character n-gram frequencies in the separate parts of an arbitrary given text can be used as text features.

If we calculate the frequencies of an arbitrary character n-gram in the separate parts of a given text and find the variance [30] of these frequencies, this variance shows the fulfillment of this character n-gram in the separate parts—at the beginning, in the middle, and at the end of that text, i.e., the stability of the character n-gram in the text. In other words, if the variance of frequencies of a character n-gram in a text, which is calculated as aforementioned, is small, this n-gram can be considered stable in that text. Even if we calculate the frequency of an arbitrary character n-gram in each of the texts of a certain author candidate in the training set and find the variance of these frequencies, the small value of this variance indicates that the character n-gram characterizes the texts of that author well. Or if we combine the known texts of each of the author candidates in the considered problem and get a single text for each author candidate (for $L$ number of authors, we obtain $L$ texts), if the variance of an arbitrary character n-gram in one of these texts is small, and the variances in the others' are large, this character n-gram characterizes one author candidate better than others, so this character n-gram can be effectively used in the considered author recognition problem. It turns out that the variance values, which indicate how character n-grams are distributed in a certain text or the stability of character n-grams, are informative in terms of author recognition. Hence, we considered that along with the frequencies of character n-grams in a given text, their variances in the text can be used as text features as well. In other words, by dividing the given text into a certain number of separate, non-intersecting parts and calculating the frequencies of an arbitrary character n-gram in these parts, the variance of these frequencies can be used as some of the features of that text.

To calculate the values of the statistical characteristics of any character n-gram in a given text for an arbitrary $n$, the text must first be divided into certain almost equally sized non-intersecting parts, the frequencies of that character n-gram in each of these parts of the text must be found, and the variance value of these frequencies must be calculated.

### 3.5. Word Frequency

Word frequencies in texts are important features that can be related to authors [3,4,14,22]. The frequency of a particular word in a given text is calculated by dividing the number of times that word occurs by the total number of words in the text.

The results of our research (see Section 7) show that if the frequency of an arbitrary word in a given text is used together with the frequencies of the unified texts of the candidate authors among the text features, it positively affects the recognition efficiency, where, by the unified text of a candidate author, we mean the text resulting from merging the author's texts in the training set. In addition to the frequencies of a given word in the unified texts of the candidate authors, the frequency of this word in the unified text obtained as the result of merging all the texts in the training set can be used among the text features. The rules for calculating the frequencies of an arbitrary word in the combined texts of the candidate authors and in the text resulting from merging all the texts of the training set are described below.

The total usage frequency of an arbitrary word by any author is obtained by dividing the sum of the number of that word in the author's texts in the training set by the total number of words in the author's texts in the training set. The total frequency of an arbitrary word in all texts in the training set is calculated by dividing the total number of that word in the texts in the training set by the total number of words in the texts in the training set.

## 4. Feature Selection Procedures

Various feature selection procedures have been proposed [1,2,6,16,31]. Here, two different feature selection procedures for word selection and two for selecting character n-grams whose frequencies will be used as text features are proposed, as described below. Recall that these feature selection procedures are performed on the training set texts whose authors are known.

### 4.1. Procedure for Selecting Frequently Used Words by Authors (Procedure 1)

During the selection of words, the frequencies of which are to be used as text features in author recognition with the help of this procedure, the total frequencies of words used by each of the authors are taken into account separately. This first feature selection procedure differs from the second feature selection procedure (see Section 4.2), i.e., in procedure 2, word selection is carried out based on the total number of times the words are used in the texts in the training set without considering the authors of the texts; in procedure 1, the most or average or least used words of the author $A^i$ were selected, where $i = 1, 2, \ldots, L$, then words from authors' lexicons are combined into a final set of words.

The determination of the most or average or least used words in the authors' lexicons is based on the total usage frequencies of the words in the $A^i$ author's $T^i_j \in \overline{T}^i$, $j = 1, 2, \ldots, l_i$, texts, here $\overline{T}^i = \overline{T} \cap T^i$, where $\overline{T}$ is the set of texts in the training set, $T^i$ is the set of the author's texts in the dataset $T$, and $l_i$ is the number of texts of $A^i$ in dataset T. Let us denote the total usage frequency of an arbitrary word $\omega_v \in W$ in $A^i$ author's texts $\overline{T}^i$ by $\phi^{1i}_v$, where $W$ is the set of all words in the training set $\overline{T}$, and $v \in \{1, \ldots, |W|\}$, $i = 1, 2, \ldots, L$.

In order to select the most or average or least used words by an author $A^i$ from among the elements of the word set $W$, at first, $W$ has to be sorted according to the descending order of the usage frequency of the words by the author $A^i$, where $i = 1, 2, \ldots, L$. Let us denote the set of words arranged according to the descending order of usage frequency of the words by the author $A^i$ by $W^i$. For given $\left|\overset{\sim}{W}^i\right|$, $i = 1, 2, \ldots, L$, consider the set of most frequently used words of author $A^i$ as $\overset{\sim}{W}^i \subset W^i$ and the final set of most frequently used words of authors $A^i$, $i = 1, 2, \ldots, L$, as $\overset{\sim}{W}$, where

$$W^i = \left\{\omega_{k_j} : \phi^{1i}_{k_1} \geq \ldots \geq \phi^{1i}_{k_{|W|}},\ \omega_{k_j} \in W,\ j = 1, 2, \ldots, |W|\right\}, \quad (1)$$

$$\overset{\sim}{W}^i = \left\{\omega^i_j : \omega^i_j \in W^i,\ j = 1, 2, \ldots, \left|\overset{\sim}{W}^i\right|,\ \omega^i_j \notin W^k,\ i \neq k,\ i, k = 1, 2, \ldots, L\right\}, \quad (2)$$

$$\overset{\sim}{W} = \bigcup_{i=1}^{L} \overset{\sim}{W}^i. \quad (3)$$

The most frequently used words of authors should be selected in such a way that authors' lexicons do not intersect, i.e., $\overset{\sim}{W}^{i_1} \cap \overset{\sim}{W}^{i_2} = \varnothing$, $i_1 \neq i_2$, $i_1, i_2 = 1, 2, \ldots, L$.

It is possible that the most used words of a certain author $A^i$, although not included in the set of most used words of $A^j$, are also used a lot by another author $A^j$, where $i \neq j$, $i, j = 1, 2, \ldots, L$. These kinds of words may not have a discriminatory character between authors $A^i$ and $A^j$. Therefore, in the author recognition problem considered in the study, in addition to the most frequently used words in the authors' lexicons, the selection of words that are used on average was also used. These words are neither at the beginning nor at the end of a sorted list $W^i$, where $i = 1, 2, \ldots, L$. This is analogous to the way described above, where the most frequently used words of authors are selected, except the following Formula (4) has to be used instead of the aforementioned (2):

$$\overset{\sim}{W}^i = \left\{\omega^i_j : \omega^i_j \in W^i,\ j = \left\lfloor \frac{|W|}{2} \right\rfloor - \left\lfloor \frac{\left|\overset{\sim}{W}^i\right|}{2} \right\rfloor, \ldots, \left\lfloor \frac{|W|}{2} \right\rfloor + \left\lfloor \frac{\left|\overset{\sim}{W}^i\right|}{2} \right\rfloor - 1,\ \omega^i_j \notin W^k,\ i \neq k,\ i, k = 1, 2, \ldots, L\right\}, \quad (4)$$

where $\lfloor d \rfloor$ indicates an integer obtained as a result of rounding down an arbitrary positive number. For example, $\lfloor 3.7 \rfloor = 3$, $\lfloor 3.4 \rfloor = 3$.

Formula (4) was obtained by only changing the indices of words, i.e., j, in the set of words $W^i$ in Formula (2), where $i = 1, 2, \ldots, L$. This is an analogous operation not only for the most or average used words but also the words in other percentiles, e.g., those with a frequency higher than 75% can be selected.

*4.2. Procedure for Selecting Frequently Used Words in the Training Set (Procedure 2)*

During the selection of words, the frequencies of which are to be used as text features in author recognition with the help of this procedure, the total frequencies of words in the training set $\overline{T}$ is taken as a basis without taking into account the authors.

Let us denote the total usage frequency of an arbitrary word $\omega_v \in W$ in $\overline{T}$ by $\phi_v^2$, where $W$ is the set of all words in the training set $\overline{T}$, and $v \in \{1,\ldots,|W|\}$. When using this procedure, the set of all the words $W$ in the texts $T_j^i \in \overline{T}$, $j = 1,2,\ldots,l_i$, $i = 1,2,\ldots,L$, is at first sorted according to the decreasing order of the total usage frequency in the training set $\overline{T}$:

$$W' = \left\{\omega_{k_i} : \phi_{k_1}^2 \geq \ldots \geq \phi_{k_{|W|}}^2,\ \omega_{k_i} \in W,\ i = 1,2,\ldots,|W|\right\}, \tag{5}$$

where $v \in \{1,\ldots,|W|\}, i = 1,2,\ldots,L$.

The set of most frequently used given $\left|\widetilde{W}\right|$ words $\widetilde{W} \subset W$ in the training set is as follows:

$$\widetilde{W} = \left\{\omega_i : \omega_i \in W',\ j = 1,2,\ldots,\left|\widetilde{W}\right|\right\}. \tag{6}$$

In the description of the first feature selection procedure (see Section 4.1), we noted that some of the most frequently used words of one author may be used a lot by another author, and in this case, these words may not be discriminative between these authors. Therefore, in the first feature selection procedure, along with the most frequently used words by the authors, words used as average were also selected. A similar situation may arise when using feature selection procedure 2. It is possible that some words, which are generally the most used words in the training set, are commonly used by more than one author; thus, they may not have a discriminatory character. Therefore, in addition to selecting the most used words in the training set, the selection of words that are used on average, i.e., are neither at the beginning nor at the end of $W'$, is also employed. The set of these words is as follows:

$$\widetilde{W} = \left\{\omega_i : \omega_i \in W',\ j = \left\lfloor\frac{|W|}{2}\right\rfloor - \left\lfloor\frac{\left|\widetilde{W}\right|}{2}\right\rfloor,\ldots,\left\lfloor\frac{|W|}{2}\right\rfloor + \left\lfloor\frac{\left|\widetilde{W}\right|}{2}\right\rfloor - 1\right\}. \tag{7}$$

*4.3. Procedure for Selecting Frequently Used Character n-Grams in the Training Set (Procedure 3)*

During the selection of character n-grams (the frequencies of which are to be used as text features in author recognition), with the help of this procedure, the total frequencies of character n-grams in the training set $\overline{T}$ are taken as a basis without taking into account the authors. During the execution of this procedure, the set of all character n-grams $\alpha^n$ have to be sorted according to the decreasing order of the total usage frequency in the training set. The characters in these character n-grams, each with $n$ characters, are selected from the character alphabet set $\alpha^1$. Let us denote this obtained sorted set by $\dot{\alpha}^n$. Consider the set of most or average or least frequently used character n-grams used most or average or least in the training set as $\widetilde{\alpha}^n$.

We will denote the total usage frequency of a certain character n-gram $\alpha_{\hat{i}_m^n} \in \alpha^n$ in the texts in the training set $\overline{T}$ by $\phi_v^3$.

The set of all character n-grams $\dot{\alpha}^n$ obtained by sorting the character n-grams in the order of decreasing total usage frequency in the training set is as follows:

$$\begin{gathered}\dot{\alpha}^n = \left\{\alpha_{\hat{i}_m^{nj}} : \phi_{\hat{i}_m^{n1}}^3 \geq \ldots \geq \phi_{\hat{i}_m^{n|\alpha^n|}}^3,\ \hat{i}_m^{nj} = \left(i_1^j,\ldots,i_n^j\right),\ 1 \leq i_m^j \leq m,\ v = 1,2,\ldots,n,\right. \\ \left. m = \left|\alpha^1\right|,\ j = 1,2,\ldots,|\alpha^n|\right\},\end{gathered} \tag{8}$$

$\hat{i}_m^{nj}$ is the multi-index of a given arbitrary character n-gram $\alpha_{\hat{i}_m^{nj}} \in \alpha^n$ numbered with $j$ in the set of character n-grams $\alpha^n$, where $\hat{i}_m^{nj_1} \neq \hat{i}_m^{nj_2}, j_1 \neq j_2, j_1, j_2 = 1, 2, \ldots, |\alpha^n|$.

The set of most used character n-grams $\overset{\sim n}{\alpha}$ in the training set is as follows:

$$\overset{\sim n}{\alpha} = \left\{ \alpha_{\hat{i}_m^{nj}} : \alpha_{\hat{i}_m^{nj}} \in \dot{\alpha}^n,\ j = 1, 2, \ldots, \left| \overset{\sim n}{\alpha} \right| \right\}. \tag{9}$$

Feature selection procedure 3 is used to select character n-grams rather than words, unlike feature selection procedure 2. In the description of the second feature selection procedure, it was noted that the most used words in the training set may not be discriminative among authors; therefore, it is necessary to select the words that are averagely used in those texts as well. This is also typical for the third feature selection procedure used to select character n-grams.

The set of character n-grams $\overset{\sim n}{\alpha}$ that are used on average, which means they are neither at the beginning nor at the end of $\dot{\alpha}^n$ in the texts in the training set, is as follows:

$$\overset{\sim n}{\alpha} = \left\{ \alpha_{\hat{i}_m^{nj}} : \alpha_{\hat{i}_m^{nj}} \in \dot{\alpha}^n,\ j = \left\lfloor \frac{|\alpha^n|}{2} \right\rfloor - \left\lfloor \frac{\left|\overset{\sim n}{\alpha}\right|}{2} \right\rfloor, \ldots, \left\lfloor \frac{|\alpha^n|}{2} \right\rfloor + \left\lfloor \frac{\left|\overset{\sim n}{\alpha}\right|}{2} \right\rfloor - 1 \right\}. \tag{10}$$

### 4.4. *Procedure for Selecting Character n-Grams with Different Characterizing Degrees of Authors (Procedure 4)*

In solving author recognition problems, text features should be used such that the values of these features are similar in the texts of one author and different in the texts of different authors. In other words, characterizing degrees of authors per feature, the values of which are used in author recognition, have to differ from each other. This feature selection procedure was proposed for the selection of character n-grams for which the characterizing degrees of the authors differ.

During the execution of this procedure, firstly, degrees of not characterizing the authors in the sense that will be mentioned below per a given n-gram are determined, and based on these degrees of non-characterization, their complements—the characterizing degrees—are determined. Then, an indicator indicating how much the characterizing degrees of the authors differ from each other in terms of one of the following meanings per that n-gram is calculated. In the study, different metrics were used to calculate the latter.

We consider the degree of not characterizing a given author $A^i$ per an arbitrary n-gram $\alpha_{\hat{i}_m^n} \in \alpha^n$ as the average difference of characterizing degrees (mean of the pairwise differences of these frequencies) of the corresponding frequencies $f^i_{j\hat{i}_m^n}$, $j = 1, 2, \ldots, l_i$, in the texts $T^i_j \in \overline{T}^i$, $j = 1, 2, \ldots, l_i$, of author $A^i$ as:

$$d^i_{\hat{i}_m^n} = \frac{1}{\frac{(|T^i|)^2}{2}} \sum_{j_1=1}^{|T^i|} \sum_{j_2=1}^{\frac{|T^i|}{2}} \left( f^i_{j_1\hat{i}_m^n} - f^i_{j_2\hat{i}_m^n} \right)^2, \tag{11}$$

where $f^i_{j_1\hat{i}_m^n}$, $f^i_{j_2\hat{i}_m^n}$ are the frequencies of n-gram $\alpha_{\hat{i}_m^n}$ in the texts of author $A^i$ numbered with $j_1$, $j_2$ accordingly, $i = 1, 2, \ldots, L$. Considering that for the frequency of an arbitrary $\alpha_{\hat{i}_m^n} \in \alpha^n$ in a given text $T^i_j \in T$ $0 \leq f^i_{j\hat{i}_m^n} \leq 1$ is true, it is clear that $0 \leq d^i_{\hat{i}_m^n} \leq 1$. Then, the characterizing degree of an author $A^i$ per a n-gram $\alpha_{\hat{i}_m^n} \in \alpha^n$ is $\dot{d}^i_{\hat{i}_m^n} = 1 - d^i_{\hat{i}_m^n}$, where $i = 1, 2, \ldots, L$.

For simplicity, the characterizing degrees of the authors $A^i, i = 1, 2, \ldots, L$, per a n-gram $\alpha_{\hat{i}_m^n} \in \alpha^n$ $\dot{d}^i_{\hat{i}_m^n}, i = 1, 2, \ldots, L$, is sorted in decreasing order: $\dot{d}^{i_k^*}_{\hat{i}_m^n}, 1 \leq i_k^* \leq L, k = 1, 2, \ldots, L$, where $\dot{d}^{i_1^*}_{\hat{i}_m^n} \geq \ldots \geq \dot{d}^{i_L^*}_{\hat{i}_m^n}$.

The difference of characterizing degrees $\dot{d}^{\,i}_{\hat{i}^n_m}$, $i = 1,2,\dots,L$, of the authors $A^i$, $i = 1,2,\dots,L$, for an arbitrary character n-gram $\alpha_{\hat{i}^n_m} \in \alpha^n$ can be defined as one of the following:

$$\dot{\phi}^{41}_{\hat{i}^n_m} = \left(\dot{d}^{\,i^*_1}_{\hat{i}^n_m} - \dot{d}^{\,i^*_2}_{\hat{i}^n_m}\right)^2, \tag{12}$$

$$\dot{\phi}^{42}_{\hat{i}^n_m} = \frac{1}{2}\left[\left(\dot{d}^{\,i^*_1}_{\hat{i}^n_m} - \dot{d}^{\,i^*_2}_{\hat{i}^n_m}\right)^2 + \left(\dot{d}^{\,i^*_2}_{\hat{i}^n_m} - \dot{d}^{\,i^*_3}_{\hat{i}^n_m}\right)^2\right], \tag{13}$$

$$\dot{\phi}^{43}_{\hat{i}^n_m} = \frac{1}{L-1}\sum_{k=1}^{L-1}\left(\dot{d}^{\,i_k}_{\hat{i}^n_m} - \dot{d}^{\,i_{k+1}}_{\hat{i}^n_m}\right)^2. \tag{14}$$

As the difference of characterizing degrees per an n-gram $\alpha_{\hat{i}^n_m} \in \alpha^n$ $\phi^4_{\hat{i}^n_m} \in \left\{\dot{\phi}^{4l}_{\hat{i}^n_m} : l = 1,2,3\right\}$ can be used.

Sorted set of character n-grams $\dot{\alpha}^n$ ordered in the decreasing order of the difference indicators of characterizing degrees of authors per character n-grams in $\alpha^n$ is as follows:

$$\dot{\alpha}^n = \left\{\alpha_{\hat{i}^{nj}_m} : \phi^4_{\hat{i}^{n1}_m} \geq \dots \geq \phi^4_{\hat{i}^{n|\alpha^n|}_m},\ \hat{i}^{nj}_m = \left(i^j_1,\dots,i^j_n\right),\ 1 \leq i^j_m \leq m,\ v = 1,2,\dots,n,\ m = \left|\alpha^1\right|,\ j = 1,2,\dots,|\alpha^n|\right\}, \tag{15}$$

$\hat{i}^{nj}_m$ is the multi-index of a given arbitrary character n-gram $\alpha_{\hat{i}^{nj}_m} \in \alpha^n$ numbered with $j$ in $\alpha^n$, where $\hat{i}^{nj_1}_m \neq \hat{i}^{nj_2}_m, j_1 \neq j_2, j_1, j_2 = 1,2,\dots,|\alpha^n|$.

The set of character n-grams $\tilde{\alpha}^n$ with high discrimination indicator—characterizing degree difference among authors in the training set—is as follows:

$$\tilde{\alpha}^n = \left\{\alpha_{\hat{i}^{nj}_m} : \alpha_{\hat{i}^{nj}_m} \in \dot{\alpha}^n,\ j = 1,2,\dots,\left|\tilde{\alpha}^n\right|\right\}. \tag{16}$$

## 5. Characteristics of Feature Groups

Using the value of a single feature of a particular text, e.g., the frequency of 5-word sentences or the frequency of the character 2-gram "ab", is not sufficient for an effective author identification in terms of adequately identifying the authors of the texts that will be executed. Therefore, the values of more than one feature are used in a specific feature group consisting of different features for an arbitrary text; see [1,25]. The characteristics of the feature groups used in this study are detailed below.

### 5.1. *Sentence Length Frequency and Word Length Frequency Types of Feature Groups*

Only two feature groups consisting of features related to the sentence length frequency type were used. These feature groups differ according to the sentence lengths to be used and the number of these different sentence lengths, where sentence length means the number of words in a sentence. In one such feature group, there are frequencies of sentences with lengths of 5, 6, ..., 14. We will denote this feature group by the name SL10 in the study, where SL stands for "sentence length", and 10 indicates the number of features in the feature group. Naming the groups of features used in the study with such short expressions is for the reader to understand the differences in those groups and also for use in the results of computer experiments if needed. Another feature group, SL25, consists of frequencies of sentences with lengths of 5, 6, ..., 29.

The number of feature groups consisting of only word length type features is also two. These feature groups differ according to the word lengths to be used and the number of these different word lengths, where word length means the number of letters in a word. In one such feature group, there are frequencies of words with lengths of 3, 4, ..., 7. We will denote this feature group by the name WL5, where WL stands for "word length", and

5 indicates the number of features in the group. Another feature group, WL10, consists of frequencies of words with lengths of 3, 4, . . ., 12.

A mixed feature group consisting of features belonging to the types of sentence length frequency and word length frequency was also used. The values of the features in this feature group are the frequencies of sentences with lengths 5, 6, . . ., 14 and the frequencies of words with lengths 3, 4, . . ., 12. Let us denote this feature group by SL10&WL10, where the "&" symbol is used in the names of mixed feature groups.

In the study, the number of feature groups used in the considered author recognition problem, which contains features of sentence length frequency and word length frequency types, is 5:

sentence length frequency: {number of feature groups} = 2;

word length frequency: {number of feature groups} = 2;

mixed groups of sentence length frequencies and word length frequencies: {number of feature groups} = 1.

### 5.2. *Character n-Gram Frequency and Variance of Character n-Gram Frequencies Types of Feature Groups*

In the study, the character alphabet set—the set that contains the characters in character n-grams with a given $n$ used in the author recognition problem considered in the example of Azerbaijani writers—is the letters of the alphabet of the Azerbaijani language, in other words, $\alpha^1 = \{a, b, c, , \ldots, z\}$, where $|\alpha^1| = 32$. The character alphabet set is clearly the set of character 1-grams, each with 1 character. In the study, for $n = 1$, the frequencies of character 1-grams—unigrams—and for $n = 2$, the frequencies of character 2-grams—bigrams—were used in the feature groups consisting of character n-gram frequency type features.

A feature group consisting of the frequencies of all unigrams in the character alphabet set $\alpha^1$ was used. We will denote this feature group by Ch1g32 in the study, where "Ch1g" is for "character 1-grams", and 32 represents the number of features in that group.

Different subsets of all character bigrams set $\alpha^2$ were used to create feature groups. Recall that characters in these bigrams are selected from the character alphabet set $\alpha^1$. These feature groups differ from each other according to the feature selection procedure used and the variety and number of bigrams, the values of which are used in these feature groups. In the study feature selection, procedures 3 and 4 are used to select character bigrams from $\alpha^2$. For procedure 3—the procedure for selecting frequently used character n-grams in the training set—and procedure 4—the procedure for selecting character n-grams with different characterizing degrees of authors—see Formulas (8)–(10) and (11)–(16), respectively. A total of 26 and 21 different feature groups were created with the help of feature selection procedures 3 and 4, respectively. Two of these twenty-six feature groups of bigrams were selected with the help of the third feature selection procedure, each consisting of frequencies of 100 bigrams selected directly from the set $\alpha^2$. These two feature groups consist of the frequencies of the 100 most and average used bigrams in the training set selected from 1024 character bigrams in the set $\alpha^2$. We will denote these feature groups as Ch2g_p3high100 and Ch2g_p3middle100, respectively. Here, "Ch2g" stands for "character 2-grams"; "p3" indicates that the third feature selection procedure is used; and 100 indicates the number of features in each of the groups.

The other 24 feature groups were selected from the bigrams whose frequencies were used in these two feature groups—Ch2g_p3high100 and Ch2g_p3middle100. Among the high-frequency 100 bigrams in the training set 5, 10, . . ., 25, 50, the first and last bigrams in the descending list of bigrams ordered by the frequencies in the training set are selected. We denote them by Ch2g_p3high100first5, . . ., Ch2g_p3high100first50 and Ch2g_p3high100last5, . . ., Ch2g_p3high100last50. Among the middle—neither high nor low—frequency 100 bigrams in the training set 5, 10, . . ., 25, 50, the first and last bigrams in the descending list of bigrams ordered by the frequencies in the training set are also selected. We denote them by Ch2g_p3middle100first5, . . ., Ch2g_p3middle100first50 and Ch2g_p3middle100last5, . . ., Ch2g_p3middle100last50.

With the help of the fourth feature selection procedure, 21 feature groups consisting of the frequencies of character bigrams selected from the set $\alpha^2$ were created. In seven of these groups, the two best-characterized authors, the three best-characterized authors in the other seven groups, and all the $L$ authors in the remaining seven groups were taken into account during the calculation of the difference indicator of the characterizing degrees of authors (see Formulas (12)–(14)). We will denote them by 4.1, 4.2, and 4.3 in feature group names as some variants of the fourth feature selection procedure. Feature groups consisting of frequencies of 5, 10, . . ., 25, 50, 100 character bigrams with the highest indicators using each of the aforementioned metrics were created. Let us denote them as Ch2g_p4.1high5, . . ., Ch2g_p4.1high50; Ch2g_p4.2high5, . . ., Ch2g_p4.2high50; Ch2g_p4.3high5, . . ., Ch2g_p4.3high50, respectively.

Character unigrams and character bigrams selected with the help of feature selection procedure 3 are used to create feature groups consisting of variance of character n-gram frequencies as well. They are analogous to Ch1g32; Ch2g_p3high100, Ch2g_p3middle100; Ch2g_p3high100first5, . . ., Ch2g_p3high100first50; Ch2g_p3high100last5, . . ., Ch2g_p3high100last50; Ch2g_p3middle100first5, . . ., Ch2g_p3middle100first50; Ch2g_p3middle100last5, . . ., Ch2g_p3middle100last50. But instead of character n-gram frequencies, variances of character n-gram frequencies are employed in feature groups. We use " ChngVar" prefix instead of "Chng" in the names of these groups, where "Var" is for "variance".

Mixed feature groups consisting of features of character n-gram frequency and character n-gram frequency variance types were also used. In one of these mixed feature groups, the character n-gram frequencies and variances of character n-gram frequencies for all unigrams $\alpha^1$ were used, i.e., a group Ch1g&Ch1gVar64 was created consisting of all features in the Ch1g32 and Ch1gVar32 groups. In the other four mixed feature groups, character n-gram frequencies and variances of character n-gram frequencies for the most frequently used 5, 10, 15, 20 character bigrams in the training set were used. We denote these groups by Ch2g&Ch2gVar_p3high100first10, . . ., Ch2g&Ch2gVar_p3high100first40.

In this study, the number of feature groups used in the considered author recognition problem, which contains the features of character n-gram frequency and variance of character n-gram frequency types, is 79:

1-grams: {number of feature types} × {number of n-gram subsets} = 2 × 1 = 2;

2-grams selected with the help of the third feature selection procedure: {number of feature types} × ({number of multi-gram n-gram sets} × (1 + {number of selection criteria of few-gram n-gram subsets) × {few-number of n-gram subsets })) = 2 × (2 × (1 + 2 × 6)) = 52;

2-grams selected with the help of the fourth feature selection procedure: {number of feature types} × {number of metrics} × {number of n-gram subsets} = 1 × 3 × 7 = 21;

mixed groups of character n-gram frequencies and variances of character n-gram frequencies: {number of n-gram subsets} = 4.

### 5.3. Word Frequency Type of Feature Groups

In the considered author recognition problem, different feature groups consisting of features related to the type of word frequency were used.

These feature groups differ from each other according to the variety and number of words used in these groups, as well as the frequency types, i.e., in addition to the frequencies of the words in the given text, the features of the given text may also include the frequencies of these words in candidate authors' unified texts and the total usage frequencies in the training set (see Section 3.5).

We divide these feature groups into several types. It may be confusing, but it is not about the type of features but the type of feature group. We will only separate groups of features of word frequency type into such feature group types due to the large number of approaches used for the selection of words, the values of which, in these groups, are quite different from each other. Let us take a look at the characteristics of each of the different feature group types in the study, which consist of features belonging to the word frequency feature type used:

1. With the help of feature selection procedure 1—the procedure for selecting frequently used words by authors (see Formulas (1)–(4))—the most frequently used words of the authors in their own texts in the training set are determined separately per each author. Using procedure 1, all the words in the training set are sorted $L$ times for $L$ number of authors each to the order of the decreasing total usage frequency by an appropriate author, which gives $L$ sets of words. Then, an almost equal number of words is selected from each of the word sets. Finally, selected words are collected together as a final set of words selected with feature selection procedure 1. In the study, 15, 25, 45, and 50 high frequent and middle frequent words of authors are used as feature groups. We denote these feature groups by the names W_p1high15, . . ., W_p1high50, W_p1middle15, . . ., W_p1middle50, where "W" is "word", "p1" indicates that the first feature selection procedure is used, "high" and "middle" indicates that the most and middle frequently used words by the authors are selected, and 15, . . ., 50 indicate counts of features in these groups.

2. Words that are rarely used in everyday life can be more effective in author recognition in terms of discriminating texts of different authors than words that are often used in daily life. Taking this into account, among the most used words by the authors individually, the frequencies of which were used in groups W_p1high15, . . ., W_p1high50, we manually selected the words that we assume are used less often in everyday life and manually selected the feature groups consisting of the frequencies of these words. In other words, we removed words that are often used in everyday life among the words selected with the help of the first feature selection procedure. The numbers of words in such groups are 3, 15, 25, 40, and 45, and let us denote these groups by the names W_p1highMAN3, . . ., W_p1highMAN45, respectively, where "MAN" is for "manual", which means that after selecting the most used words by the authors with the help of feature selection procedure 1, some of these words were manually selected from this word set.

3. Using the second feature selection procedure—the procedure for selecting frequently used words in the training set (see Formulas (5)–(7))—5, 10, . . ., 25, 50 most and middle occurring words in the training set where the authors of the texts are not taken into account were selected and used in feature groups. Let us denote these feature groups as W_p2high5, . . ., W_p2high50, W_p2middle5, . . ., W_p2middle50.

4. In author recognition problems, such text features should be used that represent the stylistic characteristics of its author in any given text of him/her [1]. It is clear that in a given author recognition problem, if the text features effectively reflect the stylistic characteristics of any author, the features of texts of a certain author must remain invariant according to their topics.

In this study, an author recognition problem is considered in the example of Azerbaijani writers. There are two types of parts of speech in the Azerbaijani language: main and auxiliary. Based on the morphology of the Azerbaijani language, words related to auxiliary parts of speech, e.g., conjunctions, do not have lexical meaning, so they do not seriously affect the topic of a text. These words are function words that do not possess a meaning but have a function in sentences. For function words, see, e.g., [1]. So, the frequency of words related to auxiliary parts of speech can be more effective as text features than the frequency of words related to the main parts of speech because they can more adequately reflect the author's stylistics since they are independent of the text's topic.

For this type of word frequency feature group, feature selection procedure 2 is used, but the word set W, where selected words are selected, contains only words of auxiliary parts of speech in the training set instead of all the words in the training set. In this study, 5, 10, . . ., 25, 50 highest and middle frequent auxiliary parts of speech words are used for feature group creation. Let us denote them by W_p2highAUX5, . . ., W_p2highAUX50, W_p2middleAUX5, . . ., W_p2middleAUX50, where "AUX" is for "auxiliary", which means that the words whose frequencies are used in the feature groups belong only to the auxiliary parts of speech.

5. In the word frequency feature groups described above, the frequencies of words in the given text features that were intended to be extracted were used. In this type of word

frequency group, not only the frequencies of the selected words in the given text but also the total frequencies of those words in the texts of the authors in the training set and in all the texts in the training set without taking authors into account are used.

In this study, some feature groups were used in which not only the frequencies of the selected words in the given text but also the total frequencies of the words in the unified texts of the authors in the training set and the total frequency in the training set without taking authors into account were used. During the use of groups belonging to this type of feature group, among the features of an arbitrary text, there is the frequency of a given word in that text, the total frequency of the authors' texts in the training set, and the total frequency of all texts in the training set.

As is clear from the description above, the main difference between this type of word frequency group and the previous types is not about the words selected but the text(s) from which it is calculated. Using a word, the frequency of that word in a given text, the total frequencies in authors' unified texts in the training set, and the total frequency in the training set would be calculated. In the study, in addition to the word frequencies in a given text, the total frequencies obtained based on the texts in the training set used with word sets were used in the groups W_p2high50, W_p1highMAN3, W_p1highMAN15, W_p1highMAN25, W_p1highMAN40, W_p1highMAN45. Thus, W&WA&WT_p2high50, W&WA&WT_p1highMAN3, …, W&WA&WT_p1highMAN45 groups were created, where "W", "WA", and "WT" denote the frequencies of words in the given text, the total usage frequencies of words by authors, and the total usage frequencies of words in the training set, respectively.

In the study, the number of feature groups used in the considered author recognition problem that contain features related to the word frequency type is 43:

1. W_p1 feature groups—feature groups that used procedure 1 for word selection: {number of word selection criteria} × {number of word sets} = 2 × 4 = 8;
2. W_p1MAN feature groups—manually intervened feature groups that used procedure 1 for word selection: {number of word selection criteria} × {number of word sets} = 1 × 5 = 5;
3. W_p2 feature groups—feature groups that used procedure 2 for word selection: {number of word selection criteria} × {number of word sets} = 2 × 6 = 12;
4. W_p2AUX feature groups—feature groups that used procedure 2 to select words from among words belonging to some chosen parts of speech, i.e., auxiliary parts of speech: {number of word selection criteria} × {number of word sets} = 2 × 6 = 12;
5. W&WA&WT feature groups—along with the frequencies of the words in the given text, the total frequencies in the training set are used: {number of feature groups of type 3} + {number of feature groups of type 2} = 1 + 5 = 6.

The calculation of the frequency of an arbitrary word in any given text in the training set, the total frequencies of that word in the authors' texts in the training set, and the total frequency in all texts in the training set are outlined in Section 3.5.

## 6. Recognition and Dataset

The machine learning methods and text sets, e.g., the training sets or test sets used in the study, are outlined below.

### *6.1. Description of Training and Test Sets*

The dataset used in the author recognition problem considered in the study was prepared by the authors of the study as a result of the collection of large and small literary fiction works of 11 Azerbaijani writers. This dataset consists of 28 large and 123 small works, for a total of 151 works of those 11 authors (Table 1). Let us call this Dataset-0. The number of large works per author varies between one and five, and the number of small works varies between 0 and 46. In order to increase the number of observations, i.e., texts with known authorship for use in parameter identifications of mathematical models in feature selection when using one of the feature selection procedures, and so on, each of the large literary works in Dataset-0 was divided into 10 almost equal separate parts, and another dataset was created with small works and those text parts of large works. Let us call this Dataset-1. In Dataset-1, the number of texts per author varies between 25 and 56. Since there are 123 small works in Dataset-0, and each of the 28 large works in Dataset-0 was divided into 10 parts, the total number of observations in Dataset-1 is $123 + 28 \times 10 = 403$. By splitting Dataset-1, approximately 80–20% training and a test set of 325 and 78 texts with known authorship, respectively, were created (Table 2).

**Table 1.** Datasets used in the study.

| Author Number | Dataset-0 | | | | | Dataset-1 |
|---|---|---|---|---|---|---|
| | Large Works | | Small Works | | Total | |
| | Number of Works | Total Number of Words | Number of Works | Total Number of Words | | Number of Texts |
| 1 | 2 | 63,421 | 13 | 22,923 | 15 | 33 |
| 2 | 4 | 72,253 | 0 | 0 | 4 | 40 |
| 3 | 1 | 52,332 | 15 | 32,565 | 16 | 25 |
| 4 | 5 | 114,951 | 0 | 0 | 5 | 50 |
| 5 | 1 | 23,403 | 46 | 69,610 | 47 | 56 |
| 6 | 2 | 19,418 | 23 | 34,743 | 25 | 43 |
| 7 | 1 | 49,702 | 19 | 38,061 | 20 | 29 |
| 8 | 3 | 112,603 | 0 | 0 | 3 | 30 |
| 9 | 3 | 148,647 | 0 | 0 | 3 | 30 |
| 10 | 3 | 207,219 | 0 | 0 | 3 | 30 |
| 11 | 3 | 26,901 | 7 | 18,295 | 10 | 37 |
| Total | 28 | 63,421 | 123 | 22,923 | 151 | 403 |

**Table 2.** Training and test sets used in the study.

| Author Number | Number of Texts | | |
|---|---|---|---|
| | Training Set | Test Set | Total |
| 1 | 27 | 6 | 33 |
| 2 | 32 | 8 | 40 |
| 3 | 20 | 5 | 25 |
| 4 | 40 | 10 | 50 |
| 5 | 45 | 11 | 56 |
| 6 | 35 | 8 | 43 |
| 7 | 24 | 5 | 29 |
| 8 | 24 | 6 | 30 |
| 9 | 24 | 6 | 30 |
| 10 | 24 | 6 | 30 |
| 11 | 30 | 7 | 37 |
| Total | 325 | 78 | 403 |

In parametric identifications of mathematical models in feature selection, the training set was used, where the training and test sets are non-intersecting subsets of Dataset-1, $T = \overline{T} \cup \tilde{T}$, $\overline{T} \cap \tilde{T} = \varnothing$, where $\overline{T}$ and $\tilde{T}$ are the training and test sets, respectively. Author recognition approaches, each consisting of mathematical models used in author recognition, text feature groups, and so on, used in the considered author recognition problem in the study were evaluated based on the recognition accuracies obtained for the test set, which is a subset of Dataset-1 and Dataset-0—sets of large and small literary works themselves.

### 6.2. Recognition Models

Support vector machine (SVM) and random forest (RF) methods, as well as multilayer feedforward artificial neural network (ANN) models of machine learning, were used in the considered author recognition problem.

ANNs used in the study differ from each other in terms of the number of layers, the number of neurons in these layers, and the values of synapses and biases among these neurons. In ANNs used for solving the considered author recognition problem, the number of neurons at the input layer—the first layer—is equal to the number of elements of the text feature vector, i.e., the number of elements in the feature group, and the number of neurons at the output layer—the last layer—is the number of authors. Intermediate layers, i.e., layers other than input or output layers, are called hidden layers. All ANNs used in the author recognition problem considered in the study are four-layered. In other words, the number of hidden layers is two. The number of neurons in the hidden layers of the ANNs used in the study differs according to the number of neurons in the input layer, i.e., the number of neurons in the last layer is the number of authors in the problem; in other words, the same for all ANNs used in the study. Let us note that the number of neurons in the input layer equals the number of features in the feature group. The number of neurons in the hidden layers in the ANNs used in the study varies from 3 to 10, and the total number of parameters—synapses and biases in the ANNs—varies from 271 to 325.

In ANNs, SoftMax was used as the activation function for the last layer, and a rectified linear unit was used for the other layers. In the parametric identification of ANNs, the Adam optimization method [32] was used. This method should not be confused with the Adams method; the Adam method is a finite-dimensional unconstrained optimization method. For the stopping criterion, "EarlyStopping" was used [33]. This aims to stop optimization when the value of the object function does not improve. If the stopping condition "EarlyStopping" is not satisfied, an additional stopping condition is also used to stop the optimization; with this stopping condition, optimization stops when the number of epochs exceeds a sufficiently large number. By epoch, we mean at least one step using all the observations in the training set; for example, training 10 epochs means that each of the instances/observations in the training set was used 10 times in training. The upper limit for epochs was taken as 200 in the author recognition problem considered in the study.

The radial basis function was used as a kernel in SVM. The number of trees—estimators used in RF—is 100, and the maximum depth of trees is 5.

The 2-gram frequencies of the 100 most frequently used character n-grams in the texts in the training set were also used with a CNN [33] in the form of a $10 \times 10$ matrix. The other machine learning methods and models used were tested with nearly all feature groups. The architecture of the used CNN consists of three convolution layers with 4, 4, 1 filters with dimensions of $3 \times 3$, $3 \times 3$, and $2 \times 2$ with padding choices "same", "valid", or "valid", respectively, one subsampling layer after each of these convolution layers, and two fully connected layers with 4 and 11 neurons, respectively. For subsampling, layer average pooling was used.

During parametric identification, the observations in the training set were involved in training in a mixed manner; in other words, observations in the training set were "shuffled" [33]. Since the number of observations belonging to different classes, i.e., authors in the training database differ from each other, the observations in the teaching set were given different class weights during their participation in training. The weight of each observation used in training is determined based on the number of observations in the class, i.e., the author of that observation.

Excluding the character bigrams selected using feature selection procedure 4, all feature groups were used with ANN, SVM, and RF. Frequencies of character bigrams selected using feature selection procedure 4 were used with SVM and RF.

## 7. Analysis and Discussion of Results of Computer Experiments

The Python programming language and related libraries were used. Specifically, Scikit-Learn library was used to work with SVM and RF, and the Keras library in TensorFlow framework to work with ANN [34,35].

By recognition accuracy in a given set of texts whose authors are known, we mean the ratio of the number of texts whose author is correctly identified to the number of all texts in the set [33]. The sets used are as follows: Dataset-0, which consists of large and small literary works of authors; Dataset-1, which consists of small works and separate parts of each of the large works in Dataset-0; and training and test sets obtained from the division of Dataset-1. The recognition accuracies obtained for the training set and the test set, as well as for Dataset-0—a set of original large and small literary works, themselves used with different methods of machine learning with different feature groups used—are given in the tables and images below. Sometimes, recognition accuracies with a certain confidence percentage on the test set, for example, 50%, 75%, 95%, and 99%, are also given, where the confidence percentage means that texts whose author is known with a confidence that is below the percentage are accepted as not correctly recognized. Note that in the figures and tables provided in this study, we will denote Dataset-0 with the word "Works" for simplicity and immediate understanding.

### 7.1. Analysis of the Recognition Effectiveness of Character n-Gram Frequency and Variance of Character n-Gram Frequencies

In the study, the maximum recognition accuracies obtained using different methods and machine learning models with character n-gram frequency and variance of character n-gram frequency types of features on Dataset-0 are given in Table 3. For only groups of character bigram frequencies, Table 3 takes into account both feature selection procedures 3 and 4. From the recognition accuracies given in this table, it can be seen that character bigrams—2-grams—are more effective than character unigrams—1-grams—in many cases. Variance of character n-gram frequency type feature groups did not outperform character n-gram frequency type feature groups in recognition. Mixed feature groups with features belonging to both of these two types did not show a more effective result in recognition than feature groups consisting of features belonging to the character n-gram frequency type. The highest recognition accuracy was obtained in one of the bigram frequency groups among all the feature groups that belong to all the feature types using character n-grams.

**Table 3.** Recognition accuracies (%) obtained by character n-gram frequencies and variances of character n-gram frequencies.

| Feature Type | *n*=1 Character | | | *n*=2 Character | | |
|---|---|---|---|---|---|---|
| | ANN | RF | SVM | ANN | RF | SVM |
| n-gram frequencies | 1.99 | 92.72 | 43.05 | 31.13 | 96.69 | **98.01** |
| variances of n-gram frequencies | 9.93 | 60.93 | 24.50 | 31.13 | 70.20 | 48.34 |
| Mixture of n-gram frequencies and variances of n-gram frequencies | 9.93 | 85.43 | 37.75 | 9.93 | 74.17 | 58.94 |

In the study, two feature selection procedures for selecting character n-grams were used—a procedure for selecting frequently used character n-grams in the training set and a procedure for selecting character n-grams with different characterizing degrees of authors. For feature selection procedures 3 and 4, see Formulas (8)–(10) and (11)–(16), respectively.

In Figures 1 and 2, the maximum obtained recognition accuracies of bigram frequencies and variance of bigram frequencies in various machine learning methods and models for bigrams selected with feature selection procedure 3 on Dataset-0 were given. Charts (a) and (b) in each of the figures show the results for bigrams selected from the top 100 and averagely used, i.e., first and middle in the descending list of bigrams ordered by the total frequency in the training set character bigrams, respectively. In each of the charts in Figures 1 and 2, two graphs are given. One of these graphs shows the results obtained with the highest frequency 5, 10, . . ., 25, 50, 100 bigrams among 100 bigrams, i.e., first or average in descending order of total frequency in the training set, and the other graph shows the results obtained with the lowest frequency 5, 10, . . ., 25, 50, 100 bigrams.

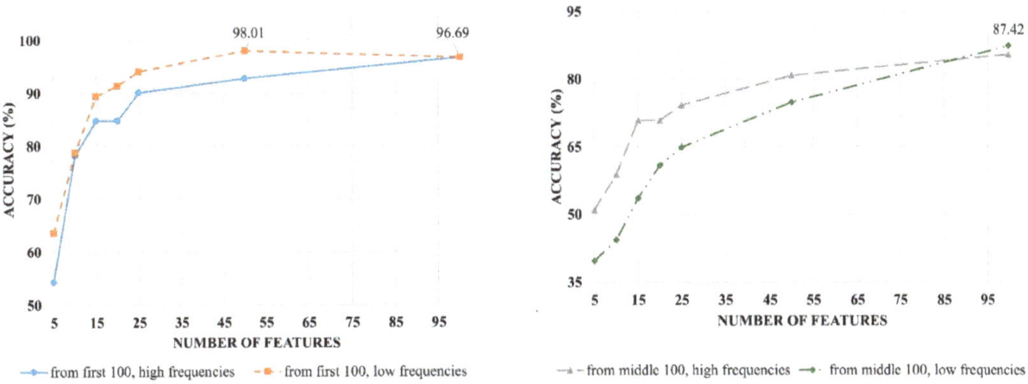


(a) (b)

**Figure 1.** Recognition accuracies obtained with variances of 2-gram frequencies in feature selection procedure 3: (**a**) frequencies of first bigrams in the descending order of total frequency in the training set; (**b**) frequencies of middle bigrams in the descending order of total frequency in the training set.

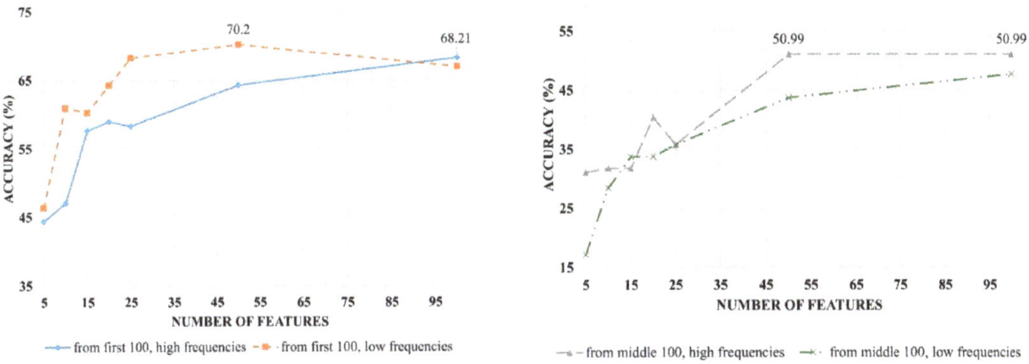


(a) (b)

**Figure 2.** Recognition accuracies obtained with 2-gram frequencies in feature selection procedure 3: (**a**) variances of frequencies of first bigrams in the descending order of total frequency in the training set; (**b**) variances of frequencies of middle bigrams in the descending order of total frequency in the training set.

From the graphs in Figure 1, it can be seen that the frequencies of the most frequently used bigrams in the training set give higher recognition accuracy than the frequencies of the averagely used n-gram characters in the training set. The second conclusion drawn from this figure is that among the first 100 bigrams in the descending order of frequency in the training set, those with lower frequencies in the training set are more effective than those with higher frequencies. This means that in order to use their frequencies in feature groups, it is advised to select character n-grams in the training set that are neither among the most used nor the least used ones in the texts. The conclusions about the recognition accuracies obtained with groups of features of character bigram frequency type in Figure 1 are analogous to the conclusions about the recognition accuracies obtained with groups of features of character bigram frequencies variance type in Figure 2. Character bigrams used to obtain results are appropriately the same for these two feature types in Figures 1 and 2.

The maximum recognition accuracies obtained on Dataset-0 by various machine learning methods and models—here, just SVM and RF were used with frequencies of bigrams selected using feature selection procedure 4 (the procedure for selecting character n-grams with different characterizing degrees of authors)—are shown in Figure 3. In each chart in Figure 3, there are two graphs. In chart (a), the results were obtained using 4.1 and 4.2 variants, and in chart (b), 4.2 and 4.3 variants of feature selection procedure 4 are represented. For a detailed description of the feature groups using 4.1, 4.2, and 4.3 variants, see Section 5.2. For 4.1–3 variants of the fourth feature selection procedure, see Formulas (12)–(14). For calculating the difference indicator characterizing degrees of authors, these variants use characterizing degrees of best-characterized two, three, and all authors, respectively.

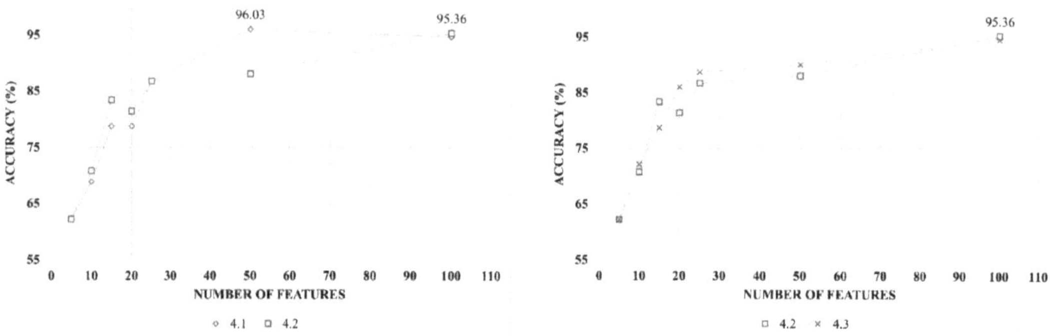


**(a)** **(b)**

**Figure 3.** Recognition accuracies obtained with 2-gram frequencies using feature selection procedure 4: (**a**) 4.1 and 4.2 variants of the feature selection procedure (see Formulas (12) and (13)); (**b**) 4.2 and 4.3 variants of the feature selection procedure (see Formulas (13) and (14)).

It can be seen from Figure 3 that as the number of best-characterized authors taken into account when calculating the difference indicator of characterizing degrees increases, in many cases, more accurate recognition results are obtained. Despite this, the procedure for selecting character n-grams with different characterizing degrees of authors—feature selection procedure 4—did not outperform the procedure for selecting frequently used character n-grams in the training set—feature selection procedure 3.

### 7.2. Analysis of the Recognition Effectiveness of Word Frequency

The maximum recognition accuracies on Dataset-0 obtained with word frequencies are shown in Figure 4: from left to right, the first column shows the word selection approaches, and the second column shows the recognition accuracies. It should be noted that in the study, two feature selection procedures were used to select words whose frequencies will be used in word frequency feature groups. For the calculation of word frequencies and for word frequency feature groups, see Sections 3.5 and 5.3, respectively. In the author recognition problem under consideration using one of these procedures, the most frequently and middle frequently used words in the lexicons of the candidate authors were selected. Using another procedure, the most frequently and middle frequently used words in the training set were selected without taking into account the author differences. For feature selection procedures 1 and 2, see Formulas (1)–(4) and (5)–(7), respectively.

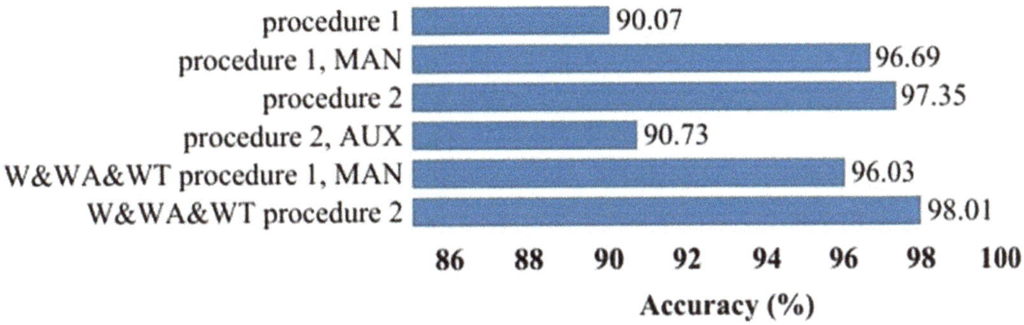


**Figure 4.** Recognition accuracies obtained with word frequencies (%).

It can be seen from Figure 4 that the frequencies of words selected using only procedure 2 turned out to be more effective in recognition than the frequencies of words selected using only procedure 1. Recognition accuracy increased when selecting words by manually removing some words—words used in everyday life, names of characters in literature works, and so on from among the words most used by authors, i.e., selected using feature selection procedure 1 (see groups "procedure 1" and "procedure 1, MAN" in Figure 4). Recognition accuracy decreased when the most common words in the training set, i.e., selected using feature selection procedure 2, were not selected from all words but only from words belonging to auxiliary parts of speech that do not have lexical meaning (see groups "procedure 2" and "procedure 2, AUX" in Figure 4). When the most frequently used words of authors are selected separately by the authors using feature selection procedure 1, in addition to the usage frequencies of words in a given text, the total usage frequency of words in each candidate author's texts, and the total usage frequency in the training set are used in recognition, recognition effectiveness decreases (see groups "procedure 1, MAN" and "W&WA&WT procedure 1, MAN" in Figure 4). This may be due to the fact that the frequencies in the authors' texts have already been taken into account when selecting words using procedure 1. In addition to the frequencies of the most frequently used words in the training set without taking into account author differences, total usage frequencies in candidate authors' texts and the overall frequency in the training set are also used, and recognition accuracy increases (see "procedure 2" and "W&WA&WT, procedure 2" groups in Figure 4).

### 7.3. Comparative Analysis of Different Types of Features

Figure 5 shows the recognition results obtained with different feature types: from left to right, the first column shows the text set on which accuracy is calculated, the second shows feature types, and the third column shows the recognition accuracies. From Figure 5, it can be seen that features belonging to the character n-gram frequency type and features belonging to the word frequency type were more effective in recognition than features belonging to other feature types. Mixed feature groups, in which features belonging to character n-gram frequency and character n-gram frequency variance types were used together, did not improve the recognition accuracy obtained with feature groups consisting of features belonging to only one of these types. Mixed feature groups that shared features belonging to the sentence length frequency and word length frequency types resulted in higher recognition accuracy than feature groups consisting of features belonging to only one of these types, i.e., using sentence length frequencies and word length frequencies together in a mixed feature group was more effective in recognition.

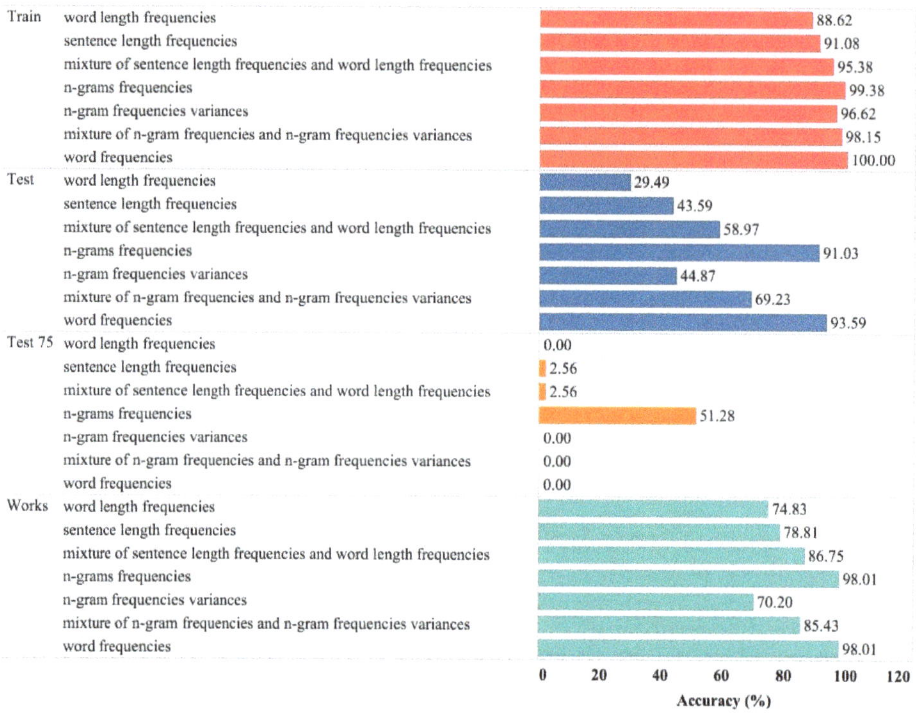


**Figure 5.** Maximum recognition accuracies obtained using different types of features.

Table 4 shows the comprehensive recognition results on different text sets and with different confidence percentages of two feature groups with the highest recognition accuracy on Dataset-0 in the author recognition problem considered in the study. One of these two feature groups contains the character n-gram frequencies, and another contains word frequencies. It is clear from the results in the table that these two feature groups caused the same accuracies in Dataset-0 (see "Works" in Table 4), but it seems recognition is performed with more confidence with character n-gram frequencies (e.g., see "Test 75"—on the test set with 75% confidence). These two cases differ not only because of obtaining different recognition accuracies with certain degrees of confidence but also because of recognition indicators for different author candidates. For these two cases, it seems from the confusion matrices [33] given in Figures 6 and 7 that they were correspondingly obtained on Dataset-0 and the test set. This can be seen from the precision and recall values on Dataset-0 for different author candidates of these two cases given in Tables 5 and 6 as well. The overall precision, recall, F1 score, and Cohen's kappa [36] values obtained on different text sets for those two cases are given in Table 7. It should be noted that the values of precision, recall, and F1 score in Table 7 are the average of per-class precision, recall, and F1 score indicators for author candidates weighted according to the number of texts of those author candidates in the text set.

**Table 4.** Maximum recognition accuracies of two best-performing feature groups (%).

| Feature Type | Number of Features | Recognition Method Type | Train | Test | Test 50 | Test 75 | Test 95 | Test 99 | Works |
|---|---|---|---|---|---|---|---|---|---|
| n-gram frequencies | 50 | SVM | 99.38 | 91.03 | 76.92 | 51.28 | 5.13 | 0.00 | 98.01 |
| word frequencies | 650 | RF | 100.00 | 93.59 | 0.00 | 0.00 | 0.00 | 0.00 | 98.01 |

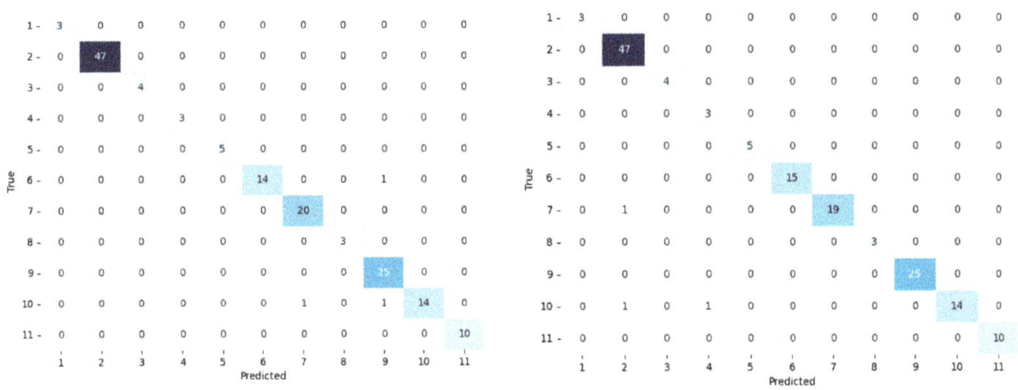


(a) (b)

**Figure 6.** Confusion matrices obtained with two best-performing feature groups on the literary works: (**a**) n-gram frequencies; (**b**) word frequencies.

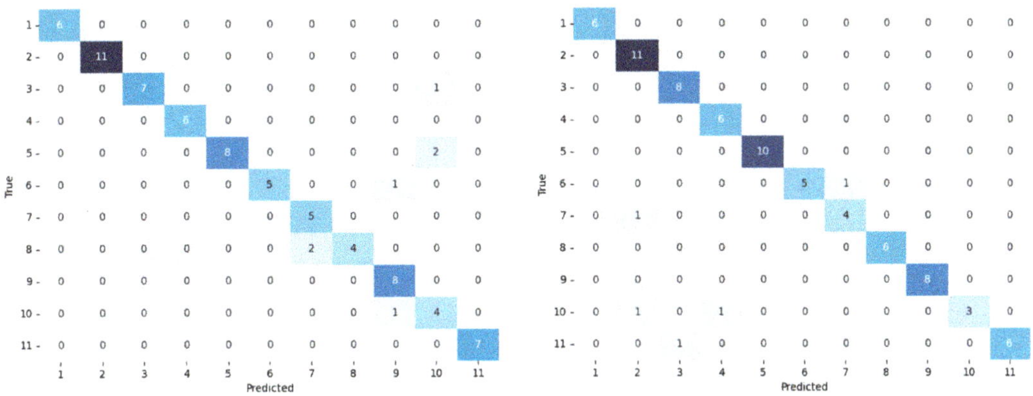


(a) (b)

**Figure 7.** Confusion matrices obtained with two best-performing feature groups on the test set: (**a**) n-gram frequencies; (**b**) word frequencies.

**Table 5.** Recognition results per different authors with n-gram frequencies on literary works.

| Author Number | Precision | Recall | F1-Score | Number of Instances |
|---|---|---|---|---|
| 1 | 1 | 1 | 1 | 3 |
| 2 | 1 | 1 | 1 | 47 |
| 3 | 1 | 1 | 1 | 4 |
| 4 | 1 | 1 | 1 | 3 |
| 5 | 1 | 1 | 1 | 5 |
| 6 | 1 | 0.933333 | 0.965517 | 15 |
| 7 | 0.952381 | 1 | 0.97561 | 20 |
| 8 | 1 | 1 | 1 | 3 |
| 9 | 0.925926 | 1 | 0.961538 | 25 |
| 10 | 1 | 0.875 | 0.933333 | 16 |
| 11 | 1 | 1 | 1 | 10 |

**Table 6.** Recognition results per different authors with word frequencies on literary works.

| Author Number | Precision | Recall | F1-Score | Number of Instances |
|---|---|---|---|---|
| 1 | 1 | 1 | 1 | 3 |
| 2 | 0.959184 | 1 | 0.979167 | 47 |
| 3 | 1 | 1 | 1 | 4 |
| 4 | 0.75 | 1 | 0.857143 | 3 |
| 5 | 1 | 1 | 1 | 5 |
| 6 | 1 | 1 | 1 | 15 |
| 7 | 1 | 0.95 | 0.974359 | 20 |
| 8 | 1 | 1 | 1 | 3 |
| 9 | 1 | 1 | 1 | 25 |
| 10 | 1 | 0.875 | 0.933333 | 16 |
| 11 | 1 | 1 | 1 | 10 |

**Table 7.** Overall recognition results.

| Feature Type | Text Set | Number of Instances | Precision (Weighted Average) | Recall (Weighted Average) | F1 (Weighted Average) | Cohen's Kappa |
|---|---|---|---|---|---|---|
| word frequencies | Train | 325 | 1 | 1 | 1 | 1 |
| word frequencies | Test | 78 | 0.943098 | 0.935897 | 0.933555 | 0.928819 |
| word frequencies | Works | 151 | 0.982329 | 0.980132 | 0.980217 | 0.975997 |
| n-gram frequencies | Train | 325 | 0.994319527 | 0.993846154 | 0.99389705 | 0.993187583 |
| n-gram frequencies | Test | 78 | 0.933699634 | 0.91025641 | 0.913092463 | 0.900763359 |
| n-gram frequencies | Works | 151 | 0.981428922 | 0.98013245 | 0.979912242 | 0.976025404 |

Figure 8 shows the maximum recognition accuracies obtained by various machine learning methods and models: from left to right, the first column shows text sets (the bases on which recognition accuracies are calculated), the second column shows machine learning methods and models, and the third column shows recognition accuracies. From this figure, it can be seen that higher recognition accuracies were obtained using SVM and RF than using ANN. From the recognition accuracies obtained with 75% confidence on the test set, it is clear that SVM recognizes with greater confidence than RF.

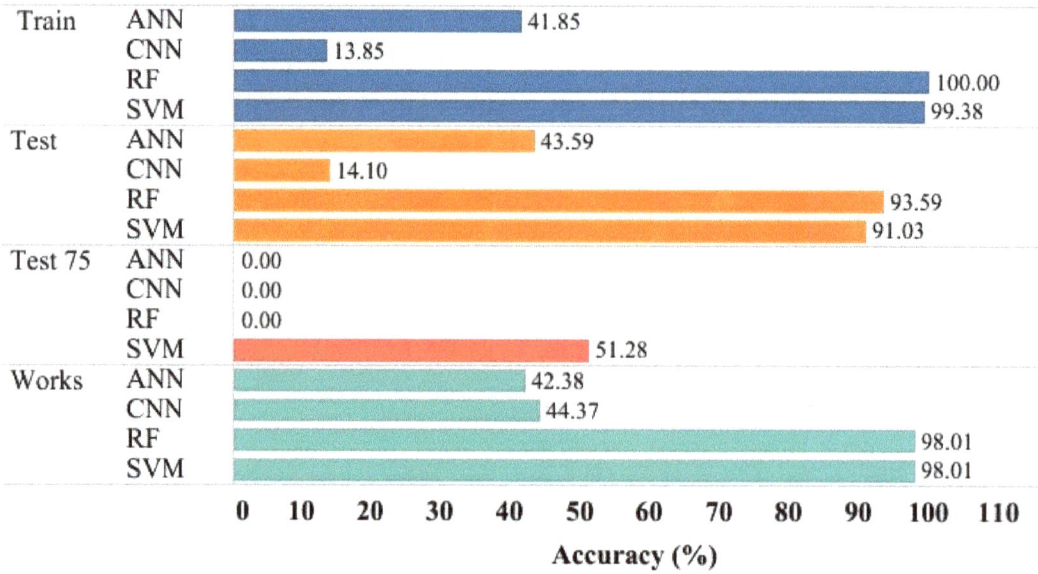


**Figure 8.** Maximum recognition accuracies obtained by different methods of machine learning.

In the study, the results of the comparative analysis of using different text feature types with different machine learning techniques were obtained on the example of a dataset consisting of texts in the Azerbaijani language. Nevertheless, the approaches used in the study and the methodology of the conducted experiments can be used in the recognition of text authors in other languages as well.

The models we have built depend strongly not only on linguistic features but also on the region (geographical location) of residence of the text authors. This was pointed out by Gore, R.J. et al., whose research is related to the dependence of the characteristics of the authors' texts on the region of their residence [37].

At the same time, we believe that the geographical factor is stable over time for the authors of texts, and the movement of authors geographically does not significantly affect the stylistic "fingerprint" of authors.

## 8. Conclusions

A comparative analysis of the effectiveness of using different machine learning classification methods with different text feature groups consisting of different feature types and their mixtures was carried out in the example of literary novels in the Azerbaijani language of several famous Azerbaijani writers.

Among the feature types, more accurate results in terms of recognition accuracy were achieved with character 2-gram frequencies and selected word frequencies. On the literary works considered, the classification methods of support vector machine and random forest with selected word frequencies had the same accuracy, but the support vector machine with character 2-gram frequencies showed more reliable results in identifying authors with higher confidence.

Since the recognition effectiveness of different machine learning methods with various groups of features of different types represents comparable results, for future work, we plan to consider using different group decision-making methods for the combined decision-making of different author recognition approaches. This is intended to increase the reliability of the to-be-developed author recognition computer system.

**Author Contributions:** Conceptualization, E.P. and R.A.; methodology, E.P. and R.A.; software, R.A.; validation, R.A.; formal analysis, E.P.; investigation, E.P. and R.A.; resources, R.A.; data curation, R.A.; writing—original draft preparation, E.P. and R.A.; writing—review and editing, E.P. and R.A.; visualization, R.A.; supervision, E.P.; project administration, E.P.; funding acquisition, E.P. All authors have read and agreed to the published version of the manuscript.

**Funding:** This research was carried out under the Erasmus+ 2022-2024 program in KA171 for learning mobility for students and staff in higher education between EU Member States and third countries [Agreement number: 2022-1-EL01-KA171-HED-000074817] between the University of Thessaly (G VOLOS01) and the Institute of Control Systems of Azerbaijan National Academy of Sciences (E10291793).

**Data Availability Statement:** The datasets presented in this article are not readily available because the data are part of an ongoing study and development process of a software for authorship attribution of texts in Azerbaijani language.

**Acknowledgments:** The authors would like to thank the anonymous reviewers for their valuable comments.

**Conflicts of Interest:** The authors declare no conflicts of interest.

## References

1. Stamatatos, E. A survey of modern authorship attribution methods. *J. Am. Soc. Inf. Sci. Technol.* **2009**, *60*, 538–556. [CrossRef]
2. He, X.; Lashkari, A.H.; Vombatkere, N.; Sharma, D.P. Authorship Attribution Methods, Challenges, and Future Research Directions: A Comprehensive Survey. *Information* **2024**, *15*, 131. [CrossRef]
3. Mosteller, F.; Wallace, D.L. Inference in an authorship problem: A comparative study of discrimination methods applied to the authorship of the disputed Federalist Papers. *J. Am. Stat. Assoc.* **1963**, *58*, 275–309.

4. Diederich, J.; Kindermann, J.; Leopold, E.; Paass, G. Authorship attribution with support vector machines. *Appl. Intell.* **2003**, *19*, 109–123. [CrossRef]
5. Doghan, S.; Diri, B. A new N-gram based classification (Ng-ind) for Turkish documents: Author, genre and gender. *Turk. Inform. Found. J. Comput. Sci. Eng.* **2010**, *3*, 11–19. (In Turkish)
6. Yasdi, M.; Diri, B. Author recognition by Abstract Feature Extraction. In Proceedings of the 20th Signal Processing and Communications Applications Conference (IEEE Xplore), Mugla, Turkey, 18–20 April 2012; pp. 1–4. (In Turkish). [CrossRef]
7. Bilgin, M. A new method proposal to increase the classification success of Turkish texts. *Uludağ Univ. Fac. Eng. J.* **2019**, *24*, 125–136. (In Turkish) [CrossRef]
8. Erdoghan, I.; Gullu, M.; Polat, H. Developing an End-to-End Author Recognition Application with Machine Learning Algorithms. *El-Cezerî J. Sci. Eng.* **2022**, *9*, 1303–1314. (In Turkish) [CrossRef]
9. Graovac, J. Text categorization using n-gram based language independent technique. *Intell. Data Anal.* **2014**, *18*, 677–695. [CrossRef]
10. Halvani, O.; Winter, C.; Pflug, A. Authorship verification for different languages, genres and topics. In Proceedings of the 3rd Annual DFRWS Europe, Lausanne, Switzerland, 29–31 March 2016; pp. 33–43.
11. Fedotova, A.; Romanov, A.; Kurtukova, A.; Shelupanov, A. Digital Authorship Attribution in Russian-Language Fanfiction and Classical Literature. *Algorithms* **2023**, *16*, 13. [CrossRef]
12. Kešelj, V.; Peng, F.; Cercone, N.; Thomas, C. N-gram-based author profiles for authorship attribution. In Proceedings of the PACLING—The Conference Pacific Association for Computational Linguistics (PACLING), Halifax, NV, Canada, 22–25 August 2003; pp. 255–264.
13. Mendenhall, T.C. A Mechanical Solution of a Literary Problem. *Pop. Sci. Mon.* **1901**, *60*, 97–105.
14. Zhao, Y.; Zobel, J. Searching with style: Authorship attribution in classic literature. In Proceedings of the Thirtieth Australasian Conference on Computer Science, Ballarat, Australia, 30 January–2 February 2007; pp. 59–68.
15. Anisimov, A.V.; Porkhun, E.V.; Taranukha, V.Y. Algorithm for construction of parametric vectors for solution of classification problems by a feed-forward neural network. *Cybern. Syst. Anal.* **2007**, *43*, 161–170. [CrossRef]
16. Howedi, F.; Mohd, M. Text classification for authorship attribution using Naive Bayes classifier with limited training data. *Comput. Eng. Intell. Syst.* **2014**, *5*, 48–56.
17. Ayda-zade, K.; Talibov, S. Analysis of The Methods for The Authorship Identification of the Text in the Azerbaijani Language. *Probl. Inf. Technol.* **2017**, *8*, 14–23. [CrossRef]
18. Marchenko, O.; Anisimov, A.; Nykonenko, A.; Rossada, T.; Melnikov, E. Authorship attribution system. In *Natural Language Processing and Information Systems, Proceedings of the 22nd International Conference on Applications of Natural Language to Information Systems, Liège, Belgium, 21–23 June 2017*; Springer International Publishing: Berlin/Heidelberg, Germany, 2018; pp. 227–231.
19. Mouratidis, D.; Kermanidis, K.L. Ensemble and Deep Learning for Language-Independent Automatic Selection of Parallel Data. *Algorithms* **2019**, *12*, 26. [CrossRef]
20. Borisov, E.S. Using artificial neural networks for classification of black-and-white images. *Cybern. Syst. Anal.* **2008**, *44*, 304–307. [CrossRef]
21. Aida-zade, K.R.; Rustamov, S.S.; Clements, M.A.; Mustafayev, E.E. Adaptive neuro-fuzzy inference system for classification of texts. In *Recent Developments and the New Direction in Soft-Computing Foundations and Applications*, 1st ed.; Zadeh, L., Yager, R., Shahbazova, S., Reformat, M., Kreinovich, V., Eds.; Studies in Fuzziness and Soft Computing; Springer: Cham, Switzerland, 2018; pp. 63–70.
22. Dabagh, R.M. Authorship attribution and statistical text analysis. *Adv. Methodol. Stat.* **2007**, *4*, 149–163.
23. Orucu, F.; Dalkilich, G. Author identification Using N-grams and SVM. In Proceedings of the ISCSE—The 1st International Symposium on Computing in Science & Engineering, Izmir, Turkey, 3–5 June 2010; pp. 3–5.
24. Stamatatos, E. Author identification using imbalanced and limited training texts. In Proceedings of the DEXA 2007—The 18th International Workshop on Database and Expert Systems Applications (IEEE), Regensburg, Germany, 3–7 September 2007; pp. 237–241.
25. Stamatatos, E. Ensemble-based author identification using character n-grams. In Proceedings of the 3rd International Workshop on Text-Based Information Retrieval, Riva del Garda, Italy, 29 August 2006; pp. 41–46.
26. Lupei, M.; Mitsa, A.; Repariuk, V.; Sharkan, V. Identification of authorship of Ukrainian-language texts of journalistic style using neural networks. *East.-Eur. J. Enterp. Technol.* **2020**, *1*, 30–36. [CrossRef]
27. Ulianovska, Y.; Firsov, O.; Kostenko, V.; Pryadka, O. Study of the process of identifying the authorship of texts written in natural language. *Technol. Audit. Prod. Reserves* **2024**, *2*, 32–37. [CrossRef]
28. Silva, K.; Can, B.; Blain, F.; Sarwar, R.; Ugolini, L.; Mitkov, R. Authorship attribution of late 19th century novels using GAN-BERT. In Proceedings of the 61st Annual Meeting of the Association for Computational Linguistics (Volume 4: Student Research Workshop), Toronto, ON, Canada, 10–12 July 2023; pp. 310–320.
29. Yule, G.U. On sentence-length as a statistical characteristic of style in prose: With application to two cases of disputed authorship. *Biometrika* **1939**, *30*, 363–390.
30. Wilcox, R.R. *Fundamentals of Modern Statistical Methods: Substantially Improving Power and Accuracy*, 2nd ed.; Springer: New York, NY, USA, 2010; 249p.

31. Ayedh, A.; Tan, G.; Alwesabi, K.; Rajeh, H. The Effect of Preprocessing on Arabic Document Categorization. *Algorithms* **2016**, *9*, 27. [CrossRef]
32. Kingma, D.P.; Ba, J. Adam: A method for stochastic optimization. *arXiv* **2014**, arXiv:1412.6980.
33. Géron, A. *Hands-on Machine Learning with Scikit-Learn, Keras, and TensorFlow*, 2nd ed.; O'Reilly Media: Sebastopol, CA, USA, 2019; 510p.
34. Pedregosa, F.; Varoquaux, G.; Gramfort, A.; Michel, V.; Thirion, B.; Grisel, O.; Blondel, M.; Prettenhofer, P.; Weiss, R.; Dubourg, V.; et al. Scikit-learn: Machine Learning in Python. *J. Mach. Learn. Res.* **2011**, *12*, 2825–2830.
35. Chollet, F. Keras. 2015. Available online: https://github.com/fchollet/keras. (accessed on 27 April 2024).
36. Vujović, Ž. Classification model evaluation metrics. *Int. J. Adv. Comput. Sci. Appl.* **2021**, *12*, 599–606. [CrossRef]
37. Gore, R.J.; Diallo, S.; Padilla, J. You are what you tweet: Connecting the geographic variation in America's obesity rate to twitter content. *PLoS ONE* **2015**, *10*, 9. [CrossRef] [PubMed]

*algorithms*

MDPI

*Article*

# Feature Extraction Based on Sparse Coding Approach for Hand Grasp Type Classification

**Jirayu Samkunta [1,*], Patinya Ketthong [1,2], Nghia Thi Mai [3], Md Abdus Samad Kamal [4], Iwanori Murakami [4] and Kou Yamada [4,*]**

1 Graduate School of Science and Technology, Gunma University, Maebashi 376-8515, Japan; patinya@tni.ac.th
2 Faculty of Engineering, Thai-Nichi Institute of Technology, 1771/1 Pattanakarn Rd. Suanluang, Bangkok 10250, Thailand
3 Department of Electrical and Electronic 1, Posts and Telecommunications Institute of Technology, Hanoi 100000, Vietnam; nghiamt@ptit.edu.vn
4 Division of Mechanical Science and Technology, Gunma University, Maebashi 376-8515, Japan; maskamal@gunma-u.ac.jp (M.A.S.K.); murakami@gunma-u.ac.jp (I.M.)
* Correspondence: t222b603@gunma-u.ac.jp (J.S.); yamada@gunma-u.ac.jp (K.Y.)

**Abstract:** The kinematics of the human hand exhibit complex and diverse characteristics unique to each individual. Various techniques such as vision-based, ultrasonic-based, and data-glove-based approaches have been employed to analyze human hand movements. However, a critical challenge remains in efficiently analyzing and classifying hand grasp types based on time-series kinematic data. In this paper, we propose a novel sparse coding feature extraction technique based on dictionary learning to address this challenge. Our method enhances model accuracy, reduces training time, and minimizes overfitting risk. We benchmarked our approach against principal component analysis (PCA) and sparse coding based on a Gaussian random dictionary. Our results demonstrate a significant improvement in classification accuracy: achieving 81.78% with our method compared to 31.43% for PCA and 77.27% for the Gaussian random dictionary. Furthermore, our technique outperforms in terms of macro-average F1-score and average area under the curve (AUC) while also significantly reducing the number of features required.

**Keywords:** feature extraction; sparse coding; human grasp types; classification; dictionary learning

## 1. Introduction

Understanding human hand characteristics involves investigating hand kinematics during various grasping actions and general patterns of hand usage. This research is critical across domains such as medicine, rehabilitation, psychology, and product design. Hand kinematics are studied to understand the characteristics of healthy hand movements [1,2] and to inform object design based on grasping patterns [3,4]. Moreover, the study of human hand manipulation has practical applications in the field of robotics, where the versatility of hand kinematics plays a crucial role. To facilitate effective manipulation, human hands exhibit coordination and a multitude of degrees of freedom (DoFs). Therefore, comprehensive hand kinematics data encompassing a wide range of DoFs are essential for studying interactions with various objects under different environmental conditions.

Existing methods for analyzing hand kinematics often fail to capture the necessary features for precise classification. The utilization of dimensionality reduction techniques becomes imperative and is implemented with all hand kinematic recording techniques. The dimensionality reduction techniques are used as a pre-processing step and can eliminate irrelevant data, noise, and redundant features. Dimensionality reduction has been performed based on two main methods, which are feature selection and feature extraction. These techniques are utilized for analyzing and interpreting intricate behavior of the human hand [5]. Feature selection involves choosing the most relevant functions that adequately describe the essential indicators. On the other hand, feature extraction entails identifying and transforming the most informative features from a given dataset. Both feature selection and feature extraction are fundamental steps in machine learning models [6], as the quality and relevance of features significantly impact the model's performance and accuracy. Feature extraction becomes a necessary method to identify and extract the essential information so that the investigation of hand kinematics can be made easier.

Due to feature extraction outperforming in terms of performance and accuracy, then feature representation is important for analyzing hand kinematics. It involves transforming raw data into a format that highlights essential characteristics, making it easier to identify patterns and perform classification tasks. Accurate feature representation can significantly enhance the performance of machine learning models used for hand kinematic analysis. Hence, this paper addresses this gap by proposing a novel sparse coding feature extraction technique based on dictionary learning. Our contributions are threefold: we introduce a new feature extraction method tailored for hand kinematics time-series data, demonstrate the effectiveness of our method through extensive experimental evaluation, and significantly improve classification accuracy while reducing the number of features compared to existing methods.

Existing hand-based feature extraction methods can be divided into four main categories. The first category includes global and local statistical-based methods [7–10] that use features like local binary histograms and graph structures to capture information from the hand image. Examples of these methods include generalized symmetric local graph structure (GSLGS) [7], local binary pattern (LBP) [8], and histogram of oriented lines (HoL) [9] and its alternatives [10]. These methods are popular for hand-based biometric recognition. Another category is coding-based methods [11–15], which focus on encoding directional information in the hand image. This information is important because hand patterns often have distinct orientations that are resistant to changes in lighting. Examples of coding-based methods include sparse coding (SC) [15], ordinal code [11], competitive code (Compcode) [12], collaborative representation_Compcode (CR_Compcode) [13], and joint discriminative sparse coding (JDSC) [14]. Subspace-learning-based approaches [16–22] are another category. These methods, like principal component analysis (PCA) [16–19,21,22] and linear discriminant analysis (LDA) [20], aim to reduce the dimensionality of the data by projecting it into a lower-dimensional space. This can help improve recognition accuracy. Finally, deep-learning based methods [23,24] have recently emerged as a powerful tool for hand-based biometric recognition. These methods have shown promising performance for capturing discriminative features from hand images.

Despite recent advancements in hand kinematic analysis, feature extraction approaches still have several limitations. For example, most feature extraction techniques are specific to hand kinematic datasets derived from hand image datasets. Additionally, some techniques are only suitable for specific hand analyses using EMG signals [24,25] and are difficult to extend to other types of hand kinematic data. Moreover, most of the traditional feature extraction methods are focused on extracting features based on subspace-learning-based approaches while not adequately exploiting the consistency and complementary information among the other types of hand kinematic data, especially hand kinematic time-series formats.

To overcome the challenges in hand kinematic analysis, we propose a methodology consisting of three primary steps. First, the hand kinematic dataset undergoes preprocessing through resampling. Next, various feature extraction techniques are applied, including raw data, PCA, sparse coding based on a Gaussian random dictionary, and our proposed sparse coding based on dictionary learning. Finally, the extracted features are used for neural network classification. Our method leverages the sparsity-inducing properties of dictionary learning to capture relevant features from hand kinematics time-series data, as detailed in Figure 1.

Our proposed method aims to enhance classification accuracy for identifying grasp types using hand kinematics in a time-series format. The proposed feature extraction technique leverages sparse coding based on dictionary learning, as illustrated in Figure 2. Building on existing sparse coding techniques, our approach provides the sparsest solution to an underdetermined linear problem by generating sparse coefficients. The process involves resampling the kinematic dataset to a specific size, vertically concatenating the resampled data, and partitioning the dataset into training and test sets using random partitioning. The training set is used to derive a dictionary through an online dictionary learning algorithm, which is then employed to extract sparse coefficients from both the training and test sets. These sparse coefficients are subsequently used as inputs for neural network classification, as depicted in Figure 3.

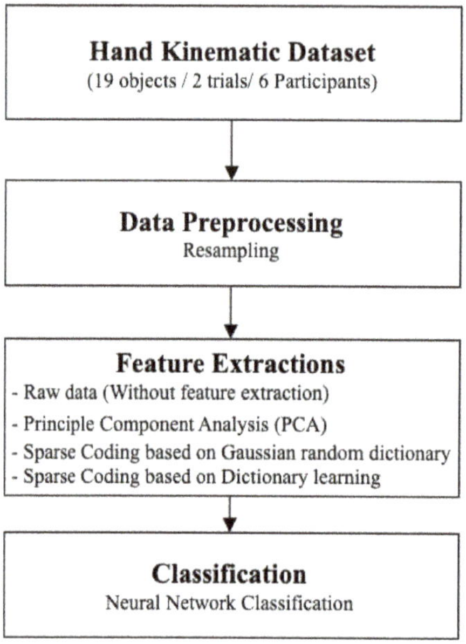


**Figure 1.** Overview of proposed methodology.

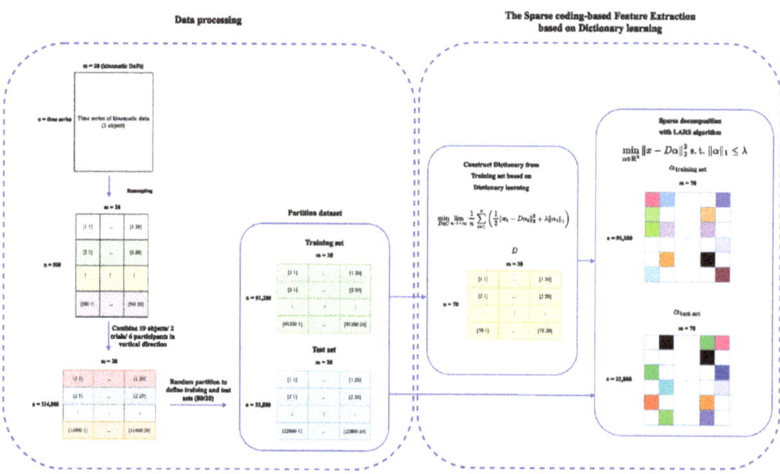


**Figure 2.** The sparse-coding-based feature extraction technique based on dictionary learning.

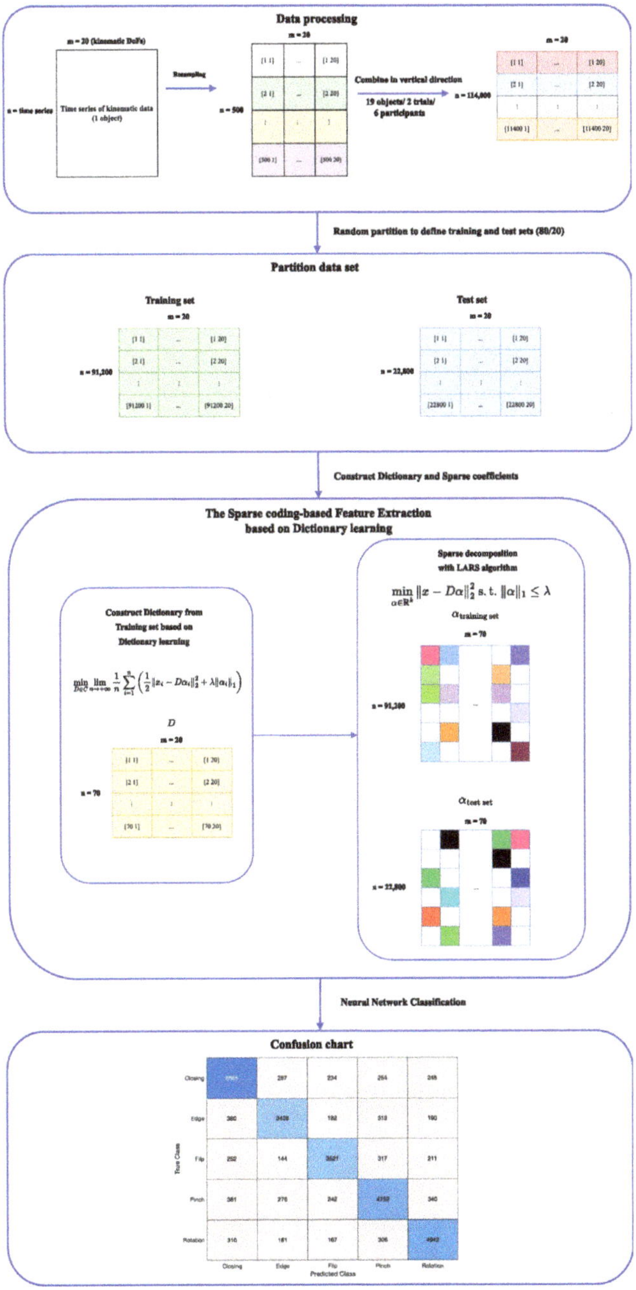


**Figure 3.** Details of proposed method.

The main contributions of this paper are summarized as follows:

- We propose a sparse coding technique based on dictionary learning to extract hand kinematic features, which is a context that has not been extensively explored before.

- Unlike most existing methods that extract features from hand datasets using images, our proposed method demonstrates the potential of using three-dimensional motion tracking using a time-series format for feature extraction.
- Our approach differs from our previous work that utilized traditional sparse coding with a dictionary based on a Gaussian random distribution. Instead, we apply a dictionary learning technique to the hand kinematics dataset in a time-series format. Extensive experimental evaluation of the publicly available UNIPI dataset demonstrates the effectiveness of our proposed method compared to existing techniques and our prior work.
- A key distinction from previous studies lies in the estimation technique used. While previous work employed the Frobenius norm for solving the optimization problem to obtain sparse coefficients, this work utilizes the L1-norm as the optimizer. This change results in a sparse representation, minimizing the number of features required.

The organization of the work is as follows. In Section 2, we review related work on feature extraction based on coding and our previous work on sparse coding for hand analysis. Section 3 details sparse coding feature extraction based on dictionary learning. In Section 4, we present the neural network classification used to evaluate the proposed technique. Section 5 describes the details of the dataset and the obtained experimental results. The discussion and limitations are presented in Section 6, while the conclusions are summarized in Section 7.

## 2. Related Work

Feature extraction based on sparse representations has been widely introduced for several tasks [26–29]. For example, Liu et al. [26] designed sparse coding based on dictionary learning with orthogonal matching pursuit (OMP) to extract sparse features for fault classification and recognition. Ma et al. [27] presented a joint sparse coding learning method for early fault feature extraction in rotating machinery with the aim of preserving weak fault features, promoting sparsity, and removing noise, thereby enhancing predictive maintenance. G. S. V. S. Sivaram et al. [28] introduced a novel speech recognition feature extraction technique using sparse coding. Speech spectro–temporal patterns are represented as sparse linear combinations of an overcomplete set of dictionaries. The proposed technique outperform conventional features in both clean and noisy conditions. H. Amintoosi et al. [29] presented a novel two-factor authentication mechanism for IoT devices, addressing the challenge of heterogeneity and security concerns. The proposed method utilizes sparse coding for feature extraction for remote user biometric authentication. By employing hash operations and an overcomplete dictionary, it efficiently stores and retrieves biometric data. Furthermore, many recent works have shown that sparse coding is well-applied to biometrics recognition and classification tasks [15,30,31], such as B. M. Whitaker et al. [30] presenting a method for classifying heart sounds using sparse coding. Preprocessed audio data are decomposed into a dictionary matrix representing key features and a sparse coefficient matrix mapping these features to each segment. M. C. Yo et al. [31] investigated the impact of sparse coding in face recognition by using PCA and sparse representation classification (SRC) with a public image dataset. The proposed method enhances face recognition with significant accuracy. In our previous work [15], we proposed a feature extraction method for hand gesture classification using sparse coding based on a Gaussian random dictionary to reduce the number of features. The optimizer in the previous work was the Frobenius norm, which was used to solve the optimization problem and obtain sparse coefficients. Additionally, the evaluation was performed on a dataset consisting of only five objects (two-Euro coin, credit card, salt shaker, screw, and marker). The results showed that the sparse-coding-based approach improved feature reduction performance. However, the classification accuracy was not satisfactory. Several related works have shown that sparse-representation-based approaches have achieved satisfactory performance and motivated various works in the feature extraction tasks [15,26–31].

Inspired by the success of the sparse-coding-based approach, this work proposes a sparse coding method based on a dictionary learning algorithm. This method utilizes the L1-norm as the optimizer to find the sparsest coefficients (the lowest number of nonzeros) for hand-grasp-type classification.

## 3. Sparse Coding Feature Extraction Based on Dictionary Learning Approach

Sparse coding represents an unsupervised learning approach with the objective of attaining a sparse representation of input data through a linear combination of fundamental elements known as atoms, which are organized in a dictionary. In this paper, we propose the utilization of sparse coding based on dictionary learning as a feature extraction method. This method is designed to capture relevant features from data. The main idea of the proposed method is related to the ability to reconstruct high-dimensional signals using only a few linear measurements under the condition that the signal exhibits sparsity or near-sparsity. The algorithm's outline is shown in Algorithm 1. Initially, an initial dictionary is generated by randomizing raw data. Subsequently, this initial dictionary is employed in the construction of an updated dictionary through the application of an online dictionary learning algorithm [32]:

$$\min_{D \in C} \lim_{n \to +\infty} \frac{1}{n} \sum_{i=1}^{n} \left( \frac{1}{2} \|x_i - D\alpha_i\|_2^2 + \lambda \|\alpha_i\|_1 \right) \tag{1}$$

Given $x_i = [x_1, \ldots, x_n] \in \mathbb{R}^{m \times n}$ is a training set of signals, $D$ is a dictionary, $\lambda$ is a sparsity-inducing regularizer, $\alpha = [\alpha_1, \ldots, \alpha_n] \in \mathbb{R}^{k \times n}$ are the coefficients of the sparse decomposition, and $C$ is the convex set of matrices verifying this constraint:

$$C \triangleq \left\{ D \in \mathbb{R}^{m \times k} \text{ s.t. } \forall j = 1, \ldots, k, d_j^T d_j \leq 1 \right\} \tag{2}$$

note that $k$ is prescribed as 70 to construct a dictionary. Assume a matrix of signals $x = [x_1, \ldots, x_n] \in \mathbb{R}^{m \times n}$ and a learned dictionary from Equation (1). To obtain a matrix of sparse coefficients $\alpha = [\alpha_1, \ldots, \alpha_n] \in \mathbb{R}^{k \times n}$, the learned dictionary was utilized by using the sparse decomposition technique [33] that implemented a least angle regression (LARS) algorithm [34] based on the L1-norm for solving the lasso problem of Equation (3). The LARS algorithm can improve the effectiveness of solving the lasso problem. Moreover, the LARS algorithm is particularly useful for feature extraction as it can reduce the number of features by the sparsest coefficients to zero and speed up the process as a matrix factorization problem:

$$\min_{\alpha \in \mathbb{R}^k} \|x - D\alpha\|_2^2 \text{ s.t. } \|\alpha\|_1 \leq \lambda \tag{3}$$

The matrix of sparse coefficients $\alpha$ from Equation (3) is represented as a significant feature of hand kinematics that will be used as the training set for classification to evaluate the performance of the feature extraction method based on the sparse coding approach.

**Algorithm 1** Online Dictionary Learning

**Require:** $x \in \mathbb{R}^m \sim p(x)$ (independent and identically distributed random variable samples of $p$), regularization parameter $\alpha \in \mathbb{R}$, initial dictionary $D_0 \in \mathbb{R}^{m \times k}$, number of iterations $T$

$A_0 \in \mathrm{R}^{k \times k} \leftarrow 0$, $B_0 \in \mathrm{R}^{m \times k} \leftarrow 0$ (reset the past information)
**for** $t = 1$ to $T$ **do**
  Draw $x_t$ from $p(x)$
  Sparse coding: compute using LARS

$$\alpha_t \triangleq \underset{\alpha \in \mathbb{R}^k}{\operatorname{argmin}} \frac{1}{2} \|x_t - D_{t-1}\alpha\|_2^2 + \lambda \|\alpha\|_1 \tag{4}$$

  $A_t \leftarrow A_{t-1} + \alpha_t \alpha_t^T$.

**Algorithm 1** *Cont.*

$B_t \leftarrow B_{t-1} + x_t \alpha_t^T$.

Compute $D_t$ based on Algorithm 2, with $D_{t-1}$ as warm restart:

$$
\begin{aligned}
D_t &\triangleq \underset{D \in C}{\text{argmin}} \frac{1}{t} \sum_{i=1}^{t} \left( \frac{1}{2} \|x_i - D\alpha_i\|_2^2 + \lambda \|\alpha_i\|_1 \right), \\
&= \underset{D \in C}{\text{argmin}} \frac{1}{t} \sum_{i=1}^{t} \left( \frac{1}{2} \|x_i - D\alpha_i\|_2^2 + \lambda \|\alpha_i\|_1 \right)
\end{aligned}
\tag{5}
$$

**end for**

Return $D_T$ (learned dictionary).

**Algorithm 2** Dictionary Update

**Require:** Input dictionary $D = [d_1, \ldots, d_k] \in \mathbb{R}^{m \times k}$,

$A = [a_1, \ldots, a_k] \in \mathbb{R}^{k \times k}, B = [b_1, \ldots, b_k] \in \mathbb{R}^{m \times k}$

**repeat**

**for** $j = 1$ to $k$ **do**

Update the $j$-th column to optimize for Equation (5)

$$
\begin{aligned}
u_j &\leftarrow \frac{1}{A[j,j]}(b_j - Da_j) + d_j, \\
d_j &\leftarrow \frac{1}{\|u_j\|_2, 1} u_j.
\end{aligned}
\tag{6}
$$

**end for**

Until convergence

Return $D$ (updated dictionary).

## 4. Neural Network Classification

Neural network classification was utilized to evaluate the efficiencies of the proposed feature extraction. The UNIPI dataset contains hand kinematics data and is composed of 2 trials from 6 participants and involves 19 objects, and it was subjected to training using the "fitcnet" function within the MATLAB 2022b and classified into five grasping types. This training process employed a feedforward neural network for classification purposes. The initial fully connected layer of the model was linked to the predictor data, with each subsequent sublayer connected to the preceding one. Within each layer, the input was multiplied by a weight matrix and subsequently had a bias vector added to it. Furthermore, the rectified linear unit (ReLU) function served as the activation function. The limited-memory Broyden–Fletcher–Goldfarb–Shanno (LBFGS) algorithm was employed as the parameter estimation solver. In the final layer, the softmax function was applied as the activation function to generate the output, which consisted of classification scores and predicted labels. A summary of all hyperparameters used in the proposed method can be found in Table 1.

**Table 1.** Hyperparameters of NN classification.

| Hyperparameter | Value |
|---|---|
| Layer size | 40 |
| Cost function | Cross-entropy |
| Activation function | Rectified linear unit (ReLU) |
| Output classifier | Softmax function |
| Parameter estimation solver | Limited-memory Broyden–Fletcher–Goldfarb–Shano algorithm (LBFGS) |
| Regularization parameter (lambda) | 0 |

## 5. Experiments

A kinematic hand dataset in a time-series format was utilized to demonstrate the effectiveness of the proposed method. The details of the dataset are described in this section. The dataset contains recordings of hand movements involving 21 objects and can be categorized into 5 grasp types, as shown in Table 2. The classification results of these five grasp types were used to evaluate the performance of the proposed method, which is also detailed in this section. All experiments were conducted on a MacBook Pro (14-inch, 2021) running macOS, equipped with an Apple M1 Pro 8-core CPU and 16 GB of unified memory, and using MATLAB 2022b.

**Table 2.** The details of 19 objects and hand grasp types.

| No. | Object | Hand Grasp Type |
|---|---|---|
| 1 | 2-Euro Coin | |
| 2 | Button Badge | Flip |
| 3 | Key | |
| 4 | Credit Card | |
| 5 | CD | Edge |
| 6 | Hair-Coloring Comb | |
| 7 | Saltshaker | |
| 8 | Tape | |
| 9 | Chess (Queen) | Closing |
| 10 | Knob | |
| 11 | Matchbox | |
| 12 | Screw | |
| 13 | Match | Pinch |
| 14 | Cigarette | |
| 15 | Rubber Band | |
| 16 | Maker | |
| 17 | Screwdriver | Rotation |
| 18 | Shashlik | |
| 19 | Glasses | |

### 5.1. Dataset

The UNIPI dataset [35] provides hand kinematics data based on visual sensors to investigate postural synergies of human grasping by six subjects during asked notification to grasp objects that can be described as a hand posture behavior from a hand kinematic perspective. Regarding the participants, six volunteers were invited to record and test in the experiments. The six volunteers, including three females and three males, were 23–27 years old and had a mean age of 25.17 years. All volunteers were tested in the experiment based on self-reported right-hand dominance. All volunteers had no neuromuscular disorders that affected the investigation's experimental purpose. Before the experiment, all volunteers signed a consent form to participate in the investigation. The acquisition setup consisted of two significant acquisition sources. First was the PhaseSpace Motion Capture system, which records kinematics data based on three-dimensional motion tracking with active LED markers. The system includes stereo cameras for tracking the 3D positions of active LED markers, which are attached to the volunteer's hand and phalanges. The second source was the set of 21 objects that were selected. In this dataset, two objects were displaced as we could not clarify the hand grasp types. Then, we considered only 19 objects and clarified them into 5 grasp types as shown in Table 2. Figure 4 depicts sequences of examples illustrating various grasping types. In the first row, the hand employs a key to execute a flip-type grasp. Moving to the second row, a credit card is utilized for a sliding grasp: guiding it across the surface to the edge of the table. In the third row, tape is employed for a robust grasp, demonstrating a closing grasp. The fourth row features a screw used for a pinch grasp. Finally, in the last row, a marker is utilized for reorientation in a rotation grasp.

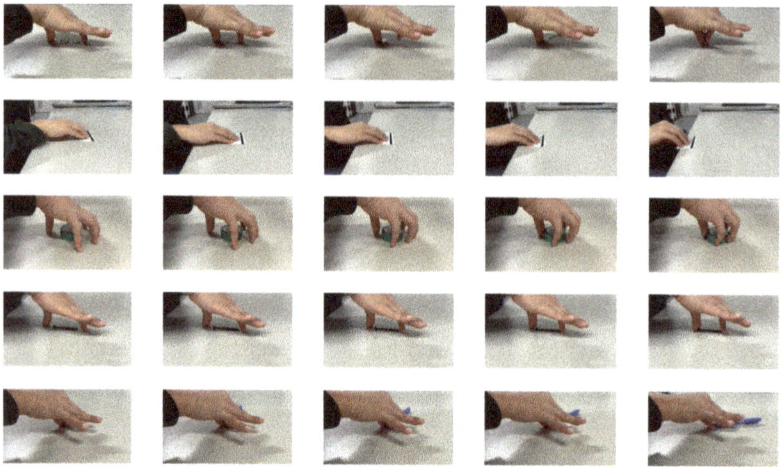

**Figure 4.** Sequences to illustrate five grasp types.

The kinematics model of the human hand has complexity that needs to be described and investigated. In this work, the kinematics model of the human hand is considered based on 20 degrees of freedom, as illustrated in Figure 5. Four long fingers, consisting of the index, middle, ring, and little, are described by four angles. Each long finger is described based on motions of the joint that have two DoFs at the metacarpophalangeal joints to describe flexion–extension and abduction–adduction mobilities along with one DoF at the proximal and distal interphalangeal joints to describe flexion–extension mobilities. The thumb is represented based on motions of four joints that have two DoFs at the trapeziometacarpal for expressing flexion–extension and abduction–adduction mobilities, along with one DoF at the metacarpophalangeal joints, and one DoF at the interphalangeal joint to describe flexion–extension mobility. The kinematic structure of the human hand model is described by Denavit–Hartenberg (DH) parameters to express the kinematic chain of each finger [35]. The description of hand kinematics based on 20 DoFs is described in Table 3.

**Table 3.** Description of degrees of freedom.

| No. | DoFs | Description |
|---|---|---|
| 1 | TA | Thumb Abduction |
| 2 | TR | Thumb Rotation |
| 3 | TM | Thumb Metacarpal |
| 4 | TI | Thumb Interphalangeal |
| 5 | IA | Index Abduction |
| 6 | IM | Index Metacarpal |
| 7 | IP | Index Proximal |
| 8 | ID | Index Distal |
| 9 | MA | Middle Abduction |
| 10 | MM | Middle Metacarpal |
| 11 | MP | Middle Proximal |
| 12 | MD | Middle Distal |
| 13 | RA | Ring Abduction |
| 14 | RM | Ring Metacarpal |
| 15 | RP | Ring Proximal |
| 16 | RD | Ring Distal |
| 17 | LA | Little Abduction |
| 18 | LM | Little Metacarpal |
| 19 | LP | Little Proximal |
| 20 | LD | Little Distal |

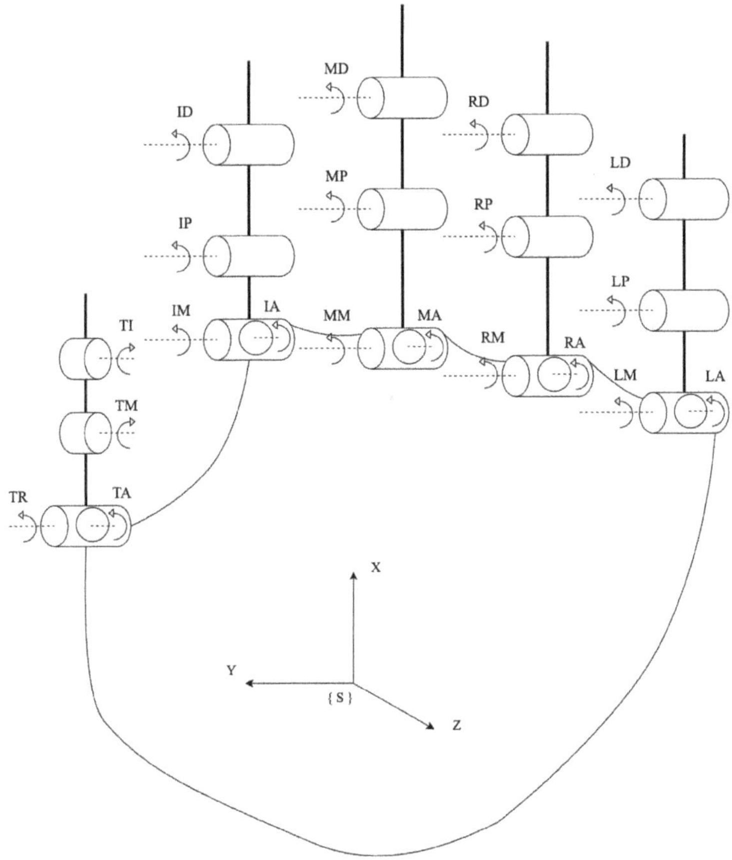


**Figure 5.** Kinematic model of the human hand.

### 5.2. Results for the UNIPI Dataset

The UNIPI dataset contributed hand kinematics data. The dataset is divided into 19 different objects, with each object subjected to 2 separate trials. In the first step, we applied data processing techniques to ensure that the kinematic data were in a suitable time-series format by adjusting for differences in data length. This involved resampling processes to effectively format the data by utilizing linear interpolation to adjust the length of the dataset to a specific size (500 time series). Before the next process, the resampled data were utilized to construct training and test sets using random partitions for holdout cross-validation. The training dataset comprised approximately 80% of the kinematic data, while the validation dataset accounted for the remaining 20%. The second step focused on feature extraction, where we employed the proposed technique based on dictionary learning constructed from the training set. The necessary parameters to construct the learned dictionary as $k$ is prescribed as 70, and the number of iterations $T$ was 100 iterations. The learned dictionary was utilized to obtain sparse coefficients based on sparse decomposition from the training and test sets. Additionally, principal component analysis (PCA) was employed to extract features from the pre-processed data, serving as a benchmark for comparing the efficiency of the proposed technique with the traditional technique for classifying grasping types. The selection of PCA as a benchmark was influenced by this research and was based on its linearity and well-known effectiveness for hand-based feature extraction tasks. Specifically, we chose two principal components for experimentation in benchmarking. This choice aimed to capture essential information while minimizing the number of components and ensuring a meaningful representation of the entire dataset's variance. These criteria provide a foundation for a meaningful and informative comparison with the proposed sparse coding approach. The final step involved classification based on neural network classification, where the goal of classification was to identify grasping types based on hand kinematic data. The sparse coefficients from the training set were used to train the NN classification model. The sparse coefficient from the test set was utilized to evaluate the performance of the NN classification model. The classification results are visualized by using a confusion matrix. The proposed feature extraction process, along with PCA as the feature extraction technique, incorporated sparse coding based on dictionary learning. The dictionary was constructed using a dictionary learning function [32]. Sparse coefficients were computed using a sparse decomposition toolbox [33], which implemented the LARS algorithm to enhance the effectiveness of solving the lasso problem and accelerate the process. To evaluate the performance of the proposed technique and compare it with PCA, we utilized a neural network classification toolbox.

The experimental results obtained from the neural network classification are presented in Table 4, which showcases a comparison of the proposed method with other approaches. These approaches include using raw data (preprocessed without feature extraction), principal component analysis (PCA), sparse coding based on a Gaussian random dictionary, and the proposed dictionary learning technique. The comparison of accuracy was evaluated using confusion matrices for four cases: without feature extraction, PCA, sparse coding based on a Gaussian random dictionary, and the proposed method, as shown in Figure 6a,b,c,d, respectively. Table 4 shows significant differences in classification accuracy. The PCA method achieved an accuracy of 31.43%, which is markedly lower than that of the proposed method, which demonstrated an accuracy of 81.78%. Additionally, it is remarkable that the accuracy of the PCA method is significantly lower than that of the raw data, which yielded an accuracy of 68.38%. Sparse coding based on the Gaussian random dictionary achieved an accuracy of 77.27%, demonstrating better performance than PCA but still lower performance than the proposed dictionary learning technique. Figure 7a–d shows the ROC curves of each feature extraction techniques, it is clearly to see that the proposed method provides higher recall rate compare with other techniques. Moreover, Table 4 includes the number of features used with raw data, PCA, the Gaussian random dictionary, and the proposed dictionary learning technique. The proposed technique achieved the highest accuracy with the fewest number of features for grasp type classification using hand kinematic data.

To further enhance the performance evaluation, the macro-average F1-scores and average area under the curve (AUC) scores, which are depicted in Figure 8, are included in Table 4. These additional metrics offer insights into the model's precision, recall, and overall discriminative ability. The proposed sparse coding technique outperforms both PCA and the Gaussian random dictionary in terms of accuracy, macro-average F1-scores, and average AUC. Specifically, the macro-average F1-scores are 79.87 for the proposed method, 66.65 for raw data, 76.06 for the Gaussian random dictionary, and only 20.12 for PCA. The average AUC values further confirm the superior performance of the proposed method, with a score of 0.9535, compared to 0.8958 for raw data, 0.93926 for the Gaussian random dictionary, and 0.5701 for PCA. These numerical results emphasize the effectiveness of the proposed sparse coding approach for achieving accurate and robust hand grasp type classification with reduced feature dimensions.

**Table 4.** Comparison of classification performance between raw data, principal component analysis (PCA), sparse coding based on Gaussian random dictionary, and dictionary learning.

| Method | Accuracy (%) | Number of Features | Macro-Average F1-Score | Average AUC |
|---|---|---|---|---|
| Raw Data | 68.38 | 1,620,299 | 66.65 | 0.8958 |
| PCA | 31.43 | 855,000 | 20.12 | 0.5701 |
| Gaussian Random | 77.27 | 1,823,449 | 76.06 | 0.93926 |
| Dictionary Learning | 81.78 | 678,678 | 79.87 | 0.9535 |

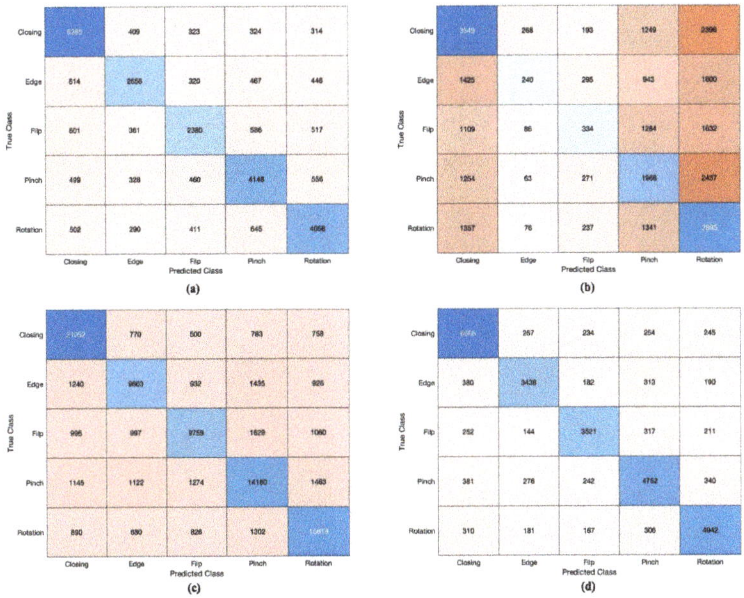


**Figure 6.** Confusion matrices for NN classification using several feature extraction techniques: (**a**) raw data, (**b**) PCA, (**c**) sparse coding based on Gaussian random dictionary, and (**d**) sparse coding based on dictionary learning.

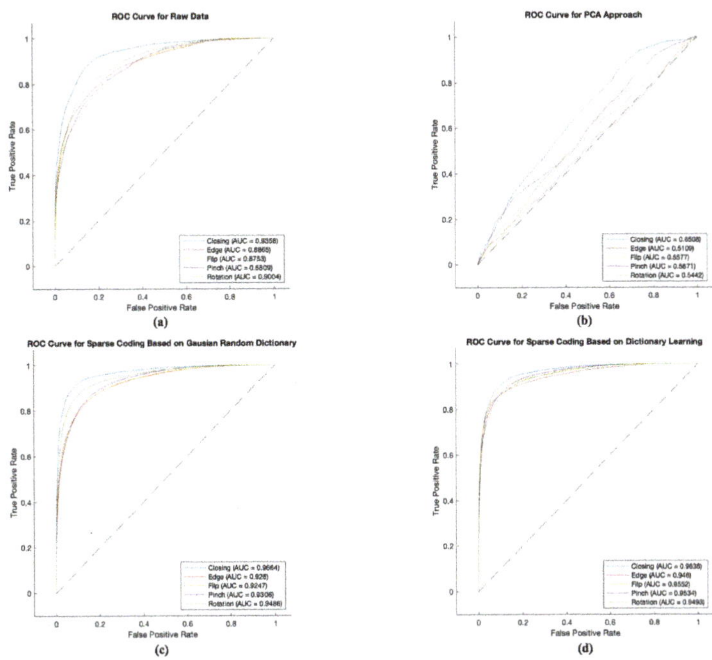


**Figure 7.** ROC curve of feature extraction techniques: (**a**) raw data, (**b**) PCA, (**c**) sparse coding based on Gaussian random dictionary, and (**d**) sparse coding based on dictionary learning.

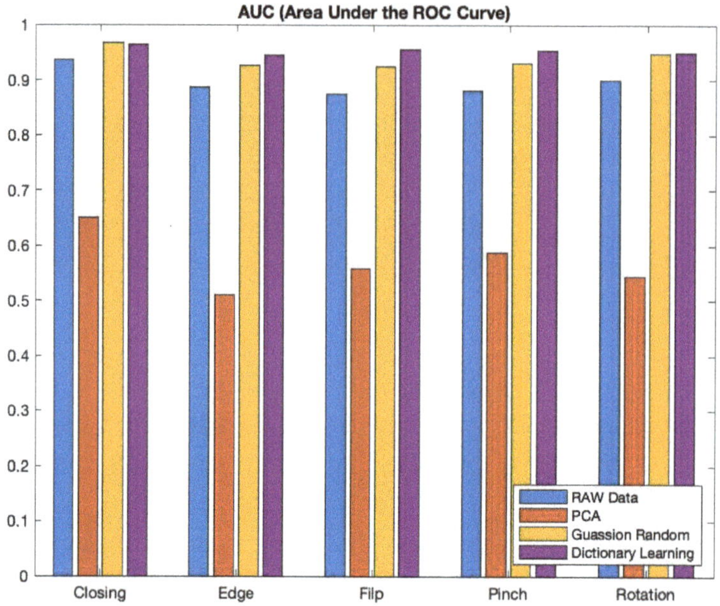


**Figure 8.** Comparison of AUC values for each class between raw data, PCA, sparse coding based on Gaussian random dictionary, and dictionary learning approach.

## 6. Discussion and Limitations

In the discussion section, we analyze and interpret the results obtained from our experiments, focusing on various performance factors and how our proposed system addresses the challenges highlighted in the introductory part of the article. Firstly, we observed significant improvements in classification accuracy with the proposed sparse-coding-based feature extraction method compared to traditional techniques such as principal component analysis (PCA). As shown in Table 4, the sparse coding approach achieved an accuracy of 81.78%, outperforming PCA by a substantial margin. This improvement can be attributed to the ability of sparse coding to capture essential features while effectively reducing data dimensionality. By representing hand kinematic data as a sparse linear combination of basis functions, the sparse coding method can extract discriminative features crucial for accurate classification.

Additionally, our proposed method offers versatility and applicability across a wide range of classification tasks. Furthermore, the number of features was significantly reduced using the proposed method (678,678 features) compared to raw data (1,620,299 features), PCA (855,000 features), and sparse coding based on Gaussian random dictionary (1,823,449). This reduction in feature dimensionality not only simplifies the computational complexity but also enhances the interpretability of the model. Moreover, the macro-average F1-scores and average AUC values for the proposed methods were substantially higher at 79.87 and 0.9535, respectively, compared to other methods, further highlighting the superior performance of our proposed approach. While the sparse coding approach using a Gaussian random dictionary (shown in Table 4) achieved a respectable accuracy of 77.27%, it fell short of the superior performance achieved by our proposed dictionary learning method (81.78% accuracy). This highlights the importance of learning an dictionary that has been optimized to the specific data for achieving the best results.

In terms of addressing the issues highlighted, the proposed technique effectively tackles the challenge of feature extraction for hand kinematic analysis. By employing sparse coding based on dictionary learning techniques, we can extract meaningful features from high-dimensional kinematic data, reducing the complexity of the dataset while preserving essential information. This approach addresses the need for efficient data representation and dimensionality reduction in hand kinematic analysis, facilitating more accurate classification of grasping types. The experimental results validate the effectiveness of the sparse-coding-based feature extraction method based on dictionary learning for hand kinematic analysis and classification. By achieving higher accuracy compared to traditional techniques, these results indicate that our method not only enhances classification accuracy but also effectively reduces feature dimensionality, making it a valuable tool for practical applications in robotics, medicine, and rehabilitation. Future work could explore the application of our method to other types of hand kinematic data and investigate its performance in real-time systems.

In this research, the proposed feature extraction technique was implemented specifically on the UNIPI dataset for classification purposes. Consequently, they may not be directly applicable to other publicly available datasets related to hand kinematics. Furthermore, while the proposed technique proves effective for hand kinematic analysis, it may not be suitable for analyzing hand synergies due to its design limitations. Future research could explore further optimizations and extensions of the proposed method as well as its application in other domains such as natural language processing.

## 7. Conclusions

In this paper, we proposed a novel sparse coding feature extraction technique based on dictionary learning for classifying human hand grasp types. Our method significantly improves classification accuracy and reduces the number of features required compared to PCA- and Gaussian-random-dictionary-based approaches. The classification accuracy of our proposed technique is compared with PCA and sparse coding based on a Gaussian random dictionary. The results from the classification experiments clearly showed that the proposed method is highly effective at classifying hand grasp types. Specifically, the classification accuracy achieved by the proposed scheme is significantly higher than that of PCA-based and other feature extraction techniques. These findings have important implications for various applications, including robotics and rehabilitation. Future research will focus on extending our technique to other types of hand kinematic data and exploring its real-time application potential. Finally, the sparse-coding-based feature extraction based on the dictionary learning approach presented in this paper provides an alternative feature extraction method for classification. Its potential for broader applications makes it a valuable contribution to the field of machine learning (ML). Particularly, in natural language processing (NLP), feature extraction is a fundamental process for converting raw text data into a proper format that can be easily processed by utilizing machine learning algorithms.

**Author Contributions:** Conceptualization, J.S. and P.K.; methodology, J.S., P.K. and N.T.M.; software, J.S. and P.K.; validation, M.A.S.K. and I.M.; formal analysis, J.S. and K.Y.; investigation, K.Y.; resources, K.Y.; data curation, J.S.; writing—original draft preparation, J.S.; writing—review and editing, P.K. and K.Y.; supervision, K.Y.; project administration, K.Y.; funding acquisition, K.Y. All authors have read and agreed to the published version of the manuscript.

**Funding:** This research received no external funding.

**Institutional Review Board Statement:** Not applicable.

**Informed Consent Statement:** Not applicable.

**Data Availability Statement:** No new data were created or analyzed in this study. Data sharing is not applicable to this article.

**Conflicts of Interest:** The authors declare no conflicts of interest. The funders had no role in the design of the study; in the collection, analyses, or interpretation of data; in the writing of the manuscript; or in the decision to publish the results.

## References


1. Santello, S.M.; Flanders, M.; Soechting, J.F. Postural hand synergies for tool use. *J. Neurosci.* **1998**, *18*, 10105–10115. [CrossRef] [PubMed]
2. Carpinella, I.; Mazzoleni, P.; Rabuffetti, M.; Thorsen, R.; Ferrarin, M. Experimental protocol for the kinematic analysis of the hand: Definition and repeatability. *Gait Posture* **2006**, *23*, 445–454. [CrossRef] [PubMed]
3. Santello, M.; Flanders, M.; Soechting, J.F. Patterns of hand motion during grasping and the influence of sensory guidance. *J. Neurosci.* **2002**, *22*, 1426–1435. [CrossRef] [PubMed]
4. Amor, H.B.; Kroemer, O.; Hillenbrand, U.; Neumann, G.; Peters, J. Generalization of human grasping for multi-fingered robot hands. In Proceedings of the IEEE International Workshop on Intelligent Robots and Systems (IROS), Vilamoura, Portugal, 7–12 October 2012; pp. 2043–2050.
5. Normani, N.; Urru, A.; Abraham, L.; Walsh, M.; Tedesco, S.; Cenedese, A.; Susto, G.A.; O'Flynn, B. A Machine learning approach for gesture recognition with a lensless smart sensor system. In Proceedings of the IEEE 15th International Conference on Wearable and Implantable Body Sensor Networks (BSN), Las Vegas, NV, USA, 4–7 March 2018; pp. 4–7.
6. Núñez, J.C.; Cabido, R.; Pantrigo, J.J.; Montemayor, A.S.; Vélez, J.F. Convolutional neural networks and long short-term memory for skeleton-based human activity and hand gesture recognition. *J. Pattern Recognit.* **2018**, *76*, 80–94. [CrossRef]
7. Li, S.; Zhang, H.; Shi, Y.; Yang, J. Novel local coding algorithm for multimodal finger feature description and recognition. *Sensors* **2019**, *19*, 2213. [CrossRef] [PubMed]
8. Ojala, T.; Pietikainen, M.; Maenpaa, T. Multiresolution gray-scale and rotation invariant texture classification with local binary patterns. *IEEE Transation Pattern Anal. Mach. Intell.* **2002**, *24*, 971–987. [CrossRef]
9. Jia, W.; Hu, R.X.; Lei, Y.K.; Zhao, Y.; Gui, J. Histogram of oriented lines for palmprint recognition. *IEEE Trans. Syst. Man Cybern. Syst.* **2014**, *44* 385–395. [CrossRef]
10. Rida, I.; AlMaadeed, S.; Mahmood, A.; Bouridane, A.; Bakshi, S. Palmprint identification using an ensemble of sparse representations. *IEEE Access* **2018**, *6*, 3241–3248. [CrossRef]
11. Sun, Z.N.; Tan, T.N.; Wang, Y.H.; Li, S.Z. Ordinal palmprint representation for personal identification. In Proceeding of the IEEE Computer Vision Pattern Recognition, San Diego, CA, USA, 20–26 June 2005; pp. 279–284.
12. Zhang, L.; Zhang, L.; Zhang, D.; Zhu, H. Online finger-knuckle-print verification for personal authentication. *Pattern Recognit.* **2010**, *43*, 2560–2571. [CrossRef]
13. Zhang, L.; Li, L.; Yang, A.; Shen, Y.; Yang, M. Towards contactless palmprint recognition: A novel device, a new benchmark, and a collaborative representation based identification approach. *Pattern Recognit.* **2017**, *69*, 199–212. [CrossRef]
14. Li, S.; Zhang, B. Joint Discriminative Sparse Coding for Robust Hand-Based Multimodal Recognition. *IEEE Trans. Inf. Forensics Secur.* **2021**, *16*, 3186–3198. [CrossRef]
15. Samkunta, J.; Ketthong, P.; Hashikura, K.; Kamal, M.A.S.; Murakami, I.; Yamada, K. Feature reduction for hand gesture classification: Sparse coding approach. In Proceedings of the 20th International Conference on Electrical Engineering/Electronics, Computer, Telecommunications and Information Technology (ECTI-CON), Nakhon Phanom, Thailand, 9–12 May 2023; pp. 1–4.
16. Todorov, E.; Ghahramani, Z. Analysis of the synergies underlying complex hand manipulation. In Proceeding of the 26th Annual International Conference of the IEEE Engineering in Medicine and Biology Society, San Francisco, CA, USA, 1–5 September 2004; pp. 4637–4640.
17. Jarque-Bou, N.J.; Scano, A.; Atzori, M.; Müller, H. Kinematic synergies of hand grasps A comprehensive study on a large publicly available dataset. *NeuroEngineering Rehabil* **2019**, *16*, 63. [CrossRef] [PubMed]
18. Lapresa, M.; Zollo, L.; Cordella, F. A user-friendly automatic toolbox for hand kinematic analysis, clinical assessment and postural synergies extraction. *Front. Bioeng. Biotechnol.* **2022**, *10*, 1010073. [CrossRef] [PubMed]
19. Hemeren, P.; Peter, V.; Swege, T.; Jiong, S. Kinematic-based classification of social gestures and grasping by humans and machine learning techniques. *Front. Robot. AI* **2021**, *8*, 699505. [CrossRef] [PubMed]
20. Wang, N.; Lao, K.; Zhang, X.; Lin, J.; Zhang, X. The recognition of grasping force using LDA. *Biomed. Signal Process. Control* **2019**, *47*, 393–400. [CrossRef]
21. Jarque-Bou, N.J.; Vergara, M.; Sancho-Bru, J.L.; Gracia-Ibanz, V.; Roda-Sales, A. Hand kinematics characterization while performing activities of daily living through kinematics reduction. *IEEE Trans. Neural Syst. Rehabil. Eng.* **2020**, *28*, 1556–1565. [CrossRef] [PubMed]
22. Battaglia, E.; Kasman, M.; Fey, A.M. Moving past principal component analysis Nonlinear dimensionality reduction towards better hand pose synthesis. In Proceedings of the International Symposium on Medical Robotics (ISMR), Atlanta, GA, USA, 13–15 April 2022.
23. He, K.; Zhang, X.; Ren, S.; Sun, J. Deep residual learning for image recognition. In Proceedings of the IEEE Conference Computer Vision Pattern Recognition (CVPR), Las Vegas, NV, USA, 27–30 June 2016; pp. 770–778.
24. Baygin, M.; Barua, P.D.; Dogan, S.; Tuncer, T.; Key, S.; Acharya, U.R.; Cheong, K.H. A Hand-Modeled Feature Extraction-Based Learning Network to Detect Grasps Using sEMG Signal. *Sensors* **2022**, *22*, 2007. [CrossRef] [PubMed]
25. Reza, B.A.; Mohammad, E.; Mehrdad, N. EMG-Based Feature Extraction and Classification for Prosthetic Hand Control. *arXiv* **2021**, arXiv:2107.00733.

26. Liu, C.; Wu, X.; Liu, T. Sparse feature extraction based on sparse representation and dictionary learning for rolling bearing fault diagnosis. In Proceedings of the International Conference on Applied System Innovation (ICASI), Sapporo, Japan, 13–17 May 2017; pp. 1733–1735.
27. Ma, S.; Han, Q.; Chu, F. Sparse representation learning for fault feature extraction and diagnosis of rotating machinery. *Expert Syst. Appl.* **2023**, *232*, 120858. [CrossRef]
28. Sivaram, G.S.V.S.; Nemala, S.K.; Elhilali, M.; Tran, T.D.; Hermansky, H. Sparse coding for speech recognition. In Proceedings of the IEEE International Conference on Acoustics, Speech and Signal Processing, Dallas, TX, USA, 14–19 March 2010; pp. 4346–4349.
29. Amintoosi, H.; Taresh, A.J. Sparse coding-based feature extraction for biometric remote authentication in Internet of Things. *SN Appl. Sci.* **2019**, *1*, 1098. [CrossRef]
30. Whitaker, B.M.; Suresha, P.B.; Liu, C.; Clifford, G.D.; Anderson, D.V. Combining sparse coding and time-domain features for heart sound classification. *Physiol. Meas.* **2017**, *38*, 1701–1713. [CrossRef] [PubMed]
31. Yo, M.C.; Chong, S.C.; Wee, K.K.; Chong, L.Y. Sparse representation with principal component analysis in face recognition. *J. Syst. Manag. Sci.* **2022**, *12*, 57–72.
32. Julien, M.; Francis, B.; Jean, P.; Guillermo, S. Online dictionary learning for matrix factorization and sparse coding. *J. Mach. Learn. Res.* **2010**, *11*, 19–60.
33. Mairal, J.; Bach, F.; Ponce, J.; Sapiro, G. Online dictionary learning for sparse coding. In Proceedings of the International Conference on Machine Learning (ICML), Montreal, QC, Canada, 14–18 June 2009; pp. 689–696.
34. Efron, B.; Hastie, T.; Johnstone, I.; Tibshirani, R. Least angle regression. *Ann. Stat.* **2004**, *32*, 407–451. [CrossRef]
35. Santina, C.D.; Bianchi, M.; Averta, G.; Ciotti, S.; Arapi, V.; Fani, S.; Battaglia, E.; Catalano, M.G.; Santello, M.; Bicchi, A. Postural Hand Synergies during Environmental Constraint Exploitation. *IEEE Trans. Robot.* **2017**, *33*, 252–269. [CrossRef]

algorithms

MDPI

*Article*

# Assessing the Ability of Genetic Programming for Feature Selection in Constructing Dispatching Rules for Unrelated Machine Environments

**Marko Đurasević [1,*,†], Domagoj Jakobović [1,†], Stjepan Picek [2,†] and Luca Mariot [3,†]**

[1] Faculty of Electrical Engineering and Computing, University of Zagreb, 10000 Zagreb, Croatia; domagoj.jakobovic@fer.hr
[2] Digital Security Group, Radboud University, 6525 XZ Nijmegen, The Netherlands; stjepan.picek@ru.nl
[3] Semantics, Cybersecurity and Services Group, University of Twente, 7522 NB Enschede, The Netherlands; l.mariot@utwente.nl
* Correspondence: marko.durasevic@fer.hr
† These authors contributed equally to this work.

**Abstract:** The automated design of dispatching rules (DRs) with genetic programming (GP) has become an important research direction in recent years. One of the most important decisions in applying GP to generate DRs is determining the features of the scheduling problem to be used during the evolution process. Unfortunately, there are no clear rules or guidelines for the design or selection of such features, and often the features are simply defined without investigating their influence on the performance of the algorithm. However, the performance of GP can depend significantly on the features provided to it, and a poor or inadequate selection of features for a given problem can result in the algorithm performing poorly. In this study, we examine in detail the features that GP should use when developing DRs for unrelated machine scheduling problems. Different types of features are investigated, and the best combination of these features is determined using two selection methods. The obtained results show that the design and selection of appropriate features are crucial for GP, as they improve the results by about 7% when only the simplest terminal nodes are used without selection. In addition, the results show that it is not possible to outperform more sophisticated manually designed DRs when only the simplest problem features are used as terminal nodes. This shows how important it is to design appropriate composite terminal nodes to produce high-quality DRs.

**Keywords:** genetic programming; feature selection; unrelated machine problem; feature selection; scheduling

## 1. Introduction

The unrelated parallel machine scheduling problem is an important combinatorial optimisation problem with frequent applications in the real world [1], such as task scheduling [2], device scheduling [3], and manufacturing [4]. Since the problem is NP-hard, it is traditionally solved using various metaheuristic optimisation methods [5,6]. However, since real-world problems are often dynamic in nature, traditional optimisation approaches that continuously improve potential solutions are usually not directly applicable. The reason for this is that not all information about the problem under consideration may be known, and in this case, it is not possible to construct a complete solution. This was the motivation for researching alternative methods that can be used to solve dynamic problems such as dispatching rules.

Dispatching rules (DRs) have emerged as an alternative solution method for solving various scheduling problems, mostly dynamic problem variants [7]. They represent simple constructive heuristics that solve the problem incrementally by making decisions about which job to schedule next based solely on the information currently available in the system. Therefore, such rules can react quickly to the changing problem environment, as they construct the solution based only on the currently available information. As new information becomes available, they can take it into account when constructing the solution. Although many DRs have been proposed over the years [7], they have been developed for a limited number of problem variants and scheduling criteria. In addition, the developed DRs perform scheduling decisions using simple heuristic strategies, which affects the quality of the plans they produce.

To address the above problems, various methods based on evolutionary computation and machine learning have been used over the years to automatically design new DRs for various problems [8–10]. One of the most commonly used methods for this purpose is genetic programming [11]. GP is an evolutionary computational method developed to enable the generation of various mathematical expressions and even computer programmes [12]. It has been applied in many fields, where it has achieved competitive results with humans [13], proving its effectiveness. In recent years, however, GP has established itself as the leading hyperheuristic method [14,15], a method used to automatically develop new heuristics.

In the context of DRs, GP is used to generate an expression, often referred to as a priority function, that is used by the DR to rank all decisions at each decision point and select the appropriate decision [16]. GP generates the expression based on a set of defined problem characteristics, which it attempts to combine in a meaningful way to determine the optimal scheduling decision at each decision point. Therefore, it is necessary to provide GP with all the relevant information about the problem in the form of terminal nodes representing certain features of the problem. However, an incomplete or wrong choice of terminal nodes can result in myopic DRs that offer poor performance [17]. Regardless, this step is often overlooked, and quite often only the most basic problem information is used as terminal nodes without a selection of appropriate nodes. Naturally, providing too many terminal nodes again has the drawback that the search space of the method grows exponentially, making it more difficult to find high-quality solutions. Although the definition and choice of appropriate terminal nodes is an important decision that significantly affects the quality and complexity of DRs, it has not yet been investigated in the context of the automated design of DRs for unrelated machine environments. Thus, there is no guarantee that the terminal nodes currently applied in the literature are really the most appropriate or whether the results could be improved by applying a different set of terminal nodes.

The aim of this study is to perform a detailed investigation of the influence of different problem properties on the quality of DRs automatically developed by GP for unrelated machine scheduling problems. The motivation for this is to determine the set of the most suitable terminal nodes, with which GP can generate DRs that perform well across a wide range of problem instances. This is done in a sequential manner, where first, simple atomic features are analysed, representing only the most basic information about the problem. Then, composite features are added to the set of terminals to investigate whether by including more sophisticated terminal nodes, either designed automatically or manually, they can improve the performance of the generated DRs. Naturally, only providing the terminal nodes is not enough, since a too-large terminal set can negatively affect the results simply due to a too-large solution space that the algorithm needs to traverse. Therefore, to select the appropriate feature set, we use the backward sequential feature selection method, which is commonly used in the literature for this purpose, but also investigate the ability of GP to perform feature selection by using the frequency of occurrence of nodes in the expressions as a criterion for selecting the appropriate features. From the obtained results, we investigate how the different node sets that were obtained influence not only the performance and complexity of the generated DRs but also the performance of different methods in selecting the appropriate features.

The contributions of this study can be summarised as follows:

- Analysis of how different types of terminal nodes influence the effectiveness of GP to generate good quality DRs and their complexity.
- Construction of new terminal nodes based on the frequency of occurrence of sub-expressions in the generated DRs.
- Application and comparison of two feature selection methods to determine appropriate terminal node sets.

The rest of this study is organised as follows. Section 2 outlines the relevant literature on the generation of DRs with GP. The necessary background information about the problem under consideration and the application of GP to generate DRs is given in Section 3. The methodology used to conduct the investigation in this paper is described in Section 4. Section 5 describes the design of the experimental study and discusses the results obtained. A more in-depth analysis of the results obtained is presented in Section 6. Finally, Section 7 concludes this paper and provides guidance for future research.

## 2. Literature Review

The automated generation of DRs has its roots in the pioneering studies of Miyashita [18] and Dimopoulos and Zalzala [19]. These studies showed that GP can be efficiently used to design new DRs for various scheduling problems. Since then, GP has been applied in numerous studies to generate DRs for various problems, such as the parallel machine scheduling problem [20], flexible job shop problem [21], resource-constrained project scheduling problem [22], and one-machine variable capacity problem [23].

Over the years, many research directions have been explored in the context of the automated design of DRs. One line of research has focused on investigating different representations for DRs. In [24], the authors compared three DR representations: one that generates an expression that selects an existing DR based on system properties to make the scheduling decision, one that generates a new DR from basic system information, and one that combines the previous two approaches. The results showed that the first approach was inferior to the other two approaches. In [25], the potential of GP to generate DRs was compared with that of artificial neural networks. The results showed that both methods performed similarly, but GP developed interpretable and more user-friendly DRs. In [26], the authors investigated several evolutionary algorithms for developing DRs and found that their performance was similar in most cases, although some resulted in simpler DRs. Another line of research focused on the generation of DRs for multi-objective scheduling problems, which were considered in [27–29] for the job shop problem and [30] for the unrelated machine scheduling problem.

Ensemble learning is one of the most widely considered topics related to DR creation, as it has the potential to significantly improve the performance of individual DRs. This topic has been studied from many aspects, including methods used to construct ensembles [31–33], methods used to aggregate the decisions of individual DRs in the ensemble [34,35], and the application of ensemble learning for multi-objective problems [36]. Another way to improve the performance of automatically generated DRs is the application of surrogate models [37,38] and local search [39], both of which have been shown to improve the performance of GP. Another recent research trend is the application of multitask learning in GP, which enables knowledge transfer between individuals to solve different types of problems [40].

Only limited attention has been given to the issues of feature selection and construction in the context of automatic generation of DRs, and this has focused mainly on the job shop scheduling problem. In [41], the authors proposed a feature selection algorithm that is embedded in GP and based on niching. This feature selection method takes into account both the fitness of the individuals in which the features occur and the frequency of occurrence of these features. The experimental results showed that the proposed approach can select features that lead to better results compared to using the entire feature set. In [42], the authors considered feature selection in the context of developing DRs for the flexible job shop problem. In this approach, two terminal sets are used and, therefore, features need to be selected for each of them simultaneously. A GP approach with adaptive search based on the frequency of features was proposed in [43] and was shown to perform better compared to standard GP in some scenarios. Another feature selection approach was proposed in [44], which led to simpler DRs that achieved comparable performance to those developed without feature selection. Finally, in [45], the authors considered feature construction in addition to feature selection, but no follow-ups or extensions to this original research were conducted. Overviews of the literature on the remaining studies dealing with the automated design of DRs for various scheduling problems can be found in [8–10].

The importance of selecting suitable problem features when using GP to create DRs was discussed in [17]. However, studies in this field rarely explore the definition of the features used in solving a particular problem. On the contrary, a particular set of features is usually defined based on previous user experiences, without further investigation into whether this terminal set is really the most appropriate. As can be seen from the previous literature review, although several studies deal with feature selection, they focus on the algorithmic aspect rather than on which features should be used or how they should be designed. Therefore, this study provides a deeper investigation into the definition and selection of features in the automated development of DRs for unrelated machine environments.

## 3. Background

As mentioned previously, the unrelated machine environment appears in many real-world scenarios, such as the manufacturing of pipes, manufacturing cells, distributing jobs in heterogeneous systems, and scheduling in the textile industry, among others [6]. Many of those problems are dynamic in nature, meaning that certain aspects of the problem are not known at the beginning of the system's execution. In such cases, DRs represent the method of choice for solving such problems [7]. However, the performance of existing DRs is quite limited, and they are usually designed for very specific problem variants, thus limiting their performance and generalisation ability. This means that it is required to design DRs for all the different problem variants that are considered. Since it is difficult to manually design DRs for all the available problem variants, the concept of the automated design of DRs has garnered significant attention. One of the most prominent and commonly used approaches for this purpose is GP, which has been successfully used to generate new DRs for various problems.

### 3.1. Unrelated Parallel Machine Scheduling Problem

In the unrelated machine scheduling problem, a set of jobs must be scheduled and executed on a scarce set of machines [46]. Each job contains certain properties that are taken into account in scheduling decisions, such as:

- $p_{ij}$—the processing time of job $j$ on machine $i$.
- $r_j$—the release time of job $j$, which specifies the earliest time at which the job can be considered for scheduling.
- $d_j$—the due date of job $j$, which specifies the time by which the job should finish with its execution.
- $w_j$—the weight of job $j$, which indicates the importance of the job.

Each machine can only process one job at a time. As soon as a machine starts executing a job, it must complete it before it can start executing another job.

Many criteria can be considered and optimised for this problem. In this study, we focus on minimising the total weighted tardiness criterion ($Twt$), defined as $Twt = \sum_j w_j T_j$, which is one of the most frequently optimised criteria in the literature, especially when considering dynamic environments [6]. $T_j$ represents the tardiness of job $j$ and is defined as $T_j = \max(C_j - d_j, 0)$, where $C_j$ indicates the time at which job $j$ was completed. The tardiness, therefore, represents the time the job has been completed after its due date, whereas the total weighted tardiness is simply the combination of all tardiness values multiplied by the corresponding weights. By minimising $Twt$, we effectively minimise the times jobs are completed after their due date.

Using the standard notation $\alpha|\beta|\gamma$ for scheduling problems [47], the problem considered in this study can be specified as $R \mid r_j \mid \sum_j w_j T_j$. In this notation, $\alpha$ represents the machine environment, which in this case, is the unrelated machine environment (denoted by $R$); $\beta$ represents the additional constraints, which in this case, include the release times of the jobs (denoted by $r_j$); and $\gamma$ represents the optimised criterion, which in this case, is the total weighted tardiness (denoted by $\sum_j w_j T_j$). Moreover, the problem is considered under dynamic conditions, which means that not all information about the problem is available during the execution of the system. More precisely, no information about the jobs, including their arrival time, is known before they are released into the system. However, once they are released into the system, all their properties are known precisely, and the jobs can then be taken into account for scheduling.

The most suitable method for solving such dynamic problems is DRs [7]. DRs consist of two parts: a schedule generation scheme (SGS) and a priority function (PF) [48]. The SGS represents the algorithmic framework of the DR, which determines when and under what conditions it performs scheduling decisions. It also ensures that it only creates feasible schedules, for example, by checking that no machine executes two jobs at the same time. Algorithm 1 provides the definition of the SGS that is used by the automatically designed DRs. This SGS performs a scheduling decision every time at least one machine is available and there are unscheduled jobs in the system. It also ensures that no job is scheduled on a machine on which a job is already in progress.

**Algorithm 1** SGS used by generated DRs

**while** true **do**
    Wait until at least one job and one machine are available
    **for** all available jobs $j$ and each machine $i$ in $m$ **do**
        Calculate the priority $\pi_{ij}$ of scheduling $j$ on machine $i$
    **end for**
    **for** all available jobs **do**
        Determine the machine with the best $\pi_{ij}$ value
    **end for**
    **while** jobs whose best available machine exists **do**
        Determine the best priority of all such jobs
        Schedule the job with the best priority
    **end while**
**end while**

One of the most important parts of the SGS is determining which scheduling decision to make at each decision time, i.e., which job should be scheduled on which machine. The SGS uses a PF to evaluate all available decisions. The best decision, determined by the lowest or highest rank, is then selected and executed. Over the years, PFs of varying complexity have been proposed in the literature [7]. For example, the earliest due date (EDD) rule uses a PF defined as $\pi = d_j$, which means that jobs are executed in order according to their due dates. The EDD selects the jobs with the earliest due dates first, where jobs that need to be completed as quickly as possible take priority. The PF can, of course, be much more complex than that defined by the EDD. In fact, the PF is the most important part of any DR, and, therefore, great care needs to be taken when developing new and efficient PFs. However, manually designing meaningful PFs has proven to be quite a difficult and tedious task, which is why only a limited number of existing PFs are available [7,8].

### 3.2. Genetic Programming and Generating DRs

GP is a metaheuristic method based on the concept of natural evolution [12]. It starts with a set, called the population, of randomly generated solutions, usually referred to as individuals. These individuals are evaluated using the fitness function, which calculates the fitness of each individual, i.e., a numerical measure of how well the individual solves a particular problem by optimising a certain criterion. GP then iteratively applies a series of genetic operators to these individuals in search of better solutions until a certain termination criterion is met. The operators that GP applies are selection, crossover, and mutation. With the selection operator, GP selects better individuals for the crossover operator and worse individuals to be eliminated from the population. The selected individuals are then used by the crossover operator, which combines their properties and creates a new individual that is potentially better than the individuals from which it was created. In addition, the newly created individual can be mutated with a certain probability to introduce random changes. The purpose of the mutation operator is to help the algorithm bypass local optima and restore lost genetic material in the population. This newly created individual then replaces one of the underperforming individuals in the population. With such a strategy, GP iteratively attempts to obtain better solutions through crossover and mutation and place them into the population, eliminating poor-quality individuals. The variant of the selection algorithm used in this study is described in Algorithm 2 [48], and the flow diagram of the algorithm is shown in Figure 1.

**Algorithm 2** The GP algorithm

Randomly create the population $P$ and evaluate all individuals in it
**while** termination criterion is not met **do**
    Randomly select 3 individuals from the population that form a tournament
    Select the two better individuals
    Crossover the selected individuals and create a new individual
    Mutate the newly created individual with a certain probability
    Evaluate the newly created individual
    Replace the worst individual from the tournament with the newly created individual
**end while**

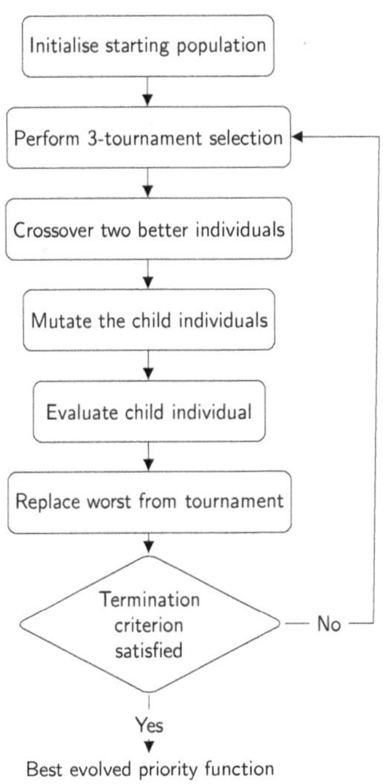


**Figure 1.** Flowchart of the GP algorithm.

As already mentioned, solutions in GP are coded as expression trees consisting of function and terminal nodes. The function nodes are the inner nodes in the tree and represent various mathematical, logical, or other types of operations. The terminal nodes, on the other hand, appear as leaf nodes in the tree and represent different features of the problem. Therefore, the definition of terminal nodes is one of the most important decisions that must be made when applying GP to any problem. Through the evolutionary process, GP searches for the most appropriate expression to solve a given problem.

GP has been successfully used as a hyperheuristic method [14,49] to automatically generate heuristics for various types of combinatorial optimisation problems, such as scheduling problems [50,51], the travelling salesman problem [52,53], vehicle and arc routing problems [54–56], the container relocation problem [57], and the cutting stock problem [15,58]. When used to generate DRs for scheduling problems, GP has the task of finding a suitable PF that can be used by the DR to evaluate scheduling decisions. Each individual represents a potential PF, which is then used by the SGS, as defined in Algorithm 1, to evaluate its effectiveness for a given set of problem instances. To be able to meaningfully rank the various decisions in the scheduling problem, e.g., which job to schedule next, GP must have access to all relevant features of the problem via its terminal nodes. Therefore, the set of terminal nodes must contain relevant problem characteristics, such as the processing times of jobs, their due dates, weights, and so on.

The entire methodology for the automatic creation of DRs is shown in Figure 2. The figure shows that GP is used to generate PFs embedded in an SGS, as outlined in Algorithm 1. This combination represents a DR, which is then used to generate a schedule based on the characteristics of the scheduling problem (job processing times, due dates, etc.). The meaning of the symbols is outlined in Tables 1 and 2. The schedule simply determines which job is assigned to which machine and the order in which they are executed on these machines. Finally, the quality of the created schedule can be evaluated using different performance criteria.

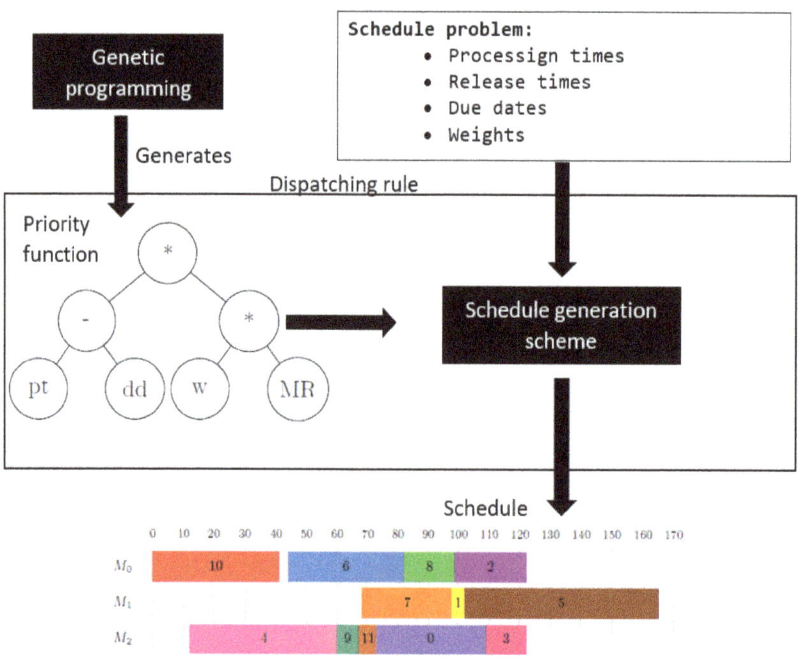


**Figure 2.** Outline of the procedure for the automated generation of DRs.

**Table 1.** The set of basic terminal nodes.

| Name | Description |
|---|---|
| dd | The due date of a job *j* |
| frma | The number of available machines |
| ma | The time when machine *i* becomes available |
| nmach | The number of machines in the scheduling environment |
| nrel | The number of currently released but not scheduled jobs |
| pt | The processing time of job *j* on machine *i* |
| rel | The release time of job *j* |
| clk | The current time of the system |
| w | The weight of job *j* |

**Table 2.** The set of extended terminal nodes.

| Name | Description |
|---|---|
| age | The time that job *j* spent in the system after being released |
| mr | The amount of time remaining until machine *i* becomes available |
| pat | The amount of time until the machine on which job *j* would be completed the soonest becomes available |
| pavg | The average execution time of job *j* across all machines |
| pmin | The minimum execution time of job *j* across all machines |
| sl | The slack of job *j*, which is defined as the remaining amount of time until it becomes tardy |

## 4. Methodology

As described in the previous section, the definition and selection of suitable terminal nodes is an important step in applying GP to develop new DRs. This is probably also the most difficult step, as it requires a certain amount of expert knowledge about the problem in order to define these terminal nodes in a meaningful way. However, even with good expert knowledge, there is no guarantee that the defined nodes will enable GP to obtain good priority functions. Therefore, the aim of this study is to investigate the process of designing the terminal set in more detail and determine how the inclusion and construction of different features and nodes affect the performance of GP.

This investigation is divided into three phases, each focusing on the influence of the following factors: (1) atomic terminal nodes, (2) composite terminal nodes constructed based on the frequency of occurrence in the previous phase, and (3) composite terminal nodes designed manually. In the following, we describe each phase in detail.

### 4.1. Atomic Terminal Nodes

In the first phase, only atomic terminal nodes, labelled in Table 1, are used. These nodes are called atomic because they represent the most basic information about the problem at hand, such as the processing times of jobs, their due dates, weights, and so on. They cannot, therefore, be broken down into sub-expressions of simpler nodes or coded in any other way. GP can combine these nodes into more complex expressions that are interpreted as PFs to determine which scheduling decision should be selected at each decision point.

Even if the previously defined set of terminal nodes is sufficient to construct any complex expression, this might prove quite difficult for GP, since it is very likely that such expressions are easily perturbed by genetic operators. Therefore, it makes sense to define composite terminal nodes, i.e., nodes that are represented as a kind of expression computed from multiple atomic nodes. However, there are several ways to define compound terminal nodes, and these are analysed in the second and third phases of the study.

### 4.2. Frequency-Based Composite Terminal Nodes

In the second phase, we analyse whether it is possible to automatically construct new terminal nodes by using the frequency of occurrence of sub-expressions from previously developed PFs that work well. This phase is, therefore, based on the results of the first phase to determine which sub-expressions occur most frequently but only in the PFs with the best performance. From the best PFs, we calculate the frequency of occurrence of all sub-expressions and select the most frequent ones. We also define new terminal nodes that encode these sub-expressions and add them to the terminal set.

### 4.3. Manually Designed Composite Terminal Nodes

In the third phase, we investigate the influence of composite, manually designed terminal nodes that combine different basic information from Table 1 in different ways. The motivation for introducing these terminals arises from several existing manually designed DRs that use similar information to that presented in Table 2. For example, these nodes represent information such as the slack of the job, a feature often used in manually designed DRs developed to optimise the $Twt$ criterion, or the time until a particular machine is available. Since such information has proven valuable in various manually created DRs, there is reason to believe that it could also be useful in the context of automatically created DRs. Therefore, we have investigated their influence on the performance of GP.

### 4.4. Feature Selection Methods

Although we have defined various terminal nodes, not all of them are equally useful for GP in designing new DRs. The problem with including unnecessary terminal nodes is that the solution space in which GP searches for a suitable PF increases exponentially. Therefore, it becomes increasingly difficult for GP to converge to good solutions. Therefore, it is not sufficient to define only a set of terminal nodes that represent all features of the problem; it is also crucial to determine whether these features are relevant for GP.

Although various algorithms and methods for feature selection have been defined in the literature [59–61], we use two simple methods: backward sequential feature selection (BSFS) and frequency-based selection (FBS). Although simple, the BSFS method is commonly used in the machine learning community to select appropriate features. The reason we select only the above-mentioned methods is that our goal is to determine the best feature set for the problem under consideration rather than compare different feature selection methods.

BSFS starts with the complete feature set and removes one feature from the feature set in each iteration. GP is then executed with this reduced feature set, and the developed PFs are evaluated. The reduced set that results in the best performance for the generated DRs is selected, and the procedure is repeated until all features are removed. So, in each iteration, this method tests the effect of removing each feature on the results and removes the feature that has the least negative effect. This process requires a quadratic number of experiments to determine the appropriate terminal set.

The FBS method also starts with the complete feature set to generate a certain number of DRs. Based on the best DRs, the frequency of occurrence of each terminal node is determined. The node that occurs the least frequently is removed, and the process is repeated until all terminal nodes are removed from the terminal set. This method, therefore, removes the node that occurs least frequently in the generated PFs in each iteration. Compared to the BSFS method, this method only requires a linear number of experiments in relation to the terminal nodes. This is because only one experiment is performed in each iteration, on the basis of which the frequency of occurrence of terminal nodes can be determined to decide which node should be removed next.

## 5. Experimental Study

In this section, we present the experimental study. First, we describe the outline of the performed experiments, and then, we outline the obtained results.

### 5.1. Setup

To conduct the experimental study, we used the dataset proposed in [16], which consists of 180 problem instances of varying sizes and complexities. The instances involve between 3 and 10 machines and between 12 and 100 jobs. Moreover, the dataset contains instances of different difficulty levels considering the $Twt$ criterion, which means that some instances are easy to solve while others are more complex. The dataset is divided into three subsets: a training set, a validation set, and a test set. Each set contains 60 instances with similar characteristics. The training dataset was used by GP to generate new DRs. After the DRs were generated, the validation set was used by the feature selection procedures to determine the best feature sets. Finally, the test dataset was used to evaluate the DRs obtained for the best feature sets, assessing their generalisation performance on unseen problems. All the results presented below were obtained with the problem instances from the test dataset. Finally, we compared the results of the automatically generated DRs with three DRs proposed in the literature [7].

The parameters used to run GP are listed in Table 3. These parameters were optimised in a previous study [16]. For each experiment, GP was run 30 times to perform a statistical analysis of the results. Due to the large number of results, only the median values from these 30 executions are presented in the tables because the Shapiro–Wilk test for normality showed that not all results followed a normal distribution. To test the statistical difference between pairs of methods, we used the Mann–Whitney test. On the other hand, to test for a statistical difference between a group of methods, we used the Kruskal–Wallis test with Dunn's post hoc test and the Bonferroni correction method. All statistical tests were conducted with a significance level of 0.05. All methods were coded in the C++ programming language using the ECF framework (http://ecf.zemris.fer.hr/, accessed on 1 May 2023). The experiments were conducted on a Windows 10 PC with an AMD Ryzen Threadripper 3990X 64-core processor and 128 GB of RAM.

**Table 3.** GP parameters.

| Parameter | Value |
|---|---|
| Population size | 1000 |
| Mutation probability | 0.3 |
| Tournament size | 3 |
| Crossover operators | subtree, uniform, context preserving, size fair, one point |
| Mutation operators | subtree, hoist, node complement, node replacement, permutation, shrink |
| Function set | addition, subtraction, multiplication, protected division (returns 1 if division by 0 is encountered), $POS(x) = \max(x, 0)$ |
| Termination criterion | 80,000 fitness evaluations |

### 5.2. Results

The results in this section are presented in three phases, corresponding to the research phases described in the methodology section. In the first phase, the set of terminal nodes consists only of the atomic features of the problem. In the second phase, this terminal set is extended with composite terminal nodes consisting of the most frequent sub-expressions of the PFs developed in the first phase. Finally, in the last phase, the basic terminal set is extended with manually designed composite nodes.

#### 5.2.1. Simple Terminal Set

In the first phase, the terminal set shown in Table 1 was used as the starting set for the construction of DRs. To determine which features were most important in this set, the BSFS and FBS methods were used to determine the optimised set of terminal nodes.

The results obtained using BSFS in this phase are shown in Table 4. The columns in the table denote the results where the corresponding feature was removed from the feature set, whereas the rows denote the steps of the algorithm. The first row indicates the results obtained when all features were used. In each subsequent row, the best result is indicated in bold, which also indicates which feature was removed from the feature set in the next iteration. In addition, each cell contains the results of the statistical test comparing the result presented in this cell with the result obtained with the entire terminal set. The symbol + means that significantly better results were achieved with the reduced set, − means that significantly worse results were achieved with the reduced set, and ≈ means that there was no significant difference between the results. We can see from the table that removing certain nodes almost always led to a significant deterioration in the results. The nodes where this happened were *dd*, *ma*, *pt*, and *w*. From this, we can conclude that these nodes represent the minimum set of features that the GP needs to construct meaningful PFs. By using only these four terminal nodes, GP achieved a value of 13.88, which was lower but not statistically better than the value obtained when using all terminal nodes. Removing all other nodes from the terminal set did not have a significant impact on the results, or in some cases, even led to a significant improvement. The best overall result was obtained for the node set that included the *clk* and *nrel* nodes in addition to the four previously mentioned terminals. The *clk* nodes, in particular, seem to be important, as they provide information about the current time in the system, which can then be used in combination with other terminal nodes to determine when a job will become late and thus prioritise it.

**Table 4.** Results obtained by BSFS for the feature set outlined in Table 1.

| Iteration | Terminals | | | | | | | | |
|---|---|---|---|---|---|---|---|---|---|
| | *clk* | *dd* | *frma* | *ma* | *nmach* | *nrel* | *pt* | *rel* | *w* |
| All nodes | | | | | 14.08 | | | | |
| 1 | 14.09 (≈) | 16.36 (−) | **13.89** (≈) | 18.78 (−) | 14.01 (≈) | 14.12 (≈) | 177.16 (−) | 13.88 (≈) | 14.49 (−) |
| 2 | 14.17 (≈) | 16.52 (−) | - | 18.81 (−) | 13.89 (≈) | 14.10 (≈) | 178.45 (−) | **13.88** (+) | 14.49 (−) |
| 3 | 13.88 (≈) | 17.53 (−) | - | 18.83 (−) | **13.69** (+) | 13.71 (+) | 176.04 (−) | - | 14.38 (−) |
| 4 | **13.81** (+) | 17.56 (−) | - | 19.31 (−) | - | 13.82 (+) | 176.21 (−) | - | 14.22 (≈) |
| 5 | - | 17.16 (−) | - | 18.69 (−) | - | **13.88** (≈) | 174.68 (−) | - | 14.66 (−) |
| 6 | - | 17.49 (−) | - | 18.59 (−) | - | - | 173.21 (−) | - | 14.57 (−) |
| 7 | - | 25.82 (−) | - | **20.86** (−) | - | - | 283.27 (−) | - | - |
| 8 | - | **44.62** (−) | - | - | - | - | 7755 (−) | - | - |

Table 5 shows the results GP achieved when the terminal nodes were removed based on the frequency of their occurrence in the generated PFs. The first row lists the removed terminal nodes, whereas the second row shows the corresponding fitness values. Again, each cell contains the result of the statistical test comparing the results of the entire set with the reduced sets. We can see that the best overall result was obtained with two terminal sets: a smaller one with the nodes *pt*, *ma*, *dd*, and *w*, and a larger one with the nodes *nmach* and *clk* in addition to these nodes. In both cases, the results are significantly better than the results obtained with the entire terminal set. This shows that it is possible to make a meaningful selection of features depending on the frequency of the terminal nodes in the obtained expressions, especially since the four most important terminal nodes consistently have the highest frequency.

**Table 5.** Results obtained by GP when selecting atomic features based on their frequency in the PFs.

| all | *nrel* | *frma* | *rel* | *clk* | *nmach* | *pt* | *ma* |
|---|---|---|---|---|---|---|---|
| 14.08 | 14.13 (≈) | 13.88 (≈) | 13.84 (+) | 13.87 (+) | 13.84 (+) | 172.92 (−) | 4942.88 (−) |

#### 5.2.2. Extended Terminal Set with Composite Features Determined by Frequency of Occurrence

Based on the best individuals from the first phase of the experiments, we calculated the frequency of sub-expressions. The sub-expressions with more than 30 occurrences are listed in Table 6. It is interesting to note that only sub-expressions of size 3 occurred, whereas larger sub-expressions were rare in several trees. This shows that there did not seem to be a larger, well-functioning sub-expression that could be reused; rather, the rules consisted of small, frequently repeated sub-expressions. The reason for this could be that either such a sub-expression did not exist or that GP had difficulty obtaining it with the given settings. If we examine which sub-expressions occurred most frequently, we can see that GP created certain sub-expressions that occurred frequently in manually created DRs. For example, the expression $ma + pt$ was often used to determine how quickly the job would be completed on each machine, using information about when the machine was available and how long the job would take on the machine. Sub-expressions such as $\frac{dd}{w}$ and $\frac{pt}{w}$ were also common, as the purpose was to schedule jobs with a lower processing time or due date adjusted for the weight of the job. Based on this frequency of occurrence, seven new terminal nodes were designed and included in the previously optimised terminal set.

**Table 6.** Frequency of occurrence of most commonly appearing sub-expressions from Phase 1.

| Expression | Occurrence Frequency |
|---|---|
| $dd * dd$ | 212 |
| $ma + pt$ | 127 |
| $ma * w$ | 110 |
| $\frac{dd}{w}$ | 99 |
| $\frac{pt}{w}$ | 48 |
| $\frac{pt}{ma}$ | 40 |
| $dd - pt$ | 36 |

Table 7 provides an overview of the results obtained through the additional use of the seven features described in Table 6. In this section, the results obtained are statistically compared with the optimised terminal set from Phase 1, the results of which are also included in the first row of the table. The results show that the inclusion of these composite features in the terminal set did not have a positive influence on the results compared to the optimised terminal set from Phase 1. In most cases, the results either remained the same or even deteriorated, which was confirmed by the statistical tests performed. The only node that seemed to have some effect on this terminal set was $dd * dd$, which occurred most frequently in the PFs from Phase 1. On the other hand, nodes such as $\frac{dd}{w}$, $ma * w$ were the first to be removed, suggesting that they were the least informative.

**Table 7.** Results obtained by BSFS for the extended terminal set with features created based on their frequency of occurrence.

| Iteration | Terminals | | | | | | |
|---|---|---|---|---|---|---|---|
| | $dd * dd$ | $dd - pt$ | $\frac{dd}{w}$ | $ma + pt$ | $\frac{pt}{ma}$ | $\frac{pt}{w}$ | $ma * w$ |
| Phase 1 optimised | 13.69 | | | | | | |
| All terminals | 13.86 (≈) | | | | | | |
| 1 | 13.84 (≈) | 13.86 (≈) | **13.83** (≈) | 14.09 (−) | 13.92 (−) | 13.95 (−) | 13.94 (−) |
| 2 | 14.07 (−) | 13.85 (≈) | - | 13.83 (≈) | 14.11 (−) | 13.96 (−) | **13.82** (≈) |
| 3 | 14.00 (−) | **13.67** (≈) | - | 13.93 (−) | 13.81 (≈) | 14.01 (−) | - |
| 4 | 14.01 (−) | - | - | 13.80 (≈) | 13.95 (−) | **13.79** (≈) | - |
| 5 | 13.86 (≈) | - | - | 13.73 (≈) | **13.66** (≈) | - | - |
| 6 | 13.83 (≈) | - | - | **13.65** (≈) | - | - | - |

Table 8 shows the selection process carried out by FBS. We can see that in this case, the order in which features were removed from the terminal set differed from that of BSFS. The results in this case showed no improvement over the terminal obtained at the end of Phase 1. Since neither method achieved a positive result, we can conclude that creating new composite features based on their frequency of occurrence in well-functioning rules does not generally lead to better results. These nodes, therefore, offer no advantages over the original set of atomic features identified in Phase 1.

**Table 8.** Results obtained by GP when selecting automatically designed composite features based on their frequency in the PFs.

| ph1 | all | $\frac{pt}{ma}$ | $\frac{pt}{w}$ | $ma * w$ | $dd - pt$ | $\frac{dd}{w}$ | $ma1 + pt$ |
|---|---|---|---|---|---|---|---|
| 13.69 | 13.85 (≈) | 14.05 (−) | 13.90 (≈) | 13.84 (≈) | 13.89 (≈) | 13.79 (≈) | 13.91 (≈) |

#### 5.2.3. Extended Terminal Set with Manually Designed Composite Features

Table 9 shows the results obtained with the BSFS method when using manually designed composite terminal nodes. Again, the statistical tests were calculated using the optimised terminal set from Phase 1. The results show that no single combination of terminal nodes was able to achieve significantly better results compared to the terminal set obtained after Phase 1. With the set from Phase 1 extended with the nodes *mr*, *pat*, *pavg*, *pmin*, and *sl*, the median value of the results achieved was improved to 13.47. In all other cases, however, it was not possible to achieve a significant improvement. The results are either equally good or even significantly worse than those achieved with the terminal set obtained in Phase 1.

**Table 9.** Results obtained using BSFS for the extended terminal set with features created based on their frequency of occurrence.

| Iteration | Terminals | | | | | |
|---|---|---|---|---|---|---|
| | *age* | *mr* | *pat* | *pavg* | *pmin* | *sl* |
| Phase 1 optimised | 13.69 | | | | | |
| All terminals | 13.93 (≈) | | | | | |
| 1 | **13.47** (≈) | 13.88 (≈) | 13.96 (≈) | 13.87 (≈) | 14.16 (−) | 14.15 (−) |
| 2 | - | **13.77** (≈) | 14.11 (−) | 13.95 (−) | 13.90 (−) | 14.30 (−) |
| 3 | - | - | 14.01 (−) | 13.80 (≈) | 13.95 (−) | **13.79** (≈) |
| 4 | - | - | 13.84 (≈) | **13.66** (≈) | 14.32 (−) | - |
| 5 | - | - | **13.72** (≈) | - | 13.80 (≈) | - |

The results when using FBS are shown in Table 10. This table shows that in all cases, the results were as good as with the basic terminal set obtained after Phase 1. Again, we can see that the order in which the terminals were removed from the set is similar to that of BSFS.

**Table 10.** Results obtained by GP when selecting manually designed composite features based on their frequency in the PFs.

| ph1 | all | *pavg* | *age* | *mr* | *pat* | *pmin* |
|---|---|---|---|---|---|---|
| 13.69 | 13.93 (≈) | 13.90 (≈) | 13.87 (≈) | 13.71 (≈) | 13.93 (≈) | (≈) |

Unfortunately, the results obtained when manually defined composite nodes were included are inconclusive. In most cases, there was no significant difference between the sets containing these features and the set obtained after Phase 1. However, some improvement in the results was observed for one feature set. This could indicate that the additional features were beneficial for GP and allowed it to generate better PFs, but at the same time, their inclusion also increased the search space, making it more difficult for GP to converge.

## 6. Analysis

### 6.1. Comparison of Results from Each Phase

Table 11 gives an overview of the best results obtained with the validation set for each terminal set, as well as the best manually developed DRs, namely EDD, COVERT, and

ATC. The initial feature set from Table 1 is labelled as Phase 0, whereas Phase 2 + 3 refers to the combination of the best feature sets from Phase 2 and Phase 3, which was used to investigate whether the combination of these two feature sets led to an improvement in the results. In addition, the table shows the average rule size obtained when using each terminal set, which represents the average number of nodes in the expressions generated by GP. Compared to the manually generated DRs, we can see that GP achieved better DRs with the best terminal set obtained after each phase compared to the three manually generated ones. Only in the cases where no optimisation was performed, or when Phases 2 and 3 were combined, did GP fail to outperform the ATC rule. This shows that even for a terminal set with atomic terminal nodes, GP can reasonably combine them to outperform the existing rules. However, for more complex terminal nodes, GP can even increase the gap between manually and automatically created DRs.

Figure 3 depicts the results from Table 11 as a box plot. The figure shows that the terminal node sets from Phase 1 and Phase 2 lead to the least scattered solutions. This is favourable, as it means that GP is more likely to produce a result close to the median. Therefore, the method is more reliable when it comes to generating solutions of expected quality. On the other hand, the solutions obtained when using the terminal node set obtained in Phase 3 are quite scattered. The results also show that GP is more likely to obtain better results with this terminal node set than with any other terminal node set.

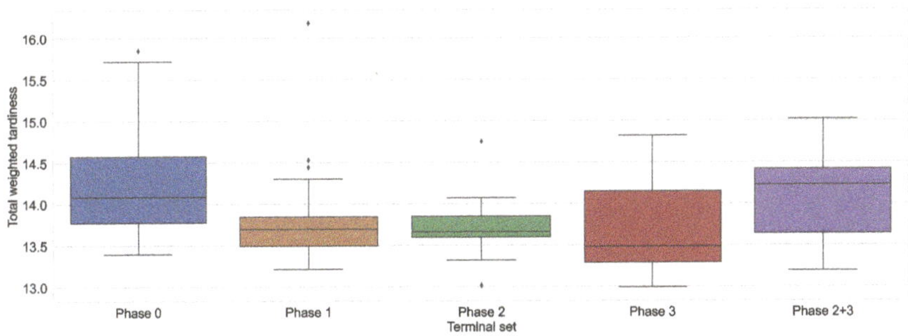


**Figure 3.** Box plot of the best results obtained by each terminal set on the validation set.

**Table 11.** Comparison of results from all phases on the validation set.

| | Median | Rule Size |
|---|---|---|
| EDD | 14.53 | 1 |
| COVERT | 14.20 | 19 |
| ATC | 13.73 | 16 |
| Phase 0 | 14.08 | 43.2 |
| Phase 1 | 13.69 | 42.7 |
| Phase 2 | 13.65 | 43.4 |
| Phase 3 | 13.47 | 43.7 |
| Phase 2 + 3 | 14.22 | 43.8 |

To determine whether there was a significant difference between the results, the statistical tests described above were used, and a $p$-value close to 0 was determined. This shows that there was a significant difference between the results obtained. To determine which of the results were significantly different, the post hoc test was used, the results of which are shown in Table 12. The table shows that the results in the row are inferior to those in the column when indicated by "<", superior when indicated by ">", or equivalent when indicated by "$\approx$". We can see that the results obtained using only the atomic nodes, without optimising the terminal set, usually led to the worst results. In contrast, there was no significant difference between the results from Phases 1, 2, and 3.

**Table 12.** Results of the statistical tests on the validation set.

| | Phase 0 | Phase 1 | Phase 2 | Phase 3 | Phase 2 + 3 |
|---|---|---|---|---|---|
| Phase 0 | - | < | < | < | ≈ |
| Phase 1 | > | - | ≈ | ≈ | ≈ |
| Phase 2 | > | ≈ | - | ≈ | ≈ |
| Phase 3 | > | ≈ | ≈ | - | > |
| Phase 2 + 3 | ≈ | ≈ | ≈ | < | - |

The above results summarise the validation set. In order to more objectively evaluate the performance of GP with the different terminal sets, the rules obtained were evaluated using the test set. These results are listed in Table 13. It can be seen from the table that the performance of the rules obtained is now quite different from before. In this case, the results before feature selection only outperformed the simplest DR but not the two more complicated ones, namely COVERT and ATC. Even after Phases 1 and 2, GP could only find rules that performed similarly well to the manually designed rules. Only when the manually designed terminal nodes were finally introduced did GP generate rules that clearly outperformed the manually designed rules. The results are also shown as a box plot in Figure 4 to better illustrate the differences between the results. The figure illustrates that the introduction of manually designed composite terminal nodes led to the greatest increase in performance.

**Table 13.** Comparison of results from all phases on the test set.

| | Median | Rule Size |
|---|---|---|
| EDD | 17.31 | 1 |
| COVERT | 16.86 | 19 |
| ATC | 16.63 | 16 |
| Phase 0 | 17.11 | 43.2 |
| Phase 1 | 16.93 | 42.7 |
| Phase 2 | 16.71 | 43.4 |
| Phase 3 | 15.89 | 43.7 |
| Phase 2 + 3 | 16.45 | 43.8 |

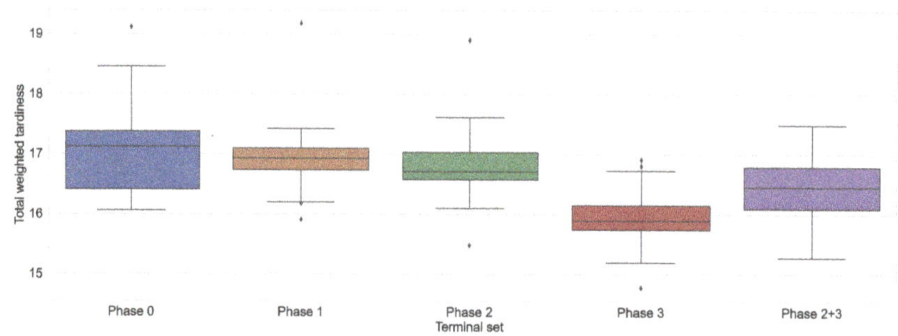


**Figure 4.** Box plot of the best results obtained by each terminal set on the test set.

To confirm that the addition of manually designed composite nodes led to a significant improvement in the results, the Kruskal–Wallis test was used, and a $p$-value of 0 was obtained, meaning that there was a significant difference. The results of the post hoc tests performed are shown in Table 14. The table shows that although in most cases there was no significant difference between the terminal sets, the use of manually designed composite terminal nodes significantly improved the results compared to those obtained in Phases 0, 1, and 2.

**Table 14.** Results of the statistical tests on the test set.

| | Phase 0 | Phase 1 | Phase 2 | Phase 3 | Phase 2 + 3 |
|---|---|---|---|---|---|
| Phase 0 | - | ≈ | ≈ | < | < |
| Phase 1 | ≈ | - | ≈ | < | < |
| Phase 2 | ≈ | ≈ | - | < | ≈ |
| Phase 3 | > | > | > | - | ≈ |
| Phase 2 + 3 | > | > | ≈ | ≈ | - |

Based on the previous results, we can see that the manually designed terminal nodes actually provided the most valuable information about the problem, allowing the rules to generalise well to unseen problem instances. Presumably, all methods performed similarly on the validation set, as the best terminal sets were selected for them. However, it appears that this may have led to a slight overfitting to the validation set. Based on the previous observations, it is, therefore, safe to conclude that a mixture of simple and manually designed composite terminal nodes is required to create the best DRs.

### 6.2. DR Complexity Analysis

One could assume that a potential advantage of introducing composite features into the terminal set could be the generation of smaller expressions. To analyse this, Figure 5 presents a scatter plot in which the fitness of the DR (x-axis) is plotted against its size (y-axis) for each terminal set used. The figure illustrates that the solutions are very widely scattered and only a very small number of rules below size 30 were obtained. Furthermore, the smaller rules usually did not perform well, often reaching a Twt value of over 16. It seems that the generated DRs started to perform well at around size 35. However, the best overall rule had a size of more than 50, and some other well-performing rules also had sizes of more than 50 nodes. To determine whether there was a correlation between the rule size and its performance, Spearman's rho test was used. Since values between $-0.15$ and 0.1 were obtained for the results of all phases, we can conclude that there was no obvious correlation between these two measures. Although it may seem counterintuitive as to why smaller expressions were not obtained for composite terminal nodes, as more complex expressions should be represented by a smaller number of nodes, this was most likely due to the bloating of GP, and could be mitigated by using different mechanisms to control the bloating [62,63].

### 6.3. Convergence Analysis

Another interesting aspect to investigate is the rate of convergence of GP when using different terminal node sets. For this purpose, the best individual was saved after every 10,000 evaluations and later evaluated on the validation set. This was done for all 30 executions, and the median values were calculated and then used to plot Figure 6. The figure illustrates that the terminal set significantly influenced the quality of the initial solution. The worst solution quality was obtained either with the initial terminal set (Phase 0) or the one obtained from Phase 2 + 3. The reason for this could be that these terminal node sets were larger and, therefore, it was more difficult for GP to generate a good initial solution. Interestingly, the terminal set from Phase 2 achieved the best initial solution, indicating that the $dd * dd$ node used contributed to the development of good solutions. Moreover, this terminal led to the fastest convergence of the algorithm in the first half of the evolutionary process, although the algorithm started to stagnate after a certain time. When using the terminal set obtained in Phase 3, GP started with quite poor solutions; however, in the end, it reached the best overall solutions. This suggests that this terminal set might have been the most meaningful, and GP was thus able to produce high-quality DRs. However, it also seemed to be much more difficult for GP to obtain these solutions, thus requiring a longer evolution process, as it can be seen that the quality of the solutions themselves had improved by the end of the assigned number of scores. Therefore, there is a possibility that with more time, GP could achieve even better solutions with this terminal set.

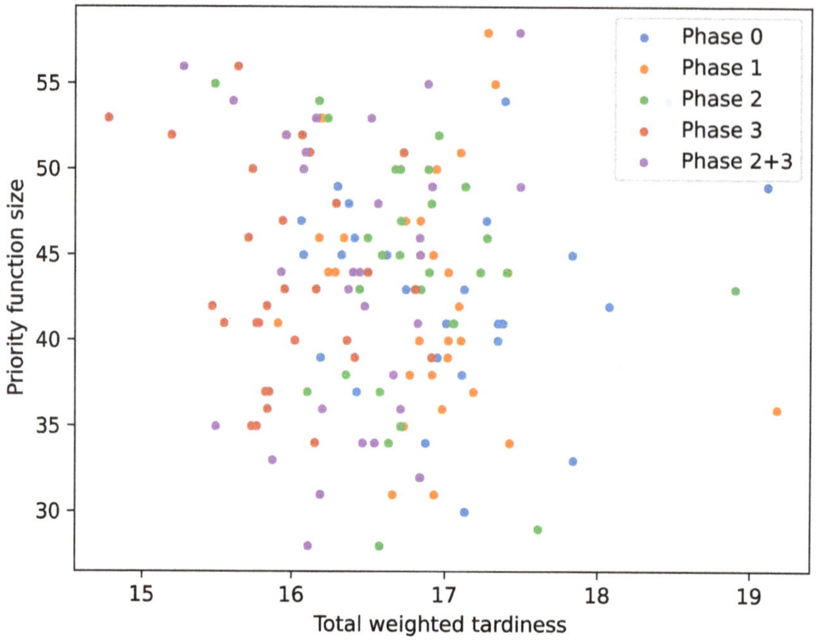


**Figure 5.** Scatter plot of DR fitness values plotted against the size of the DRs.

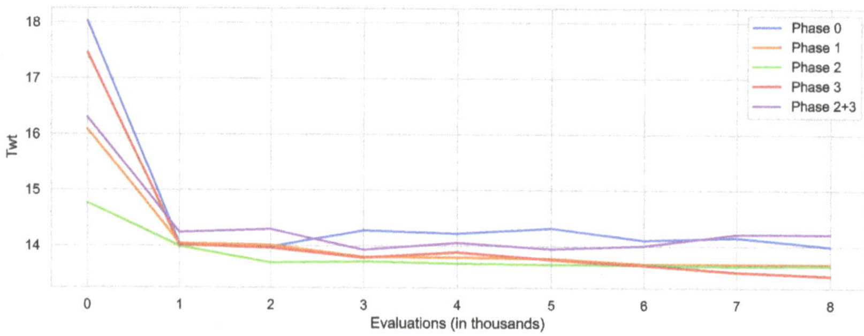


**Figure 6.** Algorithm convergence on the validation set.

### 6.4. Removal-Sequence Similarity

To analyse how similar the order in which the terminal nodes were removed from the terminal set was, the Levenshtein distance measure was used to determine the similarity of the two removal sequences. For this purpose, the removal sequences of BSFS and FBS were determined, and the Levenshtein distance for these two sequences was calculated for each phase. The Levenshtein distance values obtained, scaled between 0 and 1, were 0.666, 0.571, and 0.666 for the removal sequences obtained in Phases 1, 2, and 3, respectively. The values obtained show that there were indeed large differences between the removal sequences of the two selection methods. Thus, even if FBS could determine the nodes to be removed, it still deviated significantly from the sequence obtained by a more thorough search for the optimal feature set.

### 6.5. Run-Time Analysis

In this section, we briefly analyse the running times of the two feature selection algorithms. The complexity of FBS is linear with the number of features, i.e., to determine the best set of terminals, $N - 1$ experiments must be performed, where $N$ denotes the number of features. The $-1$ appears because it is not necessary to perform the last experiment with only a single feature. On the other hand, BSFS has a quadratic complexity and requires about $\frac{N(N-1)}{2} - 1$ experiments. This obviously represents a significant difference in execution time, as the execution time of GP for the 80,000 fitness evaluations was about 1 h. Thus, in the case where nine terminal nodes were included in the set, FBS required 8 experiments, whereas BSFS required 44. Since each experiment was executed 30 times, and each execution took 1 h, FBS was executed for a total of 240 h, whereas BFSF was executed for 1320 h. It is assumed that all experiments are run in series. However, in many cases they can be run in parallel, reducing the total execution time. Although a smaller number of evaluations could be used, this would likely lead to a degradation in performance, as previous studies have shown that GP performs best for the given number of feature evaluations [16].

## 7. Conclusions and Future Work

The aim of this study was to investigate the impact of different types of terminal nodes on the performance of GP in developing DRs for unrelated machine scheduling problems. The experimental results show that when GP is equipped with only atomic features to generate DRs, it can outperform simple DRs but has difficulty in evolving rules better than complex manually designed DRs. Therefore, two methods were used to construct composite terminal nodes and improve the performance of GP. In the first method, new terminals were constructed based on sub-expressions most commonly found in DRs developed with atomic terminals. Although with these terminals, GP matched the performance of manually constructed DRs, it still rarely outperformed them. However, the second approach, where composite terminal nodes were designed manually, proved to be more efficient and allowed GP to generate DRs that significantly outperformed manually designed DRs. Therefore, a certain level of expertise is required when designing terminal nodes, as it is necessary to define terminal nodes that provide more complex information about the scheduling problem. In addition to defining new terminals, it is also imperative to apply a feature selection method to determine the appropriate set of terminal nodes to prevent the search space from growing exponentially. The experiments showed that selecting terminal nodes based on their frequency of occurrence can help in selecting meaningful terminal nodes. However, this approach is not as robust as standard feature selection methods, such as backward sequential feature selection.

The results obtained in this study open up several avenues for future research. One possible research direction, which was only briefly explored, would be to introduce feature construction methods into the GP algorithm so that it can automatically design new features. In addition, better measures for identifying relevant features and sub-expressions are needed, aside from frequency of occurrence. Finally, another option would be to manually construct additional terminal nodes, as such nodes usually lead to better results compared to those constructed based on the frequency of occurrence.

**Author Contributions:** Conceptualization, M.Đ., D.J., S.P. and L.M.; methodology, M.Đ., D.J., S.P. and L.M.; software, M.Đ., D.J., S.P. and L.M.; validation, M.Đ., D.J., S.P. and L.M.; formal analysis, M.Đ., D.J., S.P. and L.M.; investigation, M.Đ., D.J., S.P. and L.M.; resources, M.Đ., D.J., S.P. and L.M.; data curation, M.Đ., D.J., S.P. and L.M.; writing—original draft preparation, M.Đ., D.J., S.P. and L.M.; writing—review and editing, M.Đ., D.J., S.P. and L.M.; visualization, M.Đ., D.J., S.P. and L.M.; supervision, M.Đ., D.J., S.P. and L.M.; project administration, M.Đ., D.J., S.P. and L.M.; funding acquisition, M.Đ., D.J., S.P. and L.M. All authors have read and agreed to the published version of the manuscript.

**Funding:** This work was supported in part by the Croatian Science Foundation under the project IP-2019-04-4333.

**Data Availability Statement:** Dataset available on request from the authors.

**Conflicts of Interest:** The authors declare no conflicts of interest.

## References


1. Leung, J.Y.T. (Ed.) *Handbook of Scheduling*; Chapman & Hall/CRC Computer and Information Science Series; Chapman & Hall/CRC: Philadelphia, PA, USA, 2004.
2. Wu, L.; Wang, S. Exact and heuristic methods to solve the parallel machine scheduling problem with multi-processor tasks. *Int. J. Prod. Econ.* **2018**, *201*, 26–40. [CrossRef]
3. Gedik, R.; Kalathia, D.; Egilmez, G.; Kirac, E. A constraint programming approach for solving unrelated parallel machine scheduling problem. *Comput. Ind. Eng.* **2018**, *121*, 139–149. [CrossRef]
4. Yu, L.; Shih, H.M.; Pfund, M.; Carlyle, W.M.; Fowler, J.W. Scheduling of unrelated parallel machines: An application to PWB manufacturing. *IIE Trans.* **2002**, *34*, 921–931. [CrossRef]
5. Hart, E.; Ross, P.; Corne, D. Evolutionary Scheduling: A Review. *Genet. Program. Evolvable Mach.* **2005**, *6*, 191–220. [CrossRef]
6. Đurasević, M.; Jakobović, D. Heuristic and metaheuristic methods for the parallel unrelated machines scheduling problem: A survey. *Artif. Intell. Rev.* **2022**, *56*, 3181–3289. [CrossRef]
7. Đurasević, M.; Jakobović, D. A survey of dispatching rules for the dynamic unrelated machines environment. *Expert Syst. Appl.* **2018**, *113*, 555–569. [CrossRef]
8. Branke, J.; Nguyen, S.; Pickardt, C.W.; Zhang, M. Automated Design of Production Scheduling Heuristics: A Review. *IEEE Trans. Evol. Comput.* **2016**, *20*, 110–124. [CrossRef]
9. Nguyen, S.; Mei, Y.; Zhang, M. Genetic programming for production scheduling: A survey with a unified framework. *Complex Intell. Syst.* **2017**, *3*, 41–66. [CrossRef]
10. Zhang, F.; Mei, Y.; Nguyen, S.; Zhang, M. Survey on Genetic Programming and Machine Learning Techniques for Heuristic Design in Job Shop Scheduling. *IEEE Trans. Evol. Comput.* **2023**, *28*, 147–167. [CrossRef]
11. Poli, R.; Langdon, W.B.; McPhee, N.F. *A Field Guide to Genetic Programming*; Lulu Enterprises, UK Ltd.: London, UK, 2008.
12. Koza, J.R. *Genetic Programming*; Complex Adaptive Systems; Bradford Books: Cambridge, MA, USA, 1992.
13. Koza, J.R. Human-competitive results produced by genetic programming. *Genet. Program. Evolvable Mach.* **2010**, *11*, 251–284. [CrossRef]
14. Burke, E.K.; Hyde, M.R.; Kendall, G.; Ochoa, G.; Ozcan, E.; Woodward, J.R. Exploring Hyper-heuristic Methodologies with Genetic Programming. *Comput. Intell.* **2009**, *1*, 177–201. [CrossRef]
15. Burke, E.K.; Hyde, M.R.; Kendall, G.; Woodward, J. Automating the Packing Heuristic Design Process with Genetic Programming. *Evol. Comput.* **2012**, *20*, 63–89. [CrossRef]
16. Đurasević, M.; Jakobović, D.; Knežević, K. Adaptive scheduling on unrelated machines with genetic programming. *Appl. Soft Comput.* **2016**, *48*, 419–430. [CrossRef]
17. Hunt, R.; Johnston, M.; Zhang, M. Evolving "less-myopic" scheduling rules for dynamic job shop scheduling with genetic programming. In Proceedings of the GECCO '14: 2014 Annual Conference on Genetic and Evolutionary Computation, Vancouver, BC, Canada, 12–16 July 2014. [CrossRef]
18. Miyashita, K. Job-Shop Scheduling with Genetic Programming. In Proceedings of the GECCO'00: 2nd Annual Conference on Genetic and Evolutionary Computation, San Francisco, CA, USA, 10–12 July 2000; pp. 505–512.
19. Dimopoulos, C.; Zalzala, A. Investigating the use of genetic programming for a classic one-machine scheduling problem. *Adv. Eng. Softw.* **2001**, *32*, 489–498. [CrossRef]
20. Jakobović, D.; Budin, L. Dynamic Scheduling with Genetic Programming. In Proceedings of the Genetic Programming, Budapest, Hungary, 10–12 April 2006; Collet, P., Tomassini, M., Ebner, M., Gustafson, S., Ekárt, A., Eds.; Springer: Berlin/Heidelberg, Germany, 2006; pp. 73–84.
21. Ho, N.; Tay, J.C. Evolving Dispatching Rules for solving the Flexible Job-Shop Problem. In Proceedings of the 2005 IEEE Congress on Evolutionary Computation, Edinburgh, UK, 2–5 September 2005. [CrossRef]
22. Chand, S.; Huynh, Q.; Singh, H.; Ray, T.; Wagner, M. On the use of genetic programming to evolve priority rules for resource constrained project scheduling problems. *Inf. Sci.* **2018**, *432*, 146–163. [CrossRef]
23. Gil-Gala, F.J.; Varela, R. Genetic Algorithm to Evolve Ensembles of Rules for On-Line Scheduling on Single Machine with Variable Capacity. In *From Bioinspired Systems and Biomedical Applications to Machine Learning*; Springer International Publishing: Cham, Switzerland, 2019; pp. 223–233. [CrossRef]
24. Nguyen, S.; Zhang, M.; Johnston, M.; Tan, K.C. A Computational Study of Representations in Genetic Programming to Evolve Dispatching Rules for the Job Shop Scheduling Problem. *IEEE Trans. Evol. Comput.* **2013**, *17*, 621–639. [CrossRef]
25. Branke, J.; Hildebrandt, T.; Scholz-Reiter, B. Hyper-heuristic Evolution of Dispatching Rules: A Comparison of Rule Representations. *Evol. Comput.* **2015**, *23*, 249–277. [CrossRef] [PubMed]
26. Planinić, L.; Backović, H.; Đurasević, M.; Jakobović, D. A Comparative Study of Dispatching Rule Representations in Evolutionary Algorithms for the Dynamic Unrelated Machines Environment. *IEEE Access* **2022**, *10*, 22886–22901. [CrossRef]
27. Nguyen, S.; Zhang, M.; Johnston, M.; Tan, K.C. Dynamic Multi-objective Job Shop Scheduling: A Genetic Programming Approach. In *Studies in Computational Intelligence*; Springer: Berlin/Heidelberg, Germany, 2013; pp. 251–282. [CrossRef]
28. Nguyen, S.; Zhang, M.; Tan, K.C. Enhancing genetic programming based hyper-heuristics for dynamic multi-objective job shop scheduling problems. In Proceedings of the 2015 IEEE Congress on Evolutionary Computation (CEC), Sendai, Japan, 25–28 May 2015; pp. 2781–2788. [CrossRef]

29. Masood, A.; Mei, Y.; Chen, G.; Zhang, M. Many-objective genetic programming for job-shop scheduling. In Proceedings of the 2016 IEEE Congress on Evolutionary Computation (CEC), Vancouver, BC, Canada, 24–29 July 2016; pp. 209–216. [CrossRef]
30. Đurasević, M.; Jakobović, D. Evolving dispatching rules for optimising many-objective criteria in the unrelated machines environment. *Genet. Program. Evolvable Mach.* **2017**, *19*, 9–51. [CrossRef]
31. Park, J.; Nguyen, S.; Zhang, M.; Johnston, M. Evolving Ensembles of Dispatching Rules Using Genetic Programming for Job Shop Scheduling. In Proceedings of the Genetic Programming, Copenhagen, Denmark, 8–10 April 2015; Machado, P., Heywood, M.I., McDermott, J., Castelli, M., García-Sánchez, P., Burelli, P., Risi, S., Sim, K., Eds.; Springer: Cham, Switzerland, 2015; pp. 92–104.
32. Hart, E.; Sim, K. A Hyper-Heuristic Ensemble Method for Static Job-Shop Scheduling. *Evol. Comput.* **2016**, *24*, 609–635. [CrossRef]
33. Đurasević, M.; Jakobović, D. Comparison of ensemble learning methods for creating ensembles of dispatching rules for the unrelated machines environment. *Genet. Program. Evolvable Mach.* **2017**, *19*, 53–92. [CrossRef]
34. Park, J.; Mei, Y.; Nguyen, S.; Chen, G.; Zhang, M. An Investigation of Ensemble Combination Schemes for Genetic Programming based Hyper-heuristic Approaches to Dynamic Job Shop Scheduling. *Appl. Soft Comput.* **2017**, *63*, 72–86. [CrossRef]
35. Đurasević, M.; Gil-Gala, F.J.; Planinić, L.; Jakobović, D. Collaboration methods for ensembles of dispatching rules for the dynamic unrelated machines environment. *Eng. Appl. Artif. Intell.* **2023**, *122*, 106096. [CrossRef]
36. Đurasević, M.; Gil-Gala, F.J.; Jakobović, D.; Coello, C.A.C. Combining single objective dispatching rules into multi-objective ensembles for the dynamic unrelated machines environment. *Swarm Evol. Comput.* **2023**, *80*, 101318. [CrossRef]
37. Nguyen, S.; Zhang, M.; Tan, K.C. Surrogate-Assisted Genetic Programming with Simplified Models for Automated Design of Dispatching Rules. *IEEE Trans. Cybern.* **2017**, *47*, 2951–2965. [CrossRef]
38. Zhang, F.; Mei, Y.; Nguyen, S.; Zhang, M.; Tan, K.C. Surrogate-Assisted Evolutionary Multitask Genetic Programming for Dynamic Flexible Job Shop Scheduling. *IEEE Trans. Evol. Comput.* **2021**, *25*, 651–665. [CrossRef]
39. Gil-Gala, F.J.; Sierra, M.R.; Mencía, C.; Varela, R. Genetic programming with local search to evolve priority rules for scheduling jobs on a machine with time-varying capacity. *Swarm Evol. Comput.* **2021**, *66*, 100944. [CrossRef]
40. Zhang, F.; Mei, Y.; Nguyen, S.; Tan, K.C.; Zhang, M. Multitask Genetic Programming-Based Generative Hyperheuristics: A Case Study in Dynamic Scheduling. *IEEE Trans. Cybern.* **2021**, *52*, 10515–10528 . [CrossRef]
41. Mei, Y.; Nguyen, S.; Xue, B.; Zhang, M. An Efficient Feature Selection Algorithm for Evolving Job Shop Scheduling Rules with Genetic Programming. *IEEE Trans. Emerg. Top. Comput. Intell.* **2017**, *1*, 339–353. [CrossRef]
42. Zhang, F.; Mei, Y.; Zhang, M. A two-stage genetic programming hyper-heuristic approach with feature selection for dynamic flexible job shop scheduling. In Proceedings of the GECCO'19: Genetic and Evolutionary Computation Conference, Prague, Czech Republic, 13–17 July 2019. [CrossRef]
43. Zhang, F.; Mei, Y.; Nguyen, S.; Zhang, M. Genetic Programming with Adaptive Search Based on the Frequency of Features for Dynamic Flexible Job Shop Scheduling. In *Lecture Notes in Computer Science*; Springer International Publishing: Cham, Switzerland, 2020; pp. 214–230. [CrossRef]
44. Zhang, F.; Mei, Y.; Nguyen, S.; Zhang, M. Evolving Scheduling Heuristics via Genetic Programming with Feature Selection in Dynamic Flexible Job-Shop Scheduling. *IEEE Trans. Cybern.* **2021**, *51*, 1797–1811. [CrossRef]
45. Yska, D.; Mei, Y.; Zhang, M. Feature construction in genetic programming hyper-heuristic for dynamic flexible job shop scheduling. In Proceedings of the GECCO'18: Genetic and Evolutionary Computation Conference Companion, Kyoto, Japan, 15–19 July 2018. [CrossRef]
46. Pinedo, M.L. *Scheduling*; Springer: New York, NY, USA, 2012. [CrossRef]
47. Graham, R.; Lawler, E.; Lenstra, J.; Kan, A. Optimization and Approximation in Deterministic Sequencing and Scheduling: A Survey. In *Discrete Optimization II*; Annals of Discrete Mathematics; Hammer, P., Johnson, E., Korte, B., Eds.; Elsevier: Amsterdam, The Netherlands, 1979; Volume 5, pp. 287–326. [CrossRef]
48. Đurasević, M.; Jakobović, D. Comparison of schedule generation schemes for designing dispatching rules with genetic programming in the unrelated machines environment. *Appl. Soft Comput.* **2020**, *96*, 106637. [CrossRef]
49. Burke, E.K.; Gendreau, M.; Hyde, M.; Kendall, G.; Ochoa, G.; Özcan, E.; Qu, R. Hyper-heuristics: A survey of the state of the art. *J. Oper. Res. Soc.* **2013**, *64*, 1695–1724. [CrossRef]
50. Nguyen, S.; Mei, Y.; Xue, B.; Zhang, M. A Hybrid Genetic Programming Algorithm for Automated Design of Dispatching Rules. *Evol. Comput.* **2019**, *27*, 467–496. [CrossRef]
51. Zhang, F.; Mei, Y.; Nguyen, S.; Zhang, M. Guided Subtree Selection for Genetic Operators in Genetic Programming for Dynamic Flexible Job Shop Scheduling. In *Lecture Notes in Computer Science*; Springer International Publishing: Cham, Switzerland, 2020; pp. 262–278. [CrossRef]
52. Duflo, G.; Kieffer, E.; Brust, M.R.; Danoy, G.; Bouvry, P. A GP Hyper-Heuristic Approach for Generating TSP Heuristics. In Proceedings of the 2019 IEEE International Parallel and Distributed Processing Symposium Workshops (IPDPSW), Rio de Janeiro, Brazil, 20–24 May 2019; pp. 521–529. [CrossRef]
53. Gil-Gala, F.J.; Durasević, M.; Sierra, M.R.; Varela, R. Evolving ensembles of heuristics for the travelling salesman problem. *Nat. Comput.* **2023**, *22*, 671–684. [CrossRef]
54. Jacobsen-Grocott, J.; Mei, Y.; Chen, G.; Zhang, M. Evolving heuristics for Dynamic Vehicle Routing with Time Windows using genetic programming. In Proceedings of the 2017 IEEE Congress on Evolutionary Computation (CEC), Donostia, Spain, 5–8 June 2017; pp. 1948–1955. [CrossRef]

55. Wang, S.; Mei, Y.; Park, J.; Zhang, M. Evolving Ensembles of Routing Policies using Genetic Programming for Uncertain Capacitated Arc Routing Problem. In Proceedings of the 2019 IEEE Symposium Series on Computational Intelligence (SSCI), Xiamen, China, 6–9 December 2019; pp. 1628–1635. [CrossRef]
56. Liu, Y.; Mei, Y.; Zhang, M.; Zhang, Z. A Predictive-Reactive Approach with Genetic Programming and Cooperative Coevolution for the Uncertain Capacitated Arc Routing Problem. *Evol. Comput.* **2020**, *28*, 289–316. [CrossRef]
57. Đurasević, M.; Đumić, M. Automated design of heuristics for the container relocation problem using genetic programming. *Appl. Soft Comput.* **2022**, *130*, 109696. [CrossRef]
58. Burke, E.K.; Hyde, M.R.; Kendall, G. Evolving Bin Packing Heuristics with Genetic Programming. In *Parallel Problem Solving from Nature—PPSN IX*; Springer: Berlin/Heidelberg, Germany, 2006; pp. 860–869. [CrossRef]
59. DASH, M.; LIU, H. Feature selection for classification. *Intell. Data Anal.* **1997**, *1*, 131–156. [CrossRef]
60. Jovic, A.; Brkic, K.; Bogunovic, N. A review of feature selection methods with applications. In Proceedings of the 2015 38th International Convention on Information and Communication Technology, Electronics and Microelectronics (MIPRO), Opatija, Croatia, 25–29 May 2015. [CrossRef]
61. Abiodun, E.O.; Alabdulatif, A.; Abiodun, O.I.; Alawida, M.; Alabdulatif, A.; Alkhawaldeh, R.S. A systematic review of emerging feature selection optimization methods for optimal text classification: The present state and prospective opportunities. *Neural Comput. Appl.* **2021**, *33*, 15091–15118. [CrossRef]
62. Luke, S.; Panait, L. A Comparison of Bloat Control Methods for Genetic Programming. *Evol. Comput.* **2006**, *14*, 309–344. [CrossRef]
63. Alfaro-Cid, E.; Merelo, J.J.; de Vega, F.F.; Esparcia-Alcázar, A.I.; Sharman, K. Bloat Control Operators and Diversity in Genetic Programming: A Comparative Study. *Evol. Comput.* **2010**, *18*, 305–332. [CrossRef]

MDPI AG
Grosspeteranlage 5
4052 Basel
Switzerland
Tel.: +41 61 683 77 34

*Algorithms* Editorial Office
E-mail: algorithms@mdpi.com
www.mdpi.com/journal/algorithms

www.ingramcontent.com/pod-product-compliance
Lightning Source LLC
Chambersburg PA
CBHW040839250926
51850CB00007BA/1354